AMERICAN
EXCEPTION

AMERICAN EXCEPTION

EMPIRE AND THE DEEP STATE

AARON GOOD

FOREWORD BY PETER PHILLIPS

Skyhorse Publishing

Skyhorse Publishing books may be purchased in bulk at special discounts for sales promotion, corporate gifts, fund-raising, or educational purposes. Special editions can also be created to specifications. For details, contact the Special Sales Department, Skyhorse Publishing, 307 West 36th Street, 11th Floor, New York, NY 10018 or info@skyhorsepublishing.com.

Skyhorse® and Skyhorse Publishing® are registered trademarks of Skyhorse Publishing, Inc.®, a Delaware corporation.

Visit our website at www.skyhorsepublishing.com.

10 9 8 7 6 5 4 3 2

Library of Congress Cataloging-in-Publication Data is available on file.

ISBN: 978-1-5107-6913-7
eBook ISBN: 978-1-5107-6914-4

Cover art by Abby Martin
Jacket design by Casey Moore

Printed in the United States of America

CONTENTS

For Kim and Asher

ACKNOWLEDGMENTS

It is challenging for me to express my sentiments here. This book represents much more than my political science doctoral work. It also is the product of more than a decade of training and research—from my enrollment in Temple's PhD program in 2010 to the 2022 publication date. But more than that, it represents my somewhat traumatic political education. I went from being the son of a Democratic congressional staffer, to an Obama campaign organizer in 2008—even attending the Inauguration and Staff Ball in 2009—to becoming a staunch critic of the fundamental lawlessness and avarice that animates the American state. So with all that in mind, I want to convey my gratitude to some of the people who helped along the way. Forgive me if this is overlong.

Thanks to my mom and dad—Day Smith and Tom Good—for giving me a great start in life. And my sisters Jill and Betsy, both kind souls. I couldn't ask for better in-laws than Jim and Liz McGlynn. Before and after the pandemic, our animals—Zeppo (RIP), Zadie, and Neo—have been indispensable. Most significantly I am grateful beyond words for my wife, Kim, and our son, Asher.

I am lucky to have had such great students. I could name many more, but here I'll just mention Aqua, Carley, Dylan, Helen, Sarah, Tenzin, Tommy, Will, and Zoya. You all helped to make it wonderful to be in the classroom.

A shoutout for my friends from Indiana and/or from Indiana days—Brian, Cynthia, Dan, Duany, Ger, Heath, Jason, Joe, Kevin, Krista, Stacey, and Steven!

From Bloomington, I want to thank my top undergraduate professor at Indiana University, Jeffrey Isaac. We are not so politically aligned these days, but he is a brilliant thinker and a fantastic lecturer who taught me a lot.

From Temple, I want to express my gratitude to Orfeo Fioretos and Gary Mucciaroni. They are very accomplished scholars with integrity. I benefitted greatly from their invaluable feedback and scrutiny of my dissertation. And there is Joseph Schwartz—a true mensch. My greatest regret about Temple is that I was not able to take his political theory graduate course. He was a major source of support during my exams and the prospectus phases before his health placed him on indefinite leave.

I cannot thank Sean Yom enough. I was very fortunate to have such an exceptional scholar as my committee chair. More than that, he gave me support and guidance, without which I may not have been able to complete such a radical doctoral project. I could not be happier for Sean and Zeynep here in the Spring of 2022!

Gary Wamsley is a gentleman and a scholar. I have to give him credit and much gratitude for his role in getting the original "American Exception" article published at *Administration & Society*. Of course, I must also thank Tony Lyons and Hector Carosso of Skyhorse for bringing this book into existence!

Big thanks to Liz Franczak, Brace Belden, and Yung Chomsky of TrueAnon. Somehow, they have done as much as anyone to wake large numbers of people up to the reality of elite lawlessness. I must also thank Felix Biederman for bringing Oliver Stone and me onto Chapo for "Assassination Day."

The American Exception podcast crew is growing, but at this point I must give thanks to Ben Howard, Casey Moore, Dana Chavarria, and the insightful and charming Hailey Rounsaville. Dana's sound engineering has been invaluable—a very high learning curve under tough time constraints. In terms of both technique and content, Casey's graphic artwork ranges from great to phenomenal. With so much on his plate, Ben Howard has somehow found the time to contribute his formidable writing, research, and speaking skills. When it comes to the podcasting medium, Ben is far ahead of most of the people who do it full time.

A stellar academic, Jack Bratich has been a good friend since we met at the Films of Oliver Stone conference. Joan Mellen is a role model for her courage and her persistence when it comes to getting research and writing published. Anthony Monteiro is a scholar whose integrity and courage are inspirational. David Talbot has been a big help to me in a number of ways—namely: his outstanding books, his encouragement, and his time.

Oliver Stone stands alone among American directors when it comes to holding a mirror up to the empire, even when it is most unpopular. He has also been very helpful to me personally in a number of ways. Jim DiEugenio has been a good friend and collaborator. He is also one of the most tireless and thorough historians you could imagine; it's almost superhuman.

Mickey Huff of Project Censored has been an enormous source of support over the last ten years—on top of being an admirable scholar and tireless advocate for truth and justice. Peter Phillips not only shines a light on *The Global Power Elite*, he was also a valuable member of my dissertation committee and he generously agreed to write the introduction to this book.

Abby Martin has been a joy and a privilege to work with. Her artwork—combined with Casey Moore's graphic design—exceeded my high expectations for the cover to this book. Given Abby's intelligence and charisma, she could make loads of money if she sold out. Instead, she chooses to fight for humanity. We are all the better for it.

Working with Peter Kuznick has been a thrill. No historian has done more to illuminate for Americans the truth of Hiroshima and Nagasaki. I have been enriched through our trips to Moscow and Japan, and through Peter's contributions to my peace studies class and my dissertation committee.

Getting to know Daniel Ellsberg has been an honor. History will remember Ellsberg's efforts to expose the Pentagon Papers and the nuclear "Doomsday Machine." But as our mutual friend Peter Dale Scott pointed out, decades from now—if the human race is still around—Daniel Ellsberg may be most remembered for his commitment to peace and nonviolence. On a personal level, Dan and I appeared at some events which for me were unforgettable. He also provided me with crucial source material for this book's section on the rise of the military industrial complex.

Speaking of Peter Dale Scott, like Daniel Ellsberg, Peter is an international treasure. With his deep political insights and body of work, he is peerless. Furthermore, it takes tremendous courage and psychic strength to "mind the darkness" decade after decade. He is, simultaneously, a poet with the mind of an historian—and an historian with the soul of a poet. I read and listened to Peter for years and was amazed by his insight and erudition. Befriending him and collaborating with him has been heartening and rewarding beyond what I can express.

I owe a great debt to all the SCAD theorists—Laurie Manwell, the late Kym Thorne, and Matthew Witt. I will always fondly remember attending public administration conferences with these fine academics. In particular, Matt is not just an excellent scholar—he has been a collaborator and stalwart friend through many ups and downs. I would add Mark Crispin Miller as an honorary member of this group. Mark is a brilliant and clever individual who also, notably, has the strength of his convictions.

Lastly, I must acknowledge the enormous debt of gratitude that I owe to Lance deHaven-Smith. He was already as well established in his field as one could be before taking a radical turn in order to address the criminality at the pinnacle of the American state. Lance took the time respond to me when I first reached out to him before even starting graduate school, and we soon began talking or exchanging emails on a daily basis. His support, encouragement, and friendship were priceless. Whatever I have done or might do as a scholar or writer, I carry Lance with me.

FOREWORD
BY PETER PHILLIPS

Aaron Good's *American Exception Empire and the Deep State* is a fresh look at a long tradition of research regarding power and control inside the United States empire. While Americans often take pride in a mythical belief in democracy and governmental transparency, increasing exceptions to our prideful understandings are self-evident. US wars, invasions, and unilateral aggressions in the last seventy years alone bely any rational belief in American democratic humanitarianism. The US—a country that massacred its own indigenous populations—has pursued a global dominance agenda since World War II. America has built a global empire of repressive military power in service to private capital that has cost the lives millions in Korea, Vietnam, Afghanistan, Iraq, Syria, and numerous other places.

A long tradition of social science research documents the existence of a dominant ruling class in the United States. These elites set policy and determine national political priorities. The American ruling class is complex and competitive. It perpetuates itself through interacting families of high social standing with similar lifestyles, corporate affiliations, and memberships in elite social clubs and private schools.

The American ruling class has long been determined to be mostly self-perpetuating, maintaining its influence through policymaking institutions such as the National Association of Manufacturers, US Chamber of

Commerce, Business Council, Business Roundtable, Conference Board, American Enterprise Institute for Public Policy Research, Council on Foreign Relations, and other business-centered policy groups. These associations have long dominated policy decisions within the US government.

In his 1956 book *The Power Elite*, C. Wright Mills documented how World War II solidified a trinity of power in the United States that comprised corporate, military, and government elites in a centralized power structure motivated by a national capitalist class power elite working in unison through "higher circles" of contact and agreement. Mills described how the power elite were those "who decide whatever is decided" of major consequence. Mills is careful to observe that the conception of a power elite does not rest solely on personal friendship, but rather relies on a broader ideology of shared corporate system goals.

In this book, Aaron Good provides an excellent review of Mills and the hidden networks of power elites in the US. These elites operate as a non-transparent undercover network of decision makers, the movers and shakers so to speak, who are in positions of institutional importance. Good documents the continuing social science research that summarizes the theoretical understandings of a dual state in the US: an openly apparent and widely recognized public governmental bureaucracy existing in tandem with a secretive security state imbedded in public and private intelligence agencies. This parallel state operates in support of our capital empire at the bequest of a hidden sovereign power elite.

Even the *Washington Post* (Priest and Arkin) acknowledged the expanding security state in the US that comprises tens of thousands of individuals in forty-six agencies and thousands of private companies—all operating under top secret conditions. Dana Priest and William Arkin in 2011 described the United States as two governments, "one [that] the citizens are familiar with which operates more or less in the open, and the other [a] parallel top-secret government whose parts have mushroomed in less than a decade into a gigantic, sprawling universe of its own, visible to only a carefully vetted cadre—and in its entirety visible only to God."

The existence of the public and security states in the US is widely understood by social science researchers. However, less understood are the mechanisms determining how the security state operates in times of crisis and exceptional circumstances. Aaron Good follows the lead of Peter Dale Scott's work on the idea of a *deep state* within the security state that networks a selection of insiders, who covertly make decisions of significant importance. For the general public, the origins of these decisions remain unknown. This leads Aaron Good to formulate a tripartite theory of the state that includes both a public and security state in combination with a deep state network of semi-permanent policy elite operatives.

In *American Exception: Empire and the Deep State*, Aaron Good devotes significant space addressing deep state operatives of whom we had glimpses in the sixties and seventies around the assassinations of John Kennedy, Robert Kennedy, Martin Luther King—as well as Watergate. We know enough about these actors to theorize a deep state network taking exceptional collective actions that had powerful permanent consequences for which many citizens are still confused and suspicious.

Good cites *exceptionism* (i.e., elite lawlessness) as an on-going institutional circumstance affecting American overlords, who Good sees as the primary managers of global capital. He cites the top three capital firms, Black Rock, Vanguard, and State Street, who collectively control trillions of dollars of investment capital as, "The hegemony of organized money over society." He believes that this situation did not arise by accident, but rather comprised a series of "*coups d'etat profonde*, or strokes of the deep state."[1]

My own research on US investment management companies supports Aaron Good's position. The top three US capital management firms have massively consolidated wealth in the past five years doubling holdings to over $20.9 trillion dollars.

	Holdings 2017	**Holdings 2022**
1. BlackRock	$5.4 trillion	$10 trillion
2. Vanguard Group	$4.48	$7
3. State Street	$2.4	$3.9

Aaron Good's *American Exception* follows closely Peter Dale Scott's book, *The American Deep State*, where Scott describes the importance of Wall Street in offering intelligence agencies key personnel and policies. Certainly, Allen Dulles, a Wall Street lawyer and CIA director, is a key example of this close relationship between Wall Street and national intelligence. Scott and Good believe that the mushrooming of intelligence agencies after 9/11 has also allowed for the emergence of *deep state* intelligence networks with independent capabilities, even while still in support of Wall Street's agenda.

Good cites Scott's reports on how global intelligence agencies work together as deep state networks. He cites how anticommunist elites organized in the mid-1970s, when the CIA was under restrictions imposed by Congress and enforced by President Carter. Intelligence representatives from France, Egypt, Saudi Arabia, and Iran met in Kenya at the Safari Club with CIA operatives, including former CIA Director George H. W. Bush, to overcome constraints imposed by Washington. This led to the emergence of the Bank of Credit and Commerce International (BCCI) as the depository of money for off-the-books covert operations and the formation of what Scott calls a supranational deep state.

As the power elite increasingly concentrates wealth, the requirement from the overlords for security and protection has magnified. Responding to that call are the intelligence agencies of the capital-vested nation-states—cooperating with each other to coordinate regime changes, wars, occupations, assassinations, and covert actions deemed necessary.

There can be no doubt that continued concentration of wealth cannot be economically sustained. Extreme inequality and massive repression will only bring resistance and rebellion by the world's masses. The danger is that the power elite will fail to recognize the inevitability of economic and/or environmental collapse before making the necessary adjustments to prevent millions of deaths and massive civil unrest. Without significant corrective adjustments by the power elite, mass social movements and rebellions, coupled with environmental collapse, will inevitably lead to global chaos and war.

The power elite manage, facilitate, and protect concentrated capital worldwide. This consolidation of wealth is the primary cause of world poverty, starvation, malnutrition, wars, and mass human suffering. Organizing resistance and challenging the powerful is the necessary agenda for democracy movements worldwide. Addressing top-down economic controls, monopolistic power, and the specifics of the power elite's activities will require challenging mobilizations in numerous regions.

We live in a nation and world beset by crises of massive inequality, pending environmental collapse, and real threats of nuclear annihilation. The more we can understand this system of economic domination and the inner workings of key operatives inside a deep state, the greater will be our capabilities to mediate democratic solutions. Thank you Aaron Good for your vital effort in this book to help us understand the manipulations of the powerful and to recognize the threat of the deep state.

—Peter Phillips, professor emeritus Political Sociology
Sonoma State University, author of *Giants: The Global Power Elite*, 2018

CHAPTER 1

EMPIRE, HEGEMONY, AND THE STATE

The Question

Within the social sciences, it is conventional to frame research in terms of a research question or questions. This may be more or less useful depending on one's field and the issues that one is researching. The following is an attempt to distill what my dissertation sought to address in a few question: Why does US foreign policy display such continuity across administrations? Why has American democracy—most specifically the rule of law—declined inversely with the rise of US global dominance? To some extent, this formulation of the research questions was a contrivance. The scope of the project was broader than most of the mid-range theories that today predominate in the social sciences. If comparison might be useful, *American Exception* was influenced and inspired by works like *The Power Elite* by C. Wright Mills[1] (1956) and *Democracy Incorporated* by Sheldon Wolin.[2]

Political scientists have spilled much ink to create theories and definitions of *democracy*. In a broad normative sense, a country is democratic to the extent that it is the general public—rather than an elite of power—which ultimately controls the political system. Institutionally, a democracy is characterized by the rule of law, political rights, free and fair elections, and accountability.[3] Within the American social sciences, most seminal twentieth century scholars and theorists of American democracy have focused on US domestic politics and US society. This would include political scientists like Dahl and Lindblom[4] as well as sociologists like C. Wright Mills.[5] A central concerns of this book is the relationship between expansive foreign policy and democratic decline. One of the few American political scientists to focus squarely on this issue was Lasswell.[6] His neglected "garrison state" construct is worth revisiting and reassessing given the subsequent rise of US global dominance and democratic decline.

There are three larger realms in which democratic decay is most evident. The first—and a central one for the purposes of this book—is the diminishment of the rule of law. The second pertains to the drastic rise in inequality. The third is the decline in American nationalism. The decline of the rule of law relates to the rule of law as one of the chief factors which define democracy. The other two aspects—inequality and the decline of nationalism—pertain to the broad commonsense understanding of democracy. These are relevant because they are aspects that relate directly to one of the central dynamics explored in this book—the impact of America's post–World War II global orientation upon US politics and society.

The diminishment of the rule of law can be dramatically illustrated by the following separate but interrelated trends: *high criminality* or unadjudicated crimes committed by top government officials and political insiders, elite criminality or crimes committed by socioeconomic elites, and finally the abasement of constitutionally guaranteed political rights. High criminality would include the "October surprise" of 1968, the crimes associated with Watergate, the sprawling high crime spree that is truncated by the term "Iran-Contra," and stolen presidential elections of 2000[7] and possibly 2004.[8] Deserving to be included in the realm of high criminality are innumerable US foreign policy practices, including aggressive war and the overthrow of foreign governments which would on their face appear to clearly violate the UN Charter. The UN Charter outlaws aggression and even the threat of aggression against other states. The US Senate ratified the UN Charter and since the *supremacy clause* of the US Constitution deems ratified treaties to "be the supreme Law of the Land," US leaders have violated "the supreme Law of the Land" innumerable times, judicial abdication notwithstanding.

Socioeconomic elite criminality (i.e., the crimes of the superrich) is most clearly exemplified by the scores of unadjudicated crimes related to the financial crisis of 2008 and 2009. The violation of political rights is evident in the McCarthy era, FBI COINTEL programs, media manipulation, mass surveillance regimes, suppression of political movements, torture regimes, warrantless detention, and assassination programs. While the violation of democratic political rights does entail the commission of crimes by government officials, the institutionalized nature of these violations makes them distinct from the aforementioned high crimes. It is worth noting that there is considerable overlap between the decline of the rule of law and the weakening of the other institutional components of democracy. Specifically, elections have been less than "free and fair." Political rights have been infringed upon. Accountability is diminished as a result of state secrecy and the selective application of the rule of law which together prevent meaningful accountability in crucial areas.

Economic inequality in America has risen to levels not observed since before the Great Depression. This is an anti-democratic trend because it is logical that a political system controlled by the general public rather than elites would not be characterized by ever-rising levels of stratification. Additionally, America has also seen rising levels of political inequality. In the 1950s, C. Wright Mills observed that *democracy*, in any meaningful sense, had been superseded by the rise of a tripartite American power structure which had consolidated its hegemony over politics and society.[9] More recently, political scientists using quantitative methods have been able to establish that the general public has virtually no political influence relative to elites.[10] While both the middle and lower levels of US society have little influence on the political system, the lower strata of society are subject to an array of institutions that diminish their ability to enjoy "life, liberty, and the pursuit of happiness" such as could be expected in an advanced democratic country. These institutions include police surveillance and repression, mass incarceration, substandard public education, inadequate social services, widespread unemployment and underemployment, and predatory business practices.

The third realm in which America's undemocratic trajectory can be traced relates to the decline of nationalism in many important respects. In this context, "nationalism" refers to the pursuit of policies which strengthen and enrich the country's collective economy and population. One would expect nationalism to be expressed in a democratic system since it would not behoove campaigning politicians to advocate for policies which would be harmful to the nation as a whole. Yet, in many areas, officials have acted in ways that were counter to the general interest. American governments have pursued policies that facilitated deindustrialization resulting in reduced domestic production and consumption on the part of workers whose jobs have been offshored. Additionally, the state of America's physical infrastructure has declined dramatically. This is striking in a country with considerable latent productive industrial capacity. The domestic economy also suffers from a trend toward historically high levels of private and public debt. This creates an unproductive, feudalizing dynamic which benefits a rentier class at the expense of the general population's economic security and living standards. A related trend is privatization—the transformation of the public domain (education, utilities, prisons, etc.) into avenues for rent extraction. Here again, a rentier class benefits at the expense of the public at large. Collectively, these neoliberal trends are the opposite of what progressive political economists predicted would result from democracy and economic development.[11]

It is crucial to note that this democratic decline has been unfolding in an era of American *unipolarity* or global hegemony. At the very least, the US was the hegemon of the global capitalist world during the Cold War and has been the unchallenged global hegemon since the fall of the Soviet Union. American political thinkers from the Founding Fathers to contemporary scholars like Chalmers Johnson[12] have asserted that empire is not compatible with democracy. Such analysis in and of itself is not novel. The focus here is upon the forces that drive the pursuit of global dominance, and which have altered the structure of the state. An understanding of the resultant structures is essential. Specifically, the evolution of the American state should be understood both in terms of its continuity with the past as well as its relatively novel features.

Bringing the *Tripartite State* In

First put forward in a 2015 article for *Administration & Society*, the *tripartite state* theory is intended to illuminate the nature of the American state and the American power structure.[13] Fundamentally, it blends and builds upon three extant approaches to understanding the state and US society. Regarding the state, theories of the *dual state* or *double government* are given considerable weight. C. Wright Mills's theories of the tripartite structure of American power also inform the idea of the tripartite state. In effect, the three parts of the tripartite state are analogous to the "big three" institutions that comprise Mills's American power structure—big business, the military, and the political directorate. Finally, the theory utilizes and adapts Peter Dale Scott's *deep politics* approach which seeks to discern the powerful forces and actors whose decisive influence is typically not acknowledged in public discourse.

The tripartite state is comprised of three elements—the *public state* (i.e., the *democratic state*), the *security state*, and the *deep state*. The public state consists of those institutions that we learn about in high school civics classes and study in political science—the visible and formally organized institutions that comprise our elected federal, state, and local governments as well as the civil service bureaucracies associated with them. The *security state* is comprised of those institutions in charge of maintaining "security" domestically and internationally. Notable security state organizations include the Pentagon, the Central Intelligence Agency, and the Federal Bureau of Investigation.

The *deep state* is a more nebulous thing. In a 2015 article, I sparsely defined the deep state as "an obscured, dominant, supranational source of antidemocratic power."[14] Back in 2013, the *New York Times* defined the deep state as "a hard-to-perceive level of government or super-control that exists regardless of elections and that may thwart popular movements or radical change."[15] Describing the essence of what he means by the term *deep state*, Peter Dale Scott describes it as "a power not derived from the constitution but outside and above it;" the deep state is "more powerful than the public state."[16] The institutions that exercise undemocratic power over state and society collectively comprise the deep state. The deep state is an outgrowth of the *overworld* of private wealth. It includes, most notably, the institutions that advance overworld interests through the synergy between the overworld and the underworld—as well as the national security organizations that mediate between them. Collectively, the dominance of deep state has diminished US democracy to such an extent that it is justified to describe ours as a *deep state system* and to speak of the *tripartite state*. A central contention herein is that the tripartite state developed alongside postwar American *exceptionism*—"the institutionalization of the interminable state of exception" which has entailed "the institutionalization of securitized supra-sovereignty or Lockean 'prerogative' although not to a fixed or determinate source."[17] In other words, the covert lawlessness with which the US pursued international dominance after World War II had the cumulative effect of transforming an imperfect democracy into a tripartite state system characterized by covert top-down rule.

The tripartite state emerged from deep seated forces in US society. The public state existed prior to independence in the form of colonial assemblies and later the Continental Congress. Likewise, there were elements of a security state dating at least back to the continental army and Washington's network of spies in the War for Independence. Early in US history, the security state was more securely tethered to the public state and was used relatively sparingly—for example—against Barbary Pirates and American Indians and to promote expansion as in Andrew Jackson's attack on Spanish Florida or Polk's Mexican-American War. The cases of Florida and Texas are especially relevant since no official authorization was given to Andrew Jackson or the Texas rebels respectively, yet their legally dubious actions seem clearly to have emerged from deep political forces in the US. Andrew Jackson's negation of the Indian treaties and Abraham Lincoln's suspension of *habeus corpus* are other examples of the illegal and/ or unconstitutional exercises of prerogative power which were dwarfed by the *exceptionism* that emerged after World War II.

From the founding of the United States to World War II, the US could be described as having a deep political system in tandem with the more visible political system. The overworld of private wealth often comingled with an underworld political economy, and some of the most lucrative trades occupied a realm between legality and criminality. Most notably, examples include the slave trade, the opium trade, and later the fruit and sugar industries. These often-transnational enterprises could become powerful and even decisive in shaping economic fortunes and political outcomes. Domestically, the various political machines were the most obvious institutions wherein deep political forces presided, providing a nexus between overworld and underworld forces of the US and of various localities. One may conceive of political machines as the organizations which—in miniature—provide the best historical analogy to the current hypertrophied American deep state.

The period following the Civil War—i.e., Reconstruction and the Gilded Age—saw the US emerge as an industrialized economic behemoth with commercial interests quickly expanding beyond its borders. The deep political power of private wealth was ascendant but accompanied by modest political reforms which were responses to mobilized democratic elements of civil society. At the turn of the century, with *manifest destiny* and the closing of the frontier finally achieved, the US began to project its power globally. It is noteworthy that Henry Cabot Lodge, the man perhaps most responsible for steering the US into the Spanish-American War, was descended from Boston Brahmins who had made vast fortunes in the opium trade. Similarly, deep political forces were likely decisive in the US decision to unofficially abandon neutrality early in World War I and later to formally enter the war. In particular, the US entry seems to have been a function of the relationship between Britain and the pinnacle of the US financial elite, JP Morgan specifically. Had Germany not surrendered—an outcome very much in doubt after Brest-Litovsk—the US, with JP Morgan as its broker, stood to lose billions after extending vast amounts of credit to the Allies. Morgan influence went beyond US entry and victory in the war. At Versailles, illustrious financier Bernard Baruch complained that Morgan men had been in control of the proceedings.[18] As per the treaty's terms, harsh reparations were foisted on Germany which in turn enabled the Allies to repay the US.

Despite its considerable power at the close of World War I, the US did not at that time seek the mantle of global hegemony. It wasn't until the onset of World War II that deep forces in US society sought to reorient American posture toward the international realm. The US Establishment needed to reform and create institutions to manage international and domestic politics. The postwar national security state and America's sense-making institutions collectively shaped the US-led world order and the "postwar liberal consensus" that sought and legitimized US global dominance. *Anticommunism* allowed for the securitization of politics. As America's founders observed, the securitization that necessarily accompanies wars is toxic or even fatal for democratic/republican institutions.

The Cold War achieved the securitization of politics on a scale theretofore unseen in US history and was deemed—or understood to be—a twilight struggle against an implacable, amoral adversary bent on world domination. National security organizations are by design undemocratic. Hierarchy, secrecy, and expediency are structural features necessitated by the imperatives of "security." They are authoritarian responses to real, imagined, or fabricated threats—especially existential ones. The postwar US national security state did not arise from an attack against the country. It was created ostensibly to combat Soviet Communism and the supposed threat that it posed to the US and the world. However, the organizational structure of the national security state was created by elites with deep connections to the overworld of private wealth. In particular, the CIA was the brainchild of men like Allen Dulles.[19] Along with his brother, future Secretary of State John Foster Dulles, Allen Dulles was a longtime employee of Sullivan and Cromwell, the storied Wall Street law firm whose clients included the world's largest multinational corporations. Given this history, it is not difficult to grasp why so much of US foreign policy has consisted of intervening to make countries as suitable as possible for the maximization of corporate profit. The previous seven decades provide innumerable examples that demonstrate the extent to which overt and covert US interventions in foreign countries were often instigated by—and for the benefit of—the overworld of corporate wealth. These interventions have involved every expedient manner of violence and lawbreaking. It bears repeating: Foreign wars and covert operations are illegal under the UN Charter. Having ratified the treaty, US officials violate the US constitution by contravening the charter which is deemed to be "the supreme law of the land."

It has often been argued that Cold War anticommunism was to blame for the excesses of US foreign policy during the era. This would entail conceiving of *anticommunism* as an outlook and set of practices opposed to the spread of Soviet or Chinese-style communism. Such practices could be described as regrettable but necessary departures from American ideas of fair play, undertaken to confront an existential threat. Were such an understanding accurate, the *state of exception* to the rule of law would have ended with the fall of the Soviet Union. Such has not been the case. In 1996, a House Intelligence Committee report stated that CIA officials had revealed that the agency's operations arm "is the only part of the [Intelligence Community], indeed of the government, where hundreds of employees on a daily basis are directed to break extremely serious laws in countries around the world." A conservative estimate "is that several hundred times every day, [Directorate of Operations] officers engage in highly illegal activities."[20] In 2019, Secretary of State Mike Pompeo reaffirmed this, stating, "I was the CIA director. We lied, we cheated, we stole."[21] George White of OSS, Federal Bureau of Narcotics, and the CIA put it more colorfully: "[I]t was fun, fun, fun. Where else could a red-blooded American boy lie, kill, cheat, steal, rape and pillage with the sanction and blessing of the All-Highest?"[22]

There are serious problems that an exceptionalist (i.e., lawless) security state presents to a liberal democracy. The rule of law is obviously overridden. State secrecy confounds public sense-making and deliberation since the public cannot evaluate policies and governmental actions that are obscured or misrepresented through various ersatz *cover stories*. These very weighty issues are likely not the most problematic aspect of US *exceptionism*. One provocative question examined herein involves the extent to which these criminogenic political institutions and practices have been confined to the realm of foreign policy. To put it another way: Has the US been able to hermetically seal state-sanctioned lawlessness and thereby maintain the rule of law domestically even while exceptionism prevails in foreign relations? Drawing from the work of Lance deHaven-Smith (2006) and others, the answer appears to be no; there are enough documented and suspected state crimes against democracy (SCADs) to assert that at best public sovereignty has been compromised.[23] A more alarming interpretation would be that SCADs and related dynamics have collectively comprised a series of *coups d'etat* that has drastically weakened

American democracy. Progressive elements of the US government and society have been marginalized while US dominance has been pursued internationally—typically with various measures of subversion, violence, expropriation, and exploitation.

Some of these documented and suspected interventions include: the assassination of President Kennedy; the FBI's COINTEL programs against the antiwar, civil rights, and black power movements; the assassination of Malcolm X; the Gulf of Tonkin Incident; the assassination of Martin Luther King; the assassination of Robert Kennedy; Nixon's 1968 "October Surprise;" the collection of crimes known collectively as "Watergate;" the 1980 "October Surprise;" the Iran-Contra affair; the September 11, 2001 terror attacks;[24] the subsequent anthrax attacks;[25] and the "stolen" presidential elections of 2000[26] and 2004.[27] Another notable pattern of criminality that touches upon many state crimes involves the nexus between the intelligence agencies and the international drug traffic. While the evidentiary support for each of these suspected or documented SCADs differs, they each have their serious and reputable proponents, even as the prevailing discourse dismisses such suspicions as "conspiracy theory"—a term that has come to connote unseriousness and which is applied in such a way as to encourage the *a priori* rejection of critical theories and the acceptance of state-sanctioned narratives. DeHaven-Smith (2013) examined this issue and found that the term "conspiracy theory," was seldom used in public discourse until the aftermath of the John Kennedy assassination. He points to a CIA document distributed to the agency's media assets requesting their assistance in dismissing and marginalizing "conspiracy theorists" as unreliable, irrational, and/or venal. Thus, there has been what could he describes as the "conspiracy theory conspiracy" wherein state actors intervene in civil society to help create a prevailing common sense wherein reasonable suspicions of high criminality are reflexively dismissed and stigmatized by our sense-making institutions.[28]

The collective impact of SCADs is impossible to measure precisely. Addressing many of the same anomalies as deHaven-Smith, Peter Dale Scott (2015) describes some of the key phenomena as *structural deep events*,[29] history-shaping episodes that impact "the whole fabric of society, with consequences that enlarge covert government." Rather than ever being properly investigated and/or adjudicated, structural deep events "are subsequently covered up by systematic falsifications in media and internal government records."[30] Every civilization reaches a level of complexity at which point milieus and institutions emerge which wield power yet remain submerged or not fully revealed or acknowledged by the society as a whole. In the US, this dynamic is described by Scott (1993) as America's *deep political system*.[31] An argument made in this dissertation is that these SCADs or deep events have indeed altered the course of American history and transformed the US political system. In its earlier form, US governance was characterized by varying levels of coexistence and accommodation between constitutional democracy and a deep political system. Subsequently—especially after World War II—interventions from the deep political system transformed the American state and US society, giving rise to the *tripartite state*—i.e., a *deep state system* wherein *exceptionism* allows for the supra-sovereignty of undemocratic forces. Specifically, the overworld of corporate wealth has created and altered institutions to most effectively manage international and domestic politics to the effect that empire and hegemony—and thus exceptionism—are sacrosanct imperatives even as their decisive impacts are rarely acknowledged or debated candidly in public discourse.

The rise of the *tripartite state* has greatly weakened American democracy in the most fundamental sense if a system of governance is understood to be more or less democratic to the extent that sovereignty rests with the public rather than elites. The decline of US democracy has given rise to three crises to which the deep state system cannot adequately respond. The first crisis is the ever-present risk of nuclear *omnicide*—the extinction of humanity, by humanity. The second is the crisis of global climate change. The third is the crisis of inequality wherein a tiny minority owns most of the world's wealth while globally tens of thousands of people die daily from lack of adequate access to food, potable water, and/or basic healthcare.[32] Without drastic moves toward progressive and democratic structural reform, it is difficult to imagine how any (much less, all) of these crises can be resolved. With these sobering exigencies in mind, the theory of the tripartite state seeks to illuminate our current political dystopia and to place it in the appropriate historical context.

Hegemony vs. *Empire*

The scholarly foundations of this book are eclectic. Theories pertaining to hegemony, imperialism, the dual state, and administrative prerogative are examined and critiqued. The concept of hegemony is crucial in the realms of international and US politics. Scholars who address hegemony differ mostly across a dimension that places the emphasis either on coercive dominance or upon consensual leadership.[33] John Mearsheimer—the original "offensive realist" of the international relations (IR) subdiscipline of political science—emphasizes dominance.[34] Michael Sullivan focuses on the coercive aspect of US foreign policy.[35] Kindleberger and other *hegemonic stability* theorists assert that the international system can only function smoothly when there is a hegemonic state that provides public goods internationally.[36] Susan Strange's concept of structural power serves to bridge the gap between coercion and consent.[37] Structural power allows the powerful country to determine the rules of the international political economy by which others must play. Through the use of structural power, countries can constrain and control other actors without the application of overt force.[38] As a historical materialist, Robert Cox describes hegemonic world order established by dominance over three realms: material, ideational, and institutional.[39] Arrighi and Silver similarly see hegemony as not simply dominance. Instead, the hegemon's power is amplified by virtue of the fact that it is perceived by relevant others as leading in a way that is beneficial for itself and others.[40]

While hegemony and imperialism are related concepts, it is important to highlight their differences and similarities. *Imperialism* can be a term that is used pejoratively to emphasize the international exercise of power that is unaccountable or illegitimate.[41] Theories of empire and imperialism are intertwined with theories pertaining to hegemony. Maier asserts that there is little substantial conceptual difference between theories of hegemony and empire; the terms can be used almost synonymously.[42] Or there can be subtle distinction. Michael Doyle defines *empire* as "effective control, whether formal or informal, of a subordinated society by an imperial society."[43] By contrast, he defines *hegemony* as an international order in which the dominant state controls "much or all of the external, but little or none of the internal, policy of other states."[44] Ikenberry writes about hegemony and world order from a historical institution-alist perspective. He makes explicit distinction between empire and *liberal hegemony* as two ideal types of hierarchical world order. Empire is described as rule in which control is exerted over subordinate states through direct or indirect means; sovereignty is controlled by the impe-rial state. Control is maintained through networks of elites in the center and periphery states.[45]

For Ikenberry, there are three general features of *liberal hegemonic order* which differentiate it from *empire*. First, the hegemon establishes rules and institutions which are arrived at through negotiations. The hegemon sponsors the system and acts within its rules. Second, the hegemon pro-vides international "public goods" in exchange for the cooperation of the other states. Even without taxing the other states, the hegemon still ben-efits overall by providing public goods for the system. Third, the liberal hegemonic order creates and maintains channels and networks that allow states to informally influence the governance of the international sys-tem.[46] The liberal Ikenberry believes that that the postwar era of American dominance was *liberal hegemonic* in character. After the 2001 World Trade Center attacks, he asserts, "the American-led hierarchical order began to take on imperial characteristics."[47]

Historical materialists provide definitions of imperialism that may explain much of the history of great power politics and its respective impe-rial actors. Writing in the early twentieth century, John Hobson famously described imperialism as stemming from underconsumption and capital accumulation in capitalist nations.[48] Lenin expanded on Hobson's thesis with an additional emphasis on the pivotal role of finance capital.[49] In the mid-twentieth century, Joseph Schumpeter argued that although imperi-alism had some materialist motivations, its causes were also sociological and stemmed in part from aggressive parts of human nature. For reasons perhaps stemming from conformist aspects of human nature, Schumpeter reasoned that capitalism, as opposed to being inherently imperialistic, would gradually lead to further rationalization of society and thereby cur-tail humanity's imperialist tendencies.[50] In the 1960s, dependency theory emerged to describe imperialist dynamics which accounted for the political and economic disparities in the developing world.[51] This was a challenge to the dominant *modernization* paradigm which posited that countries were merely at differing stages of development or *modernization*.[52]

Following the decline of dependency theory, imperialism became a less commonly deployed concept in political theory. One exception to this trend was Michael Parenti who in the 1990s provided a usefully broad definition of imperialism as "the process whereby the dominant politico-economic interests of one nation expropriate for their own enrichment the land, labor, raw materials, and markets of another people."[53] Nominally "post-Marxist" scholars Hardt and Negri in 2000 described empire without imperialism—an agentless, postmodern world order characterized by a novel globalized sovereignty which had effectively ended state sovereignty.[54] In other words, Hardt and Negri recognized that in the neoliberal global system, countries were constrained from pursuing independent, economic development in accordance with their respective national interests. One-upping their fellow hyperstructuralist[55] scholars, they not only effectively absolve US elites from responsibility for intentionally creating and maintaining this system—they essentially removed the US from their formulation. This could be called *hegemonic erasure*!

Given subsequent history, Hardt and Negri were at best premature in declaring the nation-state irrelevant. In the early twenty-first century, more scholars began to revisit the concept of imperialism. This rediscovery was to clear, mounting evidence of structural inequalities throughout the global system as well as American militarism after 2001.[56] Materialist (i.e., Marxist) conceptions of empire became more common. Writing in 2003, David Harvey acknowledged that "imperialism" is a term that can be used for polemical rather than analytical purposes.[57] In discussing capitalist imperialism, Harvey describes empire as "a distinctly political project on the part of actors whose power is based in command of a territory and a capacity to mobilize its human and natural resources towards political, economic and military ends." The "project" is the assertion of the imperial state's interests in the larger world. [58]

In sum, the stronger case is not that *hegemony* and *empire* are opposing ends on a continuum, but that the concepts are characterized more by overlap. This point is crucial to understanding the US-dominated world order established after World War II. To recap, Ikenberry claims that prior to 2001, the US was "liberal hegemonic" and after 2001, it took on imperial characteristics. Similarly, Doyle asserts that hegemonies do not control the internal politics of sovereign states. Any assertion that the postwar US was hegemonic fails to conform to Doyle's definition, given the numerous cases in which the US did intervene to dramatically impact the internal politics of sovereign states. Similarly, Ikenberry's assertion of America's *liberal hegemony* ignores the repeated US violations of state sovereignty during this era. These US interventions served to forge an international order characterized by hierarchical relationships maintained to a considerable degree by elite networks in the hegemonic and subordinate states.[59] Even so, no dominant power can rule wholly, or even mostly, by coercion. The consensual aspects of *hegemony* are essential. Therefore, it can be said that *any empire must constantly endeavor to maintain its hegemony.*

In the case of the US-led world order, several points emerge. The US was in an historically unprecedented position of power after World War II. Capitalizing on its structural power, the US dominated the material, ideological, and institutional arenas of the world order which emerged. The US-led world order has been preserved and extended with varying degrees of consent along with covert or overt coercion, but always with the strategic goal of maintaining American hegemony.[60] That the US has striven for *imperial hegemony*—i.e., hegemony in the pursuit of empire— is a foundational assumption of this work. The forces that compel the US to pursue empire are of key significance.

Scholarship on Foreign Policy:
Alternative Explanations and Approaches

Within history and the social sciences, there are a number of approaches and paradigms that have been developed to understand and explain international politics and foreign policy. The political science subfield of international relations (IR) has produced two dominant sets of approaches: international systemic and decision-making analysis. The first, as you might guess, focuses on the structure of the international system. Its practitioners often repurpose models and insights from economics to emphasize the rational preferences and strategies of actors whose decisions are influenced by the constraints and opportunities of the international system. The second broad approach entails the analysis of decision-making processes. Its practitioners deploy insights from psychology and social psychology to explain and understand the impediments to rationality.[61] The international systemic approaches are discussed here, while the decision-making analysis approaches—along with subdiscipline of Foreign Policy Analysis—are discussed in a later chapter.

The international systemic approaches of IR scholars can be grouped by the models that they deploy. Three approaches use models that are particularly relevant: *realism*, *liberalism* (sometimes termed "global society"), and *Marxism*.[62] The oldest and most well-known is realism. In both its classical and modern versions, realists are most concerned with issues of war and peace. States are the central actors, and they operate rationally within an anarchic international system to maximize their security, power, and national interest. Classical realists in the postwar era, like Hans Morgenthau, borrowed from Thucydides by incorporating analysis from the systemic, internal (domestic politics), and individual realms to explain international politics and history.[63] So-called *neorealists*, beginning with Kenneth Waltz, shifted the focus more exclusively to the "anarchy" of the international system in which states seek to achieve security and avoid subordinating their interests to those of other states.[64] Neorealism eventually split, beginning with Mearsheimer's "offensive realism" revision wherein states—specifically, *great powers*—seek to maximize power rather than security.[65]

The second subset of systemic IR approaches can be characterized as *liberal* or *neoliberal*. Liberal IR scholars try to correct what they perceive as the excessive emphasis that realism places on war and upon states (conceived as unitary actors).[66] Contra realism: international organizations, domestic and transnational civil society organizations, and various other non-state entities are also actors in liberal IR scholarship. Issues like welfare, economic development, and the environment warrant attention. They can give rise to institutions that foster international cooperation, even though leaders of states may be motivated by self-interest rather than altruism. Most notably deriving from Kant's *democratic peace theory*, liberalism in IR—more often than realism—analyzes states' domestic politics to explain foreign policy. Beginning in the 1970s, scholars like

Krasner[67] and Kindleberger[68] produced works on the cooperative, stabilizing aspects of hegemony. In other words, they argued that stability and cooperation can result from having a powerful state that presides over an international system. The early theorists subsequently influenced the founders of what would become *neoliberal institutionalism* in IR, most notably Robert Keohane and Joseph Nye.[69] The neoliberalism of Keohane and Nye maintains that states and societies are connected through various channels and institutions that have eclipsed the Westphalian system of sovereign nation-states.

The realist and liberal schools essentially dominate mainstream IR in the US. Their practitioners disagree on various issues. Most significantly, they disagree about the nature of international institutions and whether they have real agency or are simply constructs that serve to advance states' interests. At various times, one or the other school may have seemed to have the upper hand, so to speak. The end of the Cold War was seen by many as weakening the case for realism's explanatory power. The Global War on Terror (GWOT) could be analyzed persuasively by both approaches. The GWOT-era's interstate wars and military alliance politics are the wheelhouse of realism. The significance of non-state actors, transnational networks, and international institutions provided fertile ground for liberal IR scholars.

With the present US turn toward what the Pentagon terms "great power competition," it seems that realism has new relevance. However, in recent years institutions like the Shanghai Cooperative Council (SCO) have been formed to try and create a *multipolar* world order that may gradually cause the US to recede as the global hegemon. Ironically, it is these "revisionist" powers that advocate for the observance of international law. American officials, meanwhile, have asserted that the US "will not accept policies or actions that threaten or undermine the *rules-based international order* [emphasis added],"[70] even as the US (often aided by allies) routinely conducts foreign policy in violation of international and domestic US law. Thus, it should be understood that when pro-US figures use the term, "rules-based international order," they are not referring to anything analogous to *the rule of law*. Quite the opposite, they are using Orwellian language to describe a system in which essentially no rules can be established and/or observed, given that the dominant state has the prerogative to violate and/or rewrite "rules" at its whim.

The third subset of IR's systemic approaches is Marxism. Most notable are *dependency theory*[71] and Wallerstein's *world systems theory*.[72] Marxist IR scholars focus on exploitation and inequality in the world capitalist system. The powerful *core* nations dominate the periphery, i.e., the "developing world," the "Third World," or the "Global South." Elites in the periphery benefit from their connections with the core and thus subordinate their countries' national interests to their elite class interests. Dependency theory emerged from the failure of modernization theory to explain lingering underdevelopment in the global south, especially Latin America. It fell in prominence in part due to the success of the East Asian "tiger" nations: Japan, Taiwan, and South Korea. Additionally, the debt crises of the 1980s allowed high finance to require nations to abandon dependency theory's recommended policy prescriptions of protectionism, nationalization of key industries, and import substitution industrialization.

Latin America's halting political and economic progress of the '60s ground to a halt and was reversed beginning with the Johnson administration. Effectively, JFK's liberal Alliance for Progress policies were replaced by LBJ's "Mann doctrine" which established that Latin American governments would be treated on the basis of their conformity to US interests, i.e., US business interests. A wave of *praetorianism* followed whereby the US supported military regimes that crushed progressive political forces. Eventually, the Third World debt crisis and subsequent "structural adjustments" made nationalist, state-directed strategies for economic development no longer feasible in the Global South. At that point, democracy was no longer a threat. Thus began an era of US "democracy promotion," since structural constraints no longer allowed for any meaningful democratic control over national economies. Through debt and the dominance of international finance, Latin America had been made "safe for democracy."

Prior to the era of US "democracy promotion," it was US policy under Johnson and Nixon—not domestic factors in Latin American countries—which gave rise to the military regimes.[73] Perhaps understandably, many scholars attribute this to the exigencies of the Cold War. However, the intervening years have made the Cold War explanation less tenable. The

twenty-first century "pink tide" in Latin America brought progressive governments to power in several countries. The American response is illuminating. The US in the twenty-first century has opposed and attempted to
undermine governments across the region, notably in Venezuela, Honduras,
Nicaragua, and Brazil. Under Obama and Trump administrations, the
rollback of the "pink tide" belies assertions that previous policies can be
explained merely by reference to US fears of the Soviet-led international
communist conspiracy. An honest historical appraisal points to the conclusion that the obsolescence or theoretical weaknesses of dependency theory
were greatly overstated by mainstream US academics.

The realist, liberal, and Marxist traditions in IR can all make useful
contributions to understanding international politics and specifically the
hegemonic continuity of US foreign policy. While realists are understood
to conceive of the state as a unitary actor, this is often overstated. Some
of the most interesting realist works examine domestic political processes
to discern how and why nations abandon more sober realist prescriptions
and instead pursue harmful policies. For example, Jack Snyder's *Myths of
Empire* (1991) details how domestic politics led to the disastrous policies
pursued by Germany and Japan. Similar analyses have been applied to the
US case, but more typically by historians as detailed later.

In 2007, the eminent realists John Mearsheimer and Stephen Walt
famously published *The Israel Lobby and US Foreign Policy*. It can be
argued that the authors were actually deploying a *deep politics* approach to
their analysis of US foreign policy. Lobbies are a significant component of
America's deep political system. As Walt and Mearsheimer point out, part
of the Israel Lobby's success stems from the fact that its power had been
seldom acknowledged or elaborated upon in the mainstream of academic
and public discourse. Though the authors predictably received considerable opprobrium and shrill denunciations from pro-Israel partisans and
the corporate media, the works stands as an example to those who would
seek to better inform political debates by bringing suppressed facts to light.

The liberal tradition offers a tighter focus either on domestic sources
of foreign policy or on the workings of international institutions. The
weakness of most mainstream liberal analysis perhaps stems from a reluc-
tance to acknowledge the lawlessness and violence to which US foreign

policy habitually resorts. Additionally, there seems to be a taboo against materialism—i.e., against critiques of capitalism. It is an open question whether this is due to anticommunism or post-Cold War triumphalism or the influence of capitalist-endowed foundations. The result is that the zeitgeist of academic approaches often obscures the anti-democratic total-izing effects of the corporate overworld upon foreign policy, international organizations, and global civil society. In particular, certain foreign policy phenomena are undertheorized. These include the use of "democracy promotion" to pursue undemocratic goals (i.e., to establish governments that adopt policies that benefit a small economic elite) or the weaponiza-tion of human rights (e.g., Western security services funding the so-called "White Helmets" in Syria to deploy as propaganda assets in another illegal regime change campaign).[74] In short, the mainstream of the liberal tradi-tion in IR—like American political science in general—is too credulous about official narratives, too sanguine about the autonomy of interna-tional institutions, and too reluctant to apply materialist analysis when it is warranted. In particular, the mainstream does not acknowledge the extent to which militarism, covert/paramilitary violence, state lawlessness in foreign policy, and exploitative international institutions are all of a piece—essential aspects of the US-managed global capitalist system. The explanatory power and empirical strength of materialist perspectives are wholly disproportionate to the small space they occupy in the prevailing, ostensibly pluralist, academic discourse.

Ole Holsti's effective survey of IR perspectives on foreign policy nevertheless reveals the extent to which critical scholarship such as this dissertation are anathema to American political scientists. He states, accu-rately, that realism will continue to be of use to diplomatic historians: "Those who focus on security issues can hardly neglect [realism's] central premises and concepts." Likewise, liberal IR approaches "will be helpful to historians with an interest in the evolution of the international system and with the growing disjuncture between demands on states and their ability to meet them." However, and on the other hand, "It is much less clear that [Marxism] will provide useful new insights to historians. If one has trouble accepting certain assumptions [e.g.,] that there has been and is today a 'world capitalist system' [. . .] then the kinds of analyses that follow are likely to seem flawed."[75] To wit (and to paraphrase): For the mainstream exemplar Holsti, realism and liberalism in IR are useful and vital approaches, but Marxism is markedly less so; there may not even be a *world capitalist system* anyway, so the tradition is of dubious utility.

Holsti also demonstrates in passing the political scientist's aversion to the prospect of high criminality in the US. In his otherwise trenchant critique of postmodernism, he states that, "[I]f one rejects the feasibility of research standards because they necessarily 'privilege,' some theories or methodologies, does that not also rule out judgements of works by Holocaust deniers or of conspiracy buffs who write, for example, about the Kennedy assassination [. . .]?"[76] This formulation equates or at least approvingly juxtaposes critics of the Warren Commission with Holocaust deniers. It would be noteworthy if the statement simply reflected a political scientist's deference to official narratives, however, the most recent and most extensive official investigation of the Kennedy assassination ruled the president's death to have been the result of a "probable conspiracy." Additionally, Robert Kennedy himself came to believe the CIA and its allies had killed his brother but felt powerless to act on this knowledge without control of the presidency itself. Jackie Kennedy, Lyndon Johnson, and various world leaders did not believe the Warren Commission's theory of the two *lone nuts*. Public acceptance of the Warren Commission fell into the single digits in the mid-1970s.[77] The Commission's theory of the assassination was that a 'lone nut' killed the president and was soon killed by another 'lone nut.' This explanation steadily lost credibility with the public following the Warren Report's initial release. Revelations of intelligence community abuses in the wake of Watergate further diminished its acceptance, as did the first public broadcasting of the video of the assassination in which the president appears to have been killed by a bullet coming from the wrong direction relative to the alleged position of the alleged assassin.

It is telling that while neither the public or elites found the Warren Report credible, America's liberal sense-making institutions—the media and academia—have largely defended it. In using these examples to point out the aversion of American political science to Marxism and the possibility of Western state crimes, I am not suggesting that one should instead expect from scholars the wholesale adoption of historical materialism and the subjection of every single official narrative to exhaustive forensic examination. Rather, the point is that there are normative conventions against approaches that utilize holistic critiques of (A) capitalism, (B) imperialism, and/or (C) the lawfulness of the state. Such taboos may serve to preclude or marginalize scholarship with considerable explanatory and predictive power. If it turned out that the political power of economic elites was the decisive factor that lay at the heart of some of social science's most persistent problematics, the marginalization of thusly informed scholarship greatly handicaps US social science. Analyses generated by such critical perspectives need not be demonstrably *proven* in total; intellectual pluralism should allow for a multiplicity of viable and tenable approaches. The lack of diversity begs one to question whether the political hegemony of economic elites has, through various mechanisms, somehow influenced the character of academic discourse—political science and economics in particular—by narrowing the spectrum of acceptable critique. In case it needs to be stated, this book hits the taboo trifecta: the international and domestic lawlessness of the state is driven by the corporate rich whose interests are advanced by US imperialism.

CHAPTER 2

HISTORY AND THE ISSUE
OF *THE EXCEPTION*

Diplomatic History

Outside of political science, history offers a vast amount of scholarship pertaining to the global role of the US. World War I gave rise to the first generation of US diplomatic historians. Their efforts quickly led to the creation of two schools or approaches within the field, *nationalist* and *progressive*.[1] Over time, these early approaches evolved into two traditions which can be termed *orthodox* and *progressive*, respectively. Exemplified by Samuel Flagg Bemis, the nationalist approach emphasized the continuity of American foreign policy.[2] Its practitioners offered a triumphalist account of the rise of US power and the diplomatic traditions that emerged from core principles such as those embodied in the Monroe Doctrine.[3] In general, the nationalist school focused on state-to-state diplomacy and policymaking elites while deemphasizing the domestic determinants of US foreign policy.[4] Alternatively, the progressive approach—led by Charles Beard[5]—sought to illuminate and incorporate the worldviews of US officials as well as the economic, political, and regional influences on their policymaking. Because these influences changed over time, the progressive approach emphasized change and conflict over continuity and consensus.[6]

The rise of fascism, the Holocaust, the dropping of the bomb, and the Cold War eventually came to disillusion intellectuals—including even some the formerly triumphalist nationalist historians like Bemis and Perkins. Their critiques tended to attribute bad policymaking to public opinion and excessive partisanship. Pessimism became a hallmark of the leading historians who wrote about US foreign policy in the 1950s and 1960s—realists like George Kennan[7] and Hans Morgenthau.[8] Like the earlier nationalists, realist historians focused on the state, policymaking elites, and the application of state power to advance US national interests. They also followed the nationalists in deemphasizing the elite domestic determinants of foreign policy, blaming public opinion, political partisanship, and idealism for bad policies. The antidote, the realists argued, was a professionalized elite who could use their disinterested expertise to devise rational diplomatic strategies. The realists were appealing to government officials for a number of reasons, including their celebration of elitism and power, their tendency to write prescriptively about geopolitics and grand strategy, and their disinterest in the domestic sources of US foreign policy. Their analyses served to rationalize open-ended international commitments, the further acquisition of power, and techniques of containment.[9]

The progressive tradition of Charles Beard was eventually rekindled in the 1960s and 1970s by William Appleman Williams[10] and other revisionists. Returning to an emphasis on the domestic sources of US foreign policy, the revisionists focused on American ideology and the country's liberal capitalist system. The revisionist narrative maintained that after the "closing of the frontier," US leaders pursued overseas expansion in response to political and economic crises. American imperialism qualitatively changed from being a continental enterprise justified by *manifest destiny* to a militarized maritime endeavor founded on the liberal commercial principles of John Hay's "Open Door." American leaders, the revisionists argued, had betrayed the country's core principles in creating an overseas empire. Unlike the realists, they blamed the US for the outbreak of the Cold War. Furthermore, the revisionists harshly critiqued US policy toward the developing world. Like James Beard, they sought to illuminate the influence of non-state actors—big business and finance, especially. They reemphasized the significance of ideas in the history of US foreign policy, depicting American policymakers as rational actors seeking to achieve political outcomes on the basis of a coherent, though misguided, conception of the national interest.[11]

The revisionists eventually came to be criticized by more orthodox American historians, most notably John Lewis Gaddis.[12] On somewhat predictable bases, these critics deemed that the revisionist school was too economically deterministic, paid too little attention to competing domestic political groups, and failed to acknowledge either the reasonable national security priorities of policymakers or the impact of other states' actions on US foreign policy. Calling themselves "postrevisionist," their counter-revisionist historiography returned to a realist focus on the state, policy elites and geopolitical grand strategy while emphasizing notions like national security, the national interest, and power politics.[13] The postrevisionists treated economics as one instrument of geopolitical grand strategy, not the driving force behind American foreign policy. Relative to the revisionists, they were much more sanguine about America's early Cold War foreign policy. For their counter-revisionist narrative, if there was such a thing as an "American empire," It came by invitation from overseas rather than from forces within the American political economy. Any post–World War II US empire, they maintained, was a defensive and consensual enterprise established in response to the Cold War—which the Soviet Union started.[14] The chief weakness of the postrevisionist approach was that it did not actually provide what it advertised: a synthesis of the extant historiography. This was most succinctly captured by Warren Kimball who surmised: "postrevisionism is, at best, [. . .] orthodoxy plus archives."[15]

Perhaps postrevisionism, and thus orthodoxy, reached its apex with Leffler's "national security approach."[16] The key concept, *national security*, is defined as "the protection of core values from external threats."[17] As Bruce Cumings points out, Leffler agrees with many of the revisionists' key findings: US officials distorted Soviet actions, opportunistically inflated the Soviet threat, wanted to reform rather than destroy Western colonialism, misconstrued nationalist revolutions in the Third World, and utilized every manner of fascist or retrograde Anticommunist dictator.[18] Therefore, Leffler's national security approach is an actual synthesis of sorts, unlike Gaddis's postrevisionism which essentially sought to nullify and/or delegitimize revisionism. However, as with Gaddis, Leffler sees economics as subservient to national security, not the other way around as the revisionists would have it. Therefore, Leffler's national security approach—by attributing US foreign policy to realist (rather than economic) motives—can be fairly described as a rearguard defense of orthodoxy.

The progressive tradition in diplomatic history is alternatively termed *revisionism* or the *Wisconsin School* or the *New Left*. Collectively, the progressive historians offer a much more useful approach to understanding US foreign policy, the world order it created, and the era of imperial decline we are experiencing currently. Indeed, an examination of the devastating US policies toward places like Honduras, Libya, and Venezuela demonstrates that US still pursues and maintains hegemony in part by targeting governments that enact progressive economic policies. More than any other third world countries, Libya and Venezuela measurably reduced material deprivation through state intervention in the economy. With the Soviet Union long defunct, US policy cannot be explained by recourse to the "global communist conspiracy." The policies can be easily explained (and predicted) by the Wisconsin School's approach which posits that since the closing of the frontier, the US has sought and maintained an empire of "free trade" (read: "free investment"). Twenty-first-century Libya and Venezuela transgressed in the manner of Mossedegh, Arbenz, Lumumba, Allende, Sukarno and others: they used resource rents to fund social programs to help the masses of poor people in their countries. Likewise, materialist historiography could also best explain the "puzzle" of NATO's post–Cold War persistence: the alliance is a militarized coalition that protects the economic and geopolitical interests of the US and its European client states, especially against defiant socialist states like Serbia and Libya—and now against Russian and/or Chinese influence. Just as Vietnam served to elevate William Appleman Williams' stature, the increasingly farcical history of the Global War on Terror should serve to enhance the legitimacy of materialist, progressive historiography. By "farcical" I refer to the chronology wherein the US and its client states created the Mujahideen and al Qaeda jihadi networks and deployed them against the Soviets in the 1980s and in Azerbaijan, Bosnia, Kosovo, Libya, and Chechnya in the 1990s.[19] In 2001, elements of these networks attacked the US, thereby providing pretexts for the creation of massive surveillance regimes and disastrous, dubious wars in strategically significant countries. And finally, through obscure mechanisms, these strange paramilitary jihadi forces ended up being armed, funded, and deployed in US regime change campaigns in Libya and Syria during the Obama administration.

The orthodox approach cannot adequately explain these dynamics. Leffler's national security approach could only do so if empire itself is taken as the sacrosanct core value to be protected from external threats. Such was essentially the argument put forward by the neoconservative Project for a New American Century. Admittedly, one cannot prove definitively that such ideas are borne of material causes. Perhaps interrogating potentially analogous ideas could provide some insight. Was American white supremacist ideology in the antebellum South a cause or a consequence of the persistence of slavery? Was the *divine right of kings* a cause or a consequence of feudalism? Was *manifest destiny* a cause or a consequence of western expansion? What about the *White Man's Burden* or *American exceptionalism*? Obviously, the point is that power structures give rise to legitimizing myths—not the other way around. This was recognized and illustrated as far back as the "myth of the metals" example of the "noble lie" offered by Plato who, it should be acknowledged, was not a Marxist, trying to explain things like *base* and *superstructure*. All of this is not to say that legitimizing myths cannot become so salient as to "take on a life of their own." Merely, it is to say that this should not obscure the myths' origins and their utility.

Maybe it does require an inferential leap to arrive at the assumption that wealthy and powerful elites seek to dominate their societies politically and economically in order to further aggrandize their wealth and power. The "leap" entails assuming that elites enjoy their status—a social circumstance at which they or their ancestors arrived intentionally and which they seek to maintain or improve. As C. Wright Mills pointed out, elites of power are constrained or empowered by their respective historical circumstances.[20] By virtue of postwar America's historically unprecedented economic and military strength—in absolute and relative terms—no social class has ever had the power of the postwar US elite. As with the elites of any great power, they sought hegemony over as much of human society as was feasible. In the exceptional US case, this allowed for the establishment of a unipolar world order whose institutions allowed for the amassing of vast fortunes. US hegemony, or what Dan Ellsberg calls the "covert empire," also dramatically altered and distorted American institutions—in particular democracy and the rule of law. The Wisconsin School historians were particularly adroit at developing a historiography that provides a deep understanding of how these circumstances came to be.

Despite the acuity of New Left historiography, its practitioners have come to be somewhat marginal within the discipline. As Buzzanco (1999) summarized: "The New Left [. . .] has virtually disappeared from the landscape of diplomatic history, swept away by an ideological counterrevolution from the right and an abandonment from today's so-called left."[21] The "so-called left" is a reference to the postmodern, culturalist, and social historians who have eclipsed materialists in the field. Throughout the 1990s, only around 10 percent of *Diplomatic History* articles focused on economic aspects of US foreign policy, and by Buzzanco's reading, only one of those articles could be described "as having a leftist cast."[22] In the second edition of the ubiquitous *Explaining the History of American Foreign Relations*, only three of the fifteen chapters on methods and theories focus on economic matters—dependency theory, world systems theory, and corporatism respectively.[23] Given the explanatory power of materialist historiography at this moment of imperial decline and political paralysis in the face of multiple crises, perhaps the decline of materialism in diplomatic history is, by and large, an example of "winners" getting to write the history.

Setting aside the trends in the academic mainstream of history, the New Left/progressive historians inform the *deep politics* approach applied herein. Charles Beard himself was an earlier exemplar of the deep politics approach, even if he obviously did not name it as such. His methodology sought to uncover the obscure domestic political forces that guided US policymakers. Beard famously formulated his own version of what later became known as the "conspiracy theory of the 14th Amendment" in which he suggested that, at the behest of vested interests, the 14th amendment had been written to provide a basis for subsequent judicial rulings that established corporate personhood.[24] His last book (1948) argued that Roosevelt and his administration had done tremendous damage to US democracy by manipulating events to allow for American entry into World War II.[25] Decades later, William Appleman Williams and his descendants likewise cast a critical eye toward elite US policymakers whose public pronouncements belied the powerful vested economic interests that determined policy.

Historian Bruce Cumings rejects the label "revisionist." Nonetheless, he comes from the progressive tradition and emphasizes the obscured political influence of the power elite. Various historical episodes affirm this approach. For example, many of the most powerful Americans in the mid-twentieth century like Dean Acheson and John McCloy were not given to candidly discussing the core interests and motivations behind the policies they advocated, sometimes referring to such things as "imponderables."[26] McCloy himself was known to be "a Rockefeller man."[27] The most notable "realist" policymakers of the Cold War were men with very powerful patrons. Like McCloy, Kissinger was also a Rockefeller man. Prior to campaigning for Nelson Rockefeller's 1968 presidential run, Kissinger had been his assistant. Rockefeller also commissioned him to write a book for the Council on Foreign Relations on limited warfare.[28] Kissinger married an aide to Rockefeller, owned a Georgetown mansion thanks to Rockefeller loans and gifts, and used a palatial Rockefeller-owned bomb shelter to store his secret papers when things looked grim for the Nixon administration.[29] Zbigniew Brzezinski was also a Rockefeller man. George Kennan's patron was Dean Acheson. Cumings argues that the realist Kennan never really understood his boss, the Wall Street internationalist.[30] Kennan, Kissinger, Brzezinski—each was a "realpolitik engineer for an architecture never fully articulated."[31] It is not difficult to grasp the utility of such realists. They formulate and execute grand strategy based on a conception of the "national interest" which is—surprise!—in concert with the class interests of their patrons. Even when addressing historical episodes in which the decisive elite influences are obscured, the revisionists outperform the orthodox (i.e., "postrevisionist") historians. The reason for this is best summed up by Lloyd Gardner:

> Early books on the origins of the Cold War were little more than annotated collective memoirs of Americans who participated in that

transition period. The historian's facts and conclusions had already been chosen for him before he began. Scholars personally involved in the Cold War devoted themselves to producing "White Papers" on Russian violations of their agreements with the West. The object was to see how big a list of these misdeeds one could put together. If the President said that the Soviet Union had violated forty-seven pacts and treaties, the State Department scurried around to draw up a list to conform to the accusation, and Cold War historians all too often come following after.[32]

This dynamic explains why the "postrevisionism" John Lewis Gaddis has been described as "orthodoxy plus archives"[33] and why "it can border on court history."[34]

New Left historiography also has informed important understandings about the US power structure. Michael Klare first introduced the idea of two powerful factions with the foreign-policymaking elite: the militarist *Prussians* (including oil and arms makers) and the internationalist commercial *traders* (including high finance and other transnational firms).[35] Peter Dale Scott also uses these terms and elaborates on the varying degrees of harmony and tension between the two groups.[36] Today these two broad groups could be called "neoconservatives" and "neoliberals." Both extend back in US history. The Cold War ancestors of the neoconservatives were the advocates of "rollback" like Paul Nitze and Henry "Scoop" Jackson. The neoliberals' Cold War antecedent was the "liberal internationalism" of men like George Ball. The groups today existing as neoconservatives and neoliberals have benefited enormously from US hegemony. The firms that comprise their core constituencies are the largest in the world.

The revisionists deserve credit for delineating these aspects of US elite sociology. The *deep politics* approach goes even further. Peter Dale Scott has illuminated how elements of these two factions have intruded in US politics in history-making ways that have typically been suppressed or marginalized.[37] In one sense, the issue is whether America's liberal institutions have been able to quarantine the lawlessness of imperial foreign policy in such a way as to preserve the domestic rule of law and the integrity of the democratic US political system. In finding that America's liberal institutions have failed in this regard, I have developed concepts like *exceptionism* and the *tripartite state* and have attempted to place them in historical context. Such radical scholarship, hopefully, can be valuable in part as potential contributions to new understandings of political problems that to date have frustrated sensible responses to multiple crises—namely: climate change, the nuclear "doomsday machine," and staggering levels of economic inequality.

The State, *Exceptionism*, and Political Science

In political science terms, the central "puzzle" of this book is the continuity of US foreign policy—a grand strategy of imperial hegemony. In a liberal constitutional democracy, such a course would be untenable were the rule of law to be strictly adhered to. Therefore, central to this puzzle are two additional variables with steady trajectories over the same historical era: the institutionalized abrogation of the rule of law and the decline of democratic governance. In other words, the post–World War II US decision to pursue global dominance began an historical era in which state lawlessness became standard (if denied) and meaningful democracy (such as it was) gave way to "managed democracy"[38] or top-down rule.

Chronologically hashed out beginning in Chapter 6, the course was set most decisively with the outbreak of World War II. The cycle repeats across decades and presidential administrations to reproduce the postwar political order—US hegemony *uber alles*! At the point of origin, existing factors gave rise to what would become the imperial hegemonic general thrust. These factors included US power (in absolute and relative terms), the cohesion of US elites, and the opportunities and contingencies of that particular historical moment. This process has repeated itself over decades as such: In the context of these antecedent factors, the political response is formulated. Elites then mobilize to formulate the advancement of their respective and collective interests. Their plans must accommodate and/or overcome countervailing democratic pressures, especially those that are progressive and/or nationalist in character. The resultant grand strategy synthesis is the outcome of the balance of relevant political forces. Subsequently, officials and elites implement policy and pursue institutional and structural change as needed. The creation, transformation, and co-optation of institutions is a power elite project. The outcome for political, economic, and social institutions is more or less contested according to the cohesiveness of the elite and the countervailing democratic pressures that can be brought to bear.

Political choices are *path dependent*, meaning that such decisions greatly influence subsequent events as well as the available choices with which elites can respond. The power of the US elite as a class means that its actions impact the state, civil society, the economy, and liberal institutions like the media, academia, and electoral politics. Key consequences demonstrate the path dependency inherent in the cycle. Financial accumulation produces change in the overworld of corporate wealth and thus of the power elite as well. These are key components of the resulting outcomes which comprise the new set of antecedent circumstances to which the power elite will respond. Figure 1 below illustrates this basic cycle.

Because of the power of the executive branch, it is often fruitful to look at presidential administrations as case studies. The cycle repeats and imperial hegemony gets reproduced. In its broad outlines, this could be an anodyne *historical institutionalist* rendering of postwar US politics with Millsian elite theory influences. What may be original here are the proposed mechanisms. Decisively, these include parapolitical exceptionist

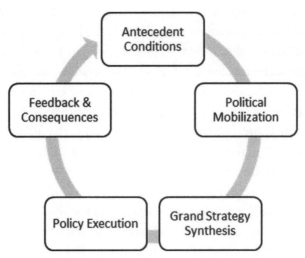

Figure 1. Hegemonic reproduction in US postwar politics.

(i.e., covert and unlawful) interventions borne of the securitization of politics and obscured by overarching state secrecy. The purportedly existential threat of the global communist conspiracy allowed for the creation of the postwar national security state. The securitization of politics, a power elite project, transformed the state and state/society relations. Unprecedented state secrecy gave the power elite vastly expanded realms in which to pursue desired political ends. Its dimensions and details obscured by state secrecy, *exceptionism*—the institutionalized abrogation of the rule of law—allowed for the state to decisively influence politics at key moments in a top-down, authoritarian manner while practices of plausible deniability preserved a degree of democratic legitimacy. Parapolitical practices became institutionalized. Sovereignty in the Schmittian sense—the power to decide *the exception*—migrated to an increasingly opaque realm: the organs of national security and the emerging deep state. In this way, the US system of governance gradually transformed.

The creation of the national security state was undertaken in pursuit of imperial hegemony along lines laid out by elite planning that began prior to US entry into World War II. Its fateful departures from earlier US institutions were explained away with reference to its communist antithesis. Internationally and domestically, deep political forces used exceptionism to neutralize opposition to imperial hegemony and to the political dominance of the overworld. It is well established that such unconstitutional practices have been utilized domestically in various forms. Perhaps most well-known is the FBI's "red scare" spectacle, collectively and misleadingly known as "McCarthyism." The FBI's infamous COINTELPRO operations against the black power movement, antiwar Americans, and other activists are also noteworthy. These are *state crimes against democracy* (SCADs), and a central contention here is that these actions have been a key mechanism to maintain the trajectory of US imperial hegemony and to manage all major course corrections in a top-down fashion. Considerable evidence indicates that pivotal events in US political history such as the Kennedy assassinations, the King assassination, and Watergate have been—or included—unadjudicated SCADs originating from the largely opaque US deep state. Though we likely don't know the half of it, similar covert US interventions in international politics are even more well-documented in the historical record. These violate ratified treaties and, thusly, the US Constitution. Even setting aside the disputed SCADs, *exceptionism* has no constitutional basis and therefore warrants a reconsideration of the nature of the American state. The historical discussion and social science theory presented herein represent such an effort.

A Note on Exceptionism

The institutionalized abrogation of the rule of law, here termed *exceptionism*, has been a key mechanism of subverting US democracy and reproducing US predominance and imperial hegemony over the global capitalist system. Said Henry Kissinger, "The illegal we do immediately, the unconstitutional takes a little longer." The most obvious ways in which the illegal and unconstitutional have been routinized involves the United Nations Charter—specifically Article 2(4) which states that "All Members shall refrain in their international relations from the threat or use of force against the territorial integrity or political independence of any state." Written with considerable input from US postwar planners, the Charter establishes that the use of force is illegal without UN Security Council authorization except in cases of self-defense.[39] Article VI, section 2 of the US Constitution states that "all treaties made, or which shall be made, under the authority of the United States, shall be the supreme law of the land." In 1967, in response to the US bombing of North Vietnam, Richard Falk and a number of other distinguished American legal scholars wrote that the US was violating the UN Charter and thus,

> [B]ecause these actions violate the supreme law of the land, the question as to which branch of the Government may authorize them, or whether one branch of the Government may delegate to another branch legal powers to authorize them, becomes irrelevant. No branch of Government is permitted directly or indirectly (by delegation) to violate the Constitution.[40]

This very straightforward logic renders innumerable US foreign policies illegal under international *and* domestic law. Notable overt examples include US aggression against Cuba, North Vietnam, Cambodia, Grenada,

Yugoslavia, Afghanistan, Iraq, Syria, and the recent assassination of Qasem Soleimani. Innumerable US covert operations also clearly constitute the "use of force against the territorial integrity or political independence of any state." These include US-orchestrated regime change operations against Iran, Guatemala, Indonesia, Congo, South Vietnam, Brazil, Chile, Nicaragua, Haiti, Azerbaijan, Venezuela, Haiti again, Ukraine, and (in all likelihood) Bolivia.

Exceptionism also abounds domestically. The US government has exercised supralegal prerogative in such ways as to repeatedly violate the US Constitution, including its prohibitions against "abridging the freedom of speech, or of the press; or the right of the people peaceably to assemble," and "against unreasonable searches and seizures, [without] Warrants [issued] upon probable cause." According to Senate investigation, domestic programs that have violated these strictures in the Bill of Rights include the FBI's COINTELPRO operations, the FBI's campaign "to 'neutralize' [Martin Luther King] as an effective civil rights leader," the CIA's mail opening program which the FBI and CIA heads declared illegal in 1970 even as it continued, the NSA collection of millions of cables sent by private citizens, widespread wiretapping and bugging without warrant, the collection and dissemination of purely political or personal information obtained through electronic surveillance, hundreds (during the 1960s alone) of warrantless CIA/FBI break-ins which often involved theft and bugging, and the widespread use of informants to infiltrate and surveil "peaceful, law-abiding groups."[41] The FBI's exceptionism was succinctly expressed by the official who ran the Bureau's Intelligence Division for ten years. He testified,

> [N]ever once did I hear anybody, including myself, raise the question: "Is this course of action which we have agreed upon lawful, is it legal, is it ethical or moral." We never gave any thought to this line of reasoning, because we were just naturally pragmatic.[42]

Similar or perhaps even more egregious/widespread abuses have occurred in the twenty-first century. The US ratified the United Nations Convention Against Torture (CAT) in 1994. Besides outlawing torture, the CAT requires signatories to "ensure in its legal system that the victim of an act of torture obtains redress and has an enforceable right to fair and adequate compensation, including the means for as full rehabilitation as possible."[43] This indicates that not only are Bush administration officials guilty under CAT provisions, subsequent US administrations are also guilty for failing to prosecute the guilty parties and for obscuring the details of the crimes behind a wall of state secrecy.

The presidency of Donald Trump brings *exceptionism* into high relief. The assassination of Qassem Soleimani was a criminal act on multiple levels. Since Soleimani was an Iranian official in Iraq at the invitation of the Iraqi government, the assassination is a violation of the UN Charter. Besides violating the post-Watergate prohibition against assassination, the act violated the War Powers Act. Arguing that the assassination "justifies a third article of impeachment," law professor Bruce Ackerman points out that the War Powers Act requires the president "in every possible instance [to] consult with Congress" before using force in "situations where imminent involvement in hostilities is clearly indicated by the circumstances." Trump neglected to consult with the Speaker of the House as the act stipulates even though the president did take time to confer with his advisors and leading Republicans. The president ignored the statutory demand that he provide the required "constitutional and legislative authority" for his action. Additionally, the War Powers Act requires the president to either (A) demonstrate that he had preexisting congressional authorization or (B) convince Congress to grant such authorization.[44]

Arguably, the Soleimani assassination and the Trump impeachment fiasco writ large confirm *exceptionism* and much of the central arguments herein. To wit: In 2014, the Obama administration backed the overthrow of Ukraine's elected government. There were no legal repercussions whatsoever for this violation of the UN Charter. In 2020, Trump illegally assassinated Qassem Soleimani with impunity. Notably, President Trump was impeached, not for the murder of Soleimani, but on the basis of two other alleged acts: he threatened not to send US weaponry to the government the US illegally helped install in Ukraine and he encouraged said Ukrainian government to investigate the dubious and lucrative activities of former Vice President Joe Biden, his son Hunter Biden, and a Ukrainian gas company. The above would appear to confirm that US officials are able to "get away with murder" in the furtherance of imperial hegemony. However, it is reasonable to conclude that US officials do risk legal sanction should they impede imperial hegemonic policies like arming Ukraine or if they threaten to make other members of the elite subject to the rule of law.

Original Contribution

In dissertation form, this work sought to make an original contribution by drawing from and building upon *power elite* theory,[45] *dual state* theory,[46] and *SCAD* theory (deHaven-Smith 2006).[47] More specifically, *exceptionism* is identified as a crucial and overlooked mechanism in the reproduction of US imperial hegemony. A *tripartite theory of the state* is formulated to account for anomalies that are not congruent with (1) a Weberian conception of the state, (2) various *dual state* theories, or (3) the *SCAD* theory literature which did not attempt to formulate a theory of the state or to address institutionalized state criminality or to theorize the relationship between economic elites and the state. For readers less steeped in social science, Max Weber's classic definition of the state describes it as *that organization in a given territory which maintains a monopoly on the legitimate use of violence.*

As discussed in greater detail in Chapter 4, *power elite* theorist C. Wright Mills and his descendants like Domhoff and Phillips focus on the overdetermining political power wielded by those like-minded, increasingly interchangeable elites who occupy the organizational command posts in politics, the military, and big business.[48] In writing *The Power Elite*, Mills was heavily influenced by the Franz Neumann's *Behemoth: The Structure and Function of National Socialism* which showed how Germany's exceptionalist state arose from the highly concentrated politico-economic power bequeathed German elites by virtue of the cartel system.[49] Mills observed that US elites were similarly unified and similarly dominant politico-economically. By virtue of US predominance, they were "commanders of power unequaled in human history."[50]

Mills was ambivalent about the role of conspiratorial elites, and he did not assert criminalization of the state. He sensibly argued against the "conspiracy theory of history." However, he described a power structure in which a highly cohesive power elite could formulate plans in secret and then see them carried out so as to aggrandize their wealth and power while furthering their dominance over US society and the postwar international scene. Mills's caution was understandable because he died in 1962. The first major CIA expose was 1964.[51] It was not until 1975 that the government declassified NSC 68, the document that most explicitly called for the privately incorporated permanent war economy described by Mills in 1956. Many more revelations would come out in the 1970s, but it is clear that Mills could not have fathomed the depths of US covert operations or the extent to which these entities mediated between the criminal underworld and the "corporate rich" he described. Domhoff, perhaps Mills's most well-known descendent, takes an oddly categorical stance on the question of conspiratorial state crimes. He states this flatly in an essay titled, "There Are No Conspiracies."[52] He substantiates this with reference to the implausibility of a number of implausible grand conspiracy theories. While refuting various notions of compact, omnipotent conspiratorial cabals, Domhoff does not address the possibility argued herein— that state criminality and parapolitical institutions are one key aspect of the way that society is governed by the elite-dominated institutions that Domhoff illuminates.

Also included in the third chapter, *dual state* theory is examined and critiqued. Thinkers as far back as John Locke have imperfectly tried to resolve the problem of *the emergency* in the context of republican/liberal political institutions. Carl Schmitt famously wrote that true sovereignty lies with the party which decides "the exception"—the instance in which the law negates itself.[53] This leads to the conclusion that alongside the liberal democratic state, there lies an authoritarian security state: the *dual state* elucidated by Ernst Fraenkel, Hans Morgenthau, Ola Tunander, and Peter Dale Scott. The exception to constitutional mandates can be seen throughout the US historical record. Notable examples include the Alien and Sedition Acts under President Adams, and Lincoln's suspension of *habeus corpus*. Woodrow Wilson presided over the Espionage and Sedition Acts as well as the Palmer Raids, ironically buttressing his status as an exemplar of American Exceptionalism. The most recent and extensive political science rendering of the dual state is from Michael Glennon. Using the less provocative term *double government*, Glennon painstakingly details and substantiates the autonomy of the national security state.[54] While the strength of his work belies mainstream theories of liberal democratic US governance, he fails to situate his autonomous national security state within a critique of state-society relations and/or within the US power structure. By presenting a dualistic Weberian state, Glennon fails to account for the overdetermining power of the corporate rich upon the general thrust of postwar US foreign policy—the pursuit and maintenance of imperial hegemony. His scholarship adroitly illustrates how the US justice system is demonstrably incapable of checking the national security state. However, he does not explore the evidence or the implications of covert securitized lawlessness in US domestic politics.

The duality of the state underwent a categorical transformation at the outset of the Cold War. The exception was institutionalized through reference to the "twilight struggle" against the global communist conspiracy—an emergency without end. In government documents—notably NSC 68 and NSC 10/2—officials asserted and authorized the use of all means that "serve the purposes of frustrating the Kremlin design."[55] National security state officials secretly authorized the practice of formulating and executing covert operations to be carried out with plausible deniability. Since these operations were not typically acknowledged even after the fact, the clandestine apparatus has confounded any realistic notion of democratic sense-making. Policies, events, and outcomes gave way to a series of cover stories and limited hangouts. Mills wrote that the power elite were "crackpot realists" who had "replaced the responsible interpretation of events with the disguise of events by a maze of public relations."[56] With no operational knowledge of the clandestine services, Mills did not know the half of it.

In Chapter 5, the limits of dual state theory are addressed and reformulated through reference to theories of *deep politics*—"all those political practices and arrangements, deliberate or not, which are usually repressed rather than acknowledged."[57] In the governance of human civilizations, two general types of power can be discerned: top-down, coercive power and power that operates through consent derived from persuasion and argument. Throughout US history, America's democratic constitutional system existed alongside a *deep political system.* This means that governance occurred with institutions that accommodated "decision-making and enforcement procedures outside as well as inside those publicly sanctioned by law and society," along with "collusive secrecy and law-breaking."[58] Of particular significance are the extraconstitutional impacts of the overworld of politico-economic elites, the underworld of organized crime, and the institutions that mediate between them.

The process by which America's deep political system evolved into the tripartite state is chronicled in Chapter 6. World War II and the Cold War served to covertly formalize what had up to that point been informal arrangements of America's deep political system. Most notably, the overworld of corporate wealth orchestrated US plans for entering World War II and the postwar imperial hegemonic project through the Wall Street-dominated Council of Foreign Relations' *War and Peace Studies Project.*[59] To assist the war effort, the US created the Office of Strategic Services (OSS)—an Eastern establishment-dominated precursor to the CIA. Its operations foreshadowed the postwar deep state by utilizing the services of "the Syndicate"—the underworld organization headed by Meyer Lansky and Charles "Lucky" Luciano, the latter of whom was released from prison at the request of the former.

Incorporating elements from across the globe, the Cold War national security state conjured up a covert netherworld allowing for the history-making application of dark power—the expanding, overworld-directed *deep state.* Over years and across administrations, it came to be supra-national and beyond the control of the office of presidency—the nominal US head of state. As US hegemony over the international capitalist system proceeded, its overworld beneficiaries accumulated more wealth and power. The organic links between the corporate rich and the covert netherworld of the national security state gave rise to the hypertrophied US deep state. The growing fecklessness of the US public state and of US liberal institutions was inversely proportional to the rise of deep state power. It is argued in Chapter 4 that eventually the US was not best described as having a deep political system whose accommodations could influence state behavior. Rather, deep political forces could covertly assert sovereignty in the Schmittian sense. In other words, the US came to have a tripartite state system in which the overworld-directed deep state came to dominate over the public state and the security state. Deep political forces consolidated this with Reagan's ascension to the presidency. Since then, the open political logic of the public state has diminished considerably. Consequently, the US came to have a deep state system in which exceptionist dark power is a key component of the overworld dominance of the American political economy and US society. Chapters 4, 5, and 6 provide historical evidence and further theoretical elaboration. In offering this explanation of the continuity of US imperial hegemonic foreign policy, the insights of the deep politics approach and SCAD theory are applied to formulate an elaborated theory of the exceptionist tripartite state.

On Methodology

In a larger sense, this work embraces the attitude and approach toward methodology articulated by C. Wright Mills, who wrote the following in a response to criticism of *The Power Elite*:

> [T]here are many literary and journalistic people who distribute larger images of the social structure in which we live. By refusing to comment on these images, much less to take them in hand, [social scientists] allow, as it were, these literary types to create and to sustain all the images that guide and all the myths that obfuscate—as the case may be—our view of social reality. [. . .] We've tried to use what we found useful of newer research techniques, but we've refused to give up the larger problems because of any initial dogma about method. Above all, we've refused to become silly about transferring the models of physical proof into the social studies. We've kept the problem, whatever it is, foremost in mind and we've felt [. . .] that we'd just have to work out the best methods we could as we went along trying to solve the problem.[60]

In practice, this means that this book's methodology and theory are drawn eclectically from social science and history on the basis of, first and foremost, their utility toward illuminating the nature of *the problem*.

Although quantitative evidence in the form social statistics and data is used when appropriate, the bulk of the historical evidence is taken from narratives within secondary sources. This is a challenging enterprise since many of the most significant issues and relevant episodes are those that are the most incomplete and obscured from historians and the public. This conundrum is explicitly addressed by the *deep politics* approach which differentiates between *archival* historiography and *deep* historiography. *Archival history* is produced by archival historians who draw from government records. *Deep history* entails the creation of a "chronology of events concerning which the public records are often either falsified or nonexistent."[61] Since this book deals with deep politics in conjunction with well-known historical events, both approaches to history are employed herein. Likewise, both approaches are found within the secondary sources which provide the bulk of the historical data.

In evaluating historical sources, the issue of selection bias is unavoidable. A social scientist is likely to select sources that conform to his theoretical framework. Lustick (1996) states that historiographical patterns must be placed at the center of the approach taken by social scientists to evaluate their sources.[62] Even with such methodological issues in mind, there are significant challenges to accumulating historical evidence by which to evaluate the theory of the tripartite state. A central concern pertains to the study of *parapolitics* in general. Parapolitics is "a system or practice of politics in which accountability is consciously diminished."[63] Any study pertaining to parapolitics faces unique challenges. Many of the most relevant actors actively strive to obscure their activities and thereby falsify contemporaneous journalistic accounts and the historical record. Qualitative social science draws considerably from documentary evidence in the form of official documents, journalistic accounts, and individual memoirs. Additionally, social scientists avail themselves of secondary sources based on those materials. Primary sources may be incorrect owing to many factors. Secondary sources often offer conflicting analyses and at any rate they must be based upon primary or other secondary sources which may be unreliable in various ways. Any evaluation of these narrative sources is arrived at through highly subjective processes.[64]

These challenges affect historically focused social science in general and parapolitical research in particular. In order to best address these issues, Gibbs advocates a "critical reading approach."[65] Using techniques similar to those used by intelligence analysts, one can study US foreign policy and arrive at reasonable conclusions even in the face of systemic biases and state secrecy. Gibbs cites the example of Kremlinologists who studied the Soviet Union with considerable success during the Cold War.[66] Such an approach is very difficult as it requires considerable erudition and research skills. The researcher must discern historical truth using an almost forensic methodology.

Some social scientists have made the case that qualitative methodology should produce research that is replicable in ways that mirror quantitative research.[67] Gibbs puts forward an opposing view. He asserts that qualitative methods employ a unique logic of inquiry which does not allow for replication in a strict sense. This does not negate the benefits of using qualitative methods.[68] Even without strict replicability, a theory can still be evaluated according to criteria including simplicity, internal consistency, and the degree to which its predictions are in accordance with the empirical record.[69] While acknowledging that strict replicability is not feasible or desirable for qualitative social inquiry, it is still a priority to provide clear and precise citations so that the interpretations and empirical evidence can be more easily evaluated. Such efforts notwithstanding, the limitations of this methodology are worth stating candidly. Given that much of the history under discussion involves the parapolitical, it is not possible to assert that any account of such matters is unimpeachable or *the* definitive theory. One cannot have absolute confidence about assessments when information is decidedly incomplete owing to state secrecy and covert operations that are rendered "plausibly deniable" by contrived cover stories. In other words, one must *satisfice*.[70]

CHAPTER 3

ACADEMIA AND THE STATE

Dual State or *Double Government?*

A defining feature of the US-dominated world order has been the crucial role of the US national security state which emerged after World War II. Various theorists have assessed the nature of the liberal democratic state when it is mobilized in response to an emergency. In Weimar Germany, Carl Schmitt referred to such a situation as a "state of exception" in which legal norms must be discarded due to a "danger to the existence of the state."[1] For Schmitt, true sovereignty rested with the entity that decided when the *state of exception* existed: "Sovereign is he who decides the exception."[2] Notoriously, Schmitt joined the Nazi party and his writings became the juridical basis for the *exceptionalist* Nazi regime. A German émigré named Ernst Fraenkel wrote about the Nazi state in a 1941 book entitled *The Dual State: A Contribution to the Study of Dictatorship*. In it, Fraenkel outlined how under the German regime, the lawful, *normative state* had been augmented by a parallel, lawless *prerogative state*. This lawless *prerogative state* was ostensibly the lawful state's guarantor of security.[3] Along lines like those laid out by Carl Schmitt, such a guarantor was deemed necessary due to Weimar Germany's "emergency" circumstances.

Observing the rise of the postwar US national security state, the "classical realist" scholar Hans Morgenthau identified, in 1955, the emergence of dictatorial forms within the US government. As "security" took precedence over all other concerns, he asserted, a *dual state* was emerging. Power may nominally rest with those holding legal authority, but the security forces hold, at the very least, veto power over decisions.[4] Tunander (2009) asserts that the dual state consists of a "democratic state" operating according to legal prescriptions and a "security state" which is more authoritarian and which exercises sovereignty most directly in cases of emergency.[5] Collectively, scholarship like this represents *dual state theory*. The *tripartite state* construct is a revision of dual state theory. Tunander's conception of the dual state is valuable in terms of comparing and contrasting the democratic state and the security/deep state. Tunander uses the terms *security state*, *sovereign*, and *deep state* more or less interchangeably. His is a radical critique of the liberal democratic state.

While Tunander's work has much to recommend it, it has failed to gain much traction in the mainstream of academia. A more prominent scholar, Michael J. Glennon, recently made what is essentially an argument for the dual state in *National Security and Double Government*.[6] Unlike Tunander, Glennon is focused on governance carried out by institutions whose structures are discernable to the public and to political leaders. Glennon does not use the term *dual state*, but his notion of *double government* is more or less the same. His theory of double government builds upon the work of Walter Bagehot, a nineteenth- century British political commentator and editor of *The Economist*. Bagehot argued that power in Britain had initially rested with the monarchy. Over time, a dual set of governing institutions emerged. The crown and the House of Lords comprised the "dignified" institutions, described as such because their traditional pomp and circumstance and their links to history served to excite and inspire the general public. Over time, the second and newer set of "efficient" institutions came to do the actual governing. These were the House of Commons, the Prime Minister, and the Cabinet.[7]

Together, the "dignified" and "efficient" governing institutions comprised a "disguised republic," obscuring what was a dramatic shift of power. The power of the efficient institutions was concealed by virtue of the fact that the dignified institutions continued to perform some governing functions while also continuing to perform according to longstanding ceremonial and ritualistic traditions. In so doing, the disguised republic was able to avert a crisis of legitimacy that would have arisen were the public to grasp the extent to which the dignified institutions were functioning as a façade which existed to generate public acceptance of rule by experts.[8] This duality is a modern analog of Plato's "Noble Lie" which Plato obliquely asserted was necessary to promote deference to the authority of the guardian class and thereby protect the republic from excessive democracy.[9]

Glennon sees a similar dynamic at work in the US. Power initially resided in dignified institutions: the presidency, Congress, and the judiciary. Over time, a second set of "efficient" institutions emerged to maintain national security. For Glennon, America's "efficient" institution is better described as a "network" comprised of hundreds of executive officials presiding in the leadership positions of "the military, intelligence, diplomatic and law enforcement departments and agencies" providing international and internal security.[10] Much of the public incorrectly believes that America's "dignified," constitutionally established institutions exercise power. The "efficient" institutions promote this false perception, since the "dignified" institutions provide legitimacy for decisions conceived and executed by the unelected national security state officials.[11]

Glennon states that national security policy-making is not only removed from the public eye, but that it is also from constitutional restrictions.[12] Thusly does Glennon implicitly make the claim that the national security state operates in a permanent *state of exception*. The United States has progressed beyond an "imperial presidency." A bifurcated system of *double government* has emerged—what others refer to as the *dual state*. It is a system in which the US president does not exercise much substantive influence over the broad thrust of American national security policy.[13] Contrasting the British and American cases, Glennon states that unlike Bagehot's Britain, the transfer of power away from constitutionally established institutions has not been achieved intentionally. On this crucial point, Glennon posits a stochastic explanation of sorts by omitting crucial history and by failing to offer a class analysis of the elites who masterminded the creation of America's national security state. Among other historical episodes, Glennon ignores the years of lobbying efforts by Wall Street-connected lawyers that preceded the creation of the CIA in the wake of the disbanding of the CIA's wartime precursor, the Office of Special Services (OSS).

On the other hand, Glennon argues that the catalysts for each country's transformation have been similar in Britain and the US. The weakness of the democratic systems was borne of the weakness of largely uninformed democratic publics. This led elites to resort to maintain what Bagehot described as "the theatrical show" or the "wonderful spectacle."[14] Similarly, vast swaths of the US population live in poverty and/or are unable to either read well or show a proficiency knowledge about history and politics.[15] Additionally, the public can never have access to all of the secret information which informs the network of national security officials. Therefore, the network internalizes the belief that transparency and public approval are unnecessary or undesirable when it comes to statecraft.

In America, the "dignified" institutions are those spelled out in the US Constitution. Since James Madison bears considerable responsibility for America's constitutional design, Glennon uses the term *Madisonian* to describe America's "dignified" institutions—the visible and legitimate face of government.[16] In accordance with the separation of powers theory, the constitution divided national security power among the three branches of government. The resulting configuration was designed so that the three branches would compete for power, thereby creating some kind of equilibrium that would prevent the rise of any centralized, authoritarian power. This balance was not to be achieved through institutional design alone. It could be maintained only in the presence of "civic virtue—an informed and engaged electorate."[17]

For much of American history, it was the dignified *Madisonian* institutions which governed, by and large. The modern institutional form of America's "efficient" institutions emerged in the aftermath of World War II, most decisively when President Truman signed the National Security Act of 1947. This legislation centralized control of the military under a newly created Secretary of Defense. The act also established the CIA, set up a new Joint Chiefs of Staff, and created the National Security Council. Also Under Truman, the National Security Agency was founded. Given the lasting import of these acts, Glennon uses the term *Trumanite* to describe America's "efficient" governing institution which is a network consisting of the hundreds of executive branch officials who make national security policy,[18] i.e., the *national security state.*

New in the American experience, the emerging national security state was justified by perceived geopolitical realities. Liberals believed that tradition had to give ground to the new reality of a totalitarian adversary capable of swiftly executing dictates of the state. The new perceived reality was that of an interminable state of imminent war.[19] Some conservatives worried about skyrocketing defense budgets and threats posed to democratic institutions by a newly securitized set of federal bureaucracies.[20] Others, including Truman, worried that the security services like the FBI and CIA could become an American "gestapo."[21] By 1949, the Hoover Commission (chaired by former president, Herbert Hoover) had found that the Joint Chiefs were functioning "virtually [as] a law unto themselves," and that "centralized civilian control scarcely exist[ed]" in particular departments within the military bureaucracy.[22]

In his memoir *The Doomsday Machine,* Daniel Ellsberg offers a chilling illustration of the US military's autonomy. While working in the Pentagon with a high security clearance, Ellsberg became aware of a document known as the Joint Strategic Capabilities Plan (JSCP). The president and secretary of defense did not know about the content or the existence of the JSCP.[23] The Joint Chiefs of Staff had actually written up a set of practices designed to keep the defense secretary from inquiring about the JSCP; in fact, the JSCP was the general war plan. Specifically, a written directive stated that the "Joint Strategic Capabilities Plan, or the capital letters JSCP, should never appear in correspondence between the JCS and any agency of the Office of the Secretary of Defense." Any JCS documents forwarded to the secretary of defense were to be retyped to remove any reference to the JSCP.[24] The key element of the JSCP was that in the event of "armed conflict" (i.e., anything beyond a small skirmish), "the basic military objective of the U.S. armed forces is the defeat of the Sino-Soviet Bloc."[25] In other words, Ellsberg became aware of the fact that the military's plan for general war meant that if conflict between the US and the Soviet Union broke out, US strategy entailed—as a matter of course—the complete destruction of the USSR *and* China with nuclear weapons.

It took a considerable amount of delicate maneuvering for Ellsberg to successfully bring this matter to the civilian leadership. Subsequently, he was tasked with drafting a seemingly more sensible set of guidelines for general nuclear war.[26] This episode demonstrates that the security state can, at times, create or perpetuate policies of tremendous import without civilian oversight or even awareness. Such policies may pertain to the gravest possible matters. In the case of the JSCP, the policy was a plan for a military response that if triggered, would have likely destroyed human civilization. A conflict in, say, Berlin would have initiated "general war," entailing the complete destruction of the Soviet Union *and* China by nuclear weapons. Though this was unknown at the time, the subsequent fires would have created an enormous shroud of smoke and ash which would have led to nuclear winter. This would have destroyed all harvests for years, causing the deaths of almost the entire human population.[27] Civilian leaders only discovered and changed this policy due to the extraordinary intervention of Ellsberg. To succeed, Ellsberg had to overcome compartmentalization, state secrecy, and systematized obfuscation—in addition to risking his professional standing in national security state circles.

Since the Cold War began, the national security state has ballooned, expanding to dimensions that Truman would not likely have imagined. A 2011 (Priest and Arkin) study was able to identify forty-six departments and agencies within the federal government that were working on classified national security matters.[28] Additionally, there were around two thousand private companies at ten thousand US locations engaged in this work.[29] Their budgets and the size of their workforces are classified, but clearly they are huge—millions of employees and a combined annual outlay of nearly $1 trillion. Presidents and other members of the Madisonian institutions have very little ability to control the Trumanite network. Out of 668,000 civilian Defense Department employees, only 247 are politically appointed. Therefore, hundreds of national security policymakers are drawn from the national security bureaucracies to oversee and manage those bureaucracies. These include some of the president's top personal assistants as well as the high-ranking staff members of the extremely powerful National Security Council.[30]

Glennon describes the Trumanites as being different from "the best and the brightest" of decades past, in that they do not owe their positions to wealth, pedigree, or an aristocratic education. They rise in the Trumanite bureaucracies because they are "smart, hard-working, and reliable," all of which makes them "unlikely to embarrass their superiors."[31] The Trumanites are efficient in comparison to Madisonians. They can act quickly and are expert summarizers, especially since their superiors have very little time and need predigested information and ideas. Although they believe in American exceptionalism, they are not ideologues. Rather, they strive to be rationalists—sober, responsible, neither too creative nor too predictable, and, most importantly, never naïve. Given that national security is their charge, it is unsurprising that Trumanites must always appear to be tough.[32]

In reference to the Trumanite mindset, Glennon quotes C. Wright Mills who wrote, "[T]his cast of mind defines reality as basically military."[33] Thus, the incentive structures within the Trumanite network encourage members to support wars in order to protect their professional and political credibility.[34] With security defined in military rather than diplomatic terms, argues Glennon, the costs of national security's overprotection can be externalized, while the costs of underprotection must be internalized by the network. This creates powerful incentives to exaggerate actual threats and to create imaginary threats.[35] It should be noted—though Glennon does not—that even underprotection may not redound to the disadvantage of the Trumanite network. The cost of "underprotection" in the wake of 9/11 manifested in no firings of responsible officials. Instead, the colossal "failure" of these organizations resulted in massive increases to their budgets. The Madisonian institutions bear the costs of these dynamics, most clearly in the form of astronomical military spending. The current US defense budget is 50 percent higher than that of an average year during the Cold War.[36] The chief driver for the rise of Trumanite power has been the persistent existence of emergency, i.e., a situation in which a threat may emerge at any moment requiring an immediate response from the security services.[37] Glennon finds that the unending perception of threats, crises, and emergency have collectively fueled the rise of America's *double government*.[38]

During this era, the Trumanite network has been held together by the same things that, according to Bagehot, held Britain's efficient institutions together. Specifically, these are: loyalty, collective responsibility, and most significantly, secrecy. The Trumanites work at rarified locations within the offices of powerful institutions like the Pentagon or CIA headquarters. They cannot speak about their work with friends or family members. Officials with access to classified information must sign nondisclosure agreements which require them to submit anything they write to prepublication review if it pertains to their work.[39] Since information is power in the network, Trumanites are "both information gluttons and information misers." Glennon cites the case of the Pentagon spy ring that stole secrets from Nixon's National Security Council (NSC) and passed them on to the Joint Chiefs of Staff.[40] Tellingly, the Nixon administration acted to halt hearings on the crime despite being its victim![41] This episode illustrates the information miserliness of the Trumanite NSC as well as the Pentagon's information lust. It also reveals the fecklessness of the Madisonian institutions when confronted with Trumanite crimes.

Collective responsibility binds the Trumanite network together by allowing it to obscure the identity of "the deciders" of crucial decisions. The most important or sensitive decisions are often not put into writing. The shield of secrecy makes the network resistant to consequences of bad policies because as long as the entire "national security team" is responsible, no one is. Among other things, this allows the Trumanites to ignore laws. For example, the US continued to supply military aid to Egypt after a 2013 military coup, despite unambiguous statutes prohibiting such actions.[42] When asked by reporters to identify the parties responsible for the decision, US State Department spokeswoman Jen Psaki demurred, stating, "This was agreed to by the national security team. Beyond that, I'm not going to . . . I don't have anything."[43]

Although the Trumanite network is cohesive, according to Glennon, it is not monolithic. It is amorphous, leaderless, and it lacks a formal structure. But while its members' worldviews may differ marginally, they do not differ at the core. Quoting Mills again, the military mindset consists of an "intensified desire, too deeply rooted to examine, to conform to type, to be indistinguishable, not to reveal loss of composure to inferiors, and above all, not to presume the right to upset the arrangements of the chain of command."[44] Since the Trumanites operate in the shadow of the military, the network's mindset is quite similar. The spectrum of opinion is exceedingly narrow.[45]

In addition to the military cast of mind, other factors also help to account for the remarkable continuity of US foreign policy. The US government has institutional interests that endure across administrations. Trumanites' highest norm is stability, which makes preserving the status quo their ultimate objective. The status quo advances US power as well as the careers of bureaucrats within Trumanite organizations. Being overburdened with administrivia and the management of various crises, Trumanites are unable to reassess the securitized cosmology which undergirds policy.[46] Advancement is typically the result of carrying out policies decided upon by superiors. Since loyalty is so prized, reconsiderations of flawed policies are rare. Thus, policy in the Trumanite realm is very much path dependent; the trajectory of today's policy planning tends to align greatly with the trajectory of past policy.[47] Career bureaucrats, as Harry Truman observed, "look upon elected officials as just temporary occupants," and this is especially true within the Trumanite network.[48]

In terms of foreign policy, the Trumanite network is not only consistent, it is also autonomous. This autonomy has been maintained by two straightforward conditions. Firstly, the Madisonian institutions appear to be in control of US national security. Secondly, the Madisonian institutions are not actually in charge.[49] Since the Trumanites' power flows from the legitimacy of the Madisonian institutions and since the Madisonian institutions' legitimacy depends upon the perception that democratically elected leaders are in charge, both institutions have strong incentives to foster the illusion of Madisonian control.[50] The maintenance of this illusion rests upon five elements: "historical pedigree, ritual, intelligibility, mystery, and harmony." Collectively, these factors create in the public a sense of duty to obey and respect the authority of the government.[51] *Pedigree* refers to the prestige enjoyed by Madisonians by virtue of their lineage, a history that traces all the way back to America's still-revered Founding Fathers. Pedigree is reified by *rituals* like the presidential inauguration which trace back to the early days in our history as a republic. *Intelligibility* enhances

Madisonian legitimacy because everyone can understand that the three branches of government exist and that they have knowable functions.[52] At the same time, Madisonians benefit from a sense of *mystery* inspired by the remove at which the government conducts its affairs.[53] Finally, the illusion of Madisonian control persists in part due to the appearance of *harmony* between Trumanite and Madisonian institutions. Trumanites are not to be seen publicly resisting Madisonians' policies; Madisonians have little incentive to highlight dissonance or the autonomy of the Trumanites.[54]

On the whole, the US public fails to recognize that Madisonian institutions do not substantially formulate much of US national security policy. By emphasizing exceptions to the general rule of double government, politicians and the media help keep the public generally unaware. These counterexamples must be highlighted to maintain the illusion that the uncanny degree of policy continuity has a human and not systemic explanation. The public needs to be able to believe that if they would but elect the right people, the policies would change.[55] The legislative, executive, and judicial branches of the government do occasionally overrule the Trumanites. This does not occur frequently enough to imperil double government, but it does bolster the illusion of Madisonian governance.[56] Existing in a state of entropy, the Madisonian institutions do not have the power to remedy their own powerlessness. Instead, they are, as Bagehot wrote, "a disguise." They exercise power "more in form than in substance," and therefore the Madisonian system has not self-corrected as it was designed to do.[57]

Alexander Hamilton referred to the judiciary as the "least dangerous" branch of the government. Today also, the courts most clearly fail to imperil the rise and continuation of double government.[58] Prior to being nominated and confirmed, appointees to the federal judiciary have been vetted by some of the same people whose cases they will eventually hear— members of the Trumanite network and their White House and Justice Department associates. Before an individual is nominated, he or she is carefully investigated for dependability. The effect of this is that appointees function as trusted allies of the Trumanite network when it comes to matters of national security.[59] It is often the case that judicial nominees are former national security officials who have participated in matters similar to cases they hear on the bench. For example, Chief Justice William

Rehnquist served in Nixon's Office of Legal Counsel (OLC), where he was a direct participant in operations involving the domestic surveillance of political groups by the military.[60] Later, as a Supreme Court Justice, his was the decisive vote in a case pertaining to Army surveillance of domestic political groups. In this instance, Rehnquist's vote very likely prevented his prior questionable activities from being discovered.[61] Similarly, Justice Antonin Scalia had previously served as an Assistant Attorney General for the OLC. In this position Scalia met with DCI William Colby and other officials to decide which classified documents should be handed over to Congress. Additionally, and according to Scalia himself, he was responsible for approving all covert actions for a time.[62]

Justice Samuel Alito was formerly a captain in Signal Corp of the US Army which is charged with handling the military's secret communication systems. He later went on to work in the OLC where he endeavored to enlarge the president's ability to influence or alter the law.[63] Chief Justice John Roberts clerked for Justice Rehnquist. He later served in in the Reagan administration's White House Office of General Counsel where he penned a presidential letter responding to Arthur Goldberg, a retired Supreme Court Justice. Goldberg had written a letter questioning the constitutionality of the US invasion of Grenada. The Roberts-written response asserted that the president had "inherent authority in international affairs" to use the military to defend US interests.[64] As Chief Justice, Roberts voted to affirm the constitutionality of the military tribunal system devised by the Bush administration.[65]

It can be argued that these judges are appointed, not because of their links to the Trumanite network, but because they have a judicial philosophy which conforms to the president's desire for a powerful executive branch.[66] Whatever the reasons might be, the result is the same: they are dependable defenders of the Trumanite network.[67] Typically, legal challenges to the Trumanites are dismissed through the invocation of various precedents, couched in obscure legal esoterica.[68] Although the courts long ago devised the "non-delegation doctrine" forbidding Congress from delegating legislative power to administrative agencies, this doctrine has never been applied to strike down a single delegation of Trumanite authority in the realm of national security policy. Instead, judges endeavor to cite "implied" congressional authorization for Trumanite initiatives.[69] The Trumanites also hold what Glennon describes as "the ultimate trump card"—the 1936 Supreme Court decision which established "the very delicate, plenary and exclusive power of the President as the sole organ of the federal government in the field of international relations—a power which does not require as a basis for its exercise an act of Congress."[70] Thus, Trumanite power is without Constitutional basis; it resides in the reality of external sovereignty—America's membership in the international community, which is deemed to grant extraconstitutional authority upon those officials who must exercise it.[71] The courts' incursions into Trumanite territory are generally insignificant and serve to preserve the illusion of Madison governance.[72] Thus, Nixon's infamous dictum, "[W]hen the president does it, that means it is not illegal," would appear to be true in the realm of national security policy and to apply not just to the president, but to the national security state as a whole.

As with the judiciary, the apparent power of Congress exceeds its actual impact on national security policy.[73] Members of Congress must be generalists. They must be knowledgeable about economic policy, social policy, and foreign policy. By comparison, Trumanites have an insurmountable informational advantage. Therefore, Trumanite threat assessments are assumed to be correct whether the threats are posed by the targets of drone strikes, Iraqi WMD, or North Vietnamese torpedoes in the Gulf of Tonkin. Members of Congress live in fear of endangering their careers by casting a vote that could be linked to any future national security disaster.[74]

Glennon finds that a lack of civic virtue is at the heart of Congress' failures. James Madison's grand design was for a self-equilibrating system with a separation of powers. Elected as they are by an ignorant and disengaged public, the chief ambition of legislators is to be reelected. Under such circumstances, there is little incentive for Congresspersons to resist infringements upon congressional authority. One consequence is that Trumanites often end up writing the national security bills introduced by members of Congress. Trumanites can oppose or approve of amendments and alterations during the legislative process. They hover near floor debates, ready to provide friendly members with information to support their positions and arguments. The net result of all this influence is that while Congress appears to make the laws, the Trumanite network creates or strongly influences virtually everything significant that national security legislation is based upon.[75]

Conversely, the Trumanite network does not allow for Congress to substantially influence Trumanite practices or decision-making.[76] The courts bear some responsibility for congressional impotence. The Supreme Court invalidated the "legislative veto" procedure in 1983. The practice had enabled Congress to disallow Trumanite weapons sales, military plans, and other defense measures. The court found the practice unconstitutional because it allowed Congress to check executive actions without providing the possible remedy of a presidential veto. It was later proposed that the Senate Intelligence Committee be granted the authority to approve or disapprove proposed covert actions. This was vetoed by President and former CIA chief George H. W. Bush on the grounds that such legislative controls had previously been invalidated by the Court.[77]

While the Constitution delegates to Congress the responsibility of declaring war, recent US wars have been fought without congressional approval in Grenada, Panama, Kosovo, and Libya. Thusly has this crucial Constitutionally designated power been stripped from Congress.[78] Additionally, Congress is unable to effectively conduct oversight of the intelligence community. In theory, oversight is provided by two congressional committees—one in each house. Defenders of the process may state that it works, but there is little to no evidence to support or disprove such statements. Information that would allow the public to evaluate the committees' efficacy is rarely available to other members of Congress, and even less accessible for the general public. The intelligence community resists even Congress' feeble attempts at providing oversight. In 1984, DCI William Casey stated that "The business of Congress is to stay out of my business."[79] The more significant and problematic a policy is, the less likely it is that the CIA will inform even the oversight committees about it. For example, the CIA began its infamous detention and interrogation program in 2002. Only in September of 2006 were the committee members briefed, excepting the Chairman and Vice Chairman who had been briefed previously. Even then, the members were briefed only hours before the program was disclosed to the general public by President Bush.[80]

Obstructionism by the intelligence community (IC) can take the form of deceptive behavior and statements. Even when agencies' activities are accurately reported, it still may not be possible to provide meaningful scrutiny, since information given to the committees is often "wildly over-classified" (according to Senator Sheldon Whitehouse). Often, the IC's activities are largely obscured. Congressmembers cannot ask too many questions about programs of which they know only vague details. Furthermore, if committee members inquire too aggressively, they may be illegally monitored by the Agency as was reported by Senator Diane Feinstein.[81] It is unclear why the CIA would bother with such surveillance given that committee members are not allowed to convey classified information to nonmember Congresspersons, even when said activities are illegal. They are also forbidden from speaking out publicly on such matters. Given these circumstances, it is not surprising that the oversight committees were generally silent about most of the Bush administration's most controversial and apparently unlawful policies.[82]

The difficulties facing committee members who could conduct actual oversight are typically irrelevant anyway because most committee members are what Loch Johnson described as "ostriches" or "cheerleaders." An "ostrich" does not want to know about intelligence activities or—like former committee member Barry Goldwater—they may not even believe that IC activities are Congress' business.[83] A "cheerleader" like Diane Feinstein approaches the process with the intention of showing her unwavering devotion to the intelligence community. "Ostriches" and "cheerleaders" today far outnumber "skeptics" and "guardians." A "skeptic" is uncertain of the benefits of our massive intelligence bureaucracy and, like Daniel Patrick Moynihan, may even wonder if its continued existence is justified on its historical merits. A "guardian," Frank Church most famously, is not content to simply respond to crises; he seeks to prevent operational fiascos and intelligence failures from occurring.[84]

Congress, according to Glennon, does not provide adequate oversight because such does not serve members' core interest—the maximization of their re-election chances. Citing political scientists Amy Zegart and Julie Quinn, he identifies three reasons why such is the case. First, voters do not vote on the basis of intelligence issues. The collective effects of the US intelligence community are not acutely felt by most citizens.[85] Second, any constituency that would be especially concerned with intelligence matters is too geographically dispersed to be significant for any individual member of Congress. Third, relative to other areas of policy, interest groups concerned with intelligence are weak and few in number. One reason for this is that state secrecy prevents even the few relevant groups from knowing enough details about IC activities to hold these agencies accountable.[86]

Some scholars, including Arthur Schlesinger and Chalmers Johnson, have argued that the issue is one of an "imperial presidency."[87] Glennon asserts that this is not the case. Although the Trumanites work for the president who could in theory order a complete reversal of national security policy, he would be very unlikely to do so because the consequences would deter him from such a course of action. The media and government officials maintain an illusion of presidential responsibility by speaking of "Obama's" decisions or policies, but truly top-down, executive decisions which reverse fundamental policies are very rare.[88] When a president issues an "order," it is typically one that originated with the Trumanites. This is often accomplished by somehow entangling a president who must then negotiate with the military. As Kennedy aide Ted Sorensen wrote, "Presidents rarely, if ever, make decisions—particularly in foreign affairs. [T]he basic decisions, which confine their choices, have all too often been previously made."[89] Justice William Douglas, who was also a friend of the Kennedy family, spoke of the relationship between President Kennedy and the generals: "I slowly realized that the military were so strong in our society that probably no President could stand against them."[90] Historian and Kennedy advisor Arthur Schlesinger Jr. stated that the Kennedy administration had been at war with "the National Security People."[91] This would seem to be at odds with the thesis of Schlesinger's own book *The Imperial Presidency* which argued that the US Presidency had far outgrown the limits and intentions outlined in the US Constitution.[92]

The "National Security People" would include the CIA, whose influence has expanded. A recent example is described in a Senate Intelligence Committee report which found that in order to justify "extreme interrogation," (i.e., torture) the agency "blatantly misled President George W. Bush, the White House, the Justice Department, and the congressional intelligence committees about the efficacy of its methods."[93] On many occasions, Trumanites have acted without presidential approval. A presidential aide testified in 1975 that the administration "didn't know half" of the legally questionable things that the intelligence agencies did. Recently, the CIA failed to inform the White House of the existence of videotapes documenting the waterboarding of detainees on the basis that the agency had determined that the White House did not "need to know."[94] Sometimes, Trumanites create presidential "directives" which they direct at themselves. Presidents endorse such policies after the fact to avoid looking like spectators.[95]

Glennon provides several recent examples illustrating presidential fecklessness in the face of Trumanite power. The Trumanites prevailed in efforts to persuade President Obama to continue the drone assassination program *and* not to discuss the broader ramifications of the policy. In the Situation Room, there were four unanimous voices representing the Pentagon and the intelligence community. All four, including Secretary of Defense Robert Gates, were holdovers from the Bush administration.[96] When Obama was considering lowering the US presence in Afghanistan, an NSC staff member suggested that if the president were to pursue such a course, he could be provoking the resignations of the commander of all allied forces in Afghanistan, the CENTCOM Commander, the Chairman of the Joint Chiefs of Staff, and possibly the Secretary of Defense.[97] When deciding on the troop levels to be deployed in Afghanistan, the military presented President Obama with three options—the option that the military officials preferred, along with two unreasonable alternatives. Eventually, the military added a fourth option largely indistinguishable from their preferred option. Said President Obama, "You guys just presented me [with] four options, two of which are not realistic [. . .] So what's my option? [. . .] You have essentially given me one option."[98]

Glennon's most detailed example is a case study of NSA surveillance. President Obama, the former constitutional law professor, continued two NSA programs which appear to be clearly unconstitutional. The first program involved collection of phone records of tens of millions of Verizon customers along with mass collection of internet communications. The second act allowed the NSA to collect internet users' information from

Google, Yahoo, Facebook, and other companies on the internet.[99] After the first program's existence was reported by *The Guardian*, US officials issued non-denials and asserted that the three branches of the US government are participants in activities of that sort. The NSA asserted that it had the statutory authority to carry out such surveillance, but that its legal interpretation was classified. A member of the Senate Intelligence Committee said the government's theory drew from the PATRIOT Act and that the theory held that the state's authority to draw personal information from third parties was "essentially limitless." The senator was prohibited from discussing the details of the legal interpretation. Thus, for all practical purposes, Congress and the public were unaware as to whether or not surveillance of this scale was authorized or if there were any checks in place.[100]

Before the leaks became public, Director of National Intelligence James Clapper was questioned by Senator Ron Wyden who inquired as to whether the NSA had been collecting any sort of data from millions or hundreds of millions of US citizens. He responded, falsely, "No, sir." After Snowden's revelations, Clapper admitted making false statements, calling his response "the least untruthful" statement that he could make. Two weeks later he revised his explanation by suggesting that he was confused about the question.[101] Senator Feinstein had been presiding when Clapper gave his original, possibly felonious response to Senator Wyden. She said nothing. President Obama and other members of the administration knew or should have known that Clapper's statement was false, yet they also remained silent for months until leaks finally revealed Clapper's perfidy.[102] The NSA also repeatedly misled the Foreign Intelligence Surveillance Court (FISC) regarding the scope of its data collection programs. The FISC had previously approved the NSA's collection of telephone data, but only after the NSA had inaccurately described the scope and scale of its activities. The court concluded that the required standard for querying was violated so routinely that the oversight was essentially ineffectual.[103] The NSA surveillance program highlights some crucial points. The Trumanite network has tremendous power when it comes to formulating and enacting national security policy. The Madisonian branches are often either kept in the dark, co-opted, or powerless. They have shown themselves to be unable to take the initiative in the creation of policy, unable to provide effective oversight, and unable or unwilling to censure the Trumanites' unlawful trespasses.

Double Government vs. **Political Science**

The Glennon version of *dual state* theory—*double government*—explains state behavior by positing the existence of a second institution (a network) that actually formulates and executes policy independently from the constitutionally established branches of government. Dovetailing with some of the approaches discussed in the first chapter of this dissertation, Glennon contrasts his *double government* theory with what he identifies as some of the more common political science approaches that seek to explain state behavior. The first approach is the *rational actor model.* This model maintains that if the information, deliberative situation, decision-making context are the same, a rational policymaker will rationally choose the same option, as the other options are irrational. The rational actor model has "thin" and "thick" variants.[104] The thinnest—"comprehensive rationality"—maintains that in a given situation there is but one rational option and any policy decision is explainable with reference to the deciders' wish to attain the maximum value of the chief preference that underpins the policy. "Thicker" variants like the "bounded rationality" approach incorporate the possibility of multiple causes for a decision, along with variables that affect actors' discernment.[105]

The rational actor model is applied across various political science approaches. *Liberalism* in international relations uses a variant of the rational actor model. Specifically, theorists of *democratic peace* assert that a state's regime type shapes its objectives, belief systems, and foreign policy preferences. After being classified as democratic or not democratic, states are then analyzed as unitary actors.[106] *Classical realists* like Hans Morgenthau start from two assumptions that are congruent with the rational actor model, specifically: (1) states are the chief unitary actors in the international sphere; and (2) states are rational utility maximizers. To these, classical realists add two further assumptions: (3) the international system is anarchical, and (4) the chief goals of states are security and power.[107] *Neorealism* refines the core assumptions of classical realism by aspiring to be more "scientific" and by placing greater emphasis on systemic variables, especially anarchy.[108] Waltz's neorealism or "structural realism" focuses on anarchy and states which differ primarily by their aggregate power relative to other states. With relative power being the decisive variable, anarchy is predicted to create a marked tendency toward systemic balance, a balance which, when disrupted, will eventually be restored in some way.[109]

International institutionalism also employs the rational actor model by accepting realist assumptions of anarchy and of the state as a rational unitary actor. To this realist foundation they add an emphasis on international institutions as major causal variables.[110] International institutions have grown in number and importance since the end of World War II. The institutions are significant because they affect the availability of information and transaction costs for cooperation among the unitary rational actors, i.e., nation-states. Keohane, the most prominent of the institutionalists, recognizes the limitations of institutionalist theory. He asserts that since the theory treats the objectives pursued by states as coming from external sources, institutionalism and neorealism should be supplemented by a better theory of the state—a theory which could address the origins of the interests, objectives, norms, and perceptions which influence state behavior.[111] This is also a valid criticism of Glennon's theory of *double government* which the tripartite state theory formulated in this book attempts to address.

The rational actor model has some fairly well-known flaws and weakness. Glennon focuses on five. First, it cannot determine which values or preferences the state ought to seek to maximize. Why does any value have a "rational" hierarchical superiority over any other value? Second, the model cannot with any degree of certainty demonstrate which objective is or was the most valued in any decision-making process.[112] Third, the government—being a massive collection of organizations and individuals—is not an individual with human emotions, mental processes, and purposes.[113] Fourth, the model entails a cost-benefit analysis without being able to determine which variables are to be weighed and how much weight each is to be accorded.[114] Finally, even were the other weaknesses accounted for, human rationality is hampered by cognitive weaknesses and distortions. There are well-known cognitive deficiencies which do not stem from human emotion. These include "bandwagon bias," "choice supportive bias," "disconfirmation bias," and "projection bias."[115]

The second political science approach cited by Glennon to explain state behavior is the "government politics model." This model is characterized as including "virtually everything that the rational actor model excludes."[116] This model was first formulated by Graham Allison in his 1971 examination of the Cuban Missile Crisis entitled *Essence of Decision*. The book was rewritten in 1999 with new coauthor Phillip Zelikow, following the declassification of much relevant documentation from the crisis. According to this model, government behavior is not the result of a unitary state, and it is not simply an organizational output. Rather, the model maintains that government behavior is the result of bargaining games. There are numerous players whose attention is divided among many domestic and international problems. The players do not act according to a single array of strategic objectives. There are various competing conceptions of interests and objectives on individual, organizational, and national levels. Thus, decisions are the result of the give and take of various bargaining games played out within the government.[117] Glennon argues that this model is not overly parsimonious like the rational actor model. Its weakness lies in the opposite direction; it identifies so many variables that it's impossible to identify the variable "*but for* which the policy result would not have occurred."[118] He acknowledges that for every national security decision, "innumerable people shape the final outcome." Without further simplification, causes cannot be isolated, and explanation is impossible.[119]

In order to isolate the actual causes of US foreign policy decisions, Glennon turns to the *organizational behavior model*.[120] This model understands government behavior as the output of organizations rather than the product of deliberate choices.[121] The basic tenets of the model parallel the central elements of Bagehot's—and thus Glennon's—approach. Unlike the rational actor model, it does not present an oversimplified, unicausal theory. And unlike the government politics model, it does not attempt to incorporate everything under the sun. Instead, the organizational behavior model focuses upon the shared characteristics that influence the behavior of organizations such as those which formulate and execute America's national security policies.[122]

Glennon identifies several key aspects of organizational behavior theory which are most relevant to the Trumanite network. The membership, culture, and purposes of an organization shape its practices and capabilities.[123] An organization's standard operating procedures (SOPs) channel members into carrying out an organization's purposes. These routines define the responses to common types of contingencies. Unforeseen events are nevertheless analogized to whatever common contingency is most relevant. These SOPs produce consistent expectations and stability, but they can also make organizations static and inflexible.[124] An organization's SOPs are formed on the basis of the likely consequences that they should bring about. This is determined by some manner of risk assessment derived from the organization's files and/or from the memories of its members. Typically, dramatic failures are most feared since they threaten an organization with cataclysmic change. Therefore, organizations are averse to risk and uncertainty. They prefer options with predictable but tolerable costs, as opposed to riskier ventures that might deliver greater benefits. In political science terms, they "satisfice," i.e., they settle for that which is "good enough" though maybe not best. The aversion to risk can allow inertia to carry programs beyond the point of loss.[125]

If an organization's benefits outweigh its costs, the organization can expect higher budgets, better personnel, and greater responsibilities. This grants an organization more power which leads to greater capabilities which leads to more power and so on. Likewise, individuals within organizations seek greater power.[126] Information flows enhance organization capabilities by reducing uncertainty. For this reason, data is not shared with the competition. This gives rise to secrecy, dissembling, and exclusivity. Data is gathered at the lower levels. Then it is filtered and reinterpreted at intermediate levels. Finally, the curated data arrives at the organization's decision-making levels. This makes information subject to "abbreviation, modification, and cognitive distortion (such as groupthink)."[127] Thus, the informational filters can damage the organization's efforts to preserve its culture and efficacy. Overall, organizational outputs serve to constrain leaders by forcing them to address problems by choosing from a narrow range of options. The lower layers identify emerging problems, and since steps are taken to deal with problems prior to leaders directing a response, leaders' decisions often appear to be unavailing. Collectively, all of these organizational tendencies give rise to preferences that remain consistent and stable. This tends to be the case regardless of changes in personnel or even leadership.[128]

All of the foregoing organizational traits are relevant to the Trumanite network. Glennon's significant departure from the *organizational behavior model* is that he is not speaking of a discrete organization, but rather a network straddling numerous organizations. Nor is the Trumanite network best described as an "institution," as Bagehot conceptualized Britain's "efficient" government. The network lacks the procedural formality implied by the term "institution," especially in the formal sense of the term.[129] The Trumanite structure is better characterized as a network for six reasons identified by Glennon. First, its boundaries are nebulous. Second, the structure as a whole has no clearly delineated formal authority to govern. Third, the network collectively has no formalized routines, standard operating procedures, or decision-making guidelines. Fourth, though organizations and individuals may specialize, there is no defined division of labor. Fifth, if a node cannot function properly, an adjustment will be made. Decision-making power will bypass the blocked node. Sixth, a network does not have stable, formally identifiable leadership. In the Trumanite case, power and responsibility can shift according to a vast array of factors.[130]

Although the Trumanite network differs from an organization in the ways listed above, it shares one important trait with an organization: its members each work within an organization. Therefore, the behavior of the members very much conforms to the expected behavior within the organizations in which they reside.[131] Within the intelligence community and the Pentagon, powerful norms hold sway. Members are expected to show loyalty to extant policy, to forgo embarrassing other network members to the public, and to demonstrate conformity by espousing commonly held assumptions and values. For these and other reasons, the Trumanite network has always been susceptible to "groupthink." This social psychology term refers to the stunted thinking that can prevail inside a very cohesive group. Members suppress dissenting voices and even thoughts in order to maintain consensus and unwavering loyalty to common mores.

Groupthink leads members to downplay the possibility of failure and of personal responsibility for actions and outcomes. The benefits of alternative policies are dismissed or given scant attention. The status quo is all too often depicted as being the self-evidently rational choice.[132] While the Trumanite network suffers from the pathologies of an organization, it has been able to maintain its power by maintaining a network structure. Were the various organizations ever consolidated into one agency, it would have been too visible to operate efficiently and survive in a political culture in which the government's legitimacy rests upon the prestige of the Madisonian institutions.[133]

This extensive review of Glennon's theory of *double government* serves a few purposes here. First, his elaboration of *double government* effectively illustrates the extent to which the Madisonian institutions (otherwise herein referred to as the *public state*) have largely abdicated—or been divested of—meaningful control and oversight of US foreign policy. Second, Glennon does indeed identify many of the dynamics that influence the behavior of the *Trumanite network* (otherwise referred to as the *security state* in this book). In sum, Glennon's *Double Government* is a devastating critique of conventional political science approaches which by and large deny the lawless anti-democratic autonomy of the national security state.

However, and most importantly, *the omissions and oversights in Glennon's theory are central to the theory of the tripartite state.* There are several questions that Glennon either does not answer or does not answer very clearly. In so doing, Glennon implicitly treats these issues as outside of his framework. These questions include: What *are* the unchanging objectives of US foreign policy? When, how, and by whom were they formulated? How unchanging have they been and what accounts for the variation that does exist? What are the foundational assumptions of the political class in the US? How did these assumptions arise? What social forces gave rise to the creation of the security state? How did these forces influence its development thereafter? Glennon fails to consider whether powerful societal interests or considerations drove and were served by past policies, resultingly becoming all the more rich and powerful—and thereby even more able to drive policy. This could describe high finance as well as the arms, aerospace, and resource extraction industries—all of which benefit enormously from US hegemony. In fact, the so-called *Trumanite* bureaucrats are lesser partners among the US elite which dominates the state. As William Domhoff points out, the subservience of national security officials to the corporate overworld is "seen most clearly in the speed with which they are fired if they disagree with the eager civilian militarists from the corporate community and associated think tanks."[134]

Foreign Policy Analysis

In sum—and setting aside its shortcomings—Glennon's *Double Government* offers a very effective critique of political science approaches to understanding the national security state. Summarized above, his critiques of *rational actor* and *governmental politics* models are relevant to assessing the growing international relations (IR) subdiscipline of foreign policy analysis (FPA). In the FPA literature, multiple approaches or levels of analysis prevail. Relevant to this discussion are the approaches that focus respectively on the individual decisionmaker, group decision-making, culture and identity, and domestic politics.[135]

In the US case, a focus on the psychology of leaders may offer plausible explanations for the odd individual policy decision. The approach could provide, say, reasonable descriptions of the idiosyncrasies like those that contributed to Woodrow Wilson's failure to get the Senate to ratify the Treaty of Versailles. However, from the beginning of US history, the continuity of US foreign policy belies any explanation that places excessive emphasis on the personality of this or that leader. If we look all the way back to colonial America, the English colonists desired more land in the West even as this led to conflicts with Britain as evidenced by the British reaction to King Philip's War or Bacon's rebellion. Perhaps as much or more than mercantilist exploitation and British despotism, the American elite revolted to be free of English restrictions (real or prophesied) on Western expansion and slave holding.[136] From independence onward, the trend was imperial expansion across the continent as presided over by figures as diverse as Thomas Jefferson (Louisiana Purchase), James Monroe (Spanish Florida), John Tyler (annexation of Texas), and James Polk (the Mexican

Session). Having achieved "manifest destiny," the US kept going West—in a sense, all the way to Japan where President Fillmore famously sent Commodore Matthew Perry. Lincoln's Secretary of State William Seward conceived of a Pacific empire, much of which the US would acquire, especially with the overthrow of the Hawaiian monarchy and the acquisitions of the Spanish-American War.

Without attempting to address each major foreign policy decision of each administration, the general trend was one of imperialist forces overcoming resistance from progressives or "isolationists" (i.e., lawful non-interventionists). This continuity belies resort to psychological explanations. However, two caveats could apply to US leaders in the twentieth and twenty-first centuries. The first is that the two progressive presidents who seemed most opposed to colonialism and neocolonialism—FDR and JFK—came from wealthy families. This suggests that during the New Deal and Bretton Woods eras, there were more opportunities for the US electoral process to produce leaders less beholden to the interests that propel imperial hegemony. The elite socialization of these reformists likely had some impact on their respective psychologies and their abilities to navigate rarefied social circles.

The other way in which psychology may impact presidential leadership pertains to those politicians who ascend from more humble origins. Specifically, presidents like Truman, Johnson, Nixon, Ford, Carter, Reagan, Clinton, and Obama may—despite obvious differences—share overarching similarities which must have been brought to bear on their respective psychologies. To rise so precipitously, these politicians must have shared, above all, a will to co-optation. This is not to argue that psychology is the decisive variable. Rather, it suggests that in a nominally democratic, technologically advanced empire, the system's elites may confer success, prestige, and patronage on the basis of psychological traits rather than those traits somehow determining the trajectory of the system. Specifically, psychological traits like ambition and moral flexibility may help a person advance by making him or her co-optable by the elites whose influence determines one's success. Alternatively, the top-flight education and economic security of progressive reformist elites (e.g., FDR, Henry Wallace, JFK, and RFK) may allow them to achieve political success without having to demonstrate corruptibility along the way. Such figures represent a real threat to the political dominance of the overworld. The risk remains that the public state could be captured by a person or persons who seek to gain power by appealing to—and serving the interests of—the general public. That is to say that the best-educated, economically secure persons have a potentially destabilizing degree of independence. America's democratic electoral system risks bringing such individuals into positions of power from which they could endanger top-down governance. As discussed in greater detail in a later chapter, structural changes in the US since the 1960s appear to have virtually eliminated this possibility.

At any rate, recent US history highlights the general weakness of psychology-based explanations of US foreign policy. Few would disagree that US presidents Bush, Obama, and Trump are possessed of considerably distinct psychologies. As such, their adherence to the general thrust of US empire is illuminating. In 2001, retired General Wesley Clark learned that the US was planning to attack and overthrow the governments of seven countries including Iraq, Libya, and Syria.[137] When the Iraq War turned into a quagmire, it appeared that this neoconservative campaign of conquest would have to be abandoned. Surprisingly to some, the campaign was resumed by President Barack Obama, disillusioning those who believed that the Nobel Peace Prize–winning president would deliver on his purported agenda of "change." On humanitarian grounds that were eventually discredited, the US under Obama led a NATO coalition that overthrew the government of Libya, plunging what had been the most prosperous country in Africa into violent chaos and lawlessness for ten years and counting.[138]

In Syria, the CIA under Obama launched Operation Timber Sycamore, a major covert operation that deployed al Qaeda and similar jihadi groups in a campaign to overthrow the Syrian government. Refuting the misleading depiction of Syria as a "civil war," Jeffrey Sachs was one of the few dissenting public figures to speak to the issue. In a 2018 appearance on MSNBC, Sachs explained that "we have made a proxy war in Syria. It's killed 500,000 people, displaced 10 million [. . .] This war continues because we to this day back rebels that are trying to overthrow a government contrary to international law, contrary to the UN charter."[139]

The US role in the conflict has not yet ended. After running as antiwar candidate who wanted to end America's "forever wars," President Trump reversed his decision to withdraw the US troops illegally occupying Syria, instead opting to occupy Syrian oil fields. Confessing to the war crime of pillage, Trump told journalist Laura Ingraham, "I left troops to take the oil. I took the oil. The only troops I have are taking the oil."[140]

While Trump's manner of explaining his policy may be novel, the policy of attacking Syria predates him and reached its deadliest levels under Obama. An even longer look at the region suggests that a psychological diagnosis of the foreign policy establishment itself may be warranted. In the 1980s, the US armed both sides in the Iran-Iraq War, a conflict which killed over a million people. The 1991 Gulf War under G. H. W. Bush was one of the most lopsided military routes in world history. The subsequent sanctions regime killed over a million Iraqi people, including over 500,000 children. When US Secretary of State Madeline Albright was asked about 500,000 dead Iraqi children, she infamously replied, "We think the price is worth it." With the sanctions' ostensible justification of Iraqi WMD now discredited, it is worth investigating what "it" was that Albright considered to be worth the price. A strong hypothesis can be derived from a story in the *San Francisco Chronicle* of February 22, 1998. Headlined "Iraq's Oil Poses Threat to the West," the article reported that if Iraqi oil were allowed on the international petroleum market, "it would devalue British North Sea oil, undermine American oil production and—much more important—it would destroy the huge profits which the United States [read: the US oil industry] stands to gain from its massive investment in Caucasian oil production, especially in Azerbaijan."[141] In sum, US foreign policy in the Gulf since the 1980s indicates that American policymakers consistently demonstrate the psychological traits associated with antisocial personality disorder—commonly referred to as "psychopathy" or "sociopathy." Such persons are able to pursue objectives without being impeded by empathy, a capacity which is either absent or attenuated in such individuals. If this seems an inappropriate way to analyze the imperial US foreign policy establishment, perhaps reference to C. Wright Mills would be more relevant from a social science perspective:

[W]hen institutions are corrupting, many of the men who live and work in them are necessarily corrupted. In the corporate era, economic relations become impersonal-and the executive feels less personal responsibility. Within the corporate worlds of business, war-making and politics, the private conscience is attenuated-and the higher immorality is institutionalized. It is not merely a question of a corrupt administration in corporation, army, or state; it is a feature of the corporate rich, as a capitalist stratum, deeply intertwined with the politics of the military state.[142]

Cultural/national identity explanations are another foreign policy analysis (FPA) approach that may produce internally consistent theories of this or that foreign policy. Samuel Huntington famously predicted that cultural factors would lead to US conflict with China and the Islamic world.[143] On the surface, this could seem apt given subsequent history. However, examined critically, the cultural arguments are less persuasive. Specifically, the culture and historical trajectory of the Muslim world has been greatly influenced by the West. The Islamist terror phenomenon derives from over a century of Western imperial meddling, most notably by Britain and the US. For example, the British supported the Wahabist Saudi royal family and created (through the Suez Canal Company) the Muslim Brotherhood specifically to combat nationalism and socialism in Egypt.[144] After World War II, the most popular statesmen across the Middle East were secular nationalists—Mossadegh and Nasser. Not coincidentally, both governments also suffered paramilitary violence from Western-backed Islamist terror organizations. Additionally, both Iran and Egypt were ultimately undone by Anglo-US imperialism—the CIA's Operation Ajax and Israel's Six Day War, respectively.[145] Other Middle Eastern states targeted by the US include secular governments in Iraq, Syria, and Libya. Additionally, the US Operation Cyclone backed the Islamist Mujahideen against the Soviets in Afghanistan. The massive campaign utilized a Saudi network for logistical assistance which eventually evolved into al Qaeda. Led by Osama bin Laden and Ayman al-Zawahiri, the paramilitary terror organization was deployed by the West in Bosnia, Kosovo, Azerbaijan, and Libya before 2001.[146] During the Obama administration, al Qaeda was used to affect regime change—successfully in Libya and unsuccessfully in Syria. The key point is that the Western use—and subsequent demonization—of Sunni Islamist terror can lend itself to Clash-of-Civilizations-style cultural explanations for international political phenomena. However, this can only occur in the context of widespread historical obscurantism and disinformation that could collectively be described as state gaslighting.

Just as the cultural explanations for the Middle East serve to obscure oily material determinants, Huntington's cultural explanation for China is similarly deficient. China's pre-modern peaks occurred during the Han and Tang dynasties when the Silk Road was most active, allowing China to thrive at the center of a vast commercial network. With China's recent resurgence, Chinese national strategists are seeking to integrate Eurasia anew through the Belt and Road Initiative. This is exactly the scenario fearfully forecast by Huntington's Trilateralist comrade Zbigniew Brzezinski in *The Grand Chessboard*.[147] The Belt and Road Initiative has obvious merits for the China's pursuit of its national interest, as well as corresponding demerits from the perspective of the US empire. Grasping the ways in which this tension could fuel conflict with the US hardly requires reference to the vagaries of Confucianism or Daoism.

None of this is to say that culture is unworthy of deep study by social scientists. However, it is remiss to treat culture as a wholly independent force. In the last years of his life, eminent sociologist C. Wright Mills sought to undertake a study of "the cultural apparatus," which he defined as:

> [A]ll the organizations and milieu in which artistic, intellectual, and scientific work goes on, and by which entertainment and information are produced and distributed. [. . .] Inside this apparatus, standing between men and events, the images, meanings, slogans that define the world in which men live are organized and compared, maintained and revised, lost and cherished, hidden, debunked, celebrated.[148]

Crucially, Mills highlighted the decisive link between power and culture by stating, "We cannot examine merely the individual workman and his choices; the cultural apparatus as a whole is established and used by dominant institutional orders."[149] Since "the prestige of culture transforms power into spellbinding authority," the cultural apparatus of every nation tends "to become a close adjunct of national authority and a leading agency of nationalist propaganda."[150] As with much else, C. Wright Mills was more prescient than could have been known at the time. Seeking funding for a large, proposed study on *The Cultural Apparatus*, Mills's request was rejected by the Ford Foundation who feared it would be "another *Power Elite*," i.e., another radical critique of US elites and their global impact.[151] Decades later, it emerged that the Ford Foundation had been a major conduit of CIA funds dispersed to influence and manipulate culture.[152] In sum, the cultural apparatus of Cold War America functioned in way that rendered it even more of a top-down instrument of power than what Mills was describing. In the case of the US foreign policy establishment, *culture* is not the determining factor. Rather, it is another crucial venue for technocratically reproducing hegemony. Furthermore, it should be noted that the top-down politico-economic power that reproduces the imperial culture of the US "foreign policy establishment" no doubt also accounts for the obscurantist orthodoxy that prevails in the foreign policy analysis subdiscipline.

FPA fares a little better with the *domestic politics* approach to under-standing foreign policy decisions. Unfortunately, the zeitgeist of the sub-discipline suffers from one of the main deficiencies of US political science in general—aversions to both elite theory and materialism. The history detailed in chapter 4 highlights just how rarefied were the decision-making circles that decided on an imperial hegemonic postwar US foreign policy. In short, the politico-economic dominance of the pro-empire coalition was largely unimpeded by any countervailing political force that could have redirected the US toward a cooperative nationalist or internationalist posture after World War II. The presidents and serious presidential can-didates who betrayed any inclination of a more progressive foreign policy were all notably prevented from doing so—Franklin Roosevelt, Henry Wallace, John Kennedy, and Robert Kennedy.

Intriguingly, FPA practitioners Hudson and Day (2020) examine the domestic factors that influenced Kennedy first to send special forces to

Vietnam and later to try and withdraw from the country—but only after being safely reelected. The authors then point out that Kennedy "probably would have been reelected, but he was assassinated instead."[153] Unmentioned is the possibility that the decidedly deadly institutions that would go on to prosecute the Vietnam War might value empire and profit over democracy and the rule of law. In other words: might not JFK's departure from the imperial consensus have been related to his abrupt departure from the presidency? This radical but reasoned interpretation suggests that at crucial points, foreign policy is formulated and executed by an elite of power operating under such secrecy that conventional approaches to studying the state's decisions may be grossly inadequate.

On the whole, FPA is an important subdiscipline with the worthy aim of illuminating the means and ends of the human decisionmakers who formulate and execute foreign policy. In this way its practitioners are following C. Wright Mills's directive that a master task of intellectuals is "to investigate the causes of war, and among them to locate the decisions and defaults of elite circles."[154] The psychological, group decision making, cultural, and domestic political approaches could all produce useful scholarship. Unfortunately, mainstream FPA has a considerable aversion to materialism and elite theory. For this study, therefore, mainstream FPA scholarship is only as useful as the extent to which US foreign policy is neither elitist nor driven by material considerations. But since US foreign policy elites demonstrably achieve their elite status through organizations dominated by the overworld of private wealth, US foreign policy is extremely elitist and driven by material considerations.

CHAPTER 4

THE AMERICAN
POWER ELITE

C. Wright Mills: Power and History

It is worth noting that while Glennon in *Double Government* cites C. Wright Mills's canny description of the military mindset, he fails to take into account the chief insight of Mills's magnum opus, *The Power Elite*. Mills's thesis is that decision-making—and thus real power—had migrated into ever loftier and increasingly opaque circles during the twentieth century. Consequently, democracy was becoming an increasingly impotent façade. Mills focused upon the "big three" American institutions: the government, the military, and big business. He noted that individuals in top organizational positions within one of these hierarchies often migrated between top positions in the other two. Thus, the leadership of these institutions formed a cohesive *power elite* which determined the conventional wisdom, assumptions, and objectives of the political class. With rise of corporate power in the US, America's *power elite* assumed control over processes of deliberation and decision-making.[1] As US hegemony spread across the globe following World War II, the power elite created the institutions necessary to effectively run the empire or the "hegemonic project" if one prefers euphemism.

Glennon's *double government* theory offers some useful insights into two of Mills's "big three" institutions—the government and the military. As discussed at length earlier, Glennon convincingly demonstrates that US foreign policy is not under the control of democratically elected officials. Instead public officials are by and large passive agents, feckless vis-à-vis the "main drift." The chief shortcoming of Glennon's framework is that it omits the power of big business—i.e., the corporate rich. This oversight represents more than just the omission of a significant variable; it likely represents the omission of the key decisive variable. As argued herein, the sustained and often coordinated influence of what Mill's calls *the corporate rich* (i.e., the *overworld*) best explains the pathological inertia and tragic continuity of US foreign policy—as well as the seemingly inexorable rightward, criminogenic, and anti-nationalist shift of politics in the US and in nations under the sway of US hegemony. This has resulted in the emergence of a *tripartite state* that has operated in a partially obscure but continuous *state of exception* to pursue and maintain the US empire. C. Wright Mills was the social scientist who most effectively elucidated these trends at an early date. It is well worth revisiting *The Power Elite* in order to reassess the most crucial trends he identified as well as the implications of those trends for society and politics in the intervening years.

Mills's 1956 book was concerned with the momentous history-making power that US elites had recently acquired and exercised. In the preceding years, small circles of US elites had decided to effect US entry into World War II, to drop atomic bombs on Japan, to intervene in Korea, and to defeat Admiral Radford's proposal to intervene at Dienbienphu.[2] Intuitively, many people, "feel that they live in a time of big decisions; they know that they are not making any." Observers feel that at the center of it all, "making decisions or failing to make them, there must be an elite of power." Many other people who follow events through the accounts of publicly visible decision makers may come to believe that there is no cohesive elite whose power is decisively consequential.[3] Mills took both perspectives into account to formulate a theory of the American power elite. In Mills's America, the means of power are the hierarchies of the government, the corporation, and the military. The command posts of modern US society reside at the summits of these *big three* hierarchies. They wield history-making power unprecedented in human history.[4] As the big three domains became larger and more centralized, their activities became more consequential and traffic between domains increased.[5] As a result, the top positions across hierarchies became increasingly interchangeable.[6]

Mills thus defined the *power elite* as "those political, economic, and military circles which as an intricate set of overlapping cliques share decisions having at least national consequences. In so far as national events are decided, the power elite are those who decide them."[7] Three major keys are identified as crucial to understanding the power elite. First, there is the common psychology that prevails among the elites. They have similar educations and backgrounds, their lifestyles are similar, they have similar social standing, and they intermingle easily. The interchangeability in the command posts across the big three serves to reinforce the shared psychology of the power elite.[8]

The second key to understanding the power elite involves the structure and mechanics of the *big three* institutional hierarchies. The larger these bureaucratic domains are, the more power afforded to their respective elites. If the hierarchies were dispersed and disconnected, the elites within each would be scattered and disconnected. If the hierarchies were interconnected to a considerable degree—and if their interests often coincided—their elites would form a more cohesive set. In Mills's America, there were "several important structural coincidences of interest between these institutional domains," the most salient being "the development of a permanent war establishment by a privately incorporated economy inside a political vacuum."[9] By the admittedly low standard of US social science, Mill's prose is quite lucid and comprehensible. But to paraphrase anyway: Mills was stating that with World War II—and the decision to go for global dominance after the war—the US economy had been transformed into a permanent war economy in which vast resources were put into the maintenance of a massive war machine. Since the supplying of the war machine was run on a for-profit basis by the corporate rich, this created a deep commonality of interest between the military and big business. This military/big business convergence took place in the context of "a political vacuum"—a situation in which democratic institutions were powerless to counter the corporate American war machine.

The third aspect of the power elite identified by Mills involves the unity achieved through direct coordination. This was not to assert that coordination is complete or constant. Nor was it to say that willful cooperation is the chief basis for the unity of the power elite or that the emergence of the power elite represented the realization of explicit plans. It was to say that the growth and centralization of power within and across the big three presented opportunities to men who, in the pursuit of their respective interests, came to grasp that they could better realize their interests by working in formal and informal ways with other members of the power elite. They have done so, and at times (e.g., during wartime, which became essentially perpetual) such coordination has been quite decisive.[10]

By focusing on the powerful synergy between the command posts of the big three, Mills cast his view of history between two ideal types. The first views history as "drift." The older version of this was "fate," or "The Unseen Hand." Imagine the tale of Oedipus as a mythical depiction of history conceived as such. The updated, sociology version of "drift" holds that since decisions are innumerable and individually inconsequential, they collectively add up to bring about an outcome that no one could have intended or controlled.[11] Mills surmised that this "view that all is blind drift is largely a fatalist projection of one's own impotence, [or] a salve of one's guilt."[12] For Mills, the problem with such a view is that not all eras are equally adrift. What if the circle of decision-makers narrows, and if the means of decision-making are centralized, and if the consequences of the decisions are tremendous? In such an era, history-making power may reside within real world circles of actors.[13]

Mills's other flawed, ideal type conceives of history as "conspiracy." Such a view holds that history unfolds according to the designs of an identifiable set of villains or, alternatively, heroes. It is a hasty projection and diversion from the more difficult effort to grasp how a shifting social structure affords opportunities to elites and to coalitions of elites who then capitalize or fail to capitalize on them. Wrote Mills, "To accept either view—of all history as conspiracy or all history as drift—is to relax the effort to understand the facts of power and the ways of the powerful."[14]

As stated above, Mills did not describe every historical epoch as equally fateful. Nor did he see America's power elite as a static configuration throughout US history. While the power system in the US has changed throughout its history, its basic legitimacy has never been challenged. By this, Mills is arguing that the alterations to the American establishment have occurred with the general acquiescence of the public, i.e., the without the state resorting to overt despotism. Changes in the power structure have been brought about by relative shifts in the positions of the political, economic, and military institutions. By Mills's reckoning, the US power elite had gone through four distinct eras and was in its fifth.[15] The first epoch spanned from the Revolution through the presidency of John Adams. The relevant aspect of this era is that the "social life, economic institutions, military establishment, and political order coincided."[16] High politicians were key economic figures who also were esteemed figures in local society. The status of politicians did not stem solely from their official positions, though prestige of politicians was high. The early nineteenth century was the second era. Jefferson's political philosophies were largely accepted, but Hamilton's economic principles came to predominate. The age of the yeoman farmer was exaggerated, but there was a broadening of the economic order which served to transform the elite into a plurality of loosely affiliated, loosely overlapping top groups.[17] Economic actors were ascendant over political power, but both politics and the economy were decentralized. This era of "romantic pluralism" lasted through the Civil War.[18]

The third epoch marked the beginning of the dominance of corporate economic power. Corporate supremacy was consolidated in 1886 when the Supreme Court ruled that the Fourteenth Amendment afforded protection to corporations. The center of initiative was transferred from the government to the corporation. It was an age of straightforward corruption, of bought up judges and senators. The military was subordinated to the political system which was dominated by the economic system. Corporate interests were immensely powerful, with Morgan interests holding 341 directorships in 112 firms whose collective holdings were in excess of $22 billion—an amount over three times larger than all the reported property in New England. Federal and state officials were so overmatched by corporate power that the governments were essentially regulated by the moneyed interests themselves. The brief and limited political shifts of the

Progressive Era foreshadowed the power structure that would emerge in the New Deal.[19]

The New Deal was the fourth epoch, and while it did not reverse the relationship between politics and the economy, it did create competing centers of power within governmental and corporate spheres. Economic elites initially opposed the expansion of government powers, though they eventually came to control and use New Deal institutions for their own benefit. That said, this era represented the first time in the US that social policy and issues related to the poor became major pillars of reformist politics. Farm, labor, and big business groups operated within an enlarged government in which officials functioned in ways that were clearly political.[20] The backdrop to this was the faltering capitalist system and the necessity of "reducing the staggering and ominous army of the unemployed."[21] The political leadership responded to the balance of pressure groups as it proceeded to craft policy going from one minor crisis to the next. Most crucially, the balancing act performed by the Roosevelt administration did not impact the foundational pillars of America's capitalist economy. FDR's policies treated some of the symptoms of capitalism and his rhetoric politically scolded the "economic royalists." The New Deal *welfare state* dealt with the crisis of the Great Depression by crafting policies that helped most segments of the population. The emerging state would change further, from a welfare state to a "new state of corporate commissars."[22]

This fifth epoch of the American power structure began with US entry into World War II. The ascendance of the power elite during this period resulted from—and exacerbated—a political decline. This decline curtailed meaningful politics, a politics which would consist of public discussion of distinct alternatives carried out by nationally responsible and politically coherent parties existing alongside independent organizations that connected lower and middle strata of power to the higher levels of decision.[23] In other words, the power elite's rise precluded meaningful democracy since major decisions were not to be arrived at through open, informed public debate in which responsible officials and political parties were influenced by a healthy civil society which could allow the informed, prevailable will of the public to become manifest in policy.

This ascendence of the power elite meant that US democracy was more a formality than a description of the social structure—and even those formal democratic institutions were weak. In the fifth epoch, business-government interpenetration increased dramatically. The power of the executive branch, including its regulatory agencies, expanded considerably, but not as any sort of autonomous bureaucracy. Instead, its rise also meant the ascendance of the corporate man as an eminent political actor with some corporate chieftains joining the New Deal political directorate. During World War II these corporate men came to dominate, most famously with the so-called "dollar-a-year men" who moved to direct the economy toward wartime production during the war and the postwar era.[24]

Both World War II and the postwar eras were characterized by what was essentially an interminable war economy. As such, the military man rose to decisive political relevance in this era. The perception of the great threat empowered the armed forces—and the men, materiel, money, and power at their command. Political and economic decisions came to be evaluated according to a militarized conception of reality. One historical fact has played a major role in these shifts in the American power structure: Since 1939, the object of elites' attention shifted away from domestic issues and toward international issues. In the 1930s, the chief issue was the economic slump. In the 1940s and '50s, the chief issues centered around war. Throughout its history up to this point, the US government had been largely shaped and formed by the balancing of domestic conflicts. It had no suitable democratic institutions for addressing international problems of immense scope. In this political vacuum, the ascendance of the power elite came to pass.[25]

Mills's power elite came to predominate in this fifth epoch of the American power structure thanks to structural facts about the economy. Namely, the economy's foundation was permanent war. Its prevailing mode of organization was the private corporation.[26] Thusly did American capitalism largely become military capitalism. The most significant link between the big corporation and the state was based in the coincidence of interests that existed between the military and the firm, as perceived by the warlords and the corporate chieftains. Among the elite collectively, the overlapping interests of the warlords and the corporate rich strengthened both parties while further subordinating the political leaders. The corporate chieftains and the warlords, not the politicians, managed the war effort. The political vacuum of the fifth epoch was created in part by the absence of any effectively institutionalized civil service vested with integrity, proficiency, and independence from monied interests.[27] Based on historical evidence, it appears that the US power structure entered a sixth epoch following the breakdown of the Bretton Woods international economic order.

Mass Society, Failed Liberalism, and the Higher Immorality

Mills uses the term *power elite* rather than *ruling class*. *Ruling class* is a politico-economic term and may be more or less apt in different eras, e.g., America's Gilded Age. The straightforward Marxist view posits that the economic man is ultimately the holder of power. The liberal perspective places the political man at the center of power. Some in Mills's time would have viewed the warlords as essentially dictators. For Mills, each of these is an oversimplification. Economic determinism should be broadened to account for military determinism and political determinism to better account for elite decisions and defaults. The most powerful agents in each of these three domains had considerable autonomy, but only as coalitions could they formulate and execute the most fateful decisions.[28]

A democratic society requires an engaged and lucid *public* whose members engage and deliberate with each other and possess some sense of agency that is not delusional. Mills saw the lower levels of power moving further away from the *public* ideal toward a *mass society*. Mass communications, metropolitan segregation, and the decline of voluntary associations were all contributing to a degeneration of the American set of publics. As a result, society was being transformed into a mass that "is sovereign only in the most formal and rhetorical sense."[29]

For Mills, the middle levels of power included unions, small property owners, white-collar groups, and "party politicians of the sovereign localities." They collectively reside within a "semi-organized stalemate" in which they might vaguely impede the power elite, but without decisively impacting important decisions.[30] Meanwhile at the top, the power elite seemed ever more unified and often purposefully coordinated. Further adding to the magnitude of the challenges to democracy posed by the power elite is the fact that unlike the middle levels of power and the mass society, the power elite are profoundly class conscious; "[N]owhere is it organized as effectively as among the power elite." While there are factions within the power elite, and while there are conflicts over policy and individual ambitions, these are all less salient than "the internal discipline and the community of interests that bind the power elite together, even across the boundaries of nations at war."[31]

By way of example, Mills refers the reader to James Stewart Martin's book *All Honorable Men* which dealt with Wall Street's prewar connections to the German cartel system and their successful postwar efforts to thwart the dismantling of the system after the war.[32] Over subsequent decades, more information came out which revealed the extent to which the US preserved and rehabilitated the Nazi power elite, including top scientists[33] and war criminals like Reinhard Gehlen,[34] Karl Wolff,[35] and Klaus Barbie.[36] Here again, Mills highlights something historically significant which only became more evident over time—the affinity between the Nazi power elite and power elite of the emerging US empire.

The liberal institutions that might have insulated democratic society against the ascendance of the power elite proved to be inadequate. Some early observers thought that modern means of communication would engage and invigorate the primary public. Instead, those means have served to inculcate widespread psychological illiteracy.[37] Mills explained a number of the symptoms for this condition. Within the public mind, there was emerging a *common sense* based on mass media stereotypes. A uniformity of opinion was taking shape, though it was masked by superficial differences which mainly serve to exacerbate confirmation bias.[38] Americans' self-images were increasingly distorted through the conjuring of an invented and sustained pseudo-world which served to distract from broader sources of individuals' tensions, anxieties, subconscious resentments, and vague hopes.[39] Unfortunately, the media are more than just a cause of America's transformation into a mass society; they are among the most significant means of increasingly expansive elite power.[40] Media manipulation is especially problematic because while there is concentrated and willful power at the top of American society, *authority* does not reside there. Small groups of men make decisions for which they need to gain acceptance or acquiescence from people they do not necessarily rule formally. Therefore, elites must try to manipulate people into accepting or supporting the elites' decisions and opinions, or at least rejecting alternatives.[41] Utilized for this purpose is the propagandist—the public relations man alongside or just below the elite.[42]

American education has not served to impede the rise of the power elite. According to Mills, the chief goal of US public education originally was political: to make citizens wise and thus more enlightened judges of public affairs. Over time, the function of education became economic, i.e., training people for jobs to help them and society economically. The political content has been reduced to the indoctrination of nationalist loyalties.[43] The liberal education was supposed to create self-educating and self-cultivating people. A knowledgeable person in a healthy public can turn his personal struggles into social issues and grasp how these issues are relevant to his community and vice versa. The knowledgeable person understands that what he perceives as his individual problems are quite often shared by others. They are not problems that can be effectively addressed by a single person, but only by changes to some level of social structure.[44] Writes Mills, "It is the task of the liberal institution, as of the liberally educated man, continually to translate troubles into issues and issues into the terms of their human meaning for the individual."[45] American educational institutions were failing at this, instead becoming politically craven institutions offering, at best, upward mobility. Rather than promoting intellectualism and cultural enrichment, they are purveyors of "the trivia of vocational tricks and *adjustment to life*—meaning the slack life of the masses."[46]

For Mills, this left the intellectual as the last line of defense against the ascendance of the power elite. Unfortunately, scholars were in default, succumbing to a "conservative mood," borne of "living in a material boom, a nationalist celebration, a political vacuum." He charged that they have given up of the overriding goal of Western humanism: "the presumptuous control by reason of man's fate."[47] Given America's history in which the bourgeois have been dominant from the beginning, neither the conservative Edmund Burke nor the classical Locke could serve as ideological fountainheads for the US. Instead, the much more pedestrian Horatio Alger seems to be the source of American ideology, such as it is.[48]

While the mood of intellectuals in Mills's time was conservative, overtly right-wing talk was usually eschewed in favor of liberal rhetoric. To satisfy this contradiction, intellectuals typically avoided acknowledging or confronting the top of the existing power structure—and they refused to imagine anything better.[49] This intellectual default occurred as American liberalism was collapsing politically. The New Deal politics of the thirties was destroyed after World War II by the "petty right"— the "political primitives" situated in the middle levels of power who exploited Anti-Communism to impugn the New Deal and the officials who formulated it.[50] The McCarthy era greatly damaged the Foreign Service and normalized secret police proceedings in US politics. Liberalism was revealed as "decayed and frightened," reduced to "defending itself from the insecure and ruthless fury of political gangsters.[51]

Romantic pluralism—also known as the *theory of* balance—allows the liberal intellectual to sustain the conservative mood. It makes it unnecessary for the intellectual of the conservative mood to address the legitimacy of the power structure. For if all actors are in democratically mediated balance against all else, each is virtually impotent; no top-down power can be responsible for events or for history-making decisions. Intellectually, the conservative mood was a rehash of classical liberalism in the decidedly unclassical twentieth century. Liberalism's "unseen hand" replaced classical conservatism's "providence." Innumerable transactions in the magic market lead to some outcome which should be allowed to unfold. From such a perspective, it follows that there is no elite of power and, hence, no elite of power that needs defending or explicit justification.[52] The dominance of these seemingly liberal perspectives served to buttress the power elite—essentially a group of sophisticated conservatives who quietly achieved power in a victory that has gone unnoticed and undebated. The default of the intellectual of the conservative mood meant that there was little scholarly resistance against "the divorce of knowledge from power," and "of mind from reality." Able to command without an ideology that they must defend, the power elite embody "the American system of organized irresponsibility."[53] The power elite can thus manipulate without even attempting to justify. Mills described the power elite's mindlessness as "the true higher immorality of our time."[54]

Elsewhere, Mills defined the *higher immorality* as "the general weakening of older values and the organization of irresponsibility."[55] This is not a case of corrupt men in honorable institutions. If institutions are themselves corrupting, the men who people them are corrupted as a matter of course. The higher immorality has become a systemic feature of the US elite; its widespread acceptance is a key aspect of the mass society.[56] In the absence of any firm prevailing morality, people in the mass are increasingly vulnerable to being manipulated and distracted by celebrity. They often derive vicarious pleasure from the power of the corporate rich, the libertine peccadillos of the celebrities, and the maudlin personal lives of the super-rich.[57]

The acquisition of money was the one value that had not been diminished. Money as a value grew while other values became less salient. As such, men became all the more unscrupulous in pursuit of easy wealth.[58] Society at the top and middle was widely believed to be a of network of clever rackets. In a society where big money is the definition of success, failure on those terms becomes the deadly sin. Such a society will aggrandize "the sharp operator and the shady deal." Within the big three hierarchies, the men at the top are men who have succeeded and who as a result may dispense with the patronage of success. That is to say that the men of the higher circles judge and bestow the criteria of success onto others.[59] From this, three facts about the higher circles can be adduced. The first fact is that success up to and within the higher circles is predicated upon self-co-optation. The second is that the hierarchies of success are not one monolithic entity, but rather a complicated array of cliques, sometimes related, sometimes adversarial. The third fact is that ambitious younger persons must convey an image of success to those in power who would select the successful. These facts created a shift in the virtues that enabled one to succeed. Diligence, integrity, and asceticism gave way to "the effective personality." Charm, self-confidence, the ability to affect empathy—these traits could enable one to be an effective public relations man for himself "to the sole end of individual success in the corporate way of life."[60] Under these conditions, starting life poor and becoming wealthy did not indicate virtue. Only if the ways of gaining wealth required virtue or led to virtue would success imply virtue. When the system is characterized by co-optation from higher levels, one's success merely reveals the principles of the men who get to anoint the successful.[61]

Not only was there an immorality of accomplishment in America; the elite had increasingly become less learned and less culturally enlightened. There had been a time in US history when the elites of power and culture coincided.[62] At the midpoint of the twentieth century, elites in the US could not be considered culturally elite or even "cultivated men of sensibility."[63] Inside the higher circles, there was no unity between knowledge and power. When learned men came in contact with powerful circles, they did so as hired men.[64] Thus, they were outsiders of a sort. Like the power elite in general, they owed their status not to virtue—intellectual acumen *per se*—but to their capacity for co-optation. Writing in the 1950s, the power elite was an essentially, perhaps exclusively, male-dominated affair. Mills's default use of the term "men" when referring to the powerful seems slightly outdated. Today, there are hired female intellectuals and officials who move in circles of power, Samantha Power being a prime example. She is a liberal academic of a sort. As the powerful did in Mills's time, Power legitimates conservative policies with liberal rhetoric. In her official positions, she advocates the frequent use of US military power—typically against the same targets favored by the superficially different neoconservatives. Thus, a woman like Samantha Power is wholly compatible with the *higher immorality* of the US power elite in the twenty-first century.

Mills also elaborated on two key aspects which operate in conjunction and are too often neglected in the social sciences: the role of power in the formation of institutions and the corrosive effects of state secrecy. Structural trends within institutions are identified as opportunities by the occupants of the commanding positions. Coordination among the *big three* was established and then grew into various going concerns, arrangements that new personnel readily accepted and perpetuated. For its purposes, the power elite typically found it easier to operate between and within existing organizations rather than establishing formal organizations comprised of its members. But where there has not been adequate organizational machinery in place, they invented and utilized such machinery as the situation called for. As an example, Mills cited the creation of the National Security Council which came about because there was no formal organization to adequately balance military and political influences upon important decisions.[65]

Such organizations exercise enormous prerogative powers in a nominal democracy. In the permanent war economy, they are aided by an attendant aspect: the assumption that national security necessarily depends upon secret plans and goals. History making events that could reveal much about the logic and workings of the power elite may be hidden from the public under a cloak of secrecy. With widespread state secrecy concealing their deliberations and actions, the power elite are able to disguise their operations, their motivations, and the further consolidation of their power. Given the foregoing, Mills suspects "that the power elite is not altogether *surfaced.*" Following this point, Mills seems to protest a little too much. He states somewhat contradictorily that, "There is nothing hidden about it, although its activities are not publicized," and that, "There is nothing conspiratorial about it, although its decisions are often publicly unknown and its mode of operation manipulative rather than explicit."[66] While this can be stated about the elite as a collective, Mills does not acknowledge an important implication of his analysis: the structural processes he has elaborated have, in conjunction with organizational secrecy, given rise to organizations comprised of members of the power elite in which conspiracy is essentially institutionalized. To some extent, his caution is understandable. Many of the historic events which most dramatically support his theoretical framework were unknown to Mills due to the very secrecy that he was attempting to illuminate.

Mills asserted that the elite don't believe in the existence of a tiny secretive elite who preside over a mass society—that they did not conceptualize it in such terms. However, the public was necessarily confused. Like children, the American people needed to allow the grown-ups to conduct foreign policy, formulate grand strategy, and carry out executive action. Obviously, some people are going to be running things; most people don't care much anyway and regardless, they are too ignorant.[67] Among these decision makers, *crackpot realism* prevails—an insular, myopic mindset and worldview. The mindlessness of the power elite is a vacuum into which platitude and dogma have been thrust.[68] By "mindlessness," Mills is referring to "the divorce of knowledge from power, of sensibilities from men of power, [and] the divorce of mind from reality."[69] Today, Mills's judgement rings prophetic to those who look aghast at humanity's inability to respond to global warming, to stop the policy of endless regime change campaigns, or to dismantle the nuclear "doomsday machine"[70] that threatens humanity with extinction.

Platitude and dogma are so widely accepted as to legitimate leaders; no countervailing worldview is able to prevail against the paranoid ersatz cosmology of crackpot realism. Capitalism is depicted as utopian. Nuanced understandings of events are supplanted by the fog of propaganda. Democratic reverence for public debate has been shunted aside by ideas and practices of psychological warfare. Erudition has been replaced by the "sound" judgement. Forbearance and foresight have given way to the "executive stance."[71] The crackpot realists are men who adhere rigidly to the dominant general principles. They focus unwaveringly on "the next step." This makes them opportunistic devotees to the main drift. In his 1959 follow up to *The Power Elite*—entitled *The Causes of World War Three*—Mills formulated an equation in which "the frenzied next step plus the altogether general principle . . ." equals US foreign policy.[72] More ominously, he argued that the hegemony of crackpot realism in the circles of power was leading to war.[73]

Three years after Mills published *The Causes of World War Three*, the factors identified by Mills nearly did cause a nuclear war. His prophesied World War III did not come to pass, despite his predictions being largely prescient in their particulars. Setting aside the remarkable restraint of key Soviet actors, it is notable that the American most responsible for preventing Mills's prophesied World War III during the Cuban Missile Crisis—President John F. Kennedy—would later be assassinated. As will be discussed in later chapters, the JFK assassination was a power elite venture. The crackpot realism of the warlords, the secrecy of the clandestine state, and the higher immorality of the corporate rich were all brought to bear on that day in Dallas—and in the cover-up ever since.

The *Tripartite State*: A Critical Theory

Mainstream scholars or critical outliers in US social science do not take seriously the possibility that anti-democratic forces could empower networks of individuals to illegally manipulate and subvert democratic institutions and democracy as a whole. Also unexamined is the possibility that the institutionalization of such dynamics could fundamentally alter the nature of the liberal democratic state. The *dual state* theorists seek to explain how the securitization of politics diminishes democratic sovereignty. On the one hand, the dual state theorists offer a critique whose validity is implicitly accepted to some degree when the "national security state" is discussed.[74] Typically, commenters and theorists do not hash out the implications of the existence of such a state. Harold Lasswell was one of the most noteworthy political scientists to address the issue of democratic decline coterminous with the rise of militarization. His *garrison state* construct is useful both for its predictive accuracy and its inaccuracy. In a state of perpetual militarism, Lasswell theorized that elites would become increasingly focused upon the manipulation of symbols for propaganda purposes. Internal violence would be aimed at unskilled laborers and anti-elitist elements. The ruling elite would seek to restrain productive technology in order to minimize consumption and living standards.[75] "Mystic democracy" would persist but such "is not [. . .] democracy at all, because [. . .] authority and control are highly concentrated."[76] These aspects did come to pass to varying degrees as the US established global dominance beginning with its entry into World War II. However, Lasswell incorrectly predicted that the military man—"the specialist on violence"—would assume a dominant position in the social hierarchy over the businessman.[77] In light of subsequent history, the opposite is the easier case to make. Nevertheless, Lasswell is noteworthy for elaborating upon the anti-democratizing effects of militarism.

C. Wright Mills's *power elite* theory perhaps comes the closest to offering a framework for understanding and explaining the sociology of the tripartite state. Mills's went against prevailing (and subsequent) trends in social science by focusing partly upon the existence of agency in a complex and advanced society and political system. He explicitly rejected views "of all history as conspiracy or all history as drift."[78] Although Mills did not address the question of state criminality at length, he identified the "higher immorality" of the emergent political order. The intertwining of the elites in the business, military, and political spheres led to the institutionalization of the higher immorality and the atrophy of private conscience in those men who hold power. The institutions themselves were corrupting. So salient was this feature of society's elite strata that Mills described it as "structural immorality."[79] Unlike Habermas and the pluralists, Mills surmised that state secrecy and the triumph of propaganda allowed the elite to game and beguile the population. "Responsible interpretation of events" was replaced by "the disguise of events," abetted by a "maze of public relations."[80] Thusly did Mills identify a political system that was assuming ever more "holographic" qualities as the state came to be defined by its "enemies"—or, rather, by the interminable, ever-present specter of allegedly existential crises in the form of communist/terrorist conspiracies.[81]

Writing before the activities of the intelligence community became known, Mills nonetheless surmised that when the institutional machinery to effect political outcomes is lacking, the elite will invent such machinery and control it. An important instance of this phenomenon involves the State Department's *War and Peace Studies Project* which was carried out prior to US entry into World War II.[82] The study was conducted in large part by the Wall Street–dominated Council on Foreign Relations and financed by the Rockefeller Foundation—an entity which itself represented an enormous accumulation of wealth acquired via Standard Oil's longtime monopoly control of the US petroleum industry. The *War and Peace Studies Project*, in essence, mapped out the plans for creating a US-dominated postwar world order as well as the institutions which would be needed to maintain it. The UN, the Bretton Woods institutions, and the US national security state all basically conformed to these prescriptions. In *The Power Elite*, Mills cited the creation of the National Security Council—one key element of the postwar US national security state—as a case in which the power elite brought a new governing institution into being.[83] Had Mills been privy to the relevant historical data, he could have cited the Central Intelligence Agency, an organization created by the same legislative act that created the National Security Council. The Central Intelligence Agency was an even more elite-engineered and elite-dominated organization. In its operation, it most greatly exemplified all of the anti-democratic trends that Mills identified in his thesis. While Mills did not specifically address the possibility of structurally impactful high criminality, it was arguably alluded to by way of reference to the illegitimacy of the rich and powerful, the racket-like ways in which they made their fortunes, the ubiquity of state secrecy, the fabrication of propaganda in lieu of realism, and the *higher immorality* that characterized the culture of the American power elite.

Opposing Mills's conception of a coherent, decisive, and self-interested power elite was *pluralism*, a perspective with a much more sanguine view of the American political system. Written at the high tide of liberalism, Dahl described America's democratic political system as one in which the government served as a mediator between various interest groups that collectively represented the whole of society.[84] In such a rendering, there was no democratic decline that needed to be explained. After the events of the 1960s and 1970s, Dahl's naïve pluralism was basically untenable. Lindblom's revised explication of pluralism viewed America's anti-democratic trajectory as the function of a lopsided competition of ideas in which big business dominated politics and indoctrinated the public by exercising an overdetermining influence on political and economic life.[85] Even Lindblom's revised, rearguard version of pluralism is problematic. At what point would the influence of the overworld of private wealth be considered so overpowering that pluralism would cease to be a viable perspective to explain US politics and society? Additionally, pluralists do not address the issue of historically impactful high criminality. Pluralism basically presupposes that the rule of law generally prevails and that the state is open, transparent, and democratic—various scandals notwithstanding.

The *critical theory* of Jurgen Habermas focused on the contradictions between capitalism and the intersubjective norms of communication. Like Lindblom, Habermas was writing in the 1970s. He argued that capitalism persisted despite the essential accuracy of Marx's predictions. The contradictions between the realities of advanced capitalism and the norms of democratic societies led to *legitimation crises* in which political and economic institutions suffered from diminishing public respect. Such crises are resolved through the power of linguistic intersubjectivity or universal communicative norms.[86] In other words—and at the risk of oversimplification—through open public discourse, the population can have some impact on the regime because the regime needs to resolve crises of legitimacy. Unexplored are the possibilities and implications of elites who collectively manipulate fundamental aspects of political reality and its perception.[87]

Postmodernist critiques have highlighted the authoritarian aspects of institutions in liberal societies, but in so doing removed actual authoritarians from the frame of analysis.[88] Foucault's (2001) theories of "governmentality" traced the modern form of government bureaucracies to the synchronous development of social scientific methods such as demography which allow for the management of populations.[89] Foucault (1970) explored and elaborated upon the connections between power and science or human systems of knowledge. It was implicitly assumed that the connections stemmed from structural forces coterminous with the rise in complexity of human civilizations. Adhering to such a perspective ignores the intentional development and deployment of "technologies of the self."[90] For example, America's "Global War on Terror" did not organically emerge as an international system of rendition, detention, and torture regimes. Such a system was organized and approved by the highest levels of government and was informed by the technical expertise of the psychology profession.[91] Additionally, the torture and interrogation techniques were based upon preexisting knowledge acquired by scientists working in the 1950s and 1960s on projects undertaken to determine the best practices for brainwashing prisoners and establishing "mind control" over human subjects.[92]

Relative to these other theoretical approaches, tripartite state theory provides an historically informed synthesis of *dual state* theories and Mills's elite-focused power structure theories. In so doing, it can better address certain historical puzzles and paradoxes. Throughout the first seven decades of the twentieth century, democratic traditions and institutions became stronger overall in the US. This represents the power of the *democratic*—or *public*—*state*, an institution that is desirable according to normative notions of progress derived from the Enlightenment. The *security state* that emerged after World War II was informed by logics of secrecy, hierarchy, and authoritarianism—all anathema to Enlightenment ideals. The US national security state was designed to bring about and defend a vision of world order formulated by a stratum of elites which had lost some of its hegemony over society following the Gilded Age and Great Depression. Perhaps the most salient anti-democratic aspect of this project has been the degree to which political economy is no longer subject to democratic deliberation. At present, the neoliberal/neoconservative bipartisan consensus so greatly narrows the spectrum of contestable policy debate that effectual public discourse is largely relegated to cultural issues with little to no bearing upon issues of justice which animated the democratic struggles of previous eras. The notion of a supranational deep state component of a tripartite state provides a theoretical construct with which to address the decisive power wielded by elites whose interests dominate the security state, the public state, and the economy—and thus society at large. The political transformation of the US and of the international system has not occurred solely by legitimate or transparent means. There is considerable documentation of anti-democratic and criminal foreign policy practices which have strengthened US hegemony and conferred ever more wealth and power upon the elites whose collective interests animate the sovereign tripartite state. Additionally, there are numerous cases of documented and suspected criminal, covert interventions into US domestic politics. Subsequent chapters of this book muster historical evidence and case studies to establish a narrative that chronicles the rise of the tripartite state and its implications for our society.

Structure and Agency

Questions of structure vs. agency loom large in the social sciences. As discussed above, Mills identified this in his formulations of two ideal type approaches to understanding history, society, and politics: all of history as "drift" or all of history as "conspiracy."[93] To posit a compact group of omnipotent conspirators directing history is not something that can be plausibly substantiated. Likewise, the *hyperstructuralism* of some critical scholars—e.g., Noam Chomsky—also evinces a stultifying myopia.[94] In short, the notion put forward here and elsewhere is that structure vs. agency is a false dichotomy. It is not a question of class *or* conspiracy which reproduces and manages overworld hegemony. Rather, it is class *and* conspiracy. As Michael Parenti states,

> The alternative is to believe that the powerful and the privileged are somnambulists, who move about oblivious to questions of power and privilege; that they always tell us the truth and have nothing to hide even when they hide so much; that although most of us ordinary people might consciously try to pursue our own interests, wealthy elites do not; that when those at the top employ force and violence around the world it is only for the laudable reasons they profess; that when they arm, train, and finance covert actions in numerous countries, and then fail to acknowledge their role in such deeds, it is because of oversight or forgetfulness or perhaps modesty; and that it is merely a coincidence how the policies of the national security state so consistently serve the interests of the transnational corporations and the capital-accumulation system throughout the world. . . .[95]

As argued herein, elite representatives of the corporate overworld transformed the American state. This did not occur through automatic or natural processes. The corporate rich do represent the pinnacle of a class structure, but like the British Empire their hegemony did not arise from "a fit of absent-mindedness." Elites have agency, the nature of which is determined in considerable part by the structure of state and society. The postwar US power elite were buttressed by vast material resources that they could efficiently mobilize and command through bureaucratic corporate organizations. "Commanders of power unequaled in human history," they set out to establish imperial hegemony over the restructured international political economy.[96] The project entailed large-scale planning for the creation and maintenance of the institutions to enable such an undertaking. While the initial architects of US hegemony allowed for some New Deal–inspired progressive institutional aspects, the elite planning of the 1970s—in the aftermath of the tumultuous and violent 1960s—reveals a power elite determined to make use of its agency by imposing what came to be referred to as *neoliberalism*. This totalizing project has—not accidentally—served to weaken democracy by greatly reducing the space in which any democratic counter-elite could emerge. Carried out through covert and overt means, these efforts furthered the rise of the US deep state system, an historically unprecedented expression of *structural power*, rightfully understood as agency of the highest order.

CHAPTER 5

THE DEEP STATE, DARK POWER, AND THE EXCEPTION

Defining the Deep State

The work of C. Wright Mills points the way toward addressing the short-comings of dual state theories. In *Double Government*, Glennon makes reference to Mills's work, but only when discussing the military mindset or the *military metaphysic* in which reality in total is understood through the lens of war. Glennon does not address the immense power of the big business, even though these men often had much to do with the creation of the national security state. Later chapters will examine some of the myriad ways in which policy has been formulated and even executed by elites outside of the public state or even outside of the formally organized security state. In Glennon's coverage of the weakness of the *Madisonian institutions* (i.e., the public state), he is essentially acknowledging the same political vacuum noted by Mills. However, for Glennon, the inertia and the lack of accountability is attributed to the internal organizational characteristics and the power of the *Trumanite network*. Like the realist IR scholars or the orthodox historians, there is no deep interrogation of the origins of geopolitical grand strategy or its beneficiaries outside of the government.

In fact, Glennon spends very little space detailing what the static *general thrust* of US foreign policy really is.

While Glennon sees two centers of power—the national security and political spheres—he has omitted Mill's third: the corporate rich or the *overworld* of private wealth. The *overworld* wields influence and power over non-state entities *and* the organizations that comprise Glennon's *double government*. Collectively exerting power over governance and history making, these institutions comprise the *deep state*. Previously, I defined the deep state as "an obscured, dominant, supranational source of antidemocratic power."[1] I would clarify this with the observation that the institutions that comprise the deep state are not uniformly obscured. Some are formally organized and transparent to varying degrees, e.g., the Council on Foreign Relations. Other entities like the Safari Club or the Bilderberg group are known to exist or to have existed, but they are largely opaque. The mainstream media must be considered part of the deep state. Its assumptions, biases, priorities, and defaults are very much a function of the interests of a tiny elite of corporate wealth whose interests the media necessarily serves regardless of this or that outlet's position along the ever-narrowing spectrum of allowable political perspective.

While the term *deep state* has become ubiquitous in the age of Trump, as yet it has no widely accepted definition. The term originally derives from Turkey where it described "a closed network said to be more powerful than the public state."[2] The Turkish deep state availed itself of false flag terror orchestrated by the security apparatus with links to organized crime.[3] It grew out of networks originally established by NATO's Operation Gladio in order to maintain stay-behind paramilitary forces that could become an insurgency following a communist takeover.[4] The Turkish example was a narrower conception of the deep state than those that would follow. It did, however, point to the existence of sovereign state power existing outside of the public state and the official security services. Collectively, therefore, the formally organized Turkish state did not exercise a monopoly on "the legitimate use of violence"—supposedly the *sine qua non* of "the state"— since the *deep state* had deemed extra-legal violence acceptable even if not explicitly "legitimate." While "legitimacy" may be a fuzzy and subjective concept, it is nevertheless stretched past the breaking point if applied to false-flag terrorism.

The *New York Times* in 2013 asserted that "deep state" was an important new term and defined it as "A hard-to-perceive level of government or super-control that exists regardless of elections and that may thwart popular movements or radical change. Some have said that Egypt is being manipulated by its deep state."[5] This is a useful definition, as it emphasizes the anti-democratic and opaque character of the deep state. In 2014, an experienced government insider penned an essay on the deep state, an entity which he described as operating "according to its own compass heading regardless of who is formally in power."[6] In his formulation, Mike Lofgren included parts of the formally organized government as well as ostensibly private organizations like Booz Allen Hamilton and the politically active wealth of Wall Street. Lofgren eventually added to this essay with a book on the deep state in which he defined it as:

> [A] hybrid association of key elements of government and parts of top level finance and industry that is effectively able to govern the United States with only limited reference to the consent of the governed as normally expressed through elections.[7]

Lofgren identifies the deep state as "the big story of our time." He describes it as the thread that connects the GWOT to the militarizing of US foreign policy. It connects both financialization and deindustrialization to the ascendant US plutocracy. This all occurs in an era of paralyzing political dysfunction.[8] By Lofgren's reckoning, the deep state was conceived at the moment that the US attained nuclear weapons. He adds that America's postwar position of unprecedented global power led to the intellectual corruption of the US political class.[9] It will be shown in a later chapter that the deep political forces identified by Lofgren were present and overwhelmingly powerful even prior to Hiroshima and Nagasaki, acting decisively to plan US entry into World War II as well as the subsequent US-led world order that was constructed after the war.

Lofgren's assessment of the deep state is a slightly sanitized formulation in comparison to the earlier, ongoing, and more provocative scholarship

of Peter Dale Scott. Despite Scott's prolific work on the subject, Lofgren
fails to cite him or make reference to his work. This may be due to the fact
that Scott, unlike Lofgren, explores and emphasizes the criminal intrigues
of the deep state. In Scott's book, *American War Machine*, he details some
complex, deep state history involving Adnan Khashoggi, the Bank of
Credit and Commerce International, and the Safari Club. Collectively,
Scott described them,

> [A]s part of a supranational deep state, whose organic links to the
> CIA may have helped consolidate it. It is clear however that deci-
> sions taken at this level by the Safari Club and BCCI were in no way
> guided by the political determinations of those elected to power in
> Washington . . . [and were instead] expressly created to overcome
> restraints established by political decisions in Washington.[10]

Scott is the most prolific and erudite deep state theorist. His conception
evolved from what he had earlier termed *parapolitics* and then *deep politics*. Scott defined *parapolitics* as "a system or practice of politics in which
accountability is consciously diminished."[11] He applied this to the study
of historical events including the CIA's covert operations, the forces and
actors that moved the US into war in Vietnam, and other episodes in which
powerful actors take politically significant action with "plausible deniability," the true facts typically being obscured through the deployment of
cover stories. Scott later coined the term *deep politics to* refer to "all those
political practices and arrangements, deliberate or not, that are usually
repressed in public discourse rather than acknowledged."[12] Examples of
deep politics include the recurrence of US foreign policy intrigues involving petroleum and narcotics traffic or the legal immunity of organized
crime in Chicago for much of the twentieth century.[13] Scott's research and
writing sought to address the problems posed by powerful forces with *sub
rosa* history-making power.

It was only relatively recently that Scott began referring to a US *deep
state*.[14] This is likely due to the difficulty of conceptualizing the nature
of obscured power in complex societies. Lofgren describes the state as an
iceberg. The visible part is the political system that we are taught about in

civics courses and in political science courses. It is theoretically controlled by elections. The larger, submerged part of the iceberg is the *deep state*. It moves according to its own inertia regardless of who nominally holds power.[15] Lofgren, like Scott, sees the deep state as a hybrid of private and governmental institutions. He also sees the overworld as an overdetermining factor in terms of controlling the deep state. "Wall Street," Lofgren writes, "may be the ultimate owner of the Deep State and its strategies, if for no other reason than that it has the money to reward government operatives with a second career that is lucrative [. . .] beyond the dreams of a salaried government employee."[16]

Scott, however, considers the iceberg metaphor to be too concrete or structurally specific. Scott asserts that the deep state is less structural and more systemic. Though difficult to define explicitly, it is "as real and powerful as a weather system."[17] Indeed, Scott acknowledges that he uses the term *deep state* to refer to what he had previously described as a "deep political system,"[18] a system "which habitually resorts to decision-making and enforcement procedures outside as well as inside those publicly sanctioned by law and society."[19] A key systemic feature of the deep state is that the largely unregulated overworld-deep state milieu not only exerts enough influence to dominate politics, but it also engages in "antisocial lawbreaking and sometimes murderous malfeasance."[20]

The empirical strength of Scott's research shows that he was justified in using the term "deep political system." Political decisions of history-making significance have been made and enforced by institutions both outside and inside those that are legally proscribed. Scott describes the deep state as the realm of accumulated extralegal powers within the government and outside it. This would include the covert agencies—as well as their allies in media, overworld, and underworld circles. In another more recent work, Scott again states explicitly that he now uses the term *deep state* roughly to refer what he previously had described as the *deep political system*.[21] There is much to suggest that the "deepness" is indeed systemic as all major political institutions increasingly exist in a world shaped by top-down power. However, when Scott describes the Khashoggi-BCCI-Safari Club milieu as "part of a supranational deep state,"[22] he is speaking about something structural. He acknowledges this problem in an endnote

where he states that previously he had wished to dissociate the idea of the
"deep state" from implications that it is a formal organization. He therefore wrote about the American deep state as "a milieu both inside and
outside government with the power to steer the history of the public state
and sometimes redirect it." In this endnote he acknowledges that indeed
there are also "extragovernmental structural components in the deep state
system." [23]

The idea of a *deep political system* accords well with tripartite state theory. I wrote in 2015 that:

> Conceptually, the tripartite state is useful[ly] if imperfectly imag-
> ined as a Venn diagram with significant overlap. An examination of
> the current political system suggests that the independent realm of
> the democratic state is small indeed. At present there is not much
> observable democratic autonomy or agency vis-à-vis the overdeter-
> mining wealth and power of the deep state. [24]

The power of the deep state is such that it is not hyperbolic to refer to the
prevailing order as the *deep state system*. The deep state has impacted the
public and security states in such a way as to prevail throughout them and
to usurp constitutionally authorized power. Thus, the power of the deep
state can be described as systemic. The Venn diagram depiction discussed
above was conceived as a way to describe the structure of the tripartite
state. However, with only a minor modification, it could be a systemic
model. Specifically, a circle representing civil society is added to the diagram, also with considerable deep state overlap. In other words, deep
political power neutralizes the ability of civil society institutions to act as
a check against top-down, anti-democratic forces.

Dark Power

No social order can rely solely or even primarily on coercion. In political
science terms, the transaction costs are too great—i.e., it is inefficient to
constantly monitor and police a hierarchy in which the subordinate members can only be compelled through force or the threat of force. Thus,
every domestic and international order rests upon a mixture of coercion

and consent. Democratic social orders owe their legitimacy to concepts of popular sovereignty and the rule of law. Hegemony in authoritarian social orders is maintained on the basis of top-down power, legitimized in various ways. Theories of hegemony in the international realm can be categorized along a continuum between consent and coercion.[25] Similarly, these two points can represent opposing modes of power within circumscribed political orders, i.e., nation-states. Hannah Arendt described them as two mindsets that can be found in every society.[26] An open society operating according to the rule of law conceives of power as "persuasion through arguments." The opposite is "coercion by force." As with Thucydides, Arendt traced these to the Greeks who used persuasion in domestic politics while using force in foreign affairs.[27] Historically speaking, it is difficult to find examples of societies wherein there exists a clean bifurcation between modes of power operant in domestic and international spheres respectively. While Arendt and others like Karl Popper[28] spoke of persuasion and deliberation as prevailing forces in open constitutional societies, Samuel Huntington (1981) advocated for coercive, top-down power as being necessary for a cohesive society.[29] Wrote Huntington, "Power remains strong when it remains in the dark; exposed to sunlight it begins to evaporate."[30] Peter Dale Scott describes this as *dark power*—"power not derived from the constitution but outside and above it."[31]

The conflict between these two modes of power can be observed as far back as the work of Plato. In *The Republic*, Plato calls obliquely for the top-down rule by the wise, legitimated by instrumental *noble lies*. In *The Laws*, Plato argued for something closer to persuasion wherein Magnesia—a hypothetical city—would be governed on the basis of painstakingly formulated laws. However, even in formulating the constitution of Magnesia, Plato returned to advocating for a form of rule by the wise. This occurs in the later sections of *The Laws* wherein Plato proposes the creation of a *nocturnal council* comprised of elites. The nocturnal council would be nominally responsible only for moderating the views of atheists and handling foreign travelers who may have been exposed to exotic and/or dangerous notions during their travels. Beyond this, the powers of the council are vaguely defined. Plato died before the work could be completed.

The vagueness of the council's power has led scholars to disagree about Plato's meaning. Most scholars have adhered to an informal view of the council—that it would operate in an informal, perhaps advisory role to those who execute the state's laws.[32] Others have argued that the council was to play an institutional or instrumental role. Argued Barker, "The nocturnal council is the perfect guardians of the Republic turned collegiate and set to control, in ways that are never explained, a system of political machinery into which they are never fitted."[33] Klosko takes the position that in the end, Plato could not discard the idea of rule by the wise. He needed to insert some mechanism to allow for the wise to wield power. At one point in *The Laws*, the members of the nocturnal council are referred to as the "real guardians of the laws." Plato also states that if such a "divine council" is created "then the state must be entrusted to it."[34]

Whether one favors the informal or institutional interpretation of the nocturnal council, either could be analogous to elements of the American deep state. The Wall Street–financed Council on Foreign Relations (CFR) could be a modern analog to the nocturnal council. Its power may have diminished since its heyday which stretched from before World War II up to the Vietnam War. However, it still retains significant influence while serving as an incubator and clearinghouse for Establishment prescriptions and conventional wisdom. In 2009, Secretary of State Hillary Clinton spoke to the CFR, stating "It's good to have an outpost of the Council right here down the street from the State Department. [. . .] This will mean I won't have as far to go to be told what we should be doing and how we should think about the future."[35] This illustrates that the CFR—like the nocturnal council as described above—has the power to exert influence "in ways that are never explained, [in] a system of political machinery into which [it is] never fitted."[36]

The institutional analogy of the nocturnal council is pregnant with even graver implications. If the council members are collectively supposed to act as the "real guardians of the laws" to which "the state must be entrusted" then the council would presumably have the capacity to formulate and execute policy in an extraconstitutional, top-down fashion. This would largely negate the basis for the legitimacy of the Magnesian state, the rule of law. However, it is not clear that such a negation would be recognized as such since the council could intervene in subtle and/or covert ways that would not necessarily be perceived by the population at large. Thus, by allowing for "wise" ruling class figures to subtly exert control over a system ostensibly regulated by a just set of laws, the elite of Magnesia could have their cake and eat it too, as it were. There is little evidence that points to anything as compact and centralized as a formally organized nocturnal council within the American deep state. There have been, however, certain entities and networks that have functioned or may have functioned as overriding centers of deep state power. Peter Dale Scott has explored the possibility that at certain fateful junctures, the *Doomsday Project*—a.k.a. *Continuity of Government*—has served as such an entity.[37]

The CIA has more infamously functioned as an instrument of dark power and as an element of the deep state. At times the agency has worked in opposition to the president. Thus, it has operated in ways that run counter to what would be expected of an organization within a hierarchical security state, nominally under the control of the public state's executive branch. Wrote former President Harry Truman one month to the day after the Kennedy assassination,

> For some time I have been disturbed by the way CIA has been diverted from its original assignment. It has become an operational and at times a *policy-making* [emphasis added] arm of the Government. This has led to trouble and may have compounded our difficulties in several explosive areas.[38]

Truman's op-ed piece was titled "Limit CIA Role To Intelligence." He claimed in the piece, with some justification, that the CIA had gone far beyond its intended purpose, which was to collate and analyze intelligence coming from various sources. While his recommendations were and still are reasonable, it is worth noting that the even in its earliest days under Truman, the agency was deployed to conduct covert operations: Infamously, Truman's CIA intervened in the Greek civil war and in Italian election rigging. The interference in the Italy's election was of a magnitude that dwarfs the alleged Russian intervention into the 2016 US election.

Regardless, Truman's 1963 editorial was ignored by the media and quickly forgotten. Subsequently, the CIA under President Johnson would reverse several Kennedy era policies in several third world countries, most notably Brazil, Congo, and Indonesia. Following the partial exposure of the high criminality of the Nixon administration, the CIA was investigated by Congress in the 1970s. Temporarily chastened, the deep state went into a remission of sorts, receding under Carter with sensitive operations handled off the books or by unaccountable entities such as the Safari Club or the World Anti-Communist League. When Reagan came into power—probably thanks to the decisive intervention of the deep state—the CIA was able to resume its former active role. This culminated in Iran-Contra which again brought the CIA under scrutiny from which it would, again, emerge largely unscathed.

Those political struggles represent the conflict between open persuasive power and coercive top-down power. The security state represented the battleground on which the public state clashed with the deep state. Although the public state has at times achieved apparent victories, these have proven fleeting and the general thrust of empire proceeds unimpeded, specifically the drive to global dominance and the dominance of wealth over society at large. As with Plato's Magnesia, US elites benefit from the legitimacy conferred by the ostensibly open constitutional order while a deep state collectively functions as the *nocturnal council* to whom the city (i.e., the nation-state) is really entrusted. In this way, US politico-economic elites enjoy the benefits of living in a society with a considerable—if declining—degree of democratic legitimacy while simultaneously retaining unacknowledged authoritarian agency. This is accomplished in part through a subset of the politically elite class,

> [H]igh ranking officials who are privy to state secrets, who decide what the public may and may not know, and who plan and authorize covert operations, foreign and domestic surveillance, and other espionage and intelligence activities.[39]

Drawing upon Plato and C. Wright Mills, Lance deHaven-Smith terms this class the *Guardian Elite*. They bear responsibility "for protecting the society from enemies foreign and domestic"—enemies which they themselves must identify.[40]

In postwar US history, such figures are typically either drawn from the ranks of America's upper classes, or they capitalize on the connections between the security state and the overworld of private wealth to attain lucrative opportunities later in life. For a recent example, former Director of National Intelligence James Clapper was an executive at Booz Allen, a private intelligence firm that is dependent on government contracts for nearly all of its revenue.[41] Famously, the Dulles brothers, John Foster and Allen, were from an elite political family; both their uncle and their grandfather had served as US Secretary of State. Before serving in the Eisenhower administration as Secretary of State and Director of Central Intelligence, respectively, the brothers were lawyers at Sullivan & Cromwell, one of the most illustrious Wall Street law firms. At Sullivan & Cromwell, the Dulles brothers did business with the most powerful US corporate interests and with international concerns including, notoriously, key figures in Nazi Germany. It would take volumes to document the ties between the mandarins of US national security and corporate America, but suffice it to state that the US Guardian Elite are very much of and for the overworld of private wealth. Since the end of World War II, the US Guardian Elite have functioned most decisively as executors of dark power. They have operated with huge budgets, under a cloak of state secrecy, and without meaningful oversight or legal restraints. Insufficient scholarly attention has been paid to the Guardian Elite as a class.

Exceptionism and the State

The contrast between dark and persuasive modes of power was evident in ancient Athens, as Thucydides observed. Open, persuasive power operated domestically while dark, coercive power was deployed in foreign policy. The distinction has been relevant in American politics as well. From the beginning, the English colonists and the early United States had comparatively open, democratic methods of handling affairs with themselves in comparison to the violent coercion deployed against "others," including American Indians, African slaves, Mexicans, Japanese, and Hawaiians. Suffice it to say that modern democracy did not eliminate the contradiction between open, persuasive, constitutional power and dark, coercive, top-down power. What has changed is the degree of candor regarding the conflict. During the Peloponnesian war, the Athenian emissary famously stated, "The strong do what they will and the weak suffer what they must." Typically, today's leaders eschew such bluntness. If they don't, it can be scandalous, such when Hillary Clinton mirthfully quipped, "We came; we saw; he died!" to an interviewer in reference to the recent death of Muammar Gaddafi. The Libyan head of state had been captured by US-sponsored militants who proceeded to videotape his torture and mutilation before murdering him and uploading the video to the internet.

Given that convention requires the cloaking of imperialist policy with liberal rhetoric, Hillary Clinton committed an unusual *faux pas* when she chose to paraphrase imperialist *par excellence* Julius Caesar. Back in the 1950s, American sociologist C. Wright Mills observed that liberal rhetoric was constantly used in the service of conservative politics. To an even greater degree, such is the case today. Prior to the Iraq War, neoconservatives used liberal rhetoric to supplement the security pretexts to justify an illegal war. "For bureaucratic reasons," Iraqi WMD were "settled on" as the war's central justification according to Paul Wolfowitz.[42] However, liberal rhetoric was deployed by liberal *and* neoconservative supporters of the war. In light of this, it is noteworthy that some of these neoconservatives, Paul Wolfowitz for example, were acolytes of Leo Strauss, a neoconservative theorist who believed that great philosophers had to speak and write esoterically since the truth was too dangerous for the uninitiated. Thus, Strauss would likely have approved of official obfuscation to promote the Iraq War. Such are the *noble lies* needed to maintain some semblance of social harmony while "the strong do what they will."

In his own writing, Leo Strauss was more straightforward:

Are the maxims of foreign policy essentially different from the maxims on which gangs of robbers act? Can they be different? Are cities not compelled to use force and fraud to take away from other cities what belongs to the latter, if they are to prosper? Do they not come into being by usurping a part of the earth's surface which by nature belongs equally to all others?[43]

Obviously, it would be even more straightforward to present these ideas in the form of declarative statements, but at times Strauss preferred to philosophize in quasi-Socratic form. Perhaps this was an homage to the esoteric style of the philosophers he regarded as his intellectual peers, namely Plato and Socrates. Alternatively, perhaps Strauss preferred a fig leaf of ambiguity given that he was advocating a foreign policy approach that was illiberal in the extreme while living in a supposedly open, liberal society.

The reflexive couching of hegemonic foreign policy in liberal terms is the signature affectation of the US empire. It is necessary not just for international public relations purposes, but because the means and ends of US foreign policy are so much at odds with America's national myths. Public figures must pantomime acceptance of these myths in their public pronouncements. For example, Council on Foreign Relations President Richard Haas recently tweeted:

International order for 4 centuries has been based on non-interference in the internal affairs of others and respect for sovereignty. Russia has violated this norm by seizing Crimea and by interfering in the 2016 US election. We must deal w Putin's Russia as the rogue state it is[.][44]

Haas makes this statement despite almost certainly knowing that no country has interfered more than the US in other countries' elections and that such interference—along with more violent subversions of democracy—has been a defining characteristic of the US-led postwar world order. Even a former CIA director demurred recently when asked to assert American innocence in election meddling. As described by antiwar blogger Caitlyn Johnstone,

"Have we ever tried to meddle in other countries' elections?" Ingraham asked in response to Woolsey's Russia remarks. "Oh, probably," Woolsey said with a grin. "But it was for the good of the system in order to avoid the communists from taking over. For example, in Europe, in '47, '48, '49, the Greeks and the Italians we CIA[. . .]." "We don't do that anymore though?" Ingraham interrupted. "We don't mess around in other people's elections, Jim?" Woolsey smiled and said "Well . . .", followed by a joking incoherent mumble, adding, "Only for a very good cause."[45]

One noteworthy aspect of these statements by Haas and Woolsey is how the mendacity and hypocrisy are effectively greeted by a collective shrug from the public. Haas' absurd *power lie* did not register as a scandal. Woolsey's glib admission did nothing to affect the general hysteria over the so-called Russiagate case, with its unsubstantiated or disproven central charges. Instead, for a handful of informed observers, these cases serve merely to highlight America's democratic impotence.

Legitimacy, Lawlessness, and Liberal Myths

Every political entity is constituted emotionally and morally through typically mythical narratives about its origins, history, and values. Together those narratives form a common biography which serves as a foundation for the group's shared common identity.[46] A state's constitutive collective identity reduces its diplomatic mendacity and its brutality in war because it entails a moral code. Violence and duplicity are also constrained by internationally accepted *meta-norms* that have emerged from the commonalities among the moral codes of other states within the world order.[47] Given that imperialism requires a kind of amorality like that articulated above in Thucydides and by Strauss, there is conflict between an empire's amoral foreign policy and its supposedly fundamental moral code. Imperialist *realpolitik* must also conflict with global meta-norms. These contradictions are becoming more glaring as the increasingly interconnected world is ever more of aware of global inequities. Former US National Security Advisor Zbigniew Brzezinski described the approaching moment as "the global political awakening," stating that,

For the first time in history almost all of humanity is politically activated, politically conscious and politically interactive. Global activism is generating a surge in the quest for cultural respect and economic opportunity in a world scarred by memories of colonial or imperial domination.[48]

In a liberal democracy, not only are liberal norms salient, they are codified. This makes the rule of law another potential impediment to the imperatives of global dominance. In order to manage affairs of state in this context, a subset of the political class must manage affairs of state, deHaven-Smith's *Guardian Elite*. This is the class, again, comprised of "high-ranking officials who are privy to state secrets, who decide what the public may and may not know, and who plan and authorize covert operations, foreign and domestic surveillance, and other espionage and intelligence activities."[49] The Guardian Elite polices—largely in secret—the political class and the mass public.[50] They serve to allow the state to overcome three potential impediments to the exigencies of empire, namely: America's moral code, global meta-norms, and the rule of law. Their amoral ethos and class consciousness allow them to be unbound from the American moral code and the norms of global society.[51] *Exceptionism*—the institutionalized suspension of legal restraints—protects them from facing legal consequences stemming from their illicit clandestine activities.[52] Exceptionism has its roots in the contradictions within liberalism, contradictions that trace back to its philosophical roots and the origins of the state.

Max Weber's classic definition of the state maintains that it is the organization which maintains a monopoly on the legitimate use of violence within a particular territory. Charles Tilly (1985) demonstrated that in the history of the rise of the modern state, the legitimacy or illegitimacy of the state's monopoly on violence is complicated by the fact that the organizations from which the modern state evolved resembled nothing so much as protection rackets. It was through war-making that these protection-racketeering, nascent states evolved.[53] "War made the state, and the state made war," wrote Tilly.[54] Thusly, the modern state emerged from institutionalized illegitimate violence, and in such a way as to allow societies to more effectively organize violence internally and externally against other societies. The modern state has sanctioned and participated in various economies of violence, including the trans-Atlantic slave trade, the Opium

Wars, and overt imperialism like colonialism. Liberals could dismiss these "as vestiges of pre-modern, absolutist political forms."[55] If such a dismissal were warranted, liberal democracy should gradually abolish these lawless aspects as public sovereignty and the rule of law are strengthened.[56]

In the latter years of colonial America, the colonists were especially aggrieved by the crown's prerogative powers. Eschewing monarchist dogma, the political philosopher John Locke is typically cited as the thinker who most influenced the Framers of the US Constitution. Locke's political philosophy is widely understood as placing sovereignty in the public through its role in selecting representatives and making a government. An elected legislature, therefore, is best able to protect life, liberty, and property while safeguarding against the arbitrary exercise of power. However, Locke contradicted his own central premise by arguing that "the Executive Power" confers the authority to act decisively in the public interest. He asserted that "accidents may happen wherein a strict and rigid observation of the laws may do harm." Locke even used the term "prerogative" to describe this discretionary power, which he admits in passing is "arbitrary power."[57]

In so doing, Locke essentially ignored the fact that the prevention of arbitrary power was the guiding principle of his prescribed constitution.[58] He most strikingly abandoned his liberal path in the instance of the "emergency," where he obliquely invokes *raison d'etat*. This is, of course, the concept offered to legitimate essentially all acts of state carried out in power contests between states—the doctrine that evolved from the "interest of state" into the "security of state," and its well-known contemporary form: "national security."[59] With these arguments, Locke placed security highest of all, just like Hobbes—the man typically considered to be his antithesis. Locke at least quibbled over the implications, asking "But who shall judge when this power is made right use of?"[60] He answered that if the legislature is unable to check the prerogatives of an executive, "[T]here can be no judge on earth."[61] In such an instance, a ruler is using a power that was never his, since people cannot consent to the rule of those who would harm them. Under such circumstances, the people are to make an "appeal to heaven" at the opportune moment.[62] This is to say that the people have the right to revolt. However, in the absence of overtly tyrannical rule, Locke and Hobbes are in general agreement regarding legal restraints to prerogative powers effecting existential security. By not defining the boundaries of prerogative power, Locke liberalized and thus legitimized what is essentially a foundation for absolutism.[63]

While Locke deemphasized the incompatible absolutism within his liberal theorizing, Carl Schmitt harkened back to Hobbes by focusing precisely on the absolutism of existential security. Schmitt is best known for his dictum, "Sovereign is he who decides on the exception."[64] The "state of exception" cannot be "codified in the existing legal order" because it is "a case of extreme peril, a danger to the existence of the state."[65] The state of exception is so perilous that "it cannot be circumscribed factually and made to conform to a preformed law."[66] Public sovereignty is essentially an illusion because true sovereignty resides with whoever decides when a state of exception exists—and when it no longer exists. The most that a liberal constitution can hope to establish is the personage of the sovereign.[67] The sovereign also determines when the situation is "normal," and only under normal circumstances can laws and the adherence to laws exist. As a less punchy corollary to his dictum, Schmitt wrote, "[I I]e is sovereign who definitely decides whether this normal situation actually exists."[68] Constitutionalist liberals can at most regulate the exception as precisely as possible, an endeavor tantamount to legally defining the circumstances that entail the law's negation of itself.[69]

Carl Schmitt was a twentieth century descendent of Thomas Hobbes, articulating a dark and illiberal conception of state power. Responding to this illiberal dynamic, other thinkers characterized the securitization of politics as a dangerous development. If unchecked, securitization would lead to increasingly authoritarian government, even if superficial democratic trappings remained.[70] Morgenthau identified the emergence of illiberal institutions in the US government, as control shifted toward the exigencies of "security." This change, Morgenthau wrote, "has occurred in all modern totalitarian states and has given rise to a phenomenon which has been aptly called the *dual state*."[71] In such a state, authority is ostensibly held by those legally empowered officeholders. In reality, Morgenthau posits that a Schmittian dynamic is in effect: "[B]y virtue of their power over life and death, the agents of the secret police—coordinated to, but independent from the official makers of decision—at the very least exert an effective veto over decisions."[72]

Ola Tunander describes a dual state with a deeper schism between the lawfully operating "democratic state" and the more autocratic "security state" whose sovereignty becomes apparent in a state of emergency.[73] Beyond the mere capacity to veto the democratic state, the security state operates to effect the "fine-tuning of democracy."[74] Such interventions are accomplished through logics that are outside liberal renderings of politics, termed *parapolitics*. As discussed previously, *parapolitics* is "a system or practice of politics in which accountability is consciously diminished."[75] For Tunander, liberalism's refusal to interrogate the duality of the state represents a serious theoretical deficiency. The problem is not that liberalism values freedoms, rights, and the rule of law; the problem is that liberalism insists that freedoms, rights, and the rule of law define Western political systems.[76] According to Tunander, this myopia has made liberal political science into "an ideology of the 'sovereign,' because indisputable evidence for the existence of the 'sovereign' [. . .] is brushed away as pure fantasy or 'conspiracy.'"[77] Carl Schmitt is typically viewed as an apologist or, worse, a philosophical midwife for the infamous exceptional state that emerged from the Weimar Republic. Tunander depicts him as something different—a theorist examining the submerged, authoritarian security state that functions in tandem with the public state.[78]

Throughout the history of liberalism, there has been a contradiction between the liberal ideal of public sovereignty under the rule of law and the dictates of "security." In fact, this tension extends further back in Western civilization as can be seen with Plato, who could never neatly reconcile the rule of law versus the rule of "the wise." This contradiction is analogous to Athenian politics. Domestically, there was some form of rule by persuasion and consent. In foreign affairs, coercion and top-down *dark power* prevailed. By the twentieth century, state behavior had in theory been legally circumscribed. But in practice, *raison d'etat* could justify exempting the state from legal restraint. Schmitt's theory of the sovereign was meant to apply to a state facing an existential crisis. Such a crisis could serve to legitimize the exceptionalist state—the state unbound by legal restraints. Schmitt could be described as an illiberal philosopher since he attempted to spell out the circumstances under which the state negates its own laws and constitutional rights. He thus argued that the state had the right—or even the obligation—to negate the very institutions that define liberalism. In Schmitt's Germany, the decidedly illiberal Nazi state emerged from circumstances and actions described and prescribed by Schmitt himself.

US *exceptionism* emerged at the high point of American liberalism. No nation in world history was as wealthy and powerful relative to the rest of the world as was the US at the end of World War II. And yet, the liberal ideal of public sovereignty proved illusory. If sovereignty rests with the party that decides both "the exception" and the "normal" situation, sovereignty shifted gradually from the public to the deep state via the deep state's dominance over the security and public states. Charles Tilly found that it was states' relations with other states which forced the evolution of pre-modern polities into modern nation-states.[79] Similarly, in the postwar era, the full US commitment to global hegemony inexorably transformed the character of the American state. The US evolved from being a constitutional democracy heavily influenced by deep political forces, into the exceptionist, behemoth, tripartite state.

Prior to the late nineteenth century, the US—like ancient Athens—was domestically governed largely through various means of persuasion, compromise, and consent among parties deemed worthy. When it came to expansion and dealing with political "others," coercive top-down power prevailed. Beginning most decisively with the closing of the frontier at the end of the nineteenth century, US elites began creating an overseas empire in earnest. Institutions were created which grew in tandem with US power—such that by the dawn of World War II, the US was poised to assume the mantle of global capitalist hegemon. The general character and institutional framework of the postwar world order was crafted by deep political forces, through a planning process that began prior to America's entry into the war. These processes led inexorably to the transformation of the American state and to the de facto abrogation of the rule of law—*exceptionism*, legitimized by myths of American exceptionalism.

CHAPTER 6

AN IMPERIAL COLOSSUS
IS BORN

Planning for an "American Century"

Less than two weeks after Germany invaded Poland and two years before Pearl Harbor, the Wall Street–dominated Council on Foreign Relations (CFR) began formulating a remarkably ambitious strategic plan for the war. But this was much more than just war planning. The planners mapped out schemes for US entry into the war, for US victory, and for the creation of a postwar world order to be dominated by the US. The CFR planning was called the War and Peace Studies Project. It was financed by the Rockefeller Foundation and carried out under the nominal auspices of the State Department. The project called for the US to act as the hegemon of a vast capitalist imperium, ensuring the predominance of the US and its junior partners over global resources and markets.[1]

To manufacture public consent for these grandiose plans, the CFR relied on council member and media tycoon, Henry Luce. His essay, "The American Century," laid out the case for the CFR's vision—without attributing it to the organization or its plutocratic backers, naturally. Most of Luce's argument was presented in banal and altruistic terms, the odd, excessively candid passage notwithstanding:

Our thinking of world trade today is on ridiculously small terms. For example, we think of Asia as being worth only a few hundred millions a year to us. Actually, in the decades to come Asia will be worth to us exactly zero—or else it will be worth to us four, five, ten billions of dollars a year. And the latter are the terms we must think in, or else confess a pitiful impotence.[2]

The CFR/Luce vision for American empire was met with some resistance. Most famously, it was opposed by Roosevelt's vice president Henry Wallace. The vice president's "Century of the Common Man" speech was a direct rebuttal to Luce. The showdown between Luce and Wallace represents a seminal conflict between progressive, democratic elements and the forces which would become the postwar exceptionist American deep state. With the benefit of hindsight, the victory of the Luce faction seems overdetermined. The defeat of Wallace's vision was made manifest by a conspiracy of political elites none as "Pauley's coup." Against the wishes of an ailing FDR, the powerful plotters removed Wallace from the 1944 Democratic ticket, replacing him with the much more pliable Harry S. Truman. It has been argued that "The attainment of the nuclear weapon was almost certainly the deep state's moment of conception."[3] Though any metaphor is imperfect, it may be more accurate to describe the atomic bombings as the deep state's birth—well after it was conceived by the War and Peace Studies Project. As the second most popular US politician, behind FDR, the progressive Wallace was a staunch anti-fascist and anti-imperialist. As such, he stood in the way of the US corporate elite and the imperial designs—hence his removal in what was effectively an anti-democratic coup.

At the end of World War II, the US was the only undamaged great power. It had a monopoly on nuclear weapons and by far the greatest industrial capacity and largest gold reserves. No country in world history has ever been as secure and unassailable as the US at that historical moment. By contrast, the Soviet Union had lost 26,600,000 people and suffered the destruction of many of its largest cities. Nevertheless, the US did nothing to compensate its former ally for bearing most of the burden when it came to defeating Nazi Germany. Instead, the US quickly settled upon the Soviet Union as a new existential foe. Those who advocated coexistence and peaceful competition with the Soviets—like Henry Wallace—were pilloried by conservatives and the emerging Cold War liberals who were considerably more bellicose than FDR and other prominent New Dealers.

To prosecute World War II, the US had created a large military bureaucracy. This was done with considerable influence from the corporate overworld, and it would eventually give rise to the globe-dominating postwar US deep state. These national security state institutions were conceived and midwifed with considerable and decisive input from the overworld of private wealth. Such was the case in a number of fateful instances in which top-down power was brought to bear in the making of history during this period—namely the War and Peace Studies Project, "Pauley's coup," the dropping of the atomic bombs, and the National Security Act of 1947.

The original structure of the US national security state was established when President Truman signed the National Security Act of 1947. Specifically, the act created the Joint Chiefs of Staff, the National Security Council, and the Central Intelligence Agency. Perhaps most notably, the CIA was willed into being through the efforts and influence of the upper strata of corporate America. The agency was conceived through the efforts of a number of Wall Street lawyers. Notably, it was a Wall Street lawyer who penned the "elastic clause" in the National Security Act. Shortly thereafter, the passage came to be interpreted as giving the CIA authority to carry out all manner of illegal covert operations—or "other duties" in the Act's oblique language.

Very early on, CIA elements began establishing illicit self-funding operations that utilized the drug trade. Specifically, the CIA's Office of Policy Coordination (OPC) collaborated with opium-trafficking Kuomintang (KMT) officers in Burma and Thailand, ostensibly so the proceeds could fund the KMT's hopelessly doomed effort to retake mainland China.[4] A transnational commercial intelligence firm known as the World Commerce Corporation (WCC) was involved in laying the groundwork for these efforts. The WCC was staffed by former British and US intelligence officers, including the former head of the wartime Office of Strategic Services, Wall Street lawyer William Donovan. WCC's financial backing came from overworld figures like Nelson Rockefeller, John McCloy, and Richard Mellon.[5] Paul Helliwell, a CIA man and OSS veteran with close connections to Meyer Lansky, was also a key WCC figure. The whole episode illustrates the deep state nexus between the overworld of private wealth, the underworld of organized crime, and the governmental or private intelligence outfits that mediate between them. State secrecy, a globe-sprawling national security state, and the operant perception that the US faced an existential threat in communism—all these elements conspired to transform the character of the American state, contributing to the rise of the *exceptionist* deep state.

NSC-68 and the Rise of the Military Industrial Complex

Around the time that a clandestine overworld/underworld milieu was impacting history through parapolitical means in Southeast Asia after the war, other events in America's *higher circles* would also influence the trajectory of the emerging American deep state. The US experienced economic downturns in the years following World War II, partly as a result of declining military spending. Additionally, there was the issue of Western Europe and the "dollar gap," i.e., the looming inability of Western Europe to continue purchasing US exports after Marshall Plan funding was to cease in the early 1950s.[6] The fundamental issues facing US policymakers at this time were not unforeseen by American elites. Wall Street's Council on Foreign Relations had been involved in the formulation of US pre-war, wartime, and postwar planning. This was done on the basis of what the CFR deemed to be the *national interest*—basically, "a capitalist system with private ownership of the productive property of society, resulting in inequality in the distribution of wealth and income and attendant class structure."[7] To create a world order in the US national interest, the CFR maintained that after the war, the US would need unrestricted access to Asian raw materials and markets—as well as to Western European markets. This was deemed essential because two-thirds of US foreign trade was outside of the Western Hemisphere. Alternatively, the need for these export markets could be negated by public ownership of essential productive sectors of the economy combined with democratically organized planning to ensure employment and healthy consumption. Any such course would be a nonstarter for the CFR since, as Shoup and Minter point out, every ruling set of elites "define[s] the national interest as the preservation of the existing set of economic, social, and political relationships and of their own rule, the national interest in a capitalist society is little more than the interest of its upper class."[8]

The key tactics and grand strategy of the American overworld would eventually be formulated in a 1950 National Security Council study known as NSC-68. The document was written largely by Paul Nitze at according to the specifications of his boss, Secretary of State Dean Acheson. Arguably the ur-neoconservative, Nitze was also a protégé of the first defense secretary, James Forrestal. NSC-68 depicted the Soviets in apocalyptic terms, calling for all manner of exceptionalist anti-Soviet measures and for a massive US rearmament campaign. The conventional view of NSC-68 is that it was an alarmist strategic paper that resulted from the twin traumas of 1949—the communist victory in China and the Soviet acquisition of the atom bomb. Further, the orthodox narrative maintains that it was the Korean War which serendipitously intervened to make America's rearmament possible. When examined critically, those events seem to have been pretexts of convenience, collectively serving as a cover story to achieve the express desired ends of the US Establishment.

In late 1949, Paul Nitze himself argued that "Nothing about the Soviets' moves indicates that Moscow is preparing to launch in the near future an all-out military attack on the West."[9] For the American power elite, the real concern was the specter of a neutral Europe. This fear is articulated in NSC-68, a document that remains a classic in the genre of American *crackpot realism*: "The idea that Germany or Japan or other important areas can exist as islands of neutrality in a divided world is unreal, given the Kremlin design for world domination." In general. the global communist meta-conspiracy theory is absurd given the historical realities at the time. In World War II, the Soviets lost 26.6 million people to America's roughly 400,000 dead. Large swaths of Soviet territory had been destroyed by the Nazi invaders. As a finale, the US ended the war with a gratuitous atomic massacre carried out largely to intimidate the Soviet Union. After the Soviets acquired the bomb, George Kennan himself said that "the damage we should be able to do in the Soviet Union is not affected by whether the Russians have the bombs themselves or not. Pointing out the obvious, Kennan added that "Russia has only recently been through a tremendously destructive war; that the Soviet economy has far less that it can afford to lose than we have; and that the Soviet leaders will not inaugurate a type of warfare bound to lead to great destruction within their country."[10]

In reality, it was not Soviet communists, but US elites who had directed all planning to achieve dominance over as much of the globe as possible. It was American planners who had decided that the US would need unfettered access to markets and raw materials in the non-communist world. In other words, to the extent that the US could engineer it, non-communist countries must not allow the Soviet bloc access to markets and raw materials. Although NSC-68 largely contrived the Soviet bogeyman for its sponsors' political purposes, one "threat" was indeed real in 1950: the possibility of a neutral Europe. In the years leading up to NSC-68, the Soviets tried to promote Western European neutrality by encouraging Soviet-Western European diplomatic relations to the extent possible.[11] NSC-68 refers to this possibility in dire terms: "If [neutrality] were to happen in Germany the effect upon Western Europe and eventually upon us might be catastrophic."[12]

Besides the geopolitical motivations behind the campaign to ratchet up the Cold War and drastically boost military spending, there were domestic political considerations as well. For one thing, the US aerospace industry was in dire straits in the years following World War II.[13] American imperialists understood that US plans for global hegemony required primacy in the aerospace industry. But US aerospace predominance was going to be difficult to achieve without massive and profitable firms. The US could have embarked upon the creation of a national R&D division that employed the services of the best engineers and gave them access to government funding and facilities. But this was anathema to the corporate American overworld. Following the exposure of massive World War I profiteering, there were calls throughout the country and in Congress to nationalize the arms industry. But as with most substantial progressive reforms, this effort was crushed in top-down fashion by corporate American forces. For all the right's rhetoric about government *inefficiency*, it seems that what the corporate overworld truly fears is *efficiency* in the public sector. If this wasn't clear in the twentieth century, it should be obvious in the present day as corporate actors have relentlessly sought to privatize everything from social security, utilities, the postal service, and even public education. Leading corporate oligarch Jeff Bezos went so far as to create his own delivery service at great expense to avoid utilizing the services of the US Postal Service. So for the mid-twentieth century corporate American hive-mind, a nationalized aerospace industry would have been a horrifying prospect. It is no coincidence that one of the men typically cited as being among the earliest neoconservatives was the Washington state's US Senator (D), Henry "Scoop" Jackson—a man sometimes mocked as being "the Senator from Boeing."

The aerospace industry had been a major beneficiary of the US war effort. Of the $3.7 billion invested in the industry's expansion between 1940 and 1944, 92 percent came from federal government spending.[14] The wartime profits were spectacular. Between 1941 to 1945, Boeing alone was earning around $12 million a year after taxes.[15] With the government funding most of the investment, it is estimated that private investment in Boeing was $15.9 million between 1941 and 1945. Therefore, Boeing's $60 million of after-tax profits in those years represent a sum "*at a minimum 3.77 times larger* than the [estimated private investment] figure of $15.9 million."[16] In other words, Boeing's profits represented a 377 percent return on investments over that period.

With the war over, aerospace profits tanked. The firms' military and commercial business declined drastically. Business strategies to reverse the firms' fortunes all failed. This left political action as the last hope for these companies. The tremendous weakness of the industry paradoxically gave its leaders an advantage when it came to persuading the ruling US corporate elite to back the campaign for vast military contracts. Leading US magazines printed articles with assessments of the industry's predicament and prospects. Such would include items like: "[The] invalid aircraft manufacturing industry [. . .] has probably received more sympathetic attention in Washington during 1947 than any other single business group," and "[T]he present state of the aircraft industry represents as grave an industrio-economic problem as exists in the US today."[17] Part of the corporate overworld's concern for aerospace stemmed from its connections to other key sectors like the steel industry as well as major firms like General Motors, General Electric, and Westinghouse—all companies that profited from large aerospace procurement contracts.[18] Perhaps most decisive was the fact that the Rockefeller family had enormous holdings in the industry. The largest investment bank in the world at the time—Chase National Bank—was acquired by John D. Rockefeller Jr. in 1930. So large was Chase's stake in aerospace that the industry's troubles posed a serious threat to the bank. During World War II and after, Chase was by far the top single creditor to the aerospace firms.[19]

Enter Winthrop W. Aldrich, chairman of Chase and brother-in-law to John D. Rockefeller Jr. Aldrich was also a friend of Defense Secretary James Forrestal, a man who had previously been the president of Wall Street's venerable Dillon, Read and Company. Previously, Aldrich's connections had led his being appointed to chair the President's Committee for Financing Foreign Trade. In this context, it is important to note that in 1948, the US Secretary of the Air Force sent a letter to Aldrich asking for help: "the problem is how to get the money to get what we want, and any advice you could give us to that end would be very much appreciated." For the air force "to get the money to get what [they wanted]" would also mean pulling the aerospace industry and its powerful creditors out of danger.[20]

The story behind the deceptive campaign to make all these things happen is too long to go into here, but it is best told in history professor Frank Kofsky's book, *Harry S. Truman and the War Scare of 1948: A Successful Campaign to Deceive the Nation.* To summarize, President Harry Truman, Secretary of Defense James Forrestal, and Secretary of State George Marshall collaborated in 1948 to contrive a war scare that would save the aerospace industry. In opportunistically misinterpreting events in Czechoslovakia, Finland, and Berlin, the three men "employed deceit and duplicity to convey the deliberately misleading impression that the USSR was poised to invade Western Europe at a moment's notice."[21] The scare tactics worked and the federal government did intervene to reverse the industry's fortunes. However, this would only be a stopgap measure—a prequel to the events of 1949 which were followed by the drafting of NSC-68 in 1950.

Another key piece of historical context related to US rearmament was the growing strength of organized labor. There were massive worker uprisings in the US after World War II. The anti-New Deal Taft-Hartley Act was passed in 1947 in response to labor militancy and couched with anti-communist pretenses. For example, under the law, union officers were required to sign anti-communist affidavits for the federal government. Orthodox historiography seems to encourage a posture of studied naivety about America's rich elites and their domination of the state. Obviously, the pronouncements of policymakers are not typically framed in terms of profit or of commercial interests' dominance over the US and the world. For mainstream journalists, historians, and social scientists, it is considered gauche to attribute elite actions to elite class interests. In other words, it is bad form to assume that the motives behind elite schemes and strategies derive from unstated, class-conscious imperatives such as (1) accruing ever more wealth and power and (2) maintaining their hegemony over society. If one is too unflinching in attributing the actions of wealthy and powerful people to a desire to aggrandize their wealth and power, one is a materialist—i.e., a Marxist—and thus beyond the pale. New Left historian Bruce Cumings is in part seemingly alluding to this when he writes about historical "imponderables," a reference to the opaque motives and decision-making processes at the top of the American power structure.[22]

At this juncture, it is time to ponder some imponderables. As C. Wright Mills pointed out in *The Power Elite*, by the mid-1950s it was clear that the *privately incorporated permanent war economy* (PIPWE, to coin an awkward acronym) had been institutionalized. For the American power elite, the PIPWE was their politico-economic cure-all. PIPWE saved US aerospace and its financiers, it ended the postwar economic slump, it served to stave off the impending "threat" of Western European neutrality, and it weakened labor by elevating anti-communism to the status of state religion. In so doing, it gave rise to the *military industrial complex* (MIC), a term coined by Eisenhower's speechwriter, a political scientist who was certainly drawing from the work of C. Wright Mills. In lieu of any sort of benevolent reforms that would first and foremost create material security and prosperity for the American people, military spending became the *alpha* and *omega* of US economic planning. The more straightforward and proximate reasons for this are outlined above, but deeper motives may also help explain this historic disaster. In 1987, old school Cold Warrior George Kennan wrote, "Were the Soviet Union to sink tomorrow under the waters of the ocean, the American military-industrial complex would have to remain, substantially unchanged, until some other adversary could be invented. Anything else would be an unacceptable shock to the American economy."[23] This is an exemplary formulation of Establishment *crackpot realism* from one of its most storied apostles. But that does not explain why the economically crucial massive government expenditure must necessarily be for the military rather than for human needs. To answer this deeper question, we must turn to literature.

In George Orwell's *1984*, there's a strange passage that provides some insight. The text is supposed to be part of a terrorist group's manifesto, but it is never clear whether or not the terrorist group is or is not some kind of stage-managed false flag operation of the state. Orwell is presenting some grim material in an obscure way. It is reminiscent of Plato's use of dialog between Socrates and Thrasymachus in *The Republic* to make Plato's own views ambiguous. Orwell writes,

> The primary aim of modern warfare (simultaneously recognized and not recognized by the directing brains of the Inner Party) is to use up the products of the machine without raising the general standard of living. Ever since the end of the nineteenth century, the problem of what to do with the surplus of consumption goods has been latent in industrial society. At present, when few human beings even have enough to eat, this problem is obviously not urgent, and it might not have become so, even if no artificial processes of destruction had been at work. The world of today is a bare, hungry, dilapidated place compared with the world that existed before 1914, and still more so if compared with the imaginary future to which the people of that period looked forward. In the early twentieth century, the vision of a future society unbelievably rich, leisured, orderly, and efficient—a glittering antiseptic world of glass and steel and snow-white concrete—was part of the consciousness of nearly every literate person.

Science and technology were developing at a prodigious speed, and it seemed natural to assume that they would go on developing.[24]

The economist Michael Hudson often writes and speaks about these issues. The aim of classical economists was to reform economies in such a way as to move toward a "free market." This is not the mythical "free market" extolled by plutocrat-sponsored right-wing economists. Rather, the free market was a market free of *economic rent* that would otherwise go to a wealthy rentier class. Defined as the sum left over when cost is subtracted from price, *economic rent* refers to "income that has no counterpart in necessary costs of production."[25] It is the "free lunch" that allows the surplus of the economy to accrue to a privileged rentier class that passively gains wealth through by way of the economy's organization. The classical economists sought to reduce and eliminate the "free lunch" and thereby bring prices more closely in line with costs. This would unleash economic productivity by eliminating the parasitism of the rentier class. At the dawn of the twentieth century, the application of classical economics combined with advances in technology led people to believe that a golden age of human progress and prosperity was approaching. But the reactionary rentier class used its rentier fortunes to launch an economic "Counter-Enlightenment." As Michael Hudson summarizes,

> To deter public regulation or higher taxation of such rent seeking, recipients of free lunches have embraced Milton Friedman's claim that There Is No Such Thing As A Free Lunch. [. . .] The actual antidote to free lunches is to make governments strong enough to tax economic rent and keep potential rent-extracting opportunities and natural monopolies in the public domain.[26]

The point here, articulated by Orwell, is that technological progress in production and in economic planning should have ushered in a golden age of civilization. Instead, activist elites recognized the implications of this dynamic and responded by using their wealth and power to maintain the inequality and material insecurity that are preconditions for their continued dominance over society.

Orwell continues in this vein:

> This [bright future] failed to happen. [. . .] Nevertheless the dangers
> inherent in the machine are still there. From the moment when
> the machine first made its appearance it was clear to all thinking
> people that the need for human drudgery, and therefore to a great
> extent for human inequality, had disappeared. If the machine were
> used deliberately for that end, hunger, overwork, dirt, illiteracy, and
> disease could be eliminated within a few generations. And in fact,
> without being used for any such purpose, but by a sort of automatic
> process—by producing wealth which it was sometimes impossible
> not to distribute—the machine did raise the living standards of the
> average human being very greatly over a period of about fifty years
> at the end of the nineteenth and the beginning of the twentieth
> centuries.

The paradox of deprivation alongside latent or even excessive productive
capacity speaks to the power of the extant regime. For example, we rarely
hear it publicly stated that our civilization does not even consider solving
easily solvable socioeconomic problems—problems that could have been
solved with technology that existed by the mid-twentieth century. Instead,
we are conditioned to be resigned to dystopian facts like the existence of
a large homeless population alongside an even larger number of vacant
homes.

But why wouldn't elites want to preside over a golden age of human
civilization? It is counterintuitive, to be sure. Orwell grapples with the
deep politics of industrialized civilization:

> [I]t was also clear that an all-round increase in wealth threatened
> the destruction—indeed, in some sense was the destruction—of
> a hierarchical society. In a world in which everyone worked short
> hours, had enough to eat, lived in a house with a bathroom and a
> refrigerator, and possessed a motor-car or even an aeroplane, the
> most obvious and perhaps the most important form of inequality
> would already have disappeared. If it once became general, wealth

would confer no distinction. It was possible, no doubt, to imagine a society in which wealth, in the sense of personal possessions and luxuries, should be evenly distributed, while power remained in the hands of a small privileged caste. But in practice such a society could not long remain stable. For if leisure and security were enjoyed by all alike, the great mass of human beings who are normally stupefied by poverty would become literate and would learn to think for themselves; and when once they had done this, they would sooner or later realize that the privileged minority had no function, and they would sweep it away. In the long run, a hierarchical society was only possible on a basis of poverty and ignorance.[27]

This gets closer to the heart of the matter. Economic insecurity and deprivation are key components of a hierarchical society. If they are eliminated, and if literacy and education are widespread, the elites have to deal with a population that is not as easily mesmerized by power and not compelled by necessity to submit to subjugation and exploitation in exchange for material security. Thus, an independent (i.e., non-imperialized) society with no underclass would likely have the wherewithal to topple the hegemony of its rentier class. It is not difficult for elites to grasp this by extrapolating. And elites in every classical, feudal, and capitalist civilization have essentially the same job description: They work to reproduce their own hegemony over society. Their class interests, elite education, and vast wealth allow them to organize and overcome the collective action problems that overwhelm non-elites.

Orwell continues:

[It was not] a satisfactory solution to keep the masses in poverty by restricting the output of goods. This happened to a great extent during the final phase of capitalism, roughly between 1920 and 1940. The economy of many countries was allowed to stagnate, land went out of cultivation, capital equipment was not added to, great blocks of the population were prevented from working and kept half alive by State charity. But this, too, entailed military weakness, and since the privations it inflicted were obviously unnecessary, it made opposition inevitable. The problem was how to keep the wheels of industry turning without increasing the real wealth of the world. Goods must be produced, but they must not be distributed. And in practice the only way of achieving this was by continuous warfare.[28]

Now Orwell is getting into the deep inner logic that informs the *privately incorporated permanent war economy*. By "real wealth," he is referring to economic institutions that provide for human life. How can the economy keep generating profits without eliminating the economic insecurity that is a prerequisite for the exploitative system over which the rentier class presides?

> The essential act of war is destruction, not necessarily of human lives, but of the products of human labour. War is a way of shattering to pieces, or pouring into the stratosphere, or sinking in the depths of the sea, materials which might otherwise be used to make the masses too comfortable, and hence, in the long run, too intelligent. Even when weapons of war are not actually destroyed, their manufacture is still a convenient way of expending labour power without producing anything that can be consumed. [. . .] In principle the war effort is always so planned as to eat up any surplus that might exist after meeting the bare needs of the population. In practice the needs of the population are always underestimated, with the result that there is a chronic shortage of half the necessities of life; but this is looked on as an advantage. It is deliberate policy to keep even the favoured groups somewhere near the brink of hardship, because a general state of scarcity increases the importance of small privileges and thus magnifies the distinction between one group and another.[29]

Obviously, Orwell's dystopia is not a perfect analogy for mid-twentieth-century America. Though it is ever shrinking, the American middle and upper-middle classes have enjoyed high living standards by many measures. But material insecurity is always looming with medical bankruptcies and homelessness and other horrors as real possibilities. With the default of the Western intellectuals, it falls to artists like the comedian George Carlin to plainly articulate matters: "The poor are there just to scare the shit out of the middle class . . . keep on showing up at those jobs."[30]

Still, the war mentality is essential, as Orwell understood:

> [T]he consciousness of being at war, and therefore in danger, makes the handing-over of all power to a small caste seem the natural, unavoidable condition of survival. War . . . accomplishes the necessary destruction . . . in a psychologically acceptable way. [. . .] What is concerned here is not the morale of masses, whose attitude is unimportant so long as they are kept steadily at work, but the morale of the Party itself. Even the humblest Party member is expected to be competent, industrious, and even intelligent within narrow limits, but it is also necessary that he should be a credulous and ignorant fanatic whose prevailing moods are fear, hatred, adulation, and orgiastic triumph. In other words it is necessary that he should have the mentality appropriate to a state of war.[31]

With the US power elite in mind, note the description of the party functionary: "a credulous and ignorant fanatic whose prevailing moods are fear, hatred, adulation, and orgiastic triumph." This cast of mind was observed in mid-twentieth century America by shrewd thinkers like C. Wright Mills. The prevailing *crackpot realism* was sometimes given explicit expression by its high priests like John Foster Dulles. In one ubiquitously quoted passage, Dulles wrote, "In order to bring a nation to support the burdens of maintaining great military establishments, it is necessary to create an emotional state akin to war psychology. There must be the portrayal of an external menace. This involves the development to a high degree of the nation-hero, nation-villain ideology and the arousing of the population to a sense of sacrifice." This was exactly the logic that was employed in the war scare hoax of 1948 and further articulated by NSC-68 in 1950.

In reality, NSC-68 was simply a grand strategic policy proposal. It took intervention from the corporate overworld to institutionalize the military industrial complex or—in a larger sense—to establish the privately incorporated permanent war economy. While Orwell's grim dystopian musings are relevant and illuminating, there are aspects of the US experience that did not conform to his depiction of the garrison state endlessly at war. To overcome the public resistance to massive remilitarization, deep state actors created a propaganda organization to promote the correct mindset in politicians and the public. Called the Committee on the Present Danger (CPD), it was formed shortly after NSC-68 was produced. Several of CPD's founding members were Establishment figures who had been involved in the drafting of NSC-68, including James Conant, Vannevar Bush, and Tracy Voorhees. The CPD lasted only a few years, disbanding in 1953 after having accomplished its mission of putting the US on a permanent war footing.[32]

For the corporate overworld, the utility of the Cold War was manifold. The military generated massive profits. Anticommunism served as a pretext for covert operations to ensure that decolonization became neocolonialism. Domestically, Anticommunism allowed for organized labor and the political left more broadly to be largely neutralized. And yet, the privately incorporated permanent war economy did not spell meager subsistence for the American people, by and large. Labor unions were relegated to the middle levels of power, with real decision-making taking place in the higher circles. Still, there was a large and growing middle class, due in part to the business of military production. In the 1950s, it was part of US propaganda to contrast high US living standards with life in the Soviet Union, as evidenced by the "kitchen debates" between Nikita Khrushchev and Richard Nixon. While the immediate postwar years were characterized in part by economic slump, the 1950s were widely, if unevenly, prosperous owing in part to the war machine.

The military Keynesian foundations for the prosperous 1950s were laid by the administration of Harry S. Truman. But whatever might be said about Truman's New Deal sympathies, the facts remain that his administration massacred over one hundred thousand with atomic bombs at Hiroshima and Nagasaki, set off an arms race with the potential to end human civilization, started the Cold War, created the CIA, and brought the military industrial complex into existence. This is not to place too much emphasis on the man himself. Rather, it speaks to the nature of

American society that prevailing forces would tragically select such a man for a such a position at such a point in history.

Eisenhower and the Growing Deep State

The American deep state was nurtured by the Truman administration. Key events under Truman were the product of elite machinations, including his ascension to the vice presidency and the creation of the CIA within the National Security Act of 1947. Networks of elites representing or controlling overworld interests comprise a crucial component, perhaps *the* crucial component, of the deep state. The conflicts between the deep state and the democratic state preceded the creation of the national security state and figured heavily in momentous events in the postwar US. President Truman claimed that he never intended for the CIA to be involved in covert operations. In the aftermath of the Kennedy assassination, Truman wrote that he "would like to see the CIA be restored to its original assignment as the intelligence arm of the President [. . .] and that its operational duties be terminated or properly used elsewhere."[33] The agency assumed operational powers only through the obscure legalese of Wall Street lawyer Clark Clifford who penned the sections of the National Security Act which created the agency in 1947.[34]

Even in the early postwar years, the cleavages in the tripartite state were emerging. The Truman administration and the oil cartels provide an important case. In 1952, the Justice Department of the Truman administration sought to end the cartel agreements and prosecute key figures in the oil industry under anti-trust laws. At the time, the global oil market was controlled by the "Seven Sisters" oil cartel, comprised of five US companies, a British company, and a Dutch company. When a US government order demanded that Exxon (Standard Oil of New Jersey) hand over relevant documents, the company's lawyer—Arthur Dean of Sullivan and Cromwell—refused to comply. To justify this defiance, Dean asserted his prerogative on grounds of "national security." The documents, he argued, were "the kind of information the Kremlin would love to get its hand on."[35]

Around the same time that this anti-trust investigation was going on, the US members of the Seven Sisters were collaborating with the British

"Sister," the Anglo-Iranian Oil Company (AIOC)—later to become British Petroleum. Their efforts were aimed at preventing the nationalization of Iranian oil.[36] Mohamed Mossadegh, the country's Prime Minister, had been elected on the basis of one issue: the nationalization of Iran's oil, theretofore controlled by the British.[37] The Seven Sisters undermined Iran by instituting a boycott of Iranian oil exports. While only one of the Seven Sisters—the AOIC—was directly affected by the nationalization of Iranian oil, they all had every incentive to oppose any example that would encourage resource nationalism. To that end, the Seven Sisters controlled 99 percent of the crude oil tankers in operation at the time. Additionally, the oil cartel dominated all the markets in which the oil could conceivably be exported. And yet, despite the tremendous power wielded by Seven Sisters, and despite a plea from Winston Churchill himself, Truman could not be convinced to authorize the CIA to overthrow the democratically elected Iranian government. However, despite Truman's refusal to authorize the policy, officials within the CIA began to plan operations in late 1952 that would involve assisting the MI6/oil cartel campaign to oust Mossadegh.[38]

The election of Eisenhower proved decisive in resolving the oil cartel's conflicts in both the US and Iran. Eisenhower had received substantial prior support from the oil industry. Upon his election, he appointed Sullivan and Cromwell partner John Foster Dulles as Secretary of State and his brother Allen Dulles as Director of Central Intelligence. The Truman Justice Department's criminal complaint against the cartel was dropped and replaced by a civil complaint. The responsibility for prosecution was transferred to Dulles' Department of State which theretofore had never prosecuted an antitrust case. On July 22, 1953 the CIA's Operation AJAX was approved by President Eisenhower.[39] The operation successfully overthrew Mossadegh and installed the Shah as a US-client dictator. For years, some accounts described the coup as being a product of Iranian domestic politics.[40] The common view today, even acknowledged by the *New York Times*, is that it was a CIA operation.[41] However, Scott's chronology suggests that it was an oil cartel operation that the CIA joined later.[42] By this rendering, the deep state began a foreign intervention—a campaign that security state elements (the CIA) tentatively joined even before receiving formal authorization from the supposedly sovereign democratic state.

With Eisenhower installed, Mossadegh uninstalled, and the Seven Sisters anti-trust investigation in the hands of Sullivan Cromwell alum John Foster Dulles, the oil cartel emerged as an even stronger pillar of the US deep state. With the Truman administration's vestigial New Deal elements removed from power, big oil could fully capitalize on its vast influence on Wall Street, in the CIA, and in the public state via Eisenhower official like Secretary of State Dulles. The deep state overcame restraints posed by democratic states—American and Iranian, respectively. In the US, this was accomplished by backing a presidential candidate who would support Wall Street interests more or less unequivocally. Such hopes were confirmed with Eisenhower's appointment of the Dulles brothers to key positions, both brothers being lawyers from Sullivan and Cromwell. The nascent Iranian democratic state was overcome by the US deep state thanks to the power of the oil cartel in conjunction with the Anglo-American clandestine services. The Mossadegh government was performing in a way that would be expected of a democratic state. It is unsurprising that the Iranian people preferred leaders who would support the national interest of Iran. The country's previously existing oil arrangement under the AIOC favored a tiny Iranian elite. It fostered and exacerbated tremendous socioeconomic inequality in the country. Iranian democracy was dealt a death blow by AJAX. The consequences have been catastrophic for Iranian society up to the present day.

Obviously, the democratic state did not retain sovereignty over Iran. Although less dramatic, the declining sovereignty of the US democratic state is also illustrated in this episode. It is noteworthy, and hard to imagine today, that the US government would have sought to prosecute oil majors for conspiratorial, criminal business practices. But the fecklessness of US democracy came to the fore. The assertion of national security privilege by an oil company lawyer form Sullivan Cromwell was profoundly anti-democratic on its face. The Seven Sisters' actions preceding the 1953 coup in Iran were tantamount to neocolonial corporate fascism. Operation AJAX was a flagrant violation of the UN Charter—and thus of the Supremacy Clause of the US Constitution. The episode marks a clear decline in American democracy—a set of traditions and institutions which had peaked during the New Deal. This decline was in considerable part due to unprecedented US power and the accompanying securitization of politics which accompanied it—all of which served to further empower the power elite of the American overworld. The formal organs of the security state are certainly an important aspect of this story. But the forces and institutions that prevailed were intertwined with—and above—the public state and the security state. All of this serves as argument for a tripartite conception of the state. Even in comparison to dual state theory, the tripartite state construct provides a way for social scientists to address elements of the political order which are typically suppressed or not given theoretical expression.

The case of Iran and the oil majors in the early 1950s is but one case in which the US deep state conflicted with the democratic state. As Eisenhower left office, he delivered a farewell address warning about the military-industrial-complex that had grown to gargantuan proportions during his administration. This was in essence a warning of the power of the deep state, though narrowly focused upon the nexus between the arms industry, the military, and Congress—though Congress was omitted from the final version of the speech. It is worth noting that each of the three represents a component of the tripartite state, while the nexus between them collectively represents a further concentration of deep state power. The military industrial complex nexus serves to make the democratic state less democratic. But it does not democratize the military, nor the deep state collectively, nor the armaments industry in particular.

Spanning the Truman and Eisenhower administrations, McCarthyism and the HUAC hearings of the early Cold War represented further consolidation of deep state power. In so doing, this second Red Scare infamously relied upon very questionable personages and constitutionally dubious methods. Multiple purposes were served. The radical left was neutralized, fanatical anti-communist elements were empowered, and formerly effectual progressive democratic voices within the elite were dispatched. In particular, the prosecution of Harry Dexter White seems to have been part of a power struggle to destroy New Deal forces. White and other like-minded figures were open to finding a modus vivendi with the Soviet

Union. Furthermore, they sought to hold accountable certain conservative, Nazi-collaborating persons and institutions like Thomas McKittrick and the Bank for International Settlements.[43]

To summarize, Dwight D. Eisenhower's ascendency to the presidency was another milestone in the rise of the American deep state. Backed by vast sums of corporate cash—especially oil money—the Eisenhower administration proceeded to devote US power toward furthering the CFR/Luce vision of American empire and thus to extinguish any remaining chances for a "century of the common man." This was most clearly epitomized by Eisenhower's appointment of the Dulles brothers to head the State Department and the CIA. The two brothers had previously been lawyers from Sullivan and Cromwell, the illustrious Wall Street law firm whose clients included the top US and Western multinational corporations. Thusly did the Wall Street overworld enjoy the deepest ties to the state department and to the CIA—collectively the pinnacle of US foreign policy decision making.

When a journalist asked CIA director Allen Dulles what the CIA was, the spymaster answered that the agency was "the State Department for unfriendly countries."[44] The "unfriendly" countries would include Iran, Guatemala, Egypt, Syria, and Indonesia. In these places, the CIA and its agents carried out all manner of covert operations, up to and including assassinations and the overthrowing of governments. While the full history of almost all of these episodes has remained at least partly submerged, it was during the Eisenhower administration that C. Wright Mills wrote *The Power Elite*. Even without the bulk of the historical evidence which supported his thesis, Mills was able to make the case that democratic sovereignty had become a façade and that control lay in the hands of an increasingly interchangeable elite of power situated at the top of the organizations which dominated big business, the federal government, and the military.[45] At the end of his presidency, Eisenhower delivered—in the passive voice—a warning about the military-industrial complex, an undemocratic pillar of the deep state that had at the very least metastasized during his administration. Eisenhower's speechwriter, political science professor Malcolm Moos, was surely influenced by Mills and *The Power Elite*. The term *military-industrial complex* was in essence a repurposing of Mills's *privately incorporated, permanent war economy*—though obviously Eisenhower, unlike Mills, did not anchor it in a deeper critique of the anti-democratic character of big business and the military. Whatever the old general may have been referring to near the end of his presidency, Eisenhower best summed up his administration when he said that to his successor, he leaves "a legacy of ashes."

The Kennedy Administration:
A Brief Departure from the Imperial Consensus

Upon inheriting his predecessor's "legacy of ashes," President John F. Kennedy pursued increasingly pursued policies that represented a serious threat to the American deep state.

Upon taking office, Kennedy immediately began grappling with the deep state. Even setting aside the CIA, the deep state permeated his administration. For example, twenty-six high-ranking Kennedy officials had previously been panelists on the Rockefeller Brothers Fund.[46] Apparently Kennedy's vocal support of Third World nationalism spurred deep political forces immediately into action. Following JFK's election but before his inauguration, Congolese President Patrice Lumumba was assassinated. His assassination had been approved previously by Eisenhower and the CIA under Dulles. Lumumba was eventually killed by Congolese opposition backed by the combined efforts of Belgium, Britain, the US, and multinational corporate interests.[47]

Kennedy had more sympathy for African independence leaders than did Eisenhower. He had supported Lumumba and he had supported Algerian independence as a senator when such positions were not politically expedient in the US.[48] Lumumba's assassination greatly dismayed President Kennedy. For Eisenhower and the Dulles brothers it would have represented the successful culmination of administration policy. Though Kennedy did not know it, his own US Treasury Secretary C. Douglas Dillon had contributed to the decision to eliminate Lumumba.[49] Dillon was from an extremely wealthy American overworld family. His family name was the Dillon of venerable Wall Street firm Dillon, Read & Company. Notably, two Dillon Read bankers, James Forrestal and Ferdinand Eberstadt, played pivotal roles in the campaign to create the

CIA in the first place.[50] In this context, it is worth noting that as JFK's Treasury Secretary, C. Douglas Dillon oversaw the Secret Service protection of the president which failed so spectacularly in Dallas.

Following soon after the Lumumba assassination, Kennedy presided over the Bay of Pigs fiasco. The ill-fated operation had been planned under Eisenhower. In this instance, the deep state and security state nearly brought the United States into an aggressive hot war. Kennedy had emphatically forbidden direct US involvement in the invasion. However, CIA director Allen Dulles and his deputy Richard Bissell had a plan to orchestrate a war in Cuba nonetheless. Their memos to the White House predicted that the Cuban exile invasion would spark a widespread anti-Castro uprising on the island. However, the CIA officials did not truly believe that such would be the case. Instead, they thought that once a beachhead was established by the exiles, the President would commit US forces due to the pressure of public opinion and his desire to avoid failure. As journalist Daniel Schorr describes, "Kennedy was the target of a CIA covert operation that collapsed when the invasion collapsed."[51] Schorr's assessment echoes what Truman wrote in the wake of the Kennedy assassination: "[The CIA] has become an operational and at times a policy-making arm of the Government."[52] As the head of the democratic state, Kennedy saw the CIA as usurping authority not legitimately vested in the organization, hence his famous remark to Arthur Schlesinger that he would "splinter the CIA into a thousand pieces and scatter it to the winds."[53]

For the purposes of this book—and so as not to derail this into a long meditation on the Kennedy administration's one thousand days—it is most worthwhile to examine the ways in which JFK's policies diverged from the Eisenhower and Johnson administrations which preceded and succeeded him, respectively. Though Kennedy has often been characterized as a dedicated "cold warrior," he pursued very different policies in key areas of the world—the USSR, Cuba, Southeast Asia, and the Third World more generally. Kennedy resisted advice from his military commanders to start hot wars in Cuba, Laos, Berlin, and Vietnam. He pursued back-channel diplomacy with Cuba and the Soviet Union with the goal of potentially normalizing US relations with the countries. In the Fall of 1963, JFK ordered a complete withdrawal from Vietnam, an order he would not live to see carried out. It cannot be proven that he would not have reversed the order, but that seems extremely unlikely.[54]

About five months before his death, JFK gave his famous "Peace Speech" at American University in which he essentially called for an end to the Cold War. In a conversation with author David Talbot, he reminded me that Kennedy officials Robert McNamara and Ted Sorensen told him explicitly that if people wanted to understand what Kennedy was trying to accomplish as president, they should listen to that speech. Said President Kennedy on Commencement Day in 1963,

> I have, therefore, chosen this time and this place to discuss a topic on which ignorance too often abounds and the truth is too rarely perceived—yet it is the most important topic on earth: world peace. What kind of peace do I mean? What kind of peace do we seek? Not a Pax Americana enforced on the world by American weapons of war. Not the peace of the grave or the security of the slave. I am talking about genuine peace, the kind of peace that makes life on earth worth living, the kind that enables men and nations to grow and to hope and to build a better life for their children—not merely peace for Americans but peace for all men and women—not merely peace in our time but peace for all time.[55]

LBJ: Empire's Return to Form

The president's assassination in Dallas brought an end to Kennedy's efforts. Almost immediately after taking office, LBJ issued an order effectively reversing JFK's withdrawal plans by allowing for the US to participate in covert paramilitary actions against North Vietnam. This led to the dubious Gulf of Tonkin incident—an episode presented to Congress as an unprovoked attack against US forces. It would have been closer to the truth to describe it as a US provocation without a Vietnamese attack. Regardless, the affair provided the pretext for the Vietnam War. Johnson also reversed Kennedy's policies in the Third World and never sought to maintain or reestablish détente negotiations with Cuba or the USSR. At

President Kennedy's funeral, Deputy Soviet Premier Anastas Mikoyan met Jacqueline Kennedy on the receiving line. According to Dean Rusk, she told the Soviet official, "My husband's dead. Now peace is up to you."[56]

Owing to a plethora of problems and seemingly impossible contrivances, neither the public nor elites accepted the government's original explanations of the Kennedy assassination and the subsequent assassination of the alleged assassin. By 1976, a Gallup poll revealed that only 11 percent of the public believed the Warren Commission theory that Oswald alone killed President Kennedy.[57] Widespread suspicions among the public ultimately led to the House Select Committee on Assassinations (HSCA) investigation. Discussed later in greater detail, the HSCA ultimately concluded that the president's death was the result of a "probable conspiracy," while leaving conspirators unidentified. In 2018, the chief counsel and staff director of the HSCA, G. Robert Blakey, was among the signatories of a statement asserting that the assassination of John Kennedy was essentially a state crime whose cover-up was facilitated by the media and elements of government.[58]

Such a conclusion could be arrived at thanks to the decades-long efforts of a small but intrepid group of scholars and researchers who examined the assassination from a critical perspective. In particular, the work of two particular scholars is utilized herein. Lance deHaven-Smith describes the John F. Kennedy assassination as a *state crime against democracy* (SCAD). Such acts are defined as "concerted actions or inactions by government insiders intended to manipulate democratic processes and undermine popular sovereignty."[59] Peter Dale Scott describes the assassination as a *structural deep event*. These are events "which violate the American social structure, have a major impact on American society, repeatedly involve lawbreaking or violence, and in many cases proceed from an unknown dark force."[60] While deHaven-Smith and Scott never collaborated, Scott conceded to me that the SCAD construct has merit, but should be amended to signify that the JFK assassination and cover-up represented a DSCAD, or a *deep state crime against democracy*. Rather than exhaustively rehashing the details of the assassination, that analysis is essentially accepted herein. For his part, deHaven-Smith conceded to me that SCAD theory lacked an explicit theory of the state. In addition to providing such a theoretical rendering, it is one of the aims of this work to reconcile and refine the formulations of these two scholars and thereby elucidate the revelatory and complementary nature of their theories.

On the eve of the JFK assassination, the political future of Lyndon Baines Johnson was imperiled. Bobby Baker, LBJ's protégé and bagman, was under investigation by the Kennedy Justice Department for myriad crimes including tax evasion, fraud, and the procuring of congressional votes through sexual favors. The scandal came to a point at which JFK himself discussed the affair with his secretary and—on the day before he left for Dallas—reportedly told her that Lyndon Johnson would not be on the ticket in 1964.[61] With the assassination of JFK and LBJ's ascendency to the presidency, the Bobby Baker investigation was dropped. Given Johnson's dramatic Dallas reprieve and his eventual early retirement from politics, his presidency illustrates the history-making power of the American deep state. On November 24, 1963—the same day that Lee Harvey Oswald was assassinated—Johnson agreed to authorize the military to carry out covert operations against North Vietnam. These operations were code-named OPLAN34A and were formally authorized in National Security Action Memorandum (NSAM) 273. Signed by President Johnson on November 26, 1963, NSAM 273 essentially marked an escalation and a thus a reversal of JFK's plan for de-escalation and withdrawal which had been made official in Kennedy's NSAM 263 of October 1963.[62] The covert operations authorized by LBJ days after Kennedy's assassination led directly to the Gulf of Tonkin incident which was eventually used to gain congressional authorization to prosecute the Vietnam War.

After winning a landslide reelection in 1964, Johnson used the Gulf of Tonkin Resolution to introduce massive numbers of ground troops into Vietnam, thereby taking the step that Kennedy had always resisted. In Latin America, JFK's moderately progressive Alliance for Progress was supplanted by the Mann Doctrine whereby Latin American governments would be judged for their promotion of US interests rather than their own national interests.[63] Johnson reversed other Kennedy policies in the Third World as well. Nationalist governments in Ghana, Brazil, and Indonesia were overthrown during the Johnson years after having been supported or at least engaged by the Kennedy administration. The consequences were especially dire in Indonesia where a bizarre abortive coup was followed by the massacre of 500,000 to 2,000,000 nominally communist and/or ethnic Chinese Sukarno supporters. The carnage unfolded with considerable US assistance and encouragement.

Lyndon Johnson himself came to suspect the CIA was somehow involved in the Kennedy assassination.[64] Likewise, Robert Kennedy and Jackie Kennedy believed that JFK was killed by domestic right-wing forces. They sent an emissary to deliver a message to that effect to the Soviets.[65] Eventually, Robert Kennedy arrived at the conclusion that his brother had been killed by elements of the CIA, organized crime, and right-wing Cuban exiles. According to RFK's confidants, he planned to reopen the investigation into the assassination once he attained the presidency.[66] These plans were derailed when RFK was assassinated on June 5, 1968 after winning the California Democratic primary. Again in the RFK case, the official explanation clashes with evidence compiled by critics. Most notably, the man convicted for the killing, Sirhan Sirhan, is essentially exonerated by RFK's autopsy. In conjunction with eyewitness testimony, the coroner's report indicates that Sirhan could not have fired the fatal shot. Additionally, there were more bullet holes in the pantry where RFK was shot than Sirhan's gun could have held. The extra shots are also apparently captured on an audio recording discovered decades later. One ballistics expert determined that the three bullets found on the scene did not match with Sirhan's pistol. The government never did make a ballistics match between the bullets and Sirhan's gun. A bullet taken by the coroner from RFK's neck simply vanished.[67] Regardless of the identity of its authors, the RFK assassination paved the way for Richard Nixon to ascend to the presidency.

CHAPTER 7

EMPIRE STRIKES
BACK, HARDER

The Rise and Fall of Tricky Dick

As with the presidency of John Kennedy, the Nixon administration presided over a time characterized by great rifts in the US public and among the elite. The Vietnam War and the political assassinations of the 1960s—especially those of the Kennedy brothers and Martin Luther King Jr.—damaged America's image domestically and internationally. The panic of US elites seemed to hit its apex in 1968. Wrote one insider decades later:

> I remembered my own encounter with the fear and trembling of what was still known as "The Establishment," four years later and 100 miles to the north at the July encampment of San Francisco's Bohemian Club. [. . .] In the summer of 1968 the misgivings were indistinguishable from panic. Martin Luther King had been assassinated; so had Robert Kennedy, and everywhere that anybody looked the country's institutional infrastructure, also its laws, customs, best-loved truths, and fairy tales, seemed to be collapsing into anarchy and chaos—black people rioting in the streets of Los Angeles and Detroit, American soldiers killing their officers in Vietnam, long-haired hippies stoned on drugs or drowned in the bathtubs of Bel

143

Air, shorthaired feminists playing with explosives instead of dolls, the Scottsdale and Pasadena sheriffs' posses preparing their palomino ponies to stand firm in the face of an urban mob.[1]

The Establishment consensus fractured first and foremost over Vietnam. Wall Street-aligned forces including Treasury officials and government economic advisors came to have deep misgivings about the war's continuation. Officials from outfits such as Citibank, Bankers Trust Company, Solomon Brothers and Goldman Sachs began making statements about the detrimental effects that war spending was having on the global economy and upon the Bretton Woods system as a whole.[2] At the same time, a minority of hawkish CFR members—most notably Paul Nitze—were determined, above all, to maintain US military primacy. In 1974, Nitze publicly appeared in front of the Senate Armed Services Committee where he attacked Nixon and Kissinger for pursuing their "myth of détente."[3]

In the pivotal year of 1968, a number of mysterious crimes involving political elites had decisive historical impact. The MLK and RFK assassinations eliminated the most powerful reformist actors among the world of social activists and political leaders, respectively. Additionally, after having run a campaign promising "Peace with Honor" in Vietnam, Nixon won the presidency in part through the commission of an arguably treasonous crime which dishonorably forestalled peace in Southeast Asia—the sabotage of the 1968 Paris Peace Accords. Through Anna Chenault, an envoy with deep ties to the opium-connected China Lobby and its Air America offshoots, Nixon persuaded the South Vietnamese delegation to hold out for his election by promising them a better deal than what they could get under Johnson.[4]

Presiding over a divided nation and a divided Establishment, Nixon pursued a middle course and limited input from much of the Washington bureaucracy while managing foreign policy from the White House.[5] He also ran a surprisingly reformist liberal domestic policy. For his efforts, Nixon won the enmity of two powerful factions of the US establishment/ *deep state*—the corporate rich and the hawkish militarists. Borrowing from Michael Klare,[6] Peter Dale Scott terms these groups "traders" and "Prussians," respectively.[7] Vietnamization, détente with the Soviets, and recognition of the People's Republic of China greatly distressed militarist hardliners. This was dramatically evidenced by the "Moorer-Radford affair" in which high ranking military officers were caught running a spy ring to obtain information about Nixon policies they opposed.[8] In addition to the financial problems caused by continuing the Vietnam War, the "traders" were opposed to Nixon's activist/liberal policies like the creation of the Environmental Protection Agency, the creation of the Occupational Safety and Health Administration, price controls, and protectionist trade policies.

Meanwhile, right-wing forces were mobilizing in response to the legitimacy crisis that had peaked in 1968. In reaction, corporate lawyer and future Supreme Court Justice Lewis Powell penned his infamous 1971 manifesto: "Confidential Memorandum: Attack on the American Free Enterprise System," more commonly known as the "Powell Memo."[9] Seemingly a response to the possibility that the corporate rich might lose their hegemony over society, the Powell Memo was initially addressed to a massive business lobby, the US Chamber of Commerce. Wrote Powell in the memo, "Strength lies in organization, in careful long-range planning and implementation, in consistency of action over an indefinite period of years, in the scale of financing available only through joint effort, and in the political power available only through united action and national organizations." With its calls for sustained, organized activism to move US politics in a more pro-business direction, the Powell Memo is often credited for inspiring or at least explaining the forces that gave rise to the New Right in America. It can also be read as a something of a manifesto of the American deep state. One might even describe it as a deep state declaration of independence from democracy. The political activism of the 1960s challenged the hegemony of the superficially liberal power elite that C. Wright Mills began exposing in the mid-1950s. The 1970s rise in right-wing activism stemmed from elements that, prior to the 1960s, had been enjoying a near monopoly on power in the US. When progressive activism threatened the power elite's monopoly on power, the response—besides a slew of assassinations—was a massive surge in right-wing elite activism, a counterrevolutionary crusade which fundamentally altered American politics and society.

Another elite response to the fallout from the Vietnam War and consequent end of Bretton Woods was a notable change in the nature of US hegemony. As Robert Buzzanco wrote, "The Bretton Woods system and military Keynesianism—which had driven economic growth in the Cold War—had been dealt a serious blow by the Vietnam War, and the United States would henceforth have to negotiate its hegemony and economic influence with Western Europe and Japan."[10] The most noteworthy establishment response to this came in the form of David Rockefeller's Trilateral Commission, an international organization comprised of compatible business elites, political figures, and intellectuals from North America (US and Canada), Western Europe, and Japan. The most concise formulation of the Trilateralist perspective can be found in *The Crisis of Democracy: Report on the Governability of Democracies to the Trilateral Commission* by Michel Crozier, Samuel P. Huntington, and Joji Watanuki, wherein the authors bemoan "an excess of democracy."[11] The book argues that

> [T]he effective operation of a democratic political system usually requires some measure of apathy and noninvolvement on the part of some individuals and groups. In the past, every democratic society has had a marginal population, of greater or lesser size, which has not actively participated in politics. In itself, this marginality on the part of some groups is inherently undemocratic, but it has also been one of the factors which has enabled democracy to function effectively. Marginal social groups, as in the case of the blacks, are now becoming full participants in the political system.[12]

The Trilateralists were in essence arguing that the decline in esteem for elites and elite institutions was in fact "a crisis of democracy"—as opposed to the legitimacy crisis being a healthy democratic response to undemocratic, top-down governance. While differing in tone and content from the Powell Memo, the Trilateralists overlapped with the nascent New Right in their fear and disdain for the progressive currents of the 1960s. It is noteworthy that the Trilateralist perspective came to dominate the Democratic Party during the Carter, Clinton, and Obama administrations. Thus, the Trilateralists—perhaps best described as the left-wing of the right-wing American political class—came to dominate the "left" side of the US political system, i.e., the Democratic Party.

Suffice it to say, Richard Nixon presided over a period in which the deep state was very much divided. Though Watergate looms as the proximate cause of his undoing, the conventional Watergate narrative seems increasingly mythical. DeHaven-Smith points to Nixon's confirmed and suspected crimes as *state crimes against democracy*. These include the burglary of Daniel Ellsberg's psychiatrist's office, the Watergate break-in, and the attempted assassination of George Wallace.[13] Such a characterization is accurate as far as it goes, but when reexamined (see Chapters 9 and 10), the Watergate mythology obscures something much deeper—a rolling coup of sorts.

Dallas and Watergate: Strange Parallels

By this reading, Watergate was another *structural deep event* that served as a crucible in the history of the deep state system's consolidation. While the two leaders would seem to be diametrically opposite in the US political system, there are striking parallels between the political fates of both John Kennedy and Richard Nixon. Both presidents failed to accommodate the antecedents of today's neoconservative and neoliberal factions of the deep state. Kennedy had outraged the militarist "Prussian" faction of the political establishment by refusing to commit the US to fighting wars during the Bay of Pigs fiasco, the crisis in Laos, the Berlin Crisis, the Cuban Missile Crisis, and in Vietnam where Kennedy had formalized a protracted (for political reasons) withdrawal process after initially boosting the US presence in the country. Kennedy also established back-channel talks with Castro and Khrushchev about improving US-Cuban relations and ending the Cold War, respectively. Nixon earned the enmity of these same forces by seeking détente and arms control with the Soviet Union, recognizing China, pursuing "Vietnamization" and the eventual end of the war, and by calling for the removal of US troops from South Korea.

Kennedy's policies also aggrieved the "traders," those representing the interests of Corporate America and transnational capital more generally. In his standoff with US Steel, Kennedy brought the power of the government to bear on the country's largest corporation, forcing its executives to back down on a price increase that nullified an agreement previously reached between the company, labor unions, and the federal government. Henry Luce's *Fortune* magazine observed that a theory circulating in the corporate world maintained that the US Steel chairman "was acting as a 'business statesman' rather than as a businessman," and that Kennedy's policies were threatening "jawbone control" of industry prices. The editorial concluded that it was in the national interest for US Steel to find "a way to break through the bland 'harmony' that has recently prevailed between government and business."[14]

As sociologist Donald Gibson describes it, Kennedy's economic policies were threatening to the established order wherein government policy served—or at least did not disrupt—"the privately organized hierarchy" whose elites, especially those affiliated with Morgan interests, have long been involved with the British establishment. These Anglo-US elites share a worldview "rooted in inherited wealth and titles and organized in the modern world around control of finance and raw materials."[15] It was in the realm of foreign policy that Kennedy most alarmed the corporate rich. His policies toward crucial Third World countries were markedly different from those of Eisenhower and Johnson. These included JFK's policies on the poor, resource-rich countries of Indonesia, Brazil, Congo, Iran, and the Dominican Republic. In Italy, Kennedy supported opening up the political system to accommodate the considerable political aspirations of the Italian left. Even prior to JFK's assassination, CIA officer William Harvey in Rome set about launching a campaign to reverse Kennedy's policy.[16] CIA officer Mark Wyatt believed Harvey himself was involved in the JFK assassination after Harvey's response on the day of the shooting and his unexplained trip to Dallas earlier in the month. In violation of the JFK Records Act, William Harvey's CIA travel records are still withheld to this day.[17]

Nixon also pursued policies anathema to the "traders," including the aforementioned price controls, creation of the EPA and OSHA, and protectionist trade policies. He sought to expand the food stamp program, and his administration established the Supplemental Security Income program to guarantee an income for America's elderly and disabled. In sum, the Nixon administration presided over considerable increases in benefits provided by Social Security, Medicare, and Medicaid. The head of Nixon's Council of Economic Advisers, Herb Stein, stated that under Nixon, "Probably more new regulation was imposed on the economy than in any other presidency since the New Deal."[18]

In addition to the above policies which alienated the main power blocs of the US Establishment, Kennedy and Nixon took measures that produced antipathy and paranoia in two crucial deep state institutions: the CIA and its colleagues in organized crime. Kennedy and Nixon famously fired two legendary CIA chiefs, Allen Dulles and Richard Helms, respectively. The two directors were Establishment to the core. From an elite family, Dulles had been an attorney for Wall Street's Sullivan and Cromwell law firm before serving as an OSS officer and later providing crucial assistance in the effort to create the CIA itself.[19] Richard McGarrah Helms was the grandson of Gates W. McGarrah, the first president of the Bank for International Settlements—the Nazi-connected bank which Roosevelt tried unsuccessfully to eliminate, and which today functions as the hub of the world's central banking system.[20] As a teenager, Helms attended an elite Swiss boarding school whose student body also included the Shah of Iran.[21] Nixon never trusted the patrician Helms and made the decision to fire him after being re-elected in 1972.

The Kennedys antagonized organized crime more than any previous administration, with Robert Kennedy leading campaigns against the organized crime syndicates that Hoover's FBI had long ignored in favor of going after other favored targets like leftists and civil rights leaders. Whereas the Kennedys clashed with figures like Teamster boss Jimmy Hoffa, Nixon actually pardoned Hoffa. However, Nixon would eventually earn the enmity of his Far Eastern, syndicate-connected, former backers from Taiwan, South Korea, and Japan. They were aggrieved by the Nixon-Kissinger pursuit of détente and by the "War on Drugs" which did impact the Asian heroin trade. In sum, the demise of the Kennedy and Nixon presidencies are best explained with reference to deep political institutions that opposed the policies and strategies pursued by the two administrations. Such an analysis illuminates much that is obscured by conventional accounts that focus on the proximate and apparent causes—the bullets in Dallas and the fallout from a botched break-in at the Watergate Hotel.

Monetary Esoterica: The Balance of Dollars

More than is commonly understood, the 1970s were a cataclysmic decade in US history and therefore in world history. Since the end of World War II, the US had presided over the international capitalist system by virtue of its de facto control of the International Monetary Fund, the World Bank, and the dollar's status as the system's gold-backed reserve currency. US leaders managed these dollar flows within the constraints imposed by the gold peg. Under Truman, the US began a massive rearmament program to save the aerospace industry, manage the "dollar gap" issue in Europe and Japan, stimulate the faltering US economy, and keep Europe on a pro-US Cold War footing. Eisenhower's "New Look" foreign policy was largely a response to balance of payments pressures stemming in part from the massive military spending he had inherited. The New Look relied relatively less on expensive conventional arms production and more on nuclear deterrence and comparatively cheap covert operations.

But Eisenhower's efforts were not very successful. When Kennedy took office, he was very concerned with the US balance of payments position and the depletion of American gold reserves. The Vietnam situation is very relevant to these matters. National Intelligence Estimates (NIE) from 1961 reflected Kennedy's intention to decrease military spending overseas. In his February 6, 1961, Special Message on the Balance of Payments, Kennedy identified these expenditures as the top factor in the balance of payments crisis that had begun in 1957. The warnings in the NIEs helped the president counter General Maxwell Taylor's request for combat troops in Vietnam in October of 1961.[22] In May of 1962, Kennedy told the US Chamber of Commerce,

> It costs the United States $3 billion a year to maintain our troops and our defense establishment and security commitments abroad. If the balance of trade is not sufficiently in our favor to finance this burden, we have two alternatives: one, to lose gold, as we have been doing; and two, to begin to withdraw our security commitments.[23]

This concern over the gold drain led to Kennedy's 1962 imposition of departmental "gold budgets" for the federal government. Peter Dale Scott argues that this concern over the gold drain also contributed to Kennedy's decision to "begin to withdraw" from Vietnam in late 1963.[24] Thus it is noteworthy that Kennedy was relying on the economist John Kenneth Galbraith to help him extricate the US from Vietnam. To Galbraith, his biographer Richard Parker writes,

> [A] potential US war in Vietnam represented more than a disastrous misadventure in foreign policy–it risked derailing the New Frontier's domestic plans for Keynesian-led full employment, and for massive new spending on education, the environment and what would become the War on Poverty. Worse, he feared, it might ultimately tear not only the Democratic Party but the nation apart–and usher in a new conservative era in American politics.[25]

John Kennedy's presidency, his Vietnam withdrawal and the New Frontier all met their end with the gunfire in Dallas. By late 1964, in the same month as the Gulf of Tonkin incidents, *Fortune* magazine reported that the arms industry was in need of new outlets. Echoing the "war scare" of 1948, aerospace outlets like *Aviation Week* began campaigning against the limitations on the "old-fashioned" air campaign the US was waging in Vietnam. Combined with similar oil industry efforts, the campaign was not something easily resisted by any US president, least of all Johnson.[26] Furthermore, the investment outflow that had been restrained by Kennedy began to hit new highs in 1964. And in the month of January 1965, the US gold drain was $262 million, a total exceeding the whole of 1964. Meanwhile, the US under Johnson was embarking on a sort of militarized Marshall Plan of sorts, "a billion-dollar American investment in . . . a greatly expanded cooperative effort for development" in Southeast Asia.[27]

Johnson's plan for massively increased private sector and military outflows of dollars to Southeast Asia also entailed measures designed to protect the US balance of payments position. Around the same time that the Rolling Thunder bombing campaign of North Vietnam began, Johnson announced his "Voluntary Program" under which US firms and banks would agree to reduce their foreign outflows in return for receiving antitrust exemptions on planning around these strictures. US financial elites apparently agreed to these measures because it secured for the largest firms a guaranteed dominant position in the realm of foreign lending—an area where the returns to investment were highest. Furthermore, these corporate statesmen could accept some restrictions because they looked forward to the very favorable investment opportunities should the US succeed in militarily securing Asia. Remarks from Federal Reserve Bank of New York president Alfred Hayes illustrate the financial establishment's shift away from Kennedy's views and toward Johnson's program.[28] As Peter Dale Scott writes,

> [O]n January 25, 1965, two weeks before the delayed war against North Vietnam began, *Mr. Hayes had already shifted towards the Johnson paradigm of* controls and expansion. Although overseas government commitments were now a far larger and more controversial issue than in 1963, Mr. Hayes concluded that "the spotlight of the moment would seem to be on capital movements," where a "more direct approach" was needed. [emphasis added; the italicized passage was inexplicably omitted from the published text and only supplied to me by the author nearly 50 years later].[29]

Despite Johnson's efforts in this regard, the US proceeded to run up enormous balance-of-payments deficits due to Vietnam War spending. Starting in the mid-1960s, European and Asian central banks began accumulating dollars in vast quantities. It soon became clear to US leaders that if the US were to adhere to the (US-crafted) Bretton Woods agreement, the national treasury would quickly exhaust its gold reserves. In response, the US under Johnson suspended informally the dollar's convertibility to gold in 1968.[30] In 1970, President Nixon appointed a new under-secretary for international monetary affairs.[31] The new appointee, Paul Volcker, was a Rockefeller man, having been vice president of David Rockefeller's Chase Manhattan Bank in the 1960s in addition to various Federal Reserve and US Treasury posts.[32] Volcker's duty was to report to another Rockefeller man, Henry Kissinger, head of the National Security Council at the time. In May of 1971, Volcker's Treasury taskforce began formulating plans for the "suspension of gold convertibility."[33] Soon thereafter, in August of

1971, President Nixon formally closed the gold window, bringing an end to the Bretton Woods era.

The closing of the gold window was the culmination of a series of ad hoc responses to monetary crises faced by US policymakers. US officials knew that their decision was a power move to address US problems in such a way as to harm other countries' interests. This was famously and most succinctly expressed at the time by US Treasury Secretary John Connolly when he told G-10 attendees in Rome, "The dollar is our currency, but it's your problem."[34] That said, the implications of the change were not fully understood at the time. Michael Hudson was the first economist to accurately assess the fundamental change after the Nixon Shock. Hudson first published *Super Imperialism: The Economic Strategy of American Empire* in 1972. The book explained how the US, by ending gold convertibility, forced the rest of the world to hold US Treasury bills as the basis for their cash reserves. Other countries recycled their surplus dollars by buying US Treasury securities, thereby financing US budget deficits. In effect, the new global financial system obliged other countries to pay for US military spending whether they wanted to or not. In the mid-1970s, the Pentagon paid a considerable sum for Hudson to explain to them just how the country was now enjoying this free financial ride.[35]

Hudson had these insights thanks to his own acumen and unique background. After earning his PhD, he worked for Chase Manhattan as the balance-of-payments economist for their economic research department. In that position, Hudson was tasked with predicting the balance of payments for Chile, Brazil, and Argentina to determine if they could take on additional debt such that the maximum amount of each country's economic surplus could be paid to US banks as debt service. Hudson also developed an accounting process to examine the US oil industry's balance of payments. His final task at Chase was to estimate the value of criminal proceeds flowing into Swiss banks and other hideouts. According to Hudson, the US State Department had requested that Chase and other US banks create branches in the Caribbean to attract "hot money" from drug dealers, embezzlers, and such. This was a desperate measure undertaken to offset the exploding US balance-of-payments deficit, which Hudson discovered to be completely due to military spending.[36]

After his illuminating experiences at Chase Manhattan, Hudson joined the New School economics department where he discovered the inadequacy of the discipline. International trade theory, he determined, was "the silliest" of the economics subdisciplines since it ignored military spending, gunboats, "errors and omissions" (i.e., "hot money"), capital flight, the various forms of smuggling, and the endemic "transfer pricing" tax avoidance scams. According to Hudson, these blind spots are necessary in order "to steer trade theory toward the perverse and destructive conclusion that any country can pay any amount of debt, simply by lowering wages enough to pay creditors."[37]

Academic monetary theory, he discovered, is even more blinkered. Friedman's "Chicago School" only factors wages and commodity prices into analysis of money supply, ignoring the impact of asset prices—specifically stocks, bonds, and real estate. Here again, the effect is to create a fictitious cosmology—"the reverse of how the world actually works"— to the benefit of a predatory, rentier financial class. His analysis led him to advocate for Third World debt cancellation. However, even leftist US economists at the time did not accept the centrality of debt service. It took another decade for Hudson to be proven right when Mexico in 1982 set off the "debt bomb" in Latin America by defaulting on its foreign debt.[38] Hudson was also the economist who perhaps most accurately predicted the subprime collapse.[39] His research and historical role in illuminating iniquities of the global financial system provide perhaps the most comprehensive critique of the post-Bretton Woods system and the economic polarization wrought by the predominance of US structural power. Additionally, by highlighting the poverty of the prevailing theories in economics, Hudson's work suggests that the academy is itself an agent of structural power by virtue of economists' *de rigueur* myopia when it comes to debt and rent.[40]

The scuttling of Bretton Woods represented an assertion of structural power unmatched in human history. The Nixon administration refused to accept the Bretton Woods stricture that the US remain in surplus. The power move of removing the gold peg was justified, according to the Nixon administration, because the deficits were caused not by US military profligacy, but by mercantilist European and Japanese practices that sought to challenge US industry.[41] Since the new dollar standard so greatly weakened Western Europe and Japan vis-à-vis the US, they opposed Nixon's moves. To manage this hostility, an IMF conference of monetary reform was convened. At meetings held between 1972 and 1974, participants deliberated about a proposed new system in which IMF Special Drawing Rights (SDRs) would serve as the anchor for the international monetary system, subordinating the dollar and other currencies. In retrospect, it is clear that the US had no intention of following through on the consensus reached at the conference. Rather, the conference was a means to stall the participating states while the US manipulated events elsewhere.[42]

War by Other Means: Oil and Finance

With the closing of the gold window as the first step, the Nixon administration took the next step toward establishing the unipolar post-Bretton Woods system. This entailed working to ensure that financial relations would no longer be controlled by states' central banks, but would instead be centered in the realm of private financial entities. The US accomplished this in large part by exploiting American dominance over the international petroleum market. Although commonly believed to be related to the Arab-Israeli conflict and the Yom Kippur War specifically, the unprecedented 1973 spike in oil prices was orchestrated by the US to serve as economic statecraft against Western Europe and Japan. The Nixon administration had been making plans to effect an OPEC price increase since 1971. Beginning in 1972, the US had been formulating plans for recycling the concomitant flood of petrodollars through private US banks. Nixon's ambassador to Saudi Arabia stated that the motivation behind the policies was to deal a severe blow to Japanese and European economies, rather than to establish a new financial world order.[43] With his administration's antipathy toward Western European and Japanese interests and his "Nixon shock" nationalistic trade policies, President Nixon was antagonizing the "trader" or neoliberal faction of the US power structure. This group was most clearly embodied in the personage of David Rockefeller, an overworld plutocrat who opposed barriers to "free trade" and whose Trilateral Commission was founded in July of 1973 to bring together elites from the US, Western Europe, and Japan in order to facilitate cooperation between these three leading centers of capitalism. Nixon's failure to accommodate these elements contributed ultimately to his downfall.

While it may seem implausible that the US could have orchestrated the OPEC crisis, there is much evidence to support such a conclusion. For starters, all the key Middle Eastern actors in the affair—Israel, Saudi Arabia, Iran—were US allies. Given the disparity in power, it would be more precise to describe them as client states. Client states do not harm the interests of their patron state. This is basically their defining characteristic. Additionally, it is clear that the oil crisis served to benefit enormously two pillars of the US power structure: oil and finance. US responsibility for the price spike was confirmed decades later by Sheikh Ahmed Zaki Yamani, the Saudi oil minister at the time. He stated that he was "100 per cent sure that the Americans were behind the increase in the price of oil," adding that the Shah of Iran said to him, "Why are you against the increase in the price of oil? That is what they want? Ask Henry Kissinger—he is the one who wants a higher price." Yamani added that documentation of these plans had emerged in papers detailing a secret meeting on a Swedish island where US and British officials outlined plans to orchestrate a fourfold increase in the price of oil.[44]

Yamani was referring to the 1973 Bilderberg meetings held in Saltjoebaden, Sweden. While he may be overstating the degree to which the meeting minutes reveal "orchestration" of the price increase, they do include discussion of a paper presented to the group which made reference to Yamani's analysis of the changing oil markets, including Yamani's recommendation that oil majors and producing countries "prevent competition [. . .] to avoid a drop in prices and revenues [and to] maintain thereby price stability , and even secure an immediate increase in world crude oil prices."[45] Participants also prophetically discussed the implications of OPEC on the global financial and monetary systems as well as the need for the US—"the most important political, economic, and military power of the Free World,"—to "continue to dominate the international oil scene [. . .] because of the world balance of power."[46] One noteworthy aspect of the conference is that it focused in large part about how to create ways for the US, Europe, Japan, the oil majors, and OPEC to devise strategies for dealing with oil price increases, even as Nixon sought to effect the oil price increase to economically weaken Japan and Europe. In July of 1973, Zbigniew Brzezinski organized the formation of David Rockefeller's aforementioned Trilateral Commission in order to bring together US, European, and Japanese elites for purposes of strategic coordination. Brzezinski had attended the May 1973 Bilderberg meeting. The Bilderberg and Trilateral Commission activities of 1973 further suggest that Nixon had lost the support of the "traders,"—i.e., the transnational capitalist class—and that he had lost control of policy to some degree as a consequence of the rolling Watergate scandal.

Eventually, the high oil prices led to a huge accumulation of petrodollars by OPEC countries. Other governments had wanted these funds recycled through the IMF. Owing to US dominance in the Persian Gulf region, it was instead decided that the banks of the Atlantic world (led by American firms, naturally) would be the conduits for petrodollar recycling.[47] To facilitate this, the US proceeded to use its power to abolish "financial repression"—the system of capital controls put in place by Bretton Woods.[48] Given that the untethered dollar was the new form of global reserves, "liberating" international financial markets like this served to preserve US financial dominance. The basis of US hegemony shifted from being a constellation of one-to-one power relationships and into being a structural, market-based type of power.[49] The system was shored up throughout the decade by secret deals struck between Saudi Arabia and US Treasury secretaries whereby the Saudis would use their petrodollars to purchase US Treasury bills at special auctions.[50] Additionally, US and Saudi officials arrived at a deal in which the kingdom agreed to extend its practice of requiring US dollars as payment for oil sales.[51]

The amount of evidence for US authorship of the oil shocks is overwhelming, and yet—as with so many other deep political episodes—historical truth cannot supplant the mythical cover story. The deep state is here again utterly unaccountable. Yannis Varoufakis sums up the affair:

> [The notion] that the OPEC countries pushed the dollar price of oil sky high against the will of the United States . . . runs counter to logic and evidence. [How else to explain that America's] closest allies, the Shah of Iran, President Suharto of Indonesia and the

Venezuelan government, not only backed the increases but led
the campaign to bring them about? [How do we explain the US]
scuttling of the Tehran negotiations between the oil companies
and OPEC just before an agreement was reached that would have
depressed prices? . . . Indeed, the Saudis have consistently claimed
that Henry Kissinger, keener to manage the flow of petrodollars to
America than to prevent the rise of energy prices, was encouraging
them all the way to push the price of oil up by a factor of between
two and four. So long as oil sales were denominated in dollars, the
U.S. administration had no quarrel with the oil price increases.[52]

The post–Bretton Woods system bequeathed to the US an historically novel
kind of empire borne of structural dominance. Peter Gowan describes the
post–Bretton Woods system as the *Dollar-Wall Street Regime* (DWSR).
The two pillars of the system are, logically, the dollar and the financial
markets.[53] With the gold-backed dollar replaced by the *petrodollar/treasury
bill standard*, the US was able to enjoy unprecedented seigniorage benefits.[54] To wit, the US is unfettered by the balance-of-payments imperatives
that constrain other countries. The US can fund its gargantuan military
colossus without worrying about budget deficits since there is no foreign
exchange constraint. US multinationals can buy up other firms around
the world, engage heavily in foreign direct investment, and direct large
amounts of funds into securities and/or portfolio investments without
consequences that would otherwise stem from massive accumulation of
the country's currency in foreign central banks. US importers and export-
ers are less affected by exchange rate fluctuations, and current account
(trade) deficits can be sustained indefinitely since they can be covered by
US dollars.[55]

    As Gowan explains, the dominance of Wall Street in the post–Bretton
Woods regime had four key consequences. Central banks were superseded by (Anglo-American) private banks in the realm of international
finance. Public supervision of international finance was greatly weakened.
Countries' currencies and financial systems—especially in the global
south—were much more vulnerable to being destabilized by activities
in US financial markets.[56] Finally, within developed countries, powerful

competitive pressures in the banking systems broke down state barriers that prevented deeper linkages between international and domestic financial systems, causing the latter to be less well-controlled by their home countries. In crises, this allowed the US to open up the economies of respective states and restructure them according to US interests.[57]

The end of Bretton Woods and the establishment of the DWSR was a spectacular victory for the maturing American deep state. Vietnam had led to a deep political conflict wherein the commercially minded *traders* (a.k.a. neoliberals) came to oppose the Prussian militarist profligacy which threatened to destroy the international capitalist order forged and maintained by the US since the end of World War II. The Nixon administration, with considerable input from the Rockefeller overworld, midwifed the DWSR even though its final form jettisoned the democratic nationalist aspects that Nixon himself favored. I surmise that Nixon was, in part, collateral damage from this conflict. What emerged was a new system that eventually repaired the rifts between the neoliberal traders and neoconservative Prussians. Wall Street and the Pentagon acquired a theretofore historically unprecedented source of structural power and financial largess.

American Glasnost: Collateral Damage from Watergate

The deep political fallout from the Establishment civil war known as "Watergate" would play itself out through the rest of the decade. Shortly after becoming head of the CIA, James Schlesinger learned about CIA involvement in the crimes of Watergate burglars James McCord and E. Howard Hunt. In response, he ordered agency employees to report any CIA activities that exceeded the agency's authority. Undertaken as a Watergate counter-offensive against the CIA, the resulting compilation became the CIA's "family jewels" files.[58] In December of 1974, some of the files' explosive contents reached the public when Seymour Hersh reported that the CIA had been violating its charter by carrying out domestic intelligence operations against antiwar activists and other dissidents.[59] In response to the article, President Ford held a meeting with Defense Secretary and ex-DCI James Schlesinger along with some other officials. At the meeting, Ford asked "Was the CIA involved in Watergate?" The reply—almost certainly from Schlesinger—was partially redacted but he did state that "There is a layer in the Agency [beyond] which you can never find out what is going on." The next day, Helms would offer a similar assessment: "I don't know everything which went on in the Agency; maybe no one really does." In response, Ford tried to get ahead of the scandals by appointing the "blue-ribbon" Rockefeller Commission.[60] Thus began 1975, the "year of intelligence."

Though the president had been warned that the commission should not be seen as a "kept" committee formed to "whitewash the problem," Ford stacked the committee with a majority of right-wing, establishment figures including Vice President Nelson Rockefeller, Douglas Dillon, Ronald Reagan and Lyman Lemnitzer.[61] From early on, the committee would face setbacks that kept it from defusing the crisis facing the US intelligence community. Watergate had led to what turned out to be a very brief historical moment in which the media sought to uncover and report on intelligence abuses, i.e., on state criminality. In February, the *CBS Evening News* aired a segment informing viewers that President Ford had "reportedly warned associates that if current investigations go too far, they could uncover several assassinations of foreign officials in which the CIA was involved."[62] As a result of the report about his warning, President Ford would have to deal with just the scenario he was trying to prevent. Over the next few months, various front-page stories exposed new abuses, including the CIA-Mafia plots to kill Castro, plots against Lumumba; Ngo Dinh Diem; and Rafael Trujillo, as well as alleged operations to assassinate Sukarno and Duvalier.[63]

Before the bizarre Watergate events that made him America's only unelected president, Ford's most historically significant accomplishment had been his service on the Warren Commission. In that capacity, he infamously rewrote the passage describing Kennedy's wounds in such a way as to erroneously move the "magic bullet's" point of entry from the president's back up to his neck, thereby making the report's single bullet theory somewhat less untenable. It is ironic, then, that the Rockefeller Commission only took up the issue of assassinations because of Ford's gaffe. Rockefeller responded to the controversy by suggesting, apparently in earnest, that the commissioners restrict their assassination inquiry to the issue of Cuban involvement in the Kennedy assassination. This was too much even for Ronald Reagan, and the commissioners overruled their chairman. Although the commission did carry out an investigation into CIA assassination plots, they were stymied in key respects. The CIA dragged its feet rather than providing the relevant documents. Secretary of State Henry Kissinger wanted to suppress the report on assassinations. Deputy assistant to the president Richard Cheney took the lead in "editing" the report. Cheney's revisions included withholding the section on assassinations and editing the report to obscure the backstory of how Ford's revelation had forced the commission to take up the issue in the first place. Additionally, Cheney changed language that described CIA abuses as "unlawful" to instead being merely beyond the CIA's statutory authority. The report did concede that the agency's drug experiments were "illegal."[64]

In addition to the revelations listed above, the US public saw the video of President Kennedy's assassination for the first time when Robert Groden and Dick Gregory screened the film on Geraldo Rivera's television show in March of 1975. Abraham Zapruder had filmed the president's death and subsequently sold the film to C. D. Jackson, a Time-Life executive. In addition to his career in the Luce media empire, Jackson had been a propagandist for the US government—a specialist in "psychological warfare" during World War II.[65] While working for Luce in the early 1950s, Jackson was paid by the CIA to coauthor a study that recommended reorganizing the US intelligence agencies. He also used Time-Life to provide cover for CIA agents.[66] After Jackson's purchase of the Zapruder Film, Time-Life kept it from the public until a bootleg version made from the copy provided to New Orleans DA Jim Garrison was finally broadcast. The film had a tremendous impact on public opinion. Much of the public in 1975 concluded what CIA director John McCone had surmised in 1963 upon seeing the film: it showed the president being hit by gunfire apparently coming from two directions.[67]

The John Kennedy assassination would subsequently be taken up by the Church Committee, the Senate's post-Watergate investigation into intelligence abuses. In its final report, the Church Committee found that the FBI and CIA investigations were "deficient" and that key facts which could have significantly impacted the investigation were withheld from the Warren Commission and even the investigators working for the CIA and FBI. In particular, the CIA's operations that plotted Castro's assassination should have been investigated. The committee's final report stated that they could not explain why the FBI/CIA let the deficient investigation proceed, nor why they then allowed the Warren Commission to arrive at its conclusion without having all the key facts. On these matters, the report concludes, "[T]he possibility exists that senior [FBI/CIA officials] made conscious decisions not to disclose potentially important information."[68]

As with the Rockefeller Commission, the White House tasked deputy assistant to the president Richard Cheney with responding to congressional investigators. His work led to the CIA adopting accommodation procedures designed explicitly to keep the agency's most important records away from the committee.[69] Despite these challenges, the committee did expose widespread abuses, including the FBI's notorious COINTELPRO operations, massive surveillance of dissidents by the CIA; FBI; military intelligence; and the theretofore largely anonymous National Security Agency. The committee's report included details of the political use of the IRS and what was, to that date, the most complete account of CIA covert operations against Chilean democracy.[70] There were additional revelations such as the development of very potent, deadly poisons derived from shellfish toxin and cobra venom. It was also exposed that the agency had created an electric dart gun that fired silently, as well as darts which could shoot poison into a target and subsequently be undetectable during a typical autopsy or physical examination.[71] A former CIA employee named Mary Embree reported that the CIA had developed a projectile made of frozen poison that could be shot into a target. The dart would melt, the target would suffer a heart attack, and there would be only a small inconspicuous mark left behind on the body of the deceased heart attack victim.[72] Despite these and other details about assassinations, including the Castro plots, the final report did not find the CIA directly responsible for a single assassination.[73]

The House conducted a separate intelligence investigation in the form of the Pike Committee. Early on, the committee nearly triggered a constitutional crisis over whether Congress had the right to investigate any elements of the executive branch. Unlike the Church Committee, the Pike Committee members refused to sign any CIA-style secrecy agreements. Pike also refused to allow the CIA to only brief the committee chair and/or co-chair on matters deemed sensitive by the agency. In the end, the committee was able to establish a process whereby the House of Representatives could declassify information in its possession.[74] The committee's final report was suppressed thanks to the efforts of the CIA's allies in Congress. However, someone had leaked the report to journalist Daniel Schorr who—after the report was suppressed—gave it to the *Village Voice* who then published it in February of 1976. Relative to the Church Committee, the report contained less sensational revelations of CIA abuses, but its conclusions and recommendations were more sweeping. The report's opening line spelled it out: "If this Committee's recent experience is any test, intelligence agencies that are to be controlled by congressional lawmaking are, today, beyond the lawmaker's scrutiny." The committee called for the creation of a permanent House intelligence committee, the prohibition of direct or indirect assassination plots and a moratorium on paramilitary operations during peacetime. Other recommendations included disclosure of the existence of the NSA, legislation to allow for civilian control of that agency, and the creation of a true director of the intelligence community to oversee and coordinate intelligence sharing and activities among the agencies. Perhaps most significantly, the report called for an end to the CIA practice of enlisting elements of civil society (journalists, religious groups, academia) in its propaganda and spying operations.[75]

Ultimately, neither congressional investigation was able to impact the lawlessness of the intelligence agencies. After Watergate, the media returned to its traditional subservient position vis-à-vis the state. The *Washington Post* was emblematic of this reversion to form, stating in an unsigned editorial that by demanding an unfettered investigation, the committee had trespassed upon "the President's prerogative to conduct foreign policy."[76] In a passage that seems ironic given the role of the media and the intelligence agencies in the age of Trump, the *Post* argued that the committee had erred by not discreetly acquiring the needed materials that "would not be forthcoming in the context of a hostile political

confrontation." Congress needed to preserve "[t]he legitimate powers of
the office of the Presidency," including "the confidentiality of the presidential decision-making process and the conduct of the nation's foreign
policy."[77]

The Church and Pike committees differed in their conclusions. After
finding no evidence of presidential authorization of plots to assassinate
foreign heads of state, Frank Church famously declared that the CIA "may
have been behaving like a rogue elephant on a rampage."[78] Congressman
Otis Pike's committee offered a very different conclusion. At one hearing,
Pike said that the CIA "was no rogue elephant," and the final report stated
that the available evidence suggested that the agency "has been utterly
responsive to the instructions of the President and the Assistant to the
President for National Security Affairs."[79] Pike knew this conclusion was a
threatening one. With Watergate, the public was confronted with a situation in which "their president had been a bad person. [Now] they are
asked to believe that their country has been evil." The problem was the
presidency and the abuse of power it facilitated through the use of the
executive branch's secret tools.[80]

While both Church and Pike committees arrived at grim conclusions
that went unheeded, neither report was able to adequately surmise what
had gone wrong and why. Judging by the experiences of Kennedy and
Nixon—two presidents who had clashed with the Pentagon and the intelligence community—it was insufficient to attribute the problems chiefly
to the presidency. Likewise, given the cross-administration continuity of
CIA activities, it would be mistaken to characterize the agency as "rogue."
Rather, the CIA and the presidency were both subject to intense pressure
for deep political forces. Created by the Wall Street overworld and invaluable to its creators, the CIA acted decisively to pursue US hegemony and
act according to a conception of the national interest that was congruent—if not identical—to the class interests of the corporate overworld.
The presidency was also forced to accommodate such forces, but with the
added imperative for the president to act as a democratic statesman seeking
the approval of the American electorate. Then as now, politicians and the
media could not diagnose the problems. The failure can be attributed to a
Cold War superstructure in which *empire* was not honestly acknowledged

or grappled with, in part because the imperial project had been legiti-mized by mythical references to the empire's antithesis and to the empire's "defensive" strategy—communism and containment, respectively. Belying liberal democratic myths about public sovereignty and the rule of law, the exceptionist pursuit of empire was driven by the pinnacle of American wealth and power. In this context, the state's crimes or "abuses" at home and abroad are much easier to comprehend, as are the media's otherwise inexplicable 1970s vacillations between being the public's watchdog and being the lapdog of official Washington, so to speak.

CHAPTER 8

TRIUMPH OF THE DEEP STATE

Ford and Carter: Disposable Stewards

The often-overlooked political watershed event of the mid-1970s happened near the end of the so-called "year of intelligence." The November 1975 "Halloween Massacre" was the denouement of Watergate as *structural deep event*. The "massacre" consisted of a number of major personnel changes in Ford's administration. Kissinger was replaced by Brent Scowcroft as National Security Advisor, though Kissinger remained as Secretary of State. William Colby was replaced by George H. W. Bush as CIA chief. Donald Rumsfeld replaced Secretary of Defense James Schlesinger. Rumsfeld's protégé, Dick Cheney, replaced Rumsfeld as Chief of Staff. Finally, Vice President Nelson Rockefeller was dropped from the 1976 ticket. At the time, Rockefeller and Kissinger believed that Rumsfeld was behind the shake-up.

With the benefit of hindsight, the end result of the shake-up was an administration that had moved so far to the right that it irreparably changed both political parties. The Republicans purged, essentially, the "liberal" Rockefeller wing of the party and became predominately neoconservative, a shift that was crystallized with Reagan's election. The Democrats became, gradually, a neoliberal party and the new home to

Rockefeller Republicans. The next Democratic presidential nominee was the Rockefeller-backed Jimmy Carter. Progressive political forces had already been greatly weakened by previous deep events like the coup against Henry Wallace, McCarthyism, and the political assassinations of the 1960s. After the right-wing takeover, begun in earnest with the Halloween Massacre and sanctified with Reagan's election, progressives were left with no real influence in the economic or foreign policy realms. The rightward shift in the two major American parties would become evident over the following presidential administrations. Kennedy, Johnson, and Nixon—regardless of their Cold War foreign policies—were the last liberal presidents.

The Last Investigation

The House Select Committee on Assassinations (HSCA) could be arguably characterized as the last significant example of democratic state resistance to the emerging deep state during the pivotal 1970s. The origins of the HSCA lay in the Church Committee's investigations, specifically Book V of the final report, "The Investigation of the Assassination of President J.F.K.: Performance of the Intelligence Agencies," more commonly known as the Schweiker-Hart Report. While the report's conclusions focused on the deeply flawed CIA and FBI investigations of the John Kennedy assassination, the incendiary statements of its lead committee member had even greater impact. Senator Schweiker told the *Village Voice* in 1975, "We do know Oswald had intelligence connections. Everywhere you look with him, there are fingerprints of intelligence."[1] Indeed, Schweiker had discovered so many indications of Oswald's ties to intelligence that it actually shocked the Republican senator. How was it possible that CIA had no records of Oswald's defection to the Soviet Union given that the marine had monitored U-2 spy flights at the CIA's biggest and most secret base in Atsugi, Japan? How could Oswald have afforded a $1500 voyage to Moscow at a time when he had but $203 in the bank? How did he obtain a visa in two weeks when the standard was a six-week wait? On the way to Russia, how did Oswald go from London to Helsinki when there weren't any commercial flights scheduled for that time? Why was there a Minox spy camera found in Oswald's possessions? And lastly, why didn't the CIA question Oswald when he came back from the Soviet Union? Schweiker was also particularly upset to discover that Warren Commissioner and former DCI Allen Dulles had withheld information of the CIA-mafia Castro assassination plots from the commission.[2]

After the Church Committee had convened and the HSCA investigation was underway, Schweiker told a BBC documentary crew that,

> The Warren Commission has in fact collapsed like a house of cards and I believe it was set up at the time to feed pablum to the American people for reasons not yet known, and one of the biggest cover-ups in the history of our country occurred at that time.[3]

Owing to the cumulative effort of Warren Commission critics (including Senator Schweiker), the revelations of the Watergate era, and the public showing of the Zapruder Film, an overwhelming majority of Americans had come to believe that the President Kennedy's death was the result of a conspiracy. In 1976, Gallup reported that 81 percent believed others were involved and 8 percent were unsure.[4] On September 17, 1976, House Resolution 1540 established a Select Committee that would "conduct a full and complete investigation and study of the circumstances surrounding the assassination and death of President John F. Kennedy . . ."[5]

The Church Committee's JFK investigation and the HSCA each faced serious and insurmountable obstacles. The CIA undermined both bodies in various ways. Additionally, the JFK investigators encountered a virtual necropolis of key witnesses who expired at suspiciously inopportune times. One week before Chicago godfather Sam Giancana was to testify to the Church Committee about the CIA-mafia assassination plots, he was shot to death in his home. CIA officer John Whitten—chief of the Mexico clandestine service desk in 1963—told the HSCA in 1978 that he suspected that CIA officer William Harvey had killed Giancana.[6]

Whitten's testimony to the HSCA was explosive on the whole. He had been assigned the job of handling the CIA's probe of the JFK assassination by director of operations Richard Helms. But Helms quickly removed Whitten from that role after the diligent officer complained that Agency men were withholding from him information on Oswald's Cuban activities. Whitten told the HSCA that Helms had withheld information about the CIA-mafia plots to assassinate Castro, and that if he had been aware of them, he would have thoroughly investigated the CIA's JMWAVE station in Miami. Testified Whitten, Helms's concealment of the plots was a "morally highly reprehensible act" which the spymaster must have done "because he realized [that revealing the plots] would have cost him his job and precipitated a crisis for the agency." Besides suspecting Harvey of killing Sam Giancana, Whitten apparently suspected him of being involved in the JFK assassination. When asked by the committee if Harvey could have been part of the plot that killed John Kennedy, he replied, "He was too young to have assassinated McKinley and Lincoln." Whitten had been alarmed to learn that the "ruthless" and "dangerous" Harvey had been chosen by Helms to handle the Castro assassination plots and that Harvey had hired the mobster Johnny Rosselli to assist. With this, Helms "violate[d] every operational precept, every bit of operational experience, every ethical consideration," according to Whitten's testimony.[7]

Prior to Whitten's appearance before the HSCA, Johnny Rosselli himself had died of decidedly unnatural causes. Rosselli was the source behind the first stories of the CIA-mafia Castro assassination plots to appear in the US media. He supplied reporter Jack Anderson with several versions of the CIA-mafia tale. In one version, members of the "Trafficante mob" sent to kill Castro were captured, brainwashed, and sent home to assassinate JFK. Rosselli testified before the Church Committee multiple times. The HSCA wanted to ascertain why Rosselli had pushed the Castro-did-it theories of Dallas, but this was impossible because he disappeared in July of 1976. In August, his dismembered body was found in a steel drum off the coast of Miami. While it appeared on the surface to be a clear mob hit, the Dade County coroner found evidence suggesting that he may have been drugged and immobilized before being asphyxiated.[8] Weeks before he was scheduled to testify to the HSCA, top FBI man William Sullivan was killed. The number three man at the Bureau in 1963, Sullivan was shot dead by a young hunter who claimed to have mistaken him for a deer. Robert Novak was a close friend of Sullivan's. In a 2007 memoir, Novak wrote that Sullivan had told him, "[S]omeday [Novak] probably would read about his death in some kind of accident, but not to believe it. It would be murder."[9]

Lee Oswald's "best friend," George de Mohrenschildt also died around this time under suspicious circumstances. On March 29 of 1977, HSCA investigator Gaeton Fonzi went to the Manalapan, Florida home where de Mohrenschildt was staying. Fonzi left a business card listing the HSCA and his name with de Mohrenschildt's daughter. Hours later, Fonzi received a phone call informing him that de Mohrenschildt had killed himself with a shotgun and that Fonzi's card was found on his person.[10] The White Russian de Mohrenschildt—sometimes called "the Baron" due to his aristocratic background—had been a globetrotting petroleum engineer, socialite, and CIA intelligence asset.[11] Just prior to his death, de Mohrenschildt told journalist Edward Epstein that he had only befriended Oswald at the request of Dallas CIA station chief J. Walton Moore. After receiving Oswald's Ft. Worth address from one of Moore's associates, de Mohrenschildt contacted Moore to request that in exchange for his help with Oswald, he be given State Department help securing a Haitian oil exploration deal. De Mohrenschildt soon received the assistance, and he did initially reach out to Oswald in what appears to have been a quid pro quo arrangement. Affirming this explanation of the otherwise inexplicable friendship between the hapless ex-Marine and "the Baron," de Mohrenschildt stated, "I would have never contacted Oswald in million years if Moore had not sanctioned it."[12] The HSCA report on de Mohrenschildt contains an unpublished manuscript that de Mohrenschildt was writing about Oswald, entitled "I AM A PATSY! I AM A PATSY!" It opens with the following sentence: "I am a patsy! I am a patsy! These last words of my friend, Lee Harvey Oswald still ring in my ears and make me think of the terrible injustice inflicted on the memory of this 'supposed assassin.'"[13]

In addition to the untimely deaths, the HSCA had other problems from the outset. Richard Sprague, the First Assistant District Attorney in Philadelphia, was chosen as the HSCA's chief counsel. In Philadelphia, he had a record of sixty-nine convictions out of seventy homicide prosecutions. Sprague intended to treat the case as if it were a homicide investigation. The attacks against him began almost immediately. He took flak in the press from congressmen who objected to the no-holds-barred approach that they believed he was going to apply. Early on, in dismay, he said, "I don't understand it. I've never been in a situation like this before, where I'm getting criticized for things I *might* do." He added, "It's nonsense, but I don't know why it's happening."[14] In January of 1977, before the new Congress had even convened, the *New York Times* ran a major story with the headline, "Counsel in Assassination Inquiry Often Target of Criticism." HSCA investigator Gaeton Fonzi described the piece as "an incredibly crude journalistic hatchet job," but stated that it "had the effect of a well-placed torpedo [that] almost blew up the Assassinations Committee."[15] After many battles during which the committee's existence was threatened by congressional refusal to fund its operations, Sprague relented to pressure and resigned in order to keep the entire HSCA from expiring. His resignation occurred on the same day as de Mohrenschildt's death. The two events collectively produced a sad victory for the HSCA in that they led to congressional support to fund, stingily, the committee's work going forward.[16]

In a 1977 interview, Sprague told a reporter, "Congress had never intended to conduct a thoroughgoing investigation in the first place." Referring to the HSCA's investigation of the MLK assassination, Sprague said that the HSCA was "a way of appeasing the Black Caucus." Sprague complained that between dealing with hostile congressmen and the belligerent press, he had spent "point zero one percent" actually examining the evidence. Asked how he would approach the investigation if he could do it all over again, Sprague said he would start by focusing on "Oswald's ties to the Central Intelligence Agency."[17] That said, Sprague also told Gaeton Fonzi that when he looked back on it all, it was clear that "the problems began only after I ran up against the CIA." In particular, Sprague found numerous inconsistencies with Oswald's visit to Mexico City, including a highly credible report of his appearance at the Dallas home of Silvia Odio when he was supposed to have been in Mexico City. Additionally, Sprague came across an FBI memo that referred to an individual—identified as Lee Harvey Oswald—photographed and recorded visiting the Russian Embassy in Mexico City. According to the memo, FBI Special Agents who knew Oswald from Dallas "are of the opinion that the above-referred-to individual was not Lee Harvey Oswald."[18] Additionally, the November 23rd date of the memo belied the CIA's assertion that the recording of Oswald had been "routinely destroyed" in October. When Sprague tried to press the CIA for information on the matter, the agency responded by offering to cooperate only if he agreed to sign a CIA Secrecy Agreement. He refused and indicated that he would obtain the CIA's records through subpoena. This led to the first congressional attempt to block the HSCA's reconstitution. One of the committee's antagonists was Illinois Congressman Robert Michael who complained that with the mandate that was being considered, "that Committee could begin a whole new investigation of the Central Intelligence Agency!"[19]

Following Sprague's resignation, retired Supreme Court Justice Arthur Goldberg considered accepting the position of the HSCA's chief counsel. He was willing to replace Sprague on the condition that he be assured full CIA cooperation. After Goldberg explained this over the phone to Stansfield Turner, Carter's new CIA chief, the phone went silent. Goldberg restated his position, to which Turner replied, "I thought my silence was my answer."[20] Eventually, an organized crime specialist named G. Robert Blakey was selected to replace Sprague as HSCA chief counsel. It would appear that he was a more acceptable choice because his organized crime expertise made him likely to attribute any evidence of conspiracy to the mob—and it made him unlikely to posit that the assassination was a state crime. The HSCA final report concluded that JFK and MLK were killed by Lee Harvey Oswald and James Earl Ray, respectively, but that in both cases there were likely unknown conspirators—which is to say that the committee found that both assassinations were probably the result of conspiracies. The report asserted that the committee found no evidence that any government agency was involved in either assassination. For JFK, the possible conspirators were individuals within organized crime and the anti-Castro Cuban community, but not any of the actual organizations therein.[21] True to form, Blakey soon after published a mob-did-it book with the spoiler-containing title, *The Plot to Kill the President: Organized Crime Assassinated JFK - The Definitive Story.*[22]

While exonerating the state, the HSCA verdict was still disconcerting to the establishment press. Responding to the HSCA conclusion that there was a second shooter (who missed the president, according to the report), a *Washington Post* editorial floated a novel hypothesis:

Could it have been some other malcontent who Mr. Oswald met casually? Could not as much as three or four societal outcasts with no ties to any one organization have developed in some spontaneous way a common determination to express their alienation in the killing of President Kennedy? It is possible that two persons acting independently attempted to shoot the President at the very same time.[23]

These were truly bizarre contrivances, but they do reveal the lengths to which the establishment media can be relied upon to defend against legitimacy crises that threaten the prevailing order.

Over time, and as with the Warren Commission, staff members of the HSCA would publicly dissent from the final report's exoneration of the state. These dissenters included Richard Sprague, Robert Tannenbaum, Edwin Lopez, Dan Hardway, and Gaeton Fonzi. Most notably, HSCA chief counsel G. Robert Blakey eventually was among the signatories of a statement attesting that:

> In the four decades since [the HSCA conclusion of a conspiracy behind the JFK assassination], a massive amount of evidence compiled by journalists, historians and independent researchers confirms this conclusion. This growing body of evidence strongly indicates that the conspiracy to assassinate President Kennedy was organized at high levels of the U.S. power structure, and was implemented by top elements of the U.S. national security apparatus using, among others, figures in the criminal underworld to help carry out the crime and cover-up.[24]

Much of Blakey's disillusionment stemmed from revelations pertaining to the CIA's HSCA liaison, George Joannides. In 1963, Joannides had been serving as the deputy director for psychological warfare at JMWAVE, the CIA's Miami station. He had been the Agency's officer in charge of the anti-Castro Cuban organization, the *Directorio Revolucionario Estudantil* (DRE). The DRE was the group which had multiple contacts with Oswald the Marxist agitator before the assassination.[25] As with Allen Dulles on the

Warren Commission, the HSCA had in Joannides a person in a key position within the investigation who himself should have been treated as a suspect or at least as an important witness. This was but one factor that led to the failure of the HSCA to satisfactorily resolve the mystery of the JFK assassination, a crucible in the conflict between American democracy and the American deep state.

Set Up to Fail: The Overmatched Jimmy Carter

In 1977, Jimmy Carter was sworn in as the 39th President of the United States. Carter's improbable rise can be attributed largely to his association with David Rockefeller's Trilateral Commission. In 1973, Carter was selected by leading establishment figures who wanted a southern Democrat to join the new organization. Carter was selected over Florida governor Reuben Askew because, according to Zbigniew Brzezinski, Carter "had opened trade offices for the state of Georgia in Brussels and Tokyo [which] seemed to fit perfectly in the concept of the Trilateral."[26] The Carter campaign followed the advice of Trilateral figures who would go on to hold important positions in his administration. As far back as 1973, Brzezinski had argued that the Democratic nominee in 1976 would need to "emphasize work, the family, religion, and, increasingly, patriotism, if he has any desire to be elected."[27] Samuel Huntington wrote in the Trilateral Commission tome, *The Crisis of Democracy*, that "the 'outsider' in politics, or the candidate who could make himself or herself appear to be an outsider, had the inside road to political office."[28]

While this accounts for Carter's strategy, it does not explain his meteoric rise. For this, the establishment press must be given considerable credit. As late as late January 1976, Carter was the favorite of only 4 percent of voters, according to a Gallup Poll. By the second week of March, he was only one percent behind the leading candidate, Hubert Humphrey. Only very favorable media coverage could account for such an historically unprecedented rise. In mid-January 1976, national media figures like Joseph Kraft and Tom Wicker noted that Carter was, as Kraft put it, "the media candidate for the Democratic presidential nomination."[29] It helped that the national media largely omitted reference to Carter's overworld sponsors. According to Project Censored, the "virtual blackout

TRIUMPH OF THE DEEP STATE 175

of information available to the public through the mass media concerning the relationships between Jimmy Carter, David Rockefeller, and the Trilateral Commission" qualified it as "the best-censored news story of 1976."[30]

Few commentators remarked upon the contradiction between Carter's elitist backing and the media image of him as a "moral" "political outsider." One notable exception in the media was Christopher Lydon who, in 1977, wrote that there were some clues that Carter was in effect a Rockefeller Republican:

> One was *Time* magazine, which gave Carter early prominence with a flattering cover portrait in 1971. Through 1975, *Time's* advertising in other magazines for its own campaign coverage looked more like an ad for Jimmy Carter: a half-page picture presented the candidate in a Kennedyesque rocking chair under the caption: "His basic strategy consists of handshaking and street-cornering his way into familiarity." Through 1976 and into 1977, *Time's* hagiographers were hard to separate from the Carter promotional staff. [. . .] I couldn't remember the weekly news magazine extending itself that way in the past except for the more eastern and international (or Rockefeller) wing of the Republican party—for Willkie in 1940, Eisenhower in 1952, and Scranton in 1964.[31]

About the Trilateral Commission Lydon observed that,

> [It] was David Rockefeller's brain child, a somewhat more energetic young cousin of the elite Bilderberg Conferences [. . .] The commission was conceived in 1972 as a private vehicle for planning the industrial world's course out of the international monetary crisis [and] into a new stability of banking relationships among the First World and of trading agreements with the Third World. [P]resumably the much greater value of [Carter's] Trilateral membership was the private reassurance it conveyed that David Rockefeller had deemed him a promising student and had gotten his education

under way. The Trilateral Commission's executive director, Zbigniew Brzezinski, became quite literally Jimmy Carter's tutor, and now, of course, directs the White House foreign policy staff, as Henry Kissinger did in the first Nixon term. How could [Rockefeller] have guessed that his Trilateralists would staff all major policy posts in the new government—including, as if by a miracle, the vice presidency and the presidency?[32]

What Lydon could not have surmised was that the Carter presidency was not a one-off event. The Democratic Party—in the aftermath of the Bretton Woods collapse and of Watergate—had been realigned by overworld forces in such a way as to render it a neoliberal-dominated party in mild opposition to the neoconservative-dominated Republican Party that was poised to deliver the "Reagan Revolution." The vaguely progressive, New Deal wing of the Democratic Party was consigned to a political wilderness from which it has not returned.

As president, Carter tried to put a greater emphasis on human rights and on a more moral foreign policy. Taking office in the wake of the "Year of Intelligence" and with the HSCA just convening, Carter sought to reign in the intelligence community. He fired George Bush as DCI and replaced him with Stansfield Turner, an admiral who graduated from the naval academy with Carter. Turner would eventually fire important deep state operatives at the CIA, "old boys" who he thought were roadblocks to reform. Among the fired officers were Ted Shackley, Ray Clines, and Ed Wilson. This would have some notable consequences.

Ultimately, Carter's presidency was undone by deep political forces. Like Kennedy and Nixon, Carter could not reconcile his political position with the accommodations demanded by the neoconservatives or even the neoliberals like his Trilateral patrons. It wasn't that Carter chose to spurn these constituencies. To the contrary, Carter pursued Reaganism before Reagan. This was in accordance with the post-Watergate rolling political coup that realigned both parties further to the right by making the GOP the party of Reagan and essentially transforming the Democrats into the party of rebranded Rockefeller Republicans. Deregulation, which began modestly under Ford, accelerated under Carter as the trucking, airline, and train industries were deregulated. Regarding banking and finance, Canova summarizes:

> [T]he similarities between the Carter and Reagan administrations far outweigh the differences. Both presidents accepted basic free-market premises that were often at odds with market realities. The result was a bipartisan dismantling of the New Deal regulatory regime in banking and finance and a relaxation of the regulatory discipline that had contained market interest rates during the period after World War II.[33]

This is to say that under Carter, the US ushered in the age of Federal Reserve–centered monetarist hegemony and financial deregulation. The former was most notably accomplished by Carter's signing of the Depository Institutions Deregulation and Monetary Control Act of 1980 (DIDMCA). This act increased insurance of deposits from $40,000 to $100,000, removed restrictions on thrift institutions (thus beginning the deregulation of savings and loan associations), and called for gradual elimination of interest rate caps on deposit accounts.[34] The latter transpired with Carter's selection of Paul Volcker to chair the Federal Reserve.

The massive interest rate hike (a.k.a., the *Volcker shock*) was another key deep state stratagem that served to strengthen US dominance after what seemed on the surface to be setbacks in the wake of Vietnam, the oil shocks, and Watergate. Again, the democratic state was suborned to the will of deep political power. Deep political forces and the Nixon administration worked in concert to create the OPEC oil shocks as a way to deal with the dollar overhang created by Vietnam War spending. Excess dollars went to oil producers' central banks and from there into US treasury bills and into US banks. Massive loans were then made to the countries of the Global South. This set the stage for the Volcker shock. With US Fed's huge interest rate hikes, excess dollars further flowed back to the US and developing countries became unable to service their debts. As Yanis Varoufakis summarizes,

> While [the Volcker shock's] did tame inflation, its harmful effects on employment and capital accumulation were profound, both

domestically and internationally. [. . .] A new phase thus began. The United States could now run an increasing trade deficit with impunity, while the new Reagan administration could also finance its hugely expanded defense budget and its gigantic tax cuts for the richest Americans. The 1980s ideology of supply-side economics, the fabled trickle-down effect, the reckless tax cuts, the dominance of greed as a form of virtue, etc.—all these were just manifestations of America's new 'exorbitant privilege': the opportunity to expand its twin deficits almost without limit, courtesy of the capital inflows from the rest of the world. American hegemony had taken a new turn.[35]

This "new turn" in American hegemony, realized early in Reagan's presidency, represents the consolidation of the deep state system, i.e., of deep state dominance over the public state and the security state.

Later in his presidency, Carter also pursued policies agreeable to neo-conservatives. After previously calling for $5–7 billion in military spending cuts, Carter in 1980 urged Congress to begin increasing the Pentagon budget to the tune of $100 billion over the following five years. Said Carter at the time, "Our forces must be increased if they are to contain Soviet aggression." He argued at the time that the budget proposals would "meet the increased threat resulting from events in Afghanistan."[36] Notably, it was a Carter policy that had served to provoke the 1979 Soviet invasion of Afghanistan in the first place. At the time, the Soviets justified the invasion in part by asserting that they were fighting against enemies secretly funded by US operations. Though US officials denied this at the time, the accusation was confirmed years later in a memoir by Robert Gates.[37] In 1998, additional confirmation came from Carter's National Security Adviser himself, Zbigniew Brzezinski, who told an interviewer:

According to the official version of history, CIA aid to the Mujahiddin began during 1980, that is to say, after the Soviet army invaded Afghanistan on December 24, 1979. But the reality, secretly guarded until now, is completely otherwise: Indeed, it was July 3, 1979 that President Carter signed the first directive for secret aid to the opponents of the pro-Soviet regime in Kabul. And that very day, I wrote a note to the president in which I explained to him that in my opinion this aid was going to induce a Soviet military intervention.[38]

The US-induced Soviet invasion served to justify another of Carter's gifts to US militarists, the so-called "Carter Doctrine" wherein the president declared that any threat to US interests in the Persian Gulf would be met with military force.

Eventually for Carter, as with Kennedy and Nixon, deep political forces would prove his undoing. His focus on human rights was perceived by Establishment imperialists as having led to the fall of two client regimes in Nicaragua and Iran. His much sought-after Salt II treaty never made it through the Senate despite Carter's various concessions like DIDMCA and the military spending hikes. The Camp David accords earned Carter the antipathy of Israelis and Saudis alike, harming Carter with powerful domestic constituencies like CIA Arabists and AIPAC's friends and beneficiaries in Congress. Elements of both the CIA and Israel were in alliance with Republican operatives working to defeat Carter by delaying the release of the hostages.[39] The hostage crisis itself only came about because Carter had bowed to a Rockefeller overworld crusade to pressure Carter into allowing the ailing Shah to come to the United States. Rockefeller financed and organized "Project Alpha," the code name given to the lobbying campaign for the Shah. Sensing the perilousness of such a course, Carter tried to resist. Prior to a meeting with Rockefeller, Carter wrote in his diary that the purpose for the meeting was "to try to induce me to let the Shah come into our country. Rockefeller, Kissinger, and Brzezinski seem to be adopting this as a joint project."[40] After months spent resisting the lobby, Carter snapped at Brzezinski and Vice President Mondale, cutting them short with the words, "Fuck the Shah. I'm not going to welcome him here when he has other places to go where he'll be safe."[41] Carter finally relented following the defection of the last of his key advisors, Cyrus Vance, to the Project Alpha side. After reluctantly agreeing to admit the Shah, the president turned to everyone in attendance and prophetically asked, "What are you guys going to advise me to do if they overrun our embassy and take our people hostage?"[42]

Not even Carter's disastrous acquiescence to his former patron could cement his support from the Rockefeller overworld. Despite Carter agreeing to admit the Shah into the US, David Rockefeller criticized Carter to the World Affairs Council in June of 1980, saying that Carter had subordinated America's "vital interests" by privileging "worthy but fuzzily defined moral issues—such as human rights and the proliferation of nuclear technologies." Pressing the cause of human rights may be "only proper" for the US, but "it should be prudent since our interference may be capable of toppling regimes whose substitutes are unknown."[43] Three months later, Rockefeller and Project Alpha veteran Joseph Reed went to Arlington to see Bill Casey at his Reagan campaign headquarters. At the time, Carter was making progress toward resolving the hostage crisis. Indications are that Rockefeller was meeting with Casey to forestall an "October Surprise"—the dramatic release of the hostages which might rescue Carter's presidency on the eve of the election. That the Rockefeller-Reed visit was October Surprise–related received confirmation in the form of sworn testimony from CIA officer Charles Cogan. Cogan was present when Reed visited William Casey early in 1981 and reportedly made remarks about how "we did something about Carter's October Surprise." In a less official setting, Cogan explained to an investigator that Reed's words to Casey were, "We fucked Carter's October Surprise."[44]

It was the summer of 2019 when the above passages were written—the material on the Rockefeller-Reagan campaign operation to sabotage Carter's "October Surprise" plan to secure the pre-election release of the hostages in Iran. This particular conspiracy theory received further corroboration in a December 2019 *New York Times* article which reported that "a newly disclosed secret history from the offices of Mr. Rockefeller" reveals how Rockefeller and his agents "worked behind the scenes to persuade the Carter administration to admit the shah, one of the bank's most profitable clients."[45] The report on the lobbying campaign confirms the previous investigatory works of people cited above like Robert Parry, Kai Bird, and Peter Dale Scott—though the *Times* article calls it Project Eagle instead of Project Alpha.

The more explosive aspect of the story is contained at the end of the article and is disappointingly if unsurprisingly not further explored or given deeper context. Specifically, the article states,

> The hostage crisis doomed Mr. Carter's presidency. And the team around Mr. Rockefeller, a lifelong Republican with a dim view of Mr. Carter's dovish foreign policy, collaborated closely with the Reagan campaign in its efforts to pre-empt and discourage what it derisively labeled an "October surprise" — a pre-election release of the American hostages, the papers show. The Chase team helped the Reagan campaign gather and spread rumors about possible payoffs to win the release, a propaganda effort that Carter administration officials have said impeded talks to free the captives. "I had given my all" to thwarting any effort by the Carter officials "to pull off the long-suspected 'October surprise,'" Mr. Reed wrote in a letter to his family after the election, apparently referring to the Chase effort to track and discourage a hostage release deal. He was later named Mr. Reagan's ambassador to Morocco.[46]

Of course, Reagan's "October Countersurprise" plot involved much more than a whisper campaign. As detailed below, the operation also included key deep state and intelligence figures like George H. W. Bush, Ted Shackley, and Robert Gates.[47] It remains one of the most well-documented *state crimes against democracy*. Its unadjudicated status, in the face of so much evidence, renders it emblematic of America's long global imperialist era— an epoch characterized by democratic decline and deep state dominance.

The Deep State Untethered: A Natural Experiment

It was during Carter's presidency that the contours of a supranational deep state can most clearly be discerned. In response to the post-Watergate intelligence investigations and to Stansfield Turner's housecleaning of the CIA's most nefarious operations officers, a new intelligence network was relied upon to do the things the CIA couldn't do at that historical juncture. Discussed further in chapter six, the Safari Club brought together the intelligence services of Egypt, Iran, Saudi Arabia, and Morocco. In addition to those foreign intelligence agencies, the Safari Club relied on current and former CIA officers, some of whom had been forced to leave the CIA during Watergate or its long aftermath. These would include Richard Helms, Ed Wilson, Tom Clines, and Ted Shackley.[48] The most common account of the Safari Club maintains that it was created by French intelligence officer Count Alexandre de Marenches in response to the post-Watergate scrutiny of intelligence operations. Other researchers argue that it began earlier, in the mid-1970s as a search for new proxies following the debacle that was US-South African intervention into the Angolan civil war.[49]

According to retired CIA officer Robert Crowley, it was Clark Clifford—the deep statesman who penned the CIA's *elastic clause* in the 1947 National Security Act—who approached Kamal Adham to request "that the Saudis consider setting up an informal intelligence network outside the United States during the investigations."[50] According to Joseph Trento, it was Watergate and the firing of James Angleton that prompted the Safari Club to start working with ex-DCI Richard Helms, then the US Ambassador to Iran. Near the end of his life, James Angleton said that,

> Colby destroyed counterintelligence. But because Colby was seen by Shackley and Helms as having betrayed the CIA to Congress, they simply began working with outsiders like Adham and Saudi Arabia. The traditional CIA answering to the president was an empty vessel having little more than technical capability.[51]

Trento claims that the Safari Club needed a banking network to fund its operations and for that purpose Kamal Adham—with CIA chief George Bush's "official blessing"—set about transforming the Bank of Credit and Commerce International into a global money-laundering operation. Bush himself reportedly created an account at the Paris branch of BCCI while he was the head of the CIA.[52] Kevin Phillips echoed some of these points, writing that upon becoming CIA chief "in January 1976, Bush cemented strong relations with the intelligence services of both Saudi Arabia and the shah of Iran. He worked closely with Kamal Adham, the head of Saudi intelligence, brother-in-law of King Faisal and an early BCCI insider."[53]

In 1977, according to Joseph Trento, CIA Associate Deputy Director for Operations Ted Shackley viewed Carter's recent election as a threat to CIA operators like himself. His solution was to act quickly to further privatize intelligence operations by making sure that the Safari Club would have access to resources which had been historically controlled by CIA's Directorate of Operations. He accomplished this by using Tom Clines to take control of Wilson's sprawling business operations and then taking Wilson out of the picture by drawing prosecutorial attention to "a former agent gone bad." Former CIA employee Shirley Brill was present with Shackley, Clines, and Wilson during this period. She had been there when the men made their plans, tampered with secret classified documents, made key payoffs, and ultimately betrayed Ed Wilson. She later surmised that it was Shackley and Clines who were the CIA officers who had gone off the reservation.[54] Speaking about Wilson's case, Shackley biographer David Corn—a journalist not unfriendly to the CIA—conceded, "They framed a guilty man. I think [Wilson is] a terrible fellow who got what he deserved, but they did frame him."[55]

After an eventful career in operations, Shackley in 1976 had risen to one of the highest clandestine jobs—associate deputy director for operations—thanks to his relationship with Ford's new CIA chief, George Bush. This cemented his loyalty to Bush and made him a potential future candidate for the top CIA post. According to notes from Reagan foreign policy adviser Richard Allen, Bush called him in October of 1980 requesting that Allen pass any information on Carter's hostage negotiations to Bush's ally Ted Shackley,[56] then operating in the realm of privatized intelligence operations. According to the indefatigable journalist and historian Robert Parry, CIA-connected individuals on the Reagan campaign like Shackley and Bush executed a successful plot whereby the Iranians held off the release of the hostages until after the election. According to Parry, a Paris meeting for Reagan's campaign manager, William Casey, was arranged by Casey's fellow Knight of Malta—the French spook, Pinay Circle member, and Safari Club organizer Alexandre de Marenches. Casey was a Wall Street lawyer, a former OSS/CIA officer, and would become CIA director under Reagan. At the Paris meeting, Casey met with Iranian and Israeli agents, promising to deliver arms that Iran needed in the war against Iraq.[57] In the end, the hostages were indeed released after the 1980 election. More precisely, the Americans were famously freed minutes after Reagan's inauguration. Within days, arms began flowing from Israel to Iran.

Over the years, many participants, insiders, and researchers have in various ways affirmed that Carter's hostage negotiations were sabotaged in what Peter Dale Scott terms "the Republican Countersurprise."[58] Notably, these include Gary Sick—the Iran desk officer of Carter's National Security Council,[59] Reagan campaign staffer and later administration analyst Barbara Honeggar,[60] Safari Club organizer Alexadre deMarenches (via his biographer David Andelman),[61] President Kennedy's press secretary Pierre Salinger,[62] Abolhassan Bani-Sadr—Iran's first president after the 1979 revolution,[63] CIA senior operations officer Duane "Dewey" Clarridge,[64] and Israeli Intelligence officer Ari Ben-Menashe.[65]

According to Ben-Menashe, longtime CIA officer and Booz-Allen Hamilton spook-in-residence Miles Copeland was present at a Georgetown meeting with Israeli intelligence officers. Attendees included David Kimche, chief of Mossad's foreign relations department, Tevel. According to Kimche, Israel opposed Carter's reelection because it was feared that in a second term, Carter would force Israel out of the occupied territories and establish a Palestinian state. As for Copeland, he told Robert Parry that any anti-Carter operation (i.e., the "October Countersurprise") would have been undertaken by "the CIA within the CIA." Parry took this to mean "the inner-most circle of powerful intelligence figures who felt they understood the strategic needs of the United States better than its elected leaders." In a discussion with Robert Parry, Copeland explained the opposition of the senior spooks to the president. Jimmy Carter "was not a stupid man," said Copeland. Worse, added Copeland in disgust and amazement, "He was a principled man . . . a Utopian. He believed, honestly, that you must do the right thing and take your chance on the consequences. He told me that. He literally believed that." Added Copeland, "There were many of us myself along with Henry Kissinger, David Rockefeller, Archie Roosevelt in the CIA at the time we believed very strongly that we were showing a kind of weakness, which people in Iran and elsewhere in the world hold in great contempt."[66]

Thanks largely to Robert Parry's tireless efforts,[67] the details around the seemingly treasonous sabotage of Carter's Iranian hostage negotiations have been well-established. This holds even as, true to form, the corporate media and the government continue to obfuscate the whole conspiratorial episode. Besides the Iran hostage crisis, Carter's defeat is often also attributed to the 1979–1980 oil shock which caused large gas price increases and long gas station lines. The gas shortage is commonly blamed on Iran's political tribulations. However, there is considerable evidence that US oil majors and Saudi Arabia were responsible for the shock. As detailed above, the Saudi decline in oil production should be viewed in the context the Safari Club, BCCI milieu in which Saudis were key figures.[68] As for the role of oil companies, petroleum industry analyst Robert Sherrill wrote that "America was importing more oil in January and February [of 1979], during the Iranian shutdown than it had during the same period in 1978." This indicates the Iranian shutdown was merely an excuse that oil importers used to slash the amount of gas they sold to US retailers. Wrote Sherrill, "A CIA study showed that during [the height of the crisis], US companies exported more oil than they had in those glut years 1977 and 1978."[69]

Consolidating the Deep State: Reagan's "Revolution"

In the election of 1980, Jimmy Carter became the first incumbent president to lose a reelection bid since Herbert Hoover. His meteoric, corporate media-fueled rise—from relative obscurity, to floundering presidential candidate, to frontrunner, to US President—is best understood as a triumph of deep state stage management of US politics. Despite his various concessions to America's neoliberal and neoconservative establishments, Carter in the end could not maintain the support of his neoliberal elite patrons, losing what Peter Dale Scott called "the Rockefeller 'Mandate from Heaven.'"[70] As president, Carter had to deal with a number of serious structural problems, many of which derived from the same deep political forces that first elevated and then destroyed his presidency. He obliquely or inadvertently alluded to this in his July 15, 1979 speech "Crisis of Confidence," the so-called "malaise speech."

> These changes did not happen overnight. They've come upon us gradually over the last generation, years that were filled with shocks

and tragedy. We were sure that ours was a nation of the ballot, not the bullet, until the murders of John Kennedy and Robert Kennedy and Martin Luther King Jr. We were taught that our armies were always invincible and our causes were always just, only to suffer the agony of Vietnam. We respected the presidency as a place of honor until the shock of Watergate.[71]

There is overwhelming evidence indicating that the political assassinations of the 1960s were not the product of "lone nuts." Rather, they were plausibly deniable covert operations with prearranged cover stories and designated patsies. In the case of JFK, it didn't even matter that the designated patsies were not cooperative. Oswald became arguably the first JFK conspiracy theorist when he said, "I'm just a patsy," i.e., *I have been set up as the fall guy for the assassination of the president.* Oswald, the most important prisoner in US history, was soon killed by Jack Ruby in a room full of policemen. Ruby—the second "lone nut"—eventually sought and was granted a new trial. He spoke to the press, saying that he had been put in his woeful position by men of power. He also claimed he was being poisoned and then proceeded to die prior to the start of the new trial he had been granted.

The assassinations of Malcolm X, RFK, and MLK followed thereafter. So did the Vietnam War, a conflict that JFK had worked to extricate the US from. Though Kennedy's Vietnam withdrawal was put forward in a regrettably protracted and deniable way owing to political calculations, historians like John Newman and James Galbraith have extensively documented JFK's efforts to defuse the Vietnam conflict with the planned denouement to occur after his reelection in 1964.[72] The specific instructions for Kennedy's Vietnam withdrawal were conveyed to the Joint Chiefs by their Chairman, General Maxwell Taylor. In an October 4, 1963 memorandum that suspiciously remained classified until 1997, Taylor explained the withdrawal orders:

> On 2 October the President *approved recommendations* on military matters contained in the report of the Secretary of Defense and the Chairman of the Joint Chiefs of Staff. The following actions derived

from these recommendations are directed: [. . .] *all planning will be directed toward preparing RVN forces for the withdrawal of all US special assistance units and personnel by the end of calendar year 1965.* The US Comprehensive Plan, Vietnam, will be revised to bring it into consonance with these objectives, and to reduce planned residual (post-1965) MAAG strengths to approximately pre-insurgency levels. . . . Execute the plan to withdraw 1,000 US military personnel by the end of 1963 [emphasis added]. . . .[73]

Note that the language, "all planning," leaves no room for the withdrawal denialists to assert that the withdrawal was contingent upon victory. The *victory* precondition argument that was made by people like Noam Chomsky—problematically in 1992 and inexplicably years later, well after declassification and McNamara's memoir should have settled the argument.[74] Like the truth of the Kennedy assassinations and of the October Countersurprise, the facts pertaining to JFK's Vietnam withdrawal are out there, yet are relegated to the realm of "historical counterfactual" or "conspiracy theory" by an ersatz mainstream which functions first and foremost to protect the legitimacy of the "liberal" empire and its elite beneficiaries.

Watergate exposed the criminality of the Nixon administration, demonstrating the reality of state criminality in a nominally democratic, open society. The fallout of Watergate led to the most significant exposure of US intelligence agency abuses. If examined objectively, the post-Watergate revelations demonstrate that Nixon and his underlings were, as criminals, bungling and amateurish in comparison to the intelligence agencies who had been carrying out similar but more systematic and egregious crimes for decades. Furthermore, critical examination of Watergate by numerous researchers indicates that the scandal was instigated and capitalized upon by right-wing, anti-Nixon elements of America's deep political system.

The public state responded to these crises with a number of investigations of the national security state, but these efforts were ultimately unsuccessful in reforming the system. Deep political forces obscured responsibility and subverted accountability, in large part through the dominance of corporate wealth over the national media and over electoral politics. The deep political dominance of the corporate overworld has been mediated by the national security state and its deep-seated connections to the underworld of organized crime. By 1968, these deep political interventions had created a democratic backlash as evidenced by the social unrest and protests in the US and around the world. At the time, the precariousness of US overworld hegemony was resolved by the MLK and RFK assassinations, as well as by Nixon's election. But these were no doubt stressful times for an Establishment whose response was perhaps best articulated in the Powell Memorandum and the Trilateral Commission's *Crisis of Democracy*. Both works demonstrate how the corporate rich and their intellectual servants had essentially come to the conclusion that America's liberal institutions needed to be better managed by the wealthy. Furthermore, and crucially, the widespread economic security of the middle-class came to be seen as destabilizing and thus undesirable.

The end of Bretton Woods was a pivotal moment in the history of the US deep state. The 1960s and 1970s saw something of a civil war within America's deep political system. The systemically destabilizing effects of Vietnam War spending created a conflict between "Prussians" and "traders," i.e., neoconservatives and neoliberals. The subsequent Petrodollar/ US Treasury Bill standard replaced the Bretton Woods gold standard and formed one of the two pillars of the subsequent *Dollar-Wall Street Regime*. This system gave America the Rumpelstiltskinian power to create money that the rest of the world would have to accept "as good as gold." Only a small number of economists and insiders recognized this at the time and in subsequent years. This historically unprecedented power led to the reconciling of the neoliberals and neoconservatives by facilitating US dominance of world trade *and* endless deficits for military spending. In the process, labor and manufacturing were jettisoned from political power. The aftermath of Watergate and the Vietnam War created a period of vulnerability for the deep state vis-à-vis the public state's brief attempts to probe the depths of the national security state. In the end, a decade that seemed like a setback for the deep state instead culminated with its decisive aggrandizement. Deep political forces brought Carter to the presidency, only to destroy his administration. Carter's downfall was overdetermined through orchestrated oil crises, the historic record-high interest rates of his Rockefeller-recommended Federal Reserve Chairman Paul Volcker,[75] and finally the deep state subversion of Carter's Iran hostage negotiations. The national media, previously the handmaiden to Carter's improbable ascension, endlessly covered the Iranian drama. Most famously the news program *Nightline* began airing in response to the hostage crisis, a depressing spectacle that the show covered every weeknight on network television.

With the election of the right-wing Ronald Reagan, the public state was largely vanquished, reduced to the largely symbolic status which it maintains to this day. The Wall Street-Dollar Regime imposed the austere Washington Consensus on the rest of the world. Meanwhile US profligacy soared to levels unprecedented in peacetime, even while median wages, savings, and general economic security plummeted. The efforts to reign in the clandestine services in the post-Watergate 1970s only served to further institutionalize the organized irresponsibility of the covert netherworld. In the wake of World War II, the embryonic deep state had seminal parapolitical institutions including banks (e.g., Castle Bank) and privatized paramilitary/intelligence outfits like the World Commerce Corporation or the various Anti-Communist Leagues. The 1970s saw more powerful iterations. Notably these included the Nugan Hand Bank and later the BCCI-Safari Club milieu which brought together right-wing Republicans, the Saudis, Israeli operators, and networks of wayward spooks. With Reagan's victory, many of these players were brought in from the cold, so to speak. Quite a few would surface in the Iran-Contra scandal, a conspiratorial mélange comprised of multiple intertwined illegal policies and operations. It is difficult to sum up the state criminality that Iran-Contra represented. A broader view of the policies and players suggests it would be more appropriate, if less pithy, to call it the *October Countersurprise-Iran-Contra-Cocaine-BCCI-Mujahideen-Heroin meta-conspiracy*.

While carrying out these exceptionist parapolitical operations in the furtherance of deep state grand strategy, the Reagan administration also presided over further planning of the Doomsday Project or Continuity of Government operations. The contours of these operations would remain obscure and largely in stasis until the events of September 11, 2001. At that point, certain emergency measures were enacted, further empowering the federal government with exceptionist emergency powers, the extent of which the public is still unaware. For all the reasons above—and for the massive, ongoing, and heretofore irreversible transfer of wealth and power to the superrich—the election of Ronald Reagan was a milestone. It represents the end of a contentious period in which the public state coexisted uneasily with the national security state as components of a visible political system which operated in tandem with a deep political system. Reagan's election marked the ascension of deep political forces to a position of sovereignty. Practically speaking, what emerged was an exceptionist tripartite state comprised of (1) a feckless public state, (2) a sprawling security state, and (3) the anti-democratic deep state to which they are subordinated. This consolidation and institutionalization of top-down power was such that US governance could thereafter be described as a *deep state system*.

CHAPTER 9

THE WATERGATE MYSTERY: WRAPPED IN A RIDDLE INSIDE AN ENIGMA

Beneath the Myth

Watergate is a singularly bizarre episode in US history. It is arguably the only instance in which high criminality was aggressively investigated by US government officials propelled forward by the vigorous efforts of the national media. In the end, the disgraced President Nixon was spared from prosecution. Ford's pardon of Nixon precluded, likely for all time, any definitive account of what Watergate was really all about. This chapter is an attempt to understand and explain Watergate by applying the political insights of tripartite state theory in the context of *exceptionism*. Of key significance are various aspects of events which belie the myth that Watergate demonstrated the strength of our liberal institutions like the "free press" and the constitutional rule of law.

Many of the key Watergate figures and events deserve to be reconsidered in light of the critical scholarship produced in the intervening decades. One important figure, Bob Woodward, today seems less of a plucky cub reporter and more of an intelligence operative of some kind. He had previously been a mentee of Admiral Robert Welander and later Communications Duty Officer to then-Chief of Naval Operations Admiral Thomas Moorer.[1] In 1970, the anti-détente Admiral Moorer authorized Admiral Welander to spy on the National Security Council—the aforementioned Moorer-Radford affair.[2] According to Admiral Welander, Woodward knew of the spy ring at least eight months before someone else broke the story in the national media.[3] It is hard to overstate the antipathy that the right-wing US militarists had toward President Nixon. Chief of Naval Operations, Admiral Elmo Zumwalt described the administration as "inimical to the security of the United States." The admiral eventually left the White House because he came to understand that "its own officials and experts reflected Henry Kissinger's world view: that the dynamics of history are on the side of the Soviet Union; that before long the USSR will be the only superpower on earth and that the duty of policy-makers, therefore, is at all costs to conceal from the people their probable fate. . . ."[4]

In the Watergate mythology, Woodward's top source "Deep Throat" is something of a conscientious insider, unhappy with the immoral lawlessness of the presidency. In fact, "Deep Throat" was a composite character—chiefly FBI officer Mark Felt. Rather than being a model of scrupulous rectitude, Felt presided over some of the FBI's most criminal and morally dubious endeavors, specifically the infamous COINTELPRO operations of the 1960s.[5]

The infamous "Plumbers" were also of a decidedly right-wing bent relative to President Nixon. The Plumbers involved in the Watergate break-in were anti-Castro Cubans, "retired" CIA officers, and persons with prior histories of working as CIA agents. The Plumbers' first operation was to break into the Beverly Hills office of Lewis J. Fielding, psychiatrist to Pentagon Papers' leaker Daniel Ellsberg. Using CIA equipment, E. Howard Hunt went with G. Gordon Liddy prior to the break-in and took a number of photographs outside the office. These images included photographs of Dr. Fielding's car in its reserved parking space, of Liddy in the rear car park of the doctor's office, and of the building where Fielding lived.[6] Though Hunt was supposedly not working for the CIA anymore, he had enlisted the help of the CIA's Technical Services Division for this task. The CIA obtained copies of the photos taken by Hunt and Liddy during their break-in. In conversation with two men who know a lot about Watergate and this incident—Daniel Ellsberg and Peter Dale Scott—both men agreed that the CIA obtained and held those photos to have a potential source of leverage over the presidency.[7]

As for the Plumbers themselves, James McCord—the chief architect of the Watergate break-in—is of particular interest. Historian and journalist Jim Hougan concluded that McCord so clearly botched the Watergate break-in that he must have intended for it to fail.[8] Likewise, Peter Dale Scott stated flatly that the break-in "was surely set up to be disclosed."[9] A cursory look at the Watergate narrative would have McCord as a hapless bungler turned whistleblower, but according to no less an authority than James Angleton, "McCord was an operator, not merely a technician."[10] With that in mind, it was McCord's inexplicable incompetence at the Watergate that led to the Plumbers' arrest. On the day of June 16th, McCord went into the Watergate while the doors were unlocked, and he placed a strip of tape across the door's latch so that it could not be locked afterwards. When the Plumbers arrived hours later, they found the door shut and the tape removed. The absence of the tape meant that the method, and thus the break-in, had been discovered. Everyone but McCord wanted to postpone the operation. He ordered Eugenio Martinez to pick open the door, during which time McCord went elsewhere for some unexplained reason. The Cubans left the door taped open for McCord believing that as one of the world's top intelligence operatives, McCord would have the wherewithal to cover his tracks by removing the tape. After McCord returned from his mysterious five-minute absence, Martinez had the presence of mind to ask him if he had remembered to remove the tape. McCord answered that he had done so, even though he had not. Soon after, the security guard who had initially found and removed the tape returned to the door. Finding it taped again, he called the police, leading to the arrest of the Plumbers.[11]

McCord's background is relevant and highly intriguing. For a time, McCord—as a colonel in the Air Force Reserve—worked as part of the Wartime Information Security Program (WISP), part of the Office of Emergency Preparedness.[12] This was a component of "the Doomsday Project," a sprawling operation which eventually morphed into "Continuity of Government" planning and organizing.[13] The function of

WISP was to formulate and activate contingency plans in the event of a declaration by either the President or the Secretary of Defense that a state of "national emergency" existed. In such an event, WISP would exercise censorship over the media, mail, and telecommunications. Additionally, civilian "security risks" like antiwar activists, union leaders, and assorted radicals would be detained and held in military facilities.[14]

McCord also worked on important CIA matters. When Allen Dulles introduced an Air Force colonel to McCord, he told the officer, "This man is the best man we have."[15] While working in the CIA's Security Office, McCord led a CIA counterintelligence operation against the Fair Play for Cuba Committee, a CIA operation illegally carried out in the US without the permission of the FBI.[16] There is much evidence that McCord never severed his ties to the CIA despite his "retirement" in 1970. One of McCord's former CIA subordinates, a man who later worked for the Secret Service in the Nixon White House, stated that the Secret Service had been "infiltrated" by McCord and the CIA from the beginning of Nixon's presidency. He asserted that "you had these guys from the [CIA's McCord-run] Office of Security working in the White House under Secret Service cover."[17] Additionally, McCord visited CIA headquarters in Langley the week before the infamous Watergate burglary.[18]

Politically, McCord was an ultra-rightist and as such did not approve of the Nixon White House. In the aftermath of Watergate, McCord issued the *McCord Washington Newsletter*—a sparsely circulated series of newsletters in which he elaborated a strange, John Birch-esque conspiracy theory positing that the Rockefellers were grasping for total control of the organs of US national security and were using Henry Kissinger and the Council on Foreign Relations to advance their nefarious ends.[19] McCord also expressed dismay at Nixon's moves against the CIA, including the firing of DCI Helms, stating that "freedom itself was never so imperiled. Nazi Germany rose and fell under exactly the same philosophy of governmental operation." In his memoir, McCord wrote of Watergate, "the whole future of the nation was at stake. If the Administration could get away with this [. . .], it would certainly stop at nothing thereafter. The precedent [. . .] would be beyond belief, beyond recovery, and a disaster beyond any possible reversal."[20]

In addition to the spying, militarist generals and the comically clumsy, CIA-connected Plumbers, there were other deep personages in the White House that served to undermine and ultimately undo Nixon. John Dean, arguably the central Watergate character, was at a minimum one of the most damaging of the Nixon officials who turned against the administration. Like James McCord, Dean had previously worked in the realm of COG operations as the associate deputy attorney general.[21] As explosive as Dean's Watergate testimony was, Nixon nevertheless might have survived were it not for the exposure of the White House taping system. That ultimately fatal revelation was made by Alexander Butterfield, the White House deputy assistant in charge of supervising the President's recording system. In 1975, Daniel Schorr of CBS News reported that Butterfield was the CIA's "man in the White House." This was denied by Butterfield, the CIA, and E. Howard Hunt. It was Hunt who had reportedly informed Schorr's source—retired Air Force Colonel L. Fletcher Prouty—of Butterfield's CIA status. The report was soon deemed by the press to be unsubstantiated.[22] However, in an Inspector-General report, the CIA admitted to a "practice of detailing CIA employees to the White House and various government agencies" and that the CIA had agents in "intimate components of the Office of the President."[23] Both Haldeman and Nixon's personal secretary, Rose Mary Woods, suspected that Butterfield was a CIA man. This is partly due to a dispute over how Butterfield came to work for the White House. Butterfield stated that Haldeman approached him initially while Haldeman maintained that Butterfield wrote a letter requesting to join the White House staff. Additionally, Haldeman came to see Butterfield's Air Force retirement as unnecessary and suspicious. He suspected that it was required per the protocol regarding the CIA's cover arrangements with the Air Force.[24] Around the time of his explosive testimony, Butterfield said that he had been hoping that he wouldn't be questioned about the tapes. Later, he privately admitted that he wanted committee members to ask about the recording system.[25]

Nixon and the CIA's "Bay of Pigs" Files

Nixon had a strained relationship with the CIA since the early days of his administration. A few days after taking office, Nixon ordered Ehrlichman to obtain from DCI Richard Helms files pertaining to the tumultuous period leading up to the Kennedy administration's end. After six months, the agency had produced nothing. Said Ehrlichman, "Those bastards in Langley are holding back something [. . .] Imagine that. The Commander-in-Chief wants to see a document and the spooks say he can't have it. [. . .] From the way they're protecting it, it must be pure dynamite."[26] So too thought Nixon, apparently. In October of 1971, the president summoned Helms to the White House. Before he arrived, Nixon and Erlichman discussed Helms's stonewalling on the president's request for those "Bay of Pigs" documents. We will return again to this matter, but apparently "Bay of Pigs" was Nixon's euphemism for the JFK assassination. In this October 1971 conversation, Ehrlichman tells Nixon that he didn't explain to Helms his true purpose for seeking the documents, saying "I was kind of mysterious about it. The two men think that they have leverage on Helms. Says Ehrlichman, "Helms is scared to death of this guy [E. Howard] Hunt we got working for us because he knows where a lot of the bodies are buried."[27]

When Helms arrives, Nixon tells him that he wants to discuss the "sensitive" matter of the documents that he's trying to obtain. He tries to reassure Helms by telling him that he is in full support of "the dirty tricks department." He says to Helms, "I know what happened in Iran and I know what happened in Guatemala and I totally approve of that. I know what happened with the planning of the Bay of Pigs." It would seem that in this instance he is not using "Bay of Pigs" as a euphemism. Nixon adds that "The problem was not the CIA. My interest there is solely to know the facts." With Helms unmoved, Nixon continued to press his case, reminding his CIA director that he is the US President. "First, this is my information [and] second, I need it for defensive reasons, for a negotiation." Still, the pensive Helms was unpersuaded. Nixon then tried a different tack—saying that he wanted the files so that he could protect the Agency.[28] Eventually, the president said,

> The "Who shot John?" angle . . . is Eisenhower to blame? Is Kennedy to blame? Is Johnson to blame? Is Nixon to blame? Etc, etc. It may become, not by me, a very vigorous issue but if it does, I need to

know what is necessary to protect frankly the intelligence gathering and the Dirty Tricks Department and I will protect it. I have done more than my share of lying to protect you, and I believe it's totally right to do it.[29]

Nixon was never able to get those CIA "Bay of Pigs" documents that he was after. His efforts and their failure reveal some important facts. Upon taking office, Nixon understood that the CIA could undermine a presidential administration. Belying their ostensible status of being subordinate to the president, they withheld documents from the rest of the government at their discretion. Furthermore, Nixon's inquiry about "Who shot John?" indicates that he thought it possible that the CIA was involved in the JFK assassination. He could not have but made the obvious inference that the agency was also a potential threat to his administration and even to his person.

A Fractured Establishment Turns to Leak Warfare

Under Nixon, the Establishment was coming apart over the Vietnam War. The formerly unified Council on Foreign Relations was emblematic of this rift, as its membership became increasingly divided over the issue. Of chief importance to drawdown proponents was the potential damage to the dollar—and thus, to US hegemony—should the war continue.[30] This conflict played out in part through the use of leaks to the press. In June of 1971, the *New York Times* began publishing the Pentagon Papers after RAND analyst Daniel Ellsberg leaked the top-secret Defense Department study to the media. Ellsberg's actions led to the creation of Nixon's Plumbers unit—a collection of dirty tricksters assembled to help the president stop leaks. Though the Pentagon Papers leak is typically cited as the impetus for the creation of the Plumbers, Nixon was initially not very concerned about it because the Papers mainly revealed the perfidy of previous administrations. In fact, it may be that a different motive was at least as decisive as the Pentagon Papers leak. Nixon worried that the leaking of sensitive Vietnam secrets could portend a more explosive revelation. Namely, Nixon was worried that documents would surface detailing how he had sabotaged the 1968 Paris peace talks in order to keep the Johnson administration from ending the Vietnam War and thereby hurting Nixon's presidential chances. On June 17, 1971, only four days after the first Pentagon Papers story was published in the *New York Times,* Nixon told Haldeman, "God damn it, get in and get those files. Blow the safe and get them." Around two weeks later, he repeated this order, saying, "I want Brookings . . . just break in, break in, and take it out. Do you understand? You're to break into the place, rifle the files, and bring them in." The following day, the president persisted: "Did they get the Brookings Institute raided last night? No? Get it done. I want it done. I want the Brookings Institute safe cleaned out."[31] For unknown reasons, the Brookings burglary apparently never happened, but as Robert Parry surmised, "Nixon's desperation to locate Johnson's peace-talk file was an important link in the chain of events that led to the creation of Nixon's Plumbers unit and then to Watergate."[32]

These struggles over the files related to the "Bay of Pigs" and to the 1968 October Surprise offer important and obscure background for understanding Watergate. For good reason, Nixon suspected that he could gain leverage over the CIA if he could acquire documentation of its role in Dallas. Also for good reason, Nixon was extremely concerned that his treasonous intervention in the 1968 Paris peace talks could derail his reelection chances. To the president's great misfortune, he erred in creating the Plumbers unit. Adding Hunt to mix was also a catastrophic error. Before Watergate, Nixon thought Hunt's presence would make the CIA wary "because [Hunt] knows where a lot of the bodies are buried." In case it needs to be stated: the opposite happened. Hunt's actions gave great leverage to Nixon's enemies, ultimately contributing in no small way to Nixon's resignation.

Nixon Ensnared

On June 23, 1972—six days after the arrest of the Watergate burglars— Nixon instructed Haldeman to speak with CIA officials. He was tasked with persuading the CIA to inform the FBI that the Watergate break-in was a CIA operation and that the Bureau should stop the investigation. Though this move led ultimately to Nixon's resignation, the initiative was not on its face dishonest or unreasonable in the context of Cold War executive prerogative. On the infamous "smoking gun tape," Nixon evinced no knowledge as to why the burglars had chosen the DNC headquarters. Haldeman was recorded saying, "[T]he FBI agents who are working the case, at this point, feel that's what it is. This is CIA." Nixon concurred: "Of course, this is a, this is a Hunt [operation that if exposed] will uncover a lot of things. You open that scab there's a hell of a lot of things and that we just feel that it would be very detrimental to have this thing go any further. This involves these Cubans, Hunt, and a lot of hanky-panky that we have nothing to do with ourselves." Nixon told Haldeman that he should inform the CIA that "the President believes that it is going to open the whole Bay of Pigs thing up again."[33]

When Haldeman made the request to the CIA, they initially stonewalled him. Then he played the president's "trump card" by stating, "The President asked me to tell you this entire affair may be connected to the Bay of Pigs, and if it opens up, the Bay of Pigs may be blown . . ." A dramatic response followed from DCI Helms who shouted, "The Bay of Pigs had nothing to do with this. I have no concern about the Bay of Pigs." After a moment of tense silence, Haldeman reminded Helms that he was merely conveying the president's message. Helms settled down and subsequently agreed to help the Nixon White House. He instructed his deputy Vernon Walters to "remind Mr. Gray of the agreement between the FBI and the CIA that if they run into or expose one another's 'assets,' they will not interfere with each other."[34] As discussed earlier, Haldeman eventually concluded that "in all of those Nixon references to the Bay of Pigs, he was actually referring to the Kennedy assassination."[35] Given that Nixon had been the action officer for the planning of the Bay of Pigs operation[36] and that the fallout from the operation had already resulted in the firing of three top CIA officials including DCI Allen Dulles, it is unclear what other explanation could account for Nixon's deployment of "the whole Bay of Pigs thing."

As CIA officers, McCord and Hunt were both veterans of the Bay of Pigs debacle. During Watergate, McCord testified that he never knew Hunt before joining the Nixon White House, but in all likelihood their relationship dated much further back, probably to before the Bay of Pigs fiasco. It has long been alleged that Hunt was in Dallas on the day of JFK's assassination.[37] According to a close associate, James McCord admitted to being in Dallas on November 22, 1963.[38] Another odd JFK assassination angle to Watergate was James McCord's hiring of Bud Fensterwald as his legal counsel. Fensterwald was most notable for running the Committee to Investigate Assassinations, a legal advocacy group working to reinvestigate the assassinations of the Kennedy brothers and Martin Luther King.[39] This raises the possibility that at different moments and with different results, both Nixon and anti-Nixon forces used the prospect of Kennedy assassination revelations to influence the course of Watergate.

One of the earliest critics of the prevailing Watergate myth was Peter Dale Scott. He began immediately looking into the connections between Dallas and Watergate following the initial arrests after the break-in. Scott's suspicions were immediately aroused because he had already been investigating several of the theretofore largely unknown burglars in the course of his research into the Kennedy assassination. For example, Watergate burglar and Bay of Pigs veteran Frank Sturgis, a.k.a. Frank Fiorini, came to be a JFK assassination suspect of sorts. In 1977, the *San Francisco Chronicle* reported, "Frank Sturgis said yesterday the CIA planned the break-in because high officials felt the then-president was becoming too powerful and was overly interested in the assassination of President Kennedy."[40] More concretely, in the immediate aftermath of the assassination, Sturgis himself was involved in a conspiracy falsely depicting Oswald as part of a Miami-based, communist Cuban plot to kill the president. At the same time that the FBI was receiving two forged letters describing such a plot, a Miami journalist named James Buchanan was publishing reports attributed to Frank Sturgis that Oswald had been in Miami where he met with Cuban intelligence agents. Buchanon's brother Jerry contributed to this effort by also publishing reports placing Oswald in Miami in 1963. The sources for the Buchanans' stories were both Miami anti-Castro groups: the CIA-sponsored Student revolutionary Directorate (DRE) and International Anti-Communist Brigade. The Buchanans themselves were both members of the latter group which was led by Bay of Pigs veteran Frank Sturgis. After the Cuban Missile Crisis, the Kennedy administration cracked down on Cuban raids launched from the US. In September of 1963, the *New York Times* reported that six individuals were issued "strong warnings" for their anti-Castro operations. Frank Sturgis was identified as one of the six.[41]

One possibility that emerges from these events is that anti-Communist militants were trying to plant evidence of Oswald as part of a communist Cuban plot to provide a pretext allowing the US to invade Cuba. A more sophisticated variant of this theory posits that the clumsy efforts were meant to be exposed. The FBI quickly ascertained that the two letters—from ostensibly different sources—were produced by the same typewriter, and the FBI's painstaking compendium of Oswald's movements showed that he had not been in Miami at the times indicated by the letters and reports. Thusly, the anti-Castro Cubans could have been enlisted in the Dallas operation, but their goal of a dangerous, potentially nuclear war with Cuba could be thwarted while subsequently justifying a massive official refutation of any Dallas conspiracy.[42] As complicated as this might seem, it is known that Warren and other key officials did agree to the "two lone nuts" theory of the assassination well before there was any basis for such a conclusion. As PBS reported in 2013,

> [Earl Warren] said that Johnson felt the argument that Khrushchev and Castro had killed Kennedy might mean nuclear war. Warren said he responded, "Well, Mr. President, if in your opinion it is that bad, surely my personal views don't count." So as the FBI record indicates, President Johnson, Deputy Attorney General Katzenbach, and FBI Director Hoover accepted that they would have to be in line with a lone-assassin scenario, a decision that was made no later than Sunday, two days after the assassination.[43]

In light of these revelations, the Miami-based plot to clumsily frame Castro would have been either overkill (since the no-conspiracy theory was already accepted), or a sop to the anti-Castro Cubans who would not—could not—be given the invasion of Cuba they were promised.

Of Felled Trees and Scorched Deserts

On December 28, 1972 McCord sent a prophetic message to the White House's Jack Caulfield stating that, "If Helms goes, and if the WG operation is laid at CIA's [feet], where it does not belong, every tree in the forest will fall. It will be a scorched desert. The whole matter is at the precipice right now."[44] Despite being employed by the Nixon White House, McCord's loyalty to the intelligence community—and to Helms in particular—seems apparent. McCord described White House attempts to blame CIA personnel for the break-in as "imply[ing] the deepest corruption and perversion of the criminal justice system in recent history."[45] In contrast to his dire assessment of the Nixon administration, McCord kept on his office wall a photograph of himself receiving an award from Richard Helms.[46] On the photograph was inscribed, "To Jim/ With *deep* appreciation" (emphasis in the original).[47] Following his arrest, McCord wrote a letter to Helms stating that he would not allow the CIA to be blamed for the Watergate break-in: "Rest assured that I will not be a patsy to this latest ploy. They will have to dream up a better one than this. . . ."[48] The CIA was later criticized harshly for failing to inform the FBI of the existence of McCord's letters.[49]

Although Helms initially acquiesced to Nixon's request for CIA help in neutralizing the FBI's investigation of Watergate, such was not the case for long. Within days of "the whole Bay of Pigs thing" confrontation between Helms and Haldeman, Helms informed the White House and the FBI that the CIA had nothing to fear from a thorough investigation.[50] This likely contributed to Nixon's firing of DCI Helms— the move that McCord warned would cause "every tree in the forest [to] fall." But after winning a landslide re-election victory over George McGovern, Nixon felt he had a mandate to make long-desired reforms. On November 20 of 1972, Nixon fired Helms. As consolation of a sort, he offered Helms the Iranian ambassadorship. As discussed in the previous chapter, this was a move that would have fateful consequences post-Nixon. But with his second term resoundingly secured, Nixon set about aggressively reforming the CIA. This was, after all, the agency that had resisted the president's demands to tailor intelligence assessments according to policy and whose director had refused to assist in the Watergate cover up. The new DCI, James Schlesinger, had previously helped Nixon pressure the agency by producing a 1971 study calling for the reorganization of the intelligence community. As Nixon's director of Central Intelligence, Schlesinger fired over a thousand agents, including much of the top leadership.[51]

In response to revelations that CIA veterans Hunt and McCord had received agency assistance with their CREEP "dirty tricks," DCI Schlesinger issued a May 9, 1973 directive calling for the compilation of what came to be known as the CIA's "family jewels." Drafted by deputy director for operations William Colby, Schlesinger's directive ordered senior CIA officers to immediately report on any conceivably unauthorized CIA activities, past or present. By the time Colby had been named as Schlesinger's successor, he had accumulated a 693-page notebook of memos.[52] With his massive downsizing of CIA personnel and his creation of the "family jewels," Schlesinger served as Nixon's instrument against the CIA and in so doing became the most unpopular DCI in the agency's history.[53] Apparently to ease White House-CIA tensions, Nixon moved Schlesinger to Secretary of Defense and Colby became CIA chief.

In the end, Nixon failed in his attempt to exert control over the CIA, an effort that was one element of broader campaigns to defuse Watergate and to bring more presidential control over the federal government. On the surface, Watergate demonstrates the historical fact of conspiratorial high criminality in the US. Within the scope the scandal, there are a vast number of criminal conspiracies. Any comprehensive account is impossible thanks to Ford's pardon. In a sense, Watergate validates deHaven-Smith's SCAD theory as well as the generic liberal perspective that views Nixon's resignation as validation of American norms relating to justice and the constitutional rule of law. However, the critical scholarship has done much to complicate, even as it affirms, deHaven-Smith's SCAD interpretation of Watergate. The liberal myth of Watergate is largely untenable.

A Media-Driven Scandal

Woodward's close connections with hawkish, anti-Nixon military intelligence circles are highly suspicious, given that in short order he changed careers to become a journalist and proceeded to break the proverbial "story of the century," reporting which led to the downfall of President Nixon and the reversal of many of his policies. Additionally, another deep state actor who proved instrumental to Nixon's removal—Mark Felt, a.k.a. "Deep Throat"—was hardly the scrupulous, concerned public servant depicted in *All the President's Men*. Rather, Felt was the man who

supervised the notorious COINTELPRO operations in the sixties. Jim
Hougan adroitly sums it up: with Felt having been "convicted for 'conspiring to injure and oppress citizens of the United States,' [and] having authorized numerous black-bag jobs and warrantless searches at the
Bureau, he seems an unlikely person to be so deeply shocked by the break-
in at the Watergate."[54] Furthermore, the *Post* itself is not an entity with
a plausible history of speaking truth to power or exposing state crimes.
When the Washington Post Company purchased *Newsweek*, *Post* publisher Philip Graham was informed by CIA officials that the agency had
a practice of using the outlet for cover purposes. This disclosure does not
likely represent the beginning of the company's relationship to the CIA.
According to a former CIA deputy director, it was common knowledge
within the agency that "Graham was somebody you could get help from.
[. . .] Frank Wisner dealt with him."[55] In fact, Carl Bernstein reported
that Graham was "probably Wisner's closest friend."[56] This is noteworthy
because as deputy director of the CIA from 1950 to 1965, Wisner was
not only CIA's top architect of "black ops," but the creator of the CIA's
propaganda apparatus. He termed this CIA disinformation machine, "the
Mighty Wurlitzer" and he ran it with the help of numerous journalists
and media outlets.[57] Likewise, Phil Graham's successor—his widowed wife
Katherine Graham—is a much more ambiguous figure than the heroine
depicted in *All the President's Men* and more recently in Steven Spielberg's
The Post. She was listed in a 1965 CIA memo as one of the journalists who
had met with CIA officer Ray Cline as part of Cline's efforts to use the
media to improve the agency's image.[58]

Post-Watergate history reveals the Watergate-era coverage to be a
very strange aberration. On the whole, the prestige media—including
the Post—took an approach after Watergate that tended to re-legitimize
the US government after Nixon's resignation. This can be seen in the US
media's unfavorable coverage of the post-Watergate congressional investigations of the intelligence community—the Pike Committee, the Church
Committee, and the House Select Committee on Assassinations.[59]

In the 1980s, matters deteriorated further. At the *Washington Post*-
owned *Newsweek*, journalist Robert Parry was discouraged from further investigating Iran-Contra. A superior told him that "we don't want

another Watergate." Parry was also prevented from covering the Contra-cocaine angle. After Senator John Kerry advanced the story with an April 1989 Senate report, *Newsweek* described the senator dismissively as "a randy conspiracy buff."[60] In 1988, Katherine Graham spoke at CIA headquarters, asserting that "We live in a dirty and dangerous world," and that there were "some things the general public does not need to know and shouldn't." Though she offered some defense of the "free press," she also stated that "official secrecy is necessary to preserve liberty," and that the government should "discipline employees who violate security regulations."[61] Also in the 1980s, Bob Woodward enjoyed a special connection with Reagan's notorious DCI William Casey, a relationship Woodward described as "a partnership over secrets," adding that "we were both obsessed with secrets."[62]

The *Washington Post* was also one of the chief newspapers that attacked the work of Gary Webb in the 1990s. Webb's articles revealed the CIA protection of Contra-cocaine traffickers whose profligate operations fueled the Los Angeles crack epidemic that began in the 1980s.[63] Though a CIA Inspector General report would later confirm and expand upon Webb's central allegations, his career and life were essentially ruined by the counterattack of the CIA and its media allies like the *Washington Post*. For historical and methodological purposes, the CIA eventually created a report detailing the way this unfolded. The agency's "Managing a Nightmare" report even presented some of the back story detailing how CIA propagandists utilized mainstream journalists. Doing the agency's biding, these CIA assets in the media launched an overwhelming counterattack against Webb that greatly diminished him and depicted the Contra-cocaine scandal as a fanciful conspiracy theory.[64]

The *Post* would go on to promote the militarism of the GWOT as well as subsequent wars and regime change campaigns, most notably in its op-ed page which offers readers a lively spectrum of opinions ranging from pro-war "liberal interventionist" to pro-war neoconservative. At present, the *Post* is owned by the world's richest man, Amazon founder Jeff Bezos. Amazon has a $600 million contract with the CIA,[65] which would appear to deepen the already problematic ties that the paper has historically maintained with the agency. And—perhaps as a subtle nod to George

Orwell—the *Washington Post* began deploying the phrase "Democracy Dies in Darkness" as its tagline in 2017.

A *Structural Deep Event* or an Establishment Civil War?

In light of all this, how then should Watergate be interpreted? Scott's characterization of Watergate as a *structural deep event* is most apt. In a similar vein, the event could be described as part of an Establishment civil war of sorts. Despite his backing by conservative forces in US society, Nixon pursued several policies that exercised key constituencies of America's deep political system, most broadly understood as the Prussian/neoconservative and trader/neoliberal portions of the US elite. The Prussians were bitterly opposed to *détente* and to rapprochement with China. They also became increasingly alarmed by their not unreasonable belief Kissinger was an agent of the internationalist David Rockefeller. As such, they believed, Kissinger was prepared to sacrifice American primacy for control of international trade.

The commercially minded traders, on the other hand, did not approve of Nixon's liberal economic policies such as the creation of the EPA, the creation of OSHA, price controls, and tariffs. It was Nixon's "economic nationalism" in response to the collapse of Bretton Woods that led to the resignation of C. Fred Bergsten, Kissinger's assistant for International Economic Affairs.[66] Bergsten went on to join forces with other representatives of transnational capital in order to promote cooperation between centers of transnational capital and to return the US to a "free trade" orientation. These efforts would soon culminate in the 1973 Rockefeller/ Brzezinski establishment of the Trilateral Commission.[67] As Jeff Frieden notes, "[I]nvolved or not in Nixon's demise, the international financiers sighed with relief when Richard Nixon made his stumbling feverish exit."[68]

It is crucial to note that this conflict between militarist neoconservatives and commercially minded neoliberals was analogous to the same conflux of forces that gave rise to the military industrial complex in the late 1940s and early 1950s. In 1950, the US "dollar gap" with Europe was cited in NSC-68 as a major factor necessitating US rearmament. This served to jumpstart the flagging US economy without strengthening any sort of social democratic public sector *and* it kept Europe and East Asia firmly in the US camp in the Cold War. The massive military spending called for in NSC-68 was achieved with the serendipitous outbreak of the Korean War. It served to solve the "dollar gap" problem in Europe and Japan.[69] This served to establish a key foundational aspect of the postwar US empire: trade and capital flows going across the Atlantic and Pacific oceans with the US at the center, rather than across Eurasia. Though Nixon was president at a cataclysmic moment with the end of Bretton Woods, he was a strong executive who pursued liberal and nationalistic policies. For Nixon, as noted earlier, the oil shocks his administrated in response to the dollar overhang were aimed at strengthening the US economy in part by beggaring Japan and Western Europe. This was precisely the opposite approach from what the capitalist elite had had sought to achieve with America's postwar rearmament. Thus David Rockefeller, a staunch Republican, created the Trilateral Commission in 1973 to promote (contra Nixon) a US foreign policy that would reintegrate these economic zones and thereby maintain US hegemony over the post–Bretton Woods capitalist world.

Wheels Within Wheels: Sex Rings and Surveillance

For all the books that have been written on Watergate, mysteries persist. One of the chief unresolved questions involves the Watergate break-in itself. Why were the Plumbers ordered to break into the DNC headquarters? Spencer Oliver, the DNC official whose phone was successfully tapped by the plumbers, offered a relatively pedestrian theory: he was a target of the Plumbers' conspiratorial mischief due to his own efforts to conspire against the pending McGovern nomination—a nomination favored by CREEP, since McGovern was seen as the weakest potential opponent in the general election.[70]

A more salacious revisionist theory is that the break-ins were related to a D.C. prostitution ring. The "call-girl theory" was first suggested by Anthony Lukas in 1976. Jim Hougan greatly expanded on the theory with his 1984 book *Secret Agenda*.[71] Authors Len Colodny and Robert Getlin built upon Hougan's work with *Silent Coup*.[72] To summarize, the theory posits that the break-ins to the Democratic National Committee Offices were carried out in order to gain intelligence pertaining to a call-girl operation. The prostitution ring was based in the nearby Columbia Plaza, and it used the office of Maxie Wells—the secretary to DNC official Spencer Oliver. Two mysteries related to Watergate have helped fuel the revisionist accounts. The first has been mentioned already; no one has ever explained who ordered the second break-in and why. The second mystery pertains to the fact that Watergate burglar Eugenio Martinez was arrested with the key to Maxie Wells's desk in his possession. This fact was unknown until discovered by Hougan who included an account in *Secret Agenda*.[73] Martinez has always suspected that James McCord set up the burglars that night. During executive session testimony in 1973, he expressly stated that he doubted he would live much longer. Instead, he was the only one of the burglars who received a pardon. At the age of ninety-six, he was asked by Shane O'Sullivan (2018) why he had the key that night. He laughed as he gave his response: "I don't remember and I don't want to remember. I want to be consistent with what I said before. I don't want it to come out, I'm sorry."[74]

The "call girl theory" is a Byzantine subject, further complicated by competing, contradictory accounts from different sources, many of whom are convicted felons and/or otherwise less than reputable. Nevertheless, critical researchers have created a coherent revisionist account—albeit one that ultimately raises more questions than can be answered definitively. The story began on April 6, 1972. On that day, the FBI raided the apartment and law offices of a Washington D.C. lawyer named Phillip Bailley. The FBI search was pursuant to alleged violations of the Mann Act, a law which prohibited interstate transport of persons for immoral purposes. One of the complainants was University of Maryland student who alleged that Bailley had plied her with wine and marijuana before taking "pornographic" pictures of her. Bailley later threatened to have the photos sent to university authorities and to the woman's parents unless she agreed to provide sexual services to Bailley's political and business associates. This led to her having sex with more than a dozen men at one of Bailley's parties in suburban Maryland. Her complaint stated that one of the men told her he had paid $20 to Bailley for the experience. Bailley offered something resembling a defense: "We pulled a train on her, [but] there wasn't any blackmail or money involved. It was just a party."[75]

The Plumbers' first Watergate break-in occurred on May 29, 1972. The phone line in the DNC headquarters that was supposed to be wire-tapped was special in that it did not go through the central switchboard. It was a line used to call the Columbia Plaza call-girl operation run by Heidi Rikan. The Columbia Plaza line was already being tapped by Lou Russell, a stringer for reporter Jack Anderson who also worked for James McCord and for McCord's attorney Bernard Fensterwald. [76] Fensterwald, as mentioned previously, was also the lawyer who ran the Committee to Investigate Assassinations (CtIA). From time to time, Lou Russell would regale Fensterwald and CtIA staffer Bob Smith with stories about salacious conversations between DNC politicians and Columbia Plaza prostitutes. [77]

On June 9, 1972, Phillip Bailley was indicted by a Washington grand jury. The *Washington Star* ran a story about the indictment with head-line "Capitol Hill Call-Girl Ring Uncovered."[78] The *Star* reported that US attorney John Rudy's investigation placed a D.C. attorney at the head of a high-priced prostitution enterprise. [79] The FBI had found that the operation involved "at least one White House secretary" and that "a White House lawyer was a client."[80] The article elicited a speedy response from White House lawyer John Dean. In the space of an hour, he arranged for a chauffeured limousine to deliver the prosecutor John Rudy to the White House where Dean photocopied Phillip Bailley's address book. [81] Within the address book, Dean recognized the name of a female lawyer working in the Office of Emergency Preparedness and she was subsequently forced to resign. According to John Rudy, the book also contained the names of Dean's girlfriend (and future wife) Maureen Biner, as well as "Cathy Dieter" an apparent alias for Biner's friend Heidi Rikan. [82] "Cathy Dieter's" Columbia Plaza apartment had been leased in the name of Bailley's ex-girlfriend (the fired lawyer), reportedly without her knowledge. The Deans dispute Heidi Rikan's identity as the "Cathy Dieter" involved in Bailley's operation. They do acknowledge that Rikan was a "close friend" and Maureen Dean's bridesmaid. [83]

In the 1980s, Rikan confided in her longtime maid, admitting "I was a call girl at the White House." Her close friend Josephine Alvarez and Rikan's sister Kathie both confirmed that Heidi had used "Kathie Dieter" as an alias. [84] After Rikan died in 1990, her sister found a "little black book" among her effects. Her phone contacts included both of the Deans, including the number of John's White House office and their unlisted home phone number. Also included were the names of Nixon officials Jeb Magruder, Maurice Stans, and Fred LaRue as well as Senator Lowell Weicker and Sam Dash—the chief counsel of the Senate Watergate Committee. Significantly, the book also contained the names of organized crime figure Joe Nesline and Irving Davidson, office-mate of Jack Anderson and D.C. lobbyist for both Jimmy Hoffa and mob boss Carlos Marcello.[85] Joe Nesline "kept" Rikan as a girlfriend. She allegedly used her friendship with Dean to intercede on behalf of Jimmy Hoffa prior to Nixon's December 1971 pardon of the Teamster president.[86] Nesline was the top underworld figure in Washington, associated at the time with Meyer Lansky and other leading mob bosses in sex-club ventures in Hamburg and Amsterdam. In other words, Nesline and his associates were at the pinnacle of prostitution, narcotics, and gambling operations that provided the basis for the underworld's political influence.[87]

The infamous second Watergate break-in occurred in the early morning hours of July 17, 1972. Again, it is still disputed as to who ordered it and why. As Jim Hougan puts it, "All the circumstantial evidence suggests that concerns about the Bailley case led to the [second break-in]."[88] On June the 9th, Magruder declared that another DNC expedition might be in the offing. That was the same day that the Bailley story broke, leading to Dean's hasty White House summons of John Rudy. The next working day—Monday, June 12—Magruder met with again with Liddy, demanding another break-in, this time saying that he was expecting to acquire scandalous information.[89] Magruder had initially stated that Liddy and Mitchell had ordered the second break-in. He eventually claimed that it was John Dean who ordered the job.[90] Jim Hougan, G. Gordon Liddy, and the authors of *Silent Coup* all believe that Dean ordered the second break-in after learning about the link between the DNC and the Columbia Plaza sex ring.[91]

In a deposition, US attorney John Rudy stated that his informant "Cathy Dieter" (presumably Heidi Rikan) had mentioned that Spencer Oliver, the bugged DNC official, "either knew of or had been involved in some way with the Columbia Plaza operation."[92] Rudy began looking for possible links between the Columbia Plaza sex-ring and the DNC, but his investigation was soon "iced" by his superior, Harold Titus. Rudy stated that he was told that the investigation might be "construed or interpreted as being politically motivated." The affair was "a political timebomb . . . very politically sensitive because of the Watergate break-in." Rudy also referred to strange goings-on at the Columbia Plaza, pointing to various parties who complicated things: "[There were] too many people involved . . . people were bugging the buggers, tape recording buggers." He added, "I believe there were [court ordered] phone taps. There were people [doing] illegal taps. . . . There were perhaps other agencies involved in some type of intelligence operations. I mean, it was a ball of wax."[93]

In spring 1973, Republicans on the Democrat-majority Ervin committee realized that Lou Russell had been playing a significant if mysterious role in the whole affair. Russell was the McCord/CREEP-employed figure who had been listening to the DNC/Columbia Plaza conversations. On May 9, the committee placed Russell under subpoena. On May 18, after refusing to comply with the subpoena, Russell had a massive heart attack. Hours later, McCord began testifying publicly before the Ervin committee. Russell told his daughter that he thought that he had been poisoned, that someone had broken into his apartment and "switched pills on me."[94] This seems paranoid, but it occurred at a pivotal time: Russell had played some part in the Watergate break-in, had very likely placed false evidence at DNC headquarters in September, and he had been helping McCord's defense. He had helped McCord to switch attorneys, the switch that brought in Bernard Fensterwald and was marked by McCord's assertion that, "We're going after the President."[95] Russell wasn't the only person at that time who voiced concerns that matters were becoming dire and possibly deadly. Nixon had threatened Dean with prison if he exposed unnamed "national security activities." Days before Russell's heart attack very late on the night of May 16th/17th, Deep Throat told Woodward that "Everyone's life is in danger." Woodward later conveyed Throat's message to Bradlee and Bernstein: "The covert activities involve the whole of the US intelligence community and are incredible. [. . .] The cover-up had little to do with Watergate, but was mainly to protect the covert operations."[96]

After his cardiac episode—which he believed to be the result of poisoning—Lou Russell seemed to have a change of heart. Though still McCord's employee, he received a retainer from John Leon, a friend who was working on a Republican counter-investigation of Watergate. Leon had surmised that Watergate was some kind of a setup, that prostitution rings were at the heart of the matter, and that the arrests of the Plumbers resulted from a tip-off to police. Russell, now Leon's employee, was the man with the first-hand knowledge of the affair. On July 2, before Russell could be of use to Leon, he died after another heart attack. Knowing about his friend's belief that he had been poisoned, Leon was frightened and despondent over his friend's death. He soon realized that the only option left for the Republicans was to go after Carmine Bellino, the chief prosecutor of the Ervin committee. Leon wanted to prove that Russell had been spying on CREEP for the Democrats and that he had tipped off the police and Bellino about the break-in.[97] Even with Russell dead, Leon and others had first-hand knowledge of Bellino's involvement in similar matters. According to sworn affidavits, Bellino had overseen illegal surveillance of Nixon's 1960 campaign. Methods deployed included the use of bugging and other eavesdropping devices. After collecting this evidence, a statement was crafted and a press conference featuring John Leon was announced for July 13. On the day the event was scheduled, John Leon suffered a heart attack. He died before the press conference could be convened. On that same day, presidential appointments secretary Alexander Butterfield offered Senate testimony revealing the existence of the White House taping system.[98]

Along with Nixon's decision not to destroy the tapes, the Butterfield revelation sealed the president's fate. Chief of Staff Alexander Haig and Fred Buzhardt persuaded Nixon not to destroy the tapes. In June of 1974, Haig ordered an Army Criminal Investigation Command (CIC) investigation into Nixon's mob ties and to his smuggling of gold into Vietnam. He received the report in late July. It is unknown whether Haig informed either Nixon or Gerald Ford about the report or its contents. The chief CIC investigator Russell Bintliff is convinced that Haig confronted both men with the report and that consequentially, Nixon's resignation followed. This can't be confirmed because Haig always refused to discuss the issue.[99] A recently published book shows that Haig was not only instrumental in Nixon's resignation; he had also been part of the anti-détente spy-ring at the heart of the Moorer-Radford affair.[100] Haig obscured his own role and prevented further investigation and public exposure of the spy-ring in various ways. He accomplished this principally by working through two men—his old West Point friend Fred Buzhardt and Bob Woodward who, as discussed earlier, had previously served as an intelligence officer under some of the same anti-détente officers in the spy ring. Notably, part of Woodward's Pentagon job in 1969 and 1970 was to brief Alexander Haig.[101] With the foregoing in mind, it is significant that a military officer previously involved in an anti-détente Pentagon spy-ring aimed at the presidency would go on to serve as Nixon's chief of staff. In that role, Haig prevented further exposure of the illegal and possibly treasonous spy-ring, utilized military intelligence to investigate the president's theretofore unsubstantiated underworld connections and activities, encouraged Nixon to make the politically suicidal decision not to destroy the White House tapes, and orchestrated the apparent denouement of Watergate—Nixon's resignation and Ford's ascension.

CHAPTER 10

WATERGATE, *QU'EST-CE QUE C'EST?*

"A Third-Rate Burglary"

The use of term "Watergate" itself is emblematic of the public's nebulous understanding of the Nixon years. "Watergate" originally referred to the actual break-in at the Watergate Hotel. The term eventually evolved, coming to encompass a swath of additional crimes committed by the ostensibly retired CIA officer E. Howard Hunt and his crew of right-wing Cuban exiles. By the time Nixon resigned in August of 1974, "Watergate" came to also include the White House efforts to cover-up the Plumbers' activities as well as Nixon's abuse of executive power writ large. Nixon's "Watergate" culpability in the second and third iterations has been well documented.[1] However, as stated previously, the authorship and aims of the Watergate burglaries remain disputed and obscure. As Tim Weiner confirms in *Legacy of Ashes*, "no one really knows if Richard Nixon authorized the break-in."[2]

Likewise, the ill-fated second break-in has been attributed to various motives and actors. The orthodox Woodward/Bernstein account depicts the break-in as a bungled crime committed on Nixon's behalf. Others like H. R. Haldeman and Jim Hougan suggest, with varying degrees of specificity, that the second break-in was a deliberately botched affair of

CIA design, intended "to draw attention to Nixon's illegal activities and political aspirations."[3] The theory posited here builds on a third alternative explanation offered by Peter Dale Scott: "the break-in was the work of a well-organized anti-détente cadre transcending any one agency, including elements close to organized crime." If correct, "the aim of the break-in, as well as the clear result, was to gain power over *both* Nixon and also the traditional CIA."[4]

Revolt of the Bureaucrats

One key aspect of Nixon's political aspirations was his administration's efforts to situate control of the federal bureaucracy more firmly in the White House. These efforts were carried out in order to give the president more power to pursue policies which could otherwise be stymied by various bureaucratic elements. In particular, détente and the "war on drugs" created fear and paranoia not merely in the public and security state bureaucracies, but among the deep political constituencies that provided political succor to those agencies. US *exceptionism* is also key to understanding Watergate, since the crimes of the Nixon administration were decidedly minor relative to the various scandals and state crimes that have been documented and/or suspected. Such would include the political assassinations of the 1960s, the Gulf of Tonkin incident/resolution, MKULTRA testing on US citizens, CIA/KMT complicity in the heroin traffic, the October surprises of 1968 and 1980 (admittedly Nixon was the bad actor in 1968, but this had no impact on the publicly understood reasons for his resignation), Iran-Contra-cocaine, Iraqi WMD, and CIA torture.

The early Nixon-Hoover conflict over the Huston Plan illustrates how Nixon threatened the deep state by encroaching upon its security state turf, the FBI in this instance. The Huston Plan mobilized the CIA, FBI, and military intelligence to increase electronic surveillance of individuals deemed to be "domestic security threats." The operation involved intercepting mail and allowed for "surreptitious entry," i.e., burglaries or "black-bag jobs." The plan was rescinded after Hoover protested. His objection was not based on moral, legal, or ethical principles. Rather, Hoover considered the plan a trespass on the FBI's domain.[5] The Joint Chiefs of Staff also strongly opposed Nixon's policies, specifically the efforts to pursue détente as discussed earlier. This opposition led to the arguably treasonous spy-ring which was never adjudicated. Nixon's also faced resistance to his efforts to restructure the CIA and bring it more firmly under presidential control. The CIA assisted and was briefed on many of the Plumbers' illegal activities. Both the firing of Helms and Schlesinger's order to compile the "family jewels" must be understood as aspects of Nixon's efforts to control the CIA and bring its power to bear in defusing Watergate. As McCord predicted, firing Helms would be disastrous for Nixon: "[E]very tree in the forest will fall. It will be a scorched desert."

As with Nixon's pursuit of détente and his efforts to restructure the CIA, the "war on drugs" also led to bureaucratic intrigue and deep state paranoia. Enforcement of drug laws at the national level had been carried out largely by the Federal Bureau of Narcotics until a serious corruption scandal at the agency's New York office led to the organization's dissolution in the late 1960s. In the early 1970s, Nixon announced a "war on drugs" to be waged especially against Asian heroin.[6] The first target of the campaign was the Turkish opium which had been supplying Corsican heroin labs—the infamous French Connection. But after a series of notable seizures and arrests in 1970 and 1971, US officials came to recognize the threat posed by East Asian heroin.[7] Most spectacularly, the Laotian ambassador to France, Prince Sopsaisana, was found to be travelling with a suitcase containing 60 kilograms of premium Laotian heroin. The heroin was likely destined for New York where it would be worth around $13 million. The prince, who was also an active member of the Asian People's Anti-Communist League (APACL), was not arrested. Reports later received by US officials stated that Sopsaisana's enterprise had been bankrolled by General Vang Pao, the leader of the CIA's secret army of Hmong tribesmen. The heroin had been at Long Tieng in a laboratory within the CIA's command center for covert operations in the region.[8] Interestingly, and perhaps as something of an aside, the APACL was founded in 1954 by Taiwanese KMT members, South Korean ultra-rightists, and Yoshio Kodama—a man suspected of drug trafficking in addition to being a notorious Japanese war criminal who the CIA sprang from prison after the war. Following the 1954 creation of the APACL, a

Latin American branch was established by none other than E. Howard Hunt.[9]

In the aftermath of the arrest of Laotian Prince Sopsaisana, Nixon and the CIA took measures to distance US officials from these operations by pressuring Laos to outlaw opium and by recalling or reassigning implicated CIA officers like Tom Clines and Ted Shackley.[10] Notably, the *New York Times* even momentarily overcame its studied reticence regarding CIA-drug matters. In June of 1971, the paper published a story based on a leaked CIA report detailing Golden Triangle heroin operations. Though not explicitly stated, the refineries in question were in areas under the control of paramilitary groups deeply involved in US covert operations going back as far as 1950.[11] A month later, the Nixon administration announced it would crack down on Southeast Asian leaders involved in the Golden Triangle heroin traffic.[12] Around this time, history PhD candidate Alfred McCoy was working on what would become his magnum opus, *The Politics of Heroin in Southeast Asia*.[13] In the book's third edition, McCoy writes that as he was working on the original edition, he was contacted by Tom Tripodi, a DEA agent and ex-CIA officer. Tripodi later visited McCoy to look over his text, eventually reviewing whole chapters and providing corrections and additional anecdotes.[14] Tripodi was actually with the Bureau of Narcotics and Dangerous Drugs (BNDD) at the time since the DEA hadn't been created yet; McCoy probably lists him as DEA to minimize confusion. Journalist and historian Doug Valentine wrote that Tripodi insists that he gave McCoy considerable help, while McCoy asserts that it was minimal.[15] In either case, the takeaway here is that the BNDD did provide support for McCoy's work, demonstrating the conflict between CIA-drug operations and other agencies involved in Nixon's "war on drugs."

A major problem for Nixon was that his détente policies and his anti-drug policies were anathema to key groups with which Nixon was associated. E. Howard Hunt and other Plumbers (especially the Cubans) were not only against détente; many had also been involved in the drug traffic in various ways. Hunt—along with Paul Helliwell, a future CIA officer and attorney for a Lansky-connected bank—was a veteran of the OSS base in Kunming, China. The Kunming OSS made payments to its agents in opium. As an OPC officer, Helliwell orchestrated the CIA's purchase of Civil Air Transport, the airline that became CIA/KMT-owned Air America. Lansky would eventually establish a Mexico-US drug running operation that utilized KMT-connected Chinese living in Mexico. As mentioned earlier, Hunt was stationed in Mexico in the mid-1950s when he set about creating a Latin American branch of the KMT's embryonic World Anti-Communist League (WACL). The Latin American WACL franchise brought together a group of ultra-rightists who soon came to agitate for the overthrow of Arbenz in Guatemala. WACL members have been involved or suspected in numerous drug trafficking episodes, most notoriously in the 1980 Bolivian "cocaine coup" during which the WACL installed a ruling junta and helped a major drug trafficker get his cousin appointed Minister of the Interior.[16] Besides Hunt, other close associates of the Cuban Watergate burglars were arrested during Nixon's anti-drug campaign.[17]

The other entity that should be considered here is the China Lobby, more accurately described as the *Far Eastern Lobby* since it came to include more than just the Taiwanese KMT. Nixon's envoy to sabotage the 1968 Paris Peace Talks was Anna Chennault, a key figure in the opium-corrupted China/Far Eastern Lobby. Her husband was Claire Chennault, the US officer whose World War II fleet of airplanes later became the Civil Air Transport and then Air America. The *Atlantic Monthly* reported in 1976 that Anna Chennault had also raised illegal Nixon campaign contributions from across the far east. These sources apparently included South Vietnamese officials who wanted the money from the US war effort to continue pouring into the country.[18] Several of Nixon's policies undoubtedly would have been seen as betrayals by the Far Eastern Lobby. Specifically, these would include Nixon's recognition of the Peoples Republic of China, "Vietnamization" and the Paris Peace Talks, the planned withdrawal of American forces from South Korea, and the war on drugs.

With all this as foreground, there are clues to suggest that the intentionally bungled Watergate break-in was one episode in an unfolding struggle over détente and the international drug traffic. Beyond McCord's conspicuously bad tradecraft, the Plumbers took other measures that made their operation and capture highly radioactive for the administration. As Peter Dale Scott has documented, the first link connecting the break-in to CREEP was Kenneth Dahlberg's $25,000 cashier's check deposited into the bank account of burglar Bernard Barker's Miami real estate firm, Ameritas. The check was discovered by an investigator for Richard E. Gerstein, the Dade County District Attorney. Gerstein told Carl Bernstein about the check. Dahlberg was soon identified as a CRP fund-raiser who had laundered funds into a cashier's check to be deposited into CRP accounts. But the check was not deposited thusly. Instead, Liddy passed the check on to Hunt, who then deposited it in the account of Barker's firm. As a result, the funds were not anonymous and untraceable, but were instead the opposite—a trail leading from the burglars to the CRP. "Trail" may not be the most apt metaphor; better to describe it as an express highway.[19]

Gerstein, the Dade County DA whose office leaked the information about the Gerstein check to Bernstein, was described by the Miami Strike Force chief as undoubtably "a knowing handmaiden of organized crime in Dade County."[20] Declassified FBI reports describe Gerstein's protection of a Lansky associate and his receipt of payoffs from mob-connected industries. An FBI informant alleged that Gerstein regularly lunched with Santo Trafficante.[21]

Additionally, the burglars had cash in their possession and in their hotel rooms. Their money was in mint, sequentially numbered hundred-dollar bills which were also easily traceable to CRP accounts.[22] Within days, the bills led investigators to the Miami bank account of Bernard Barker where the money had been given "in exchange for four Mexican checks traceable to the Finance Committee for the Re-election of the President."[23] Richard Helms—a man later convicted for lying to Congress about the CIA's Chilean operations—testified that the FBI's investigation into the Mexican checks and the Bernard Barker account was of no concern to the CIA: "The question comes up, when the President talked about getting into CIA operations in Mexico . . . people keep asking me, what did he have in mind. The answer is, I don't know what he had in mind."[24] However, documents released in 1998 show that the CIA had in fact been concerned about the FBI's investigation into the Mexican checks. Additionally, John Ehrlichman testified that Helms's deputy "General

Walters would not say that the CIA had no concern on the question of Mexican operations."[25] The embarrassment of the CIA is the likely explanation for Helms's order that the FBI investigators "confine themselves to the personalities already arrested or directly under suspicion." This belies those accounts of Watergate which maintain that the CIA refused to intervene in the FBI's Watergate investigation. The Helms order to the FBI was only in effect for two weeks, but a lot can be swept away in that time. The CIA's initial response to Watergate indicates that the agency was unprepared and exposed by aspects of the affair.[26]

Operation Eagle was an early and revealing episode in Nixon's nascent war on drugs. Starting in 1970, Operation Eagle pursued anti-Castro Cubans moving drugs from Latin America to the Florida-based Trafficante organization. Dozens were arrested and many of them turned out to be members of Operation 40, a CIA paramilitary organization originally created to carry out assassinations and other terrorist operations which were to follow the Bay of Pigs invasion. When it was discovered that CIA assets were smuggling drugs in the US, the CIA began placing officers alongside mid-level BNDD (the DEA's precursor agency) agents in order to protect the agency's assets from being exposed and to help recruit them as BNDD informants.[27] Operation 40 was discontinued in 1970 after one of its planes crashed in Southern California with large amounts of heroin and cocaine on board.[28] Shortly thereafter, Operation 40 member Juan Restoy was arrested in Miami along with Bay of Pigs veteran Alonso Pujol as part of an Operation Eagle drug bust. Cuban Watergate burglar Bernard Barker was a close associate of Guillermo Pujol, Alonso's brother. Barker's Ameritas firm employed Felipe de Diego, one of the Plumbers and an Operation 40 veteran. Watergate burglar Frank Sturgis also identified himself as part of Operation 40.[29] Like McCord, Sturgis, and Hunt, Barker also may have been involved in the John Kennedy assassination. On the day of the murder, a Dallas deputy sheriff in Dealey Plaza named Seymour Weitzman, along with officer Joe Smith, ran over to the grassy knoll after hearing the gunshots. After officer Smith pulled his pistol on a man behind the fence, the man produced credentials indicating that he was with the Secret Service. It eventually emerged that there were no Secret Service agents in the area who did not travel with the motorcade, thus the man behind the fence was wielding false credentials. In 1975, journalist Michael Canfield spoke to the retired Weitzman. Because of speculation that Watergate burglars Hunt and Sturgis had been in Dealey Plaza, Canfield showed him photos of Sturgis and Barker. Weitzman immediately pointed to the picture of Barker and stated that he was willing "to make a tape-recorded statement for official investigators." Another Dealey Plaza witness named Malcolm Summers also eventually identified Barker as the man with a gun that he had seen on the grassy knoll moments after the shooting.[30] Though the well-documented presence of Secret Service impersonators points to—or perhaps confirms—a conspiracy in Dallas, the Bernard Barker angle is provocative but unproven.

A Combustible Mix

In Richard Nixon's memoirs, he recounts what Haldeman said him less than two weeks after the break-in. Haldeman told the president that the entire affair was so absurd that John Dean had not ruled out the possibility that they were grappling with some kind of double agent who intentionally botched the operation. Otherwise, it just made no sense.[31] Writing in the December 1973 issue of *Ramparts* magazine, Peter Dale Scott argued that "the Watergate cover-up almost succeeded—not despite the exotic records of the defendants, but precisely because of them." Subsequent revelations would cause him to revise his appraisal of Watergate, but at that early date, with Nixon still ensconced in the White House, Scott was correct to note that "what makes [the disparate Miami intrigues] so dangerous and what links the scandal of Watergate to the assassination in Dallas, is the increasingly ominous symbiosis between U.S. intelligence networks and the forces of organized crime."[32]

A number of factors combined to make the bizarre Watergate caper such a debacle. The slow-burning scandal became so explosive that it not only took down a presidency—it also led to the largest and most damaging series of intelligence community revelations in US history. The Watergate break-in risked exposing the already surveilled Columbia Plaza sex-ring connected on some level to the DNC and to the DC crime boss and Lansky associate Joe Nesline. The operation bears the hallmarks of previous and subsequent scandals that collectively point to an institutionalized practice of using sexual blackmail for political purposes. Prior to Watergate, J. Edgar Hoover is known to have used sexual blackmail for various purposes. The Bobby Baker scandal, which prior to Dallas appeared poised to end Lyndon Johnson's political career, also had a significant sex angle. According to an ex-CIA officer, there was also a serious intelligence-related sexual blackmail component in the so-called "Koreagate" scandal of the 1970s.[33]

In the 1980s, the *Washington Times* ran a story on a man named Craig Spence,

> [A]n enigmatic figure who threw glittery parties for key officials of the Reagan and Bush administrations, media stars and top military officers, bugged the gatherings to compromise guests, provided cocaine, blackmailed some associates and spent up to $20,000 a month on male prostitutes, according to friends, acquaintances and records. The 48-year-old D.C. power broker has been linked to a homosexual prostitution ring currently under investigation by the U.S. Attorney's Office. Its clients included several top government and business officials from Washington and abroad.[34]

The article reported that a Chinese businessman who knew Spence described him as an odd fellow who often bragged that he worked for the CIA, on one occasion even saying that he needed to disappear for a time "because he had an important CIA assignment." Spence also told the man that he was worried the CIA would "doublecross him," murder him, and "make it look like a suicide."[35] Shortly before Spence's "suicide," he identified George H. W. Bush's National Security Advisor Donald Gregg (previously of the CIA) as his key White House contact. He also told *Washington Times* reporters that "All this stuff you've uncovered [. . .] is insignificant compared to other things I've done. But I'm not going to tell you those things, and somehow the world will carry on."[36]

More recently, mysterious billionaire Jeffrey Epstein was exposed for his role in running a sex-ring which included the trafficking of under-age girls for powerful men. He escaped prosecution in 2007 after an extraordinary plea deal. The US attorney in Miami who signed off on the deal, Alexander Acosta, was later interviewed before his nomination to be Trump's labor secretary. Asked about Epstein, Acosta explained that he was only a participant in one meeting about the case. At this meeting, Acosta "was told Epstein 'belonged to intelligence' and to leave it alone."[37] Thanks to the efforts of courageous victims and a relentless journalist in Miami, Epstein was eventually arrested again in 2019. Before a trial could be held—a trial that could have potentially exposed criminal intelligence practices as well as the grim predilections of very powerful men—Epstein died in what was reported as a suicide. Perhaps no "mysterious suicide" has ever been predicted by more people.

In examining the Columbia Plaza sex-ring, the Koreagate scandal, the Craig Spence operation, and the Epstein case, a pattern emerges. Multiple, discursive intelligence-connected, sexual blackmail operations have been partially exposed. These operations are never adjudicated, often due to untimely deaths which preclude any kind of reckoning. The Watergate sex-ring angle fits this pattern. Likewise, the inculpatory *soiling* of funds (rather than their exculpatory laundering) through Bernard Barker's drug-connected Ameritas served to needlessly implicate CREEP and the Plumbers; an exculpatory laundering of the funds could have been easily accomplished. Additionally, the composition of the Watergate burglars' team could hardly have been more radioactive. Hunt, Sturgis, McCord, and Barker were each, in all likelihood, Bay of Pigs veterans. Each of these figures has each been implicated in the JFK assassination, with various degrees of supporting evidence. Nixon himself seemed to grasp as much. The president apparently thought that this would help him if one accepts that Nixon was referring to Dallas when he sent Haldeman to warn Helms about "the Bay of Pigs thing." As Nixon said on the "smoking gun" tape, "[T]his is a . . . Hunt [operation] that will uncover a lot of things. You open that scab there's a hell of a lot of things and that we just feel that it would be very detrimental to have this thing go any further. This involves these Cubans, Hunt, and a lot of hanky-panky that we have nothing to do with ourselves."[38]

Watergate: Richard Nixon's Deep State Nemesis

Of Watergate, Nixon famously said, "I gave [my enemies] a sword, and they stuck it in and they twisted it with relish." Perhaps the key figure in terms of weaponizing Watergate against Nixon was James McCord. Prior to Watergate, he had been involved in some of the most sensitive intelligence operations of the Cold War. After MKULTRA scientist Frank Olson fell ten stories to his death in 1953, it was the CIA's James McCord of the Office of Security who was called in to make sure that no details would emerge regarding agency involvement. Decades after Olson's death, an exhumation revealed to a forensic pathologist that Olson had a hematoma above his left eye not caused by the fall, an injury suggesting that "Dr Olson was struck a stunning blow to the head by some person or instrument prior to his exiting through the window."[39] Seymour Hersh eventually learned what happened to Olson through a highly placed source in the CIA. Essentially, Olson was deemed a security risk and liquidated. The *New York Review of Books* described the agency protocol identified by Hersh as "the execution of internal dissidents by the CIA's 'Office of Security.'"[40] These recent revelations stemming from the Frank Olson case seem to confirm E. Howard Hunt's 1975 admission that the CIA had an assassination team tasked with liquidating security risks like suspected double-agents or CIA employees.[41]

Under McCord's supervision, the CIA's Office of Security launched its illegal domestic counterintelligence operation against the Fair Play for Cuba Committee (FPCC).[42] Lee Harvey Oswald's bizarre attempts to ostensibly establish an FPCC chapter in New Orleans were so inept that they only make sense if understood as a counterintelligence operation of the kind McCord was conducting. To wit: Oswald moved to New Orleans, found office space in the building occupied by ex-FBI ultra-rightist Guy Banister and the militant CIA-sponsored anti-Castro Cuban Revolutionary Council.[43] From this sensitive location, Oswald established a non-sanctioned "chapter" of the FPCC consisting of himself and his alias "Alec Hidel." He proceeded to get arrested in a scuffle with CIA-sponsored Cubans, and then further discredited the FPCC by participating in a broadcast radio debate during which he acknowledged that he had defected to the Soviet Union. That Oswald was involved in a counterintelligence operation seems obvious; it is only because of the grim implications that such an assessment is controversial. The historical consequence of all this was considerable. His New Orleans misadventures, along with his Soviet defection, served to create the Oswald "legend"—i.e., that he was a Communist malcontent.

Lastly, James McCord was involved in high level planning for the "Doomsday Project" or "Continuity of Government," in which he helped plan for the implementation of authoritarian measures like censorship, preventive detention, and mass surveillance. Such plans were to be activated in the event of a "national emergency" declared by either the president or the Secretary of Defense.[44] In sum, McCord had first-hand knowledge of many of the most sensitive "national security" operations, all of which represent *exceptionism*—both in their supralegal dimensions and by virtue of the fact that their details are to this day obscured by state secrecy. McCord's spectacular bungling of the Watergate break-in, his prophecy of the doom that would follow should Helms be fired and the CIA blamed for Watergate, his refusal to stay quiet in return for money and executive clemency, his letter to Judge Sirica, his bizarre memoir casting Nixon as a Hitler-type figure in a Bircheresque anti-Rockefeller conspiracy theory— all of these anecdotes strongly indicate that McCord was a pivotal figure in a plot to weaken and ultimately bring down the Nixon presidency. It is not plausible that McCord would have been charged with handling so many of the most sensitive national security operations if he were as inept as the James McCord who planned and performed the second Watergate break-in. Likewise, the idea that he was somehow scandalized by Nixon's lawbreaking is belied by the fact that he willingly performed even more blatantly illegal duties for the CIA. Such would include McCord's role as—at the very least—the clean-up man following Frank Olson's apparently extrajudicial execution by defenestration, as well as his work establishing protocol for an emergency transition to dictatorial governance.

In short, James McCord operated in a realm of deep state exceptionism. His high position in the CIA's Office of Security entailed exercising exceptionist prerogative in order to conceal exceptionism in general. This applies to how the apparent execution of Frank Olson and the subsequent cover-up were deemed necessary to protect "national security." What is notable is fact that the threat that Olson represented seems to have been that he might reveal the criminal horrors of the CIA's mind control and biological weapons programs. McCord's involvement in the illegal domestic counterintelligence operations against the FPCC and his key role in the Olson murder strongly suggest that he was indeed "an operator" as James Angleton asserted. In the highly compartmentalized CIA where sensitive information is held on a need-to-know basis, the Office of Security would be one of those entities where officers would *need-to-know* about the most sensitive operations throughout the intelligence community in order to be aware of the persons and operations who could pose the greatest potential risks to "security." The historical record suggests that the state deems some of the most serious security risks to be the exposure of operations that belie the liberal democratic myths related to the rule-of-law. By this reckoning, "security" entails protecting the cultivated perception that the national security state does not represent the lawless despotism in a society nominally governed by the rule of law and a sovereign public.

While détente seems to have been the decisive issue motivating Haig and the other anti-détente "Prussians" who figured in Watergate, the perceived threat represented by Nixon's efforts to restructure the national security state is illuminating. In so doing, Nixon was trying to exercise his constitutionally prescribed duty to conduct diplomacy. His departure from the deep state's Cold War orthodoxies, CREEP's White House assumption of exceptionist prerogative, and Nixon's moves to radically restructure the national security state . . . all these factors contributed to a conflict that was in part a battle over sovereignty in the Schmittian sense. If "he is sovereign who decides the exception," Nixon was to discover that he was not sovereign. McCord, on the other hand, represented those deep state forces that exercised considerable sovereignty. Given his position, it is wholly appropriate—perhaps even a prerequisite—that he held fanatical views of the existential threat to the American way posed by communism and by those who would seek a *modus vivendi* with communist governments. To the extent that it was tacitly acknowledged or grimly tolerated by the public, Cold War exceptionism demanded for its legitimation a Manichean enemy bent on global domination. In such an existential struggle, all questions of morality, legality, and transparency would necessarily be irrelevant save for public relations purposes.

Watergate had threads leading to the most legally dubious US national security operations. These include sexual blackmail, state complicity in drug trafficking, assassinations of US officials like Frank Olson and John Kennedy, operational plans to establish more overtly dictatorial governance, and longstanding links between the state and the criminal underworld. These are operations whose details are to this day controversial, obscured, unadjudicated, and likely still ongoing. Even when Nixon tasked his handpicked DCI James Schlesinger with bringing the CIA to heel by compiling the "Family Jewels" files of the agency's worst crimes, the aforementioned operations were shielded from disclosure. Instead, it was the arrested Plumbers who, in the standoff over Watergate, had the power to unleash the most explosive revelations about the US government. These were secrets whose exposure would have falsified foundational American myths, potentially destroying the legitimacy of the US government and US hegemony. In this context, Deep Throat's aforementioned cryptic and apocalyptic message that "Everyone's life is in danger" can be understood. As recounted by Woodward, Throat said, "The covert activities involve the whole U.S. intelligence community and are incredible. . . . The cover-up had little to do with Watergate, but was mainly to protect the covert operations."[45]

The assemblage of the Plumbers Unit created a felonious criminal conspiracy comprised of individuals who were participants in—or were tied to—an amazingly scandalous array of clandestine chicanery. As the former chief of the CIA's security office, these intrigues were exactly the sort of matters that McCord would have been charged with protecting from disclosure. McCord did the opposite. Rather than preventing or dissolving this highly combustible unit, he appears to have intentionally bungled the second Watergate break-in. This led to the arrest of the Plumbers which risked an unprecedented exposure of extremely sensitive state secrets—a risk that grew immeasurably by McCord's refusal to assist in the cover-up. McCord, as in the case of Frank Olson, was a deep state clean-up man. So why did he apparently make such a mess that even the full power of the presidency couldn't clean it up? Given his own ultrarightist opposition to Nixon and his loyalty to the much more urbane and inscrutable Richard Helms, it seems that McCord had to have been part of an anti-Nixon cabal that gathered more and more momentum as events unfolded.

The Watergate theory offered here is that the Plumbers were deployed in such a way as to gain leverage over Nixon through their exploits like the excessively, damningly well-documented burgling of Ellsberg's psychiatrist. The disastrous second Watergate break-in made matters more precarious. Nixon's partial grasp of the situation's sensitivity led him to think, understandably, that it would help ensure a cover-up. As DCI, Richard Helms seemed caught off-guard by some aspects of the unfolding drama. He was eventually fired and the affair ended up bringing the agency to the lowest point in its history. The post-Watergate congressional intelligence investigations represented the most significant series of intelligence community revelations that the US has experienced. For these and other reasons, Watergate cannot be understood through any theory that posits it as purely a CIA plot. Much of the deep state's operational wherewithal may have resided at the CIA, but these exceptionist prerogatives are ultimately backstopped by the prevailing power structure—the pinnacle of the politico-economic elite.

From this analysis, further hypotheses emerge related to the role of the Doomsday Project. Do Doomsday/COG provisions allow for supralegal covert actions to be carried out domestically in the name of national security? Do such provisions deem US hegemony, in some respect, to be a sacrosanct core element of national security—an element whose perpetuation must be safeguarded? Would exposure of the most egregious state crimes be considered the kind of threat to national security that would necessitate exceptionist measures? This is another way of asking whether American exceptionism extends to authorizing actions to maintain the concealment of exceptionism from US and global publics. Could such secret provisions explain McCord's role (as well as the CIA's) in Frank Olson's apparent summary execution? Could such provisions also partly explain the historically unique manner in which the press and the national security bureaucracy coalesced against Nixon? Might such policies help to illuminate other strange events such as the suspicious recent deaths of Michael Hastings or Jeffrey Epstein? Clearly, these matters are academic in the vernacular sense without the dramatic weakening of US state secrecy.

Admittedly, this look at Watergate cannot be brought to a definitive conclusion. Exactly how the various intrigues were planned and by whom cannot be clearly determined. What can be concluded—and what does merit further investigation—is that Nixon and his subordinates in the administration were the only ones held to account for these crimes. Collectively, their illegalities represent a small fraction of postwar US state criminality. Regardless of one's preferred explanation of Watergate, the historical evidence demonstrates that Nixon attempted to depart from US neoconservative and neoliberal policy prescriptions and was subsequently removed from office. Imperial hegemony was reproduced and revised in the turbulent wake of Bretton Woods's collapse. Nixon's foreign and domestic policies were reversed by his successors. As with Kennedy, Nixon was undone by his failure to either counter or accommodate powerful factions of the American deep state. And as with Carter, Nixon's efforts at statesmanship caused him to lose the neoliberal backing he had previously enjoyed, something similar to how Carter would later lose the "Rockefeller 'Mandate of Heaven.'" With no countervailing overworld support, Nixon could not withstand the assault of Prussian/neoconservative forces, the intelligence bureaucracies with their underworld allies, the national media, and Nixon's political enemies in the Democratic party. Such a theory goes further toward explaining the paradox of how Nixon's resignation, an apparent defeat for right-wing forces, served to usher in a political realignment that moved both major parties significantly rightward. Watergate was a structural deep event that contributed significantly to the destruction of American liberalism—a political order which existed precariously through the New Deal, World War II, and Bretton Woods eras.

CHAPTER 11

THE CONSTITUTION OF
THE DEEP STATE

The deep state—the overworld-dominated institutions within and without the government—is not completely hidden. An institution like the Council on Foreign Relations (CFR) is a visible, partially transparent component of the deep state. It is a nominally non-governmental entity funded by Wall Street in order to cultivate and utilize foreign policy "expertise." The tailormade expertise and policy prescriptions of the CFR logically and demonstrably serve the interests of the Wall Street overworld which funds the organization. As previously discussed, the CFR has had considerable impact on US policies including US entry into World War II, the creation of the postwar US empire, and US foreign policy in general during the Cold War and beyond. The Trilateral Commission is a transnational component of the deep state. It was founded by overworld eminence David Rockefeller, a man who was also a towering figure in the Council on Foreign Relations. The Trilateral Commission was comprised initially of political, business, and academic elites from the US, Western Europe, and Japan. The organization provided much of the personnel of the Carter administration and in retrospect clearly appears to have been at the forefront of moving the Democratic party in a neoliberal direction. The Trilateral Commission is largely transparent, perhaps excessively so with its publication *The Crisis of Democracy*. That volume contains the writings of ostensibly "liberal" academics bemoaning the emancipatory political movements of the 1960s and calling for a renewed focus on the "indoctrination of the young," among other things.[1]

Supranationality

The Safari Club was a supranational deep state organization. It was run in part by the CIA-connected Saudi arms magnate Adnan Khashoggi and comprised of intelligence officials from France, Saudi Arabia, Iran, Egypt, Israel, and Morocco. According to Saudi Prince Turki Al Faisal, the former head of Saudi intelligence:

> In 1976, after the Watergate matters took place here, your intel-ligence community was literally tied up by Congress. It could not do anything. It could not send spies, it could not write reports, and it could not pay money. In order to compensate for that, a group of countries got together in the hope of fighting communism and established what was called the Safari Club. The Safari Club included France, Egypt, Saudi Arabia, Morocco, and Iran . . . so, the Kingdom, with these countries, helped in some way, I believe, to keep the world safe when the United States was not able to do that. That, I think, is a secret that many of you don't know.[2]

This organization provides an illuminating example of deep state power. The US has had considerable sway over many foreign intelligence agencies, including those that comprised the Safari Club. For example, the CIA created Savak in Iran following the 1953 coup. Likewise, after the US-backed coup which overthrew Brazilian democracy in 1964, the CIA established a client Brazilian intelligence agency, the National Information Service (SNI).[3] When the US acted to effect the overthrow of Salvador Allende in 1973, it was the Brazilian state which took on a considerable portion of the operational duties.[4] After Chilean democracy was overthrown, the CIA created a client Chilean intelligence agency, the National Intelligence Directorate (DINA). These Southern Cone intelligence agencies func-tioned essentially as CIA franchises, carrying out Operation Condor in which tens of thousands of South American leftists, labor leaders, and religious clergy were assassinated, tortured, disappeared, or forced into exile. The creation and subsequent use of client intelligence services has been a common CIA practice. The obscuring of responsibility—in addition to the state secrecy already enjoyed by the CIA—makes these entities a crucial component of the deep state. To wit: The American public state acted to curtail the legally dubious practices of the CIA in the wake of Watergate revelations. In response, a supranational deep state availed itself of client intelligence services and private organizations to fill the vacuum, constructed as they were by the same overworld forces that created and animated the CIA.

The Underworld and the Deep State

One obscure but enduring characteristic of Western deep politics and the American deep state is the presence of organized crime. The history of collaboration between US elites and organized crime networks is long and somewhat hidden. There are numerous documented incidents of close collaboration or interpenetration between organized crime and US/Anglo political elites. In the early nineteenth century, US businessmen capitalized on the sale of opium in China. Corrupt institutions emerged to administrate this illicit commerce which was illegal under Chinese law. The opium trade was the most lucrative aspect of the "China trade," and served to finance significant portions of early US industrialization. These economic relationships had considerable long-term impacts on US politics, history, and the conception of the national interest. The prospect of trading with Asia was one of the motivations for seizing California from Mexico. The ensuing Pacific focus led, shortly thereafter, to Commodore Perry forcibly opening up Japan. In the late nineteenth and early twentieth centuries the US continued to expand across the Pacific. American business interests and US marines overthrew the Hawaiian monarchy; the US annexed the islands soon after. Following the Spanish-American War, the US seized the Philippines. American statesmen declared the "open door" policy, a doctrine originally intended to apply to China but also an apt and succinct creed for US hegemony. In Asia and elsewhere, the "door" to US investment and commerce was to be "open." Or else.

In Central America, US fruit companies came to dominate the political economy of whole societies. They did this with considerable assistance from organized crime who could use muscle to suppress dock workers or labor in general. This combination of business and organized crime dominated the region and even brought down entire governments. The addition of US military power to the equation gave rise to the term *banana republic*—a country in which the US fruit company is more powerful than the national government. Here again, a criminogenic economic realm would become so powerful as to corrupt and alter the US national interest, giving rise to "Banana Wars" fought all over Central America after the Spanish-American War and only ending with FDR's "Good Neighbor" policy.

The deep state's modern overworld/underworld nexus was forged by the World War II era US national security bureaucracy. Most notable was the Office of Strategic Services (OSS), the wartime intelligence organization which was the precursor to the CIA. With Operation Underworld, the OSS brought together organized crime figures and the patrician elites who comprised the OSS. Most infamously, the underworld figures included Meyer Lansky and Lucky Luciano—a syndicate kingpin released from prison on Lansky's insistence. Like the fruit companies discussed earlier, the US government wanted to use the mob's expertise in suppressing radical longshoreman and thereby guarantee that the logistically crucial waterfront areas would be pacified. This was more consequential than other stated aims of Operation Underworld, namely the apprehending of Nazi spies and saboteurs.[5]

In Asia, the OSS helped to broker a peaceful alliance between Thai and KMT forces in the opium rich Shan states of Burma, with fateful historical consequences.[6] After the war, the OSS was disbanded, but the former OSS chief and a former chief of British intelligence formed something of a private alternative. This outfit was called the World Commerce Corporation (WCC) and it had backing from powerful overworld figures like Nelson Rockefeller.[7] Through the activities of Kunming OSS chief and Wall Street lawyer Paul Helliwell (also Meyer Lansky's lawyer), WCC figures were able to reestablish the KMT/Thai opium production in Burma.[8] In the 1950s, under the auspices of the CIA's Office of Policy Coordination (OPC), this same milieu would bleed into Operation Paper—a self-sustaining (through drug trafficking) KMT effort to retake the Chinese mainland. Only the drug trafficking aspect of the operation was successful.[9] Later, many of the same figures, practices, and arrangements would be reconstituted during the secret war in Laos where the CIA/KMT Air America airline utilized heroin trafficking to fund an anti-communist military force.[10]

After the brief post-Watergate lull in CIA adventurism, these practices were revamped during the Reagan administration under DCI William Casey, the last surviving member of the "Old Boys" from the OSS and early CIA days. In order to fund the anti-Communist terrorist/paramilitary contras, the CIA and DEA turned a blind eye (in the most charitable assessment) to the Contra cocaine trafficking which helped fuel the crack epidemic of the 1980s and '90s.[11] Around the same time, the CIA's Operation Cyclone used Pakistani and Saudi intelligence to support the Mujahedeen—or "Arab-Afghans"—in a war against the Soviets. The largest recipient by far of these CIA funds was Gulbuddin Hekmatyar, a radically reactionary Islamist who became one of the world's largest heroin traffickers during this time.[12]

The intelligence agencies' partnership with drug trafficking organizations was not merely a Cold War peccadillo. In the early 1990s, the US—with no Cold War pretext—deployed similar measures in the former Soviet Union. The George H. W. Bush administration sought to have a pipeline built which would transport Baku oil to Turkey.[13] Around this time a front company from Atlanta named MEGA Oil appeared.[14] In Azerbaijan, MEGA Oil created a proprietary airline that secretly flew al Qaeda fighters from Afghanistan to Azerbaijan.[15] Afghan heroin also flowed through Baku and into Chechnya with the support of the Pakistani ISI.[16] These operations led eventually to a 1993 military coup that overthrew Abulfaz Elchibey, Azerbaijan's elected president. His replacement was the US-friendly Heidar Aliyev. Turkish intelligence ascertained that the Azerbaijan International Oil Consortium (comprised of BP and Amoco) were behind the coup.[17] MEGA Oil never found oil and it would appear that it was not created to do so. Rather, MEGA Oil served to lay the operational groundwork for an Azerbaijani shift that moved the country firmly into the US/Anglo camp, both as a source of petroleum profits and as a hub for the transportation of jihadis and heroin. While there is evidence that big oil was behind the coup in 1993, it is unknown to this author what persons or organizations were ultimately behind the creation of MEGA Oil.

It is important to note that one of the founders of MEGA oil was Richard Secord,[18] a veteran of both Iran-Contra and the "secret war" in Laos.[19] Secord was already formally retired by the time of his Iran-Contra involvement. He eventually pled guilty of lying to Congress about the $2 million he had personally received during the operation.[20] The overlapping personnel and the recurring *modi operandi* demonstrate that these operations are deep state institutions that bring together elements of the security state, the criminal underworld, and the overworld of the corporate rich. An exception to the rule of law generally applies to those practices carried out in furtherance of US hegemony. Thus, again, the *national interest* appears to be defined as being largely synonymous with the interests of the overworld of private wealth.

Besides arms and commodities industries, the drug traffic (often with covert state sanction) must also be considered a significant element of the Dollar Wall Street Regime. The true extent of this may be impossible to quantify, but occasionally facts surface which illuminate this aspect of the global economy. In 2009, *The Guardian* reported that the top official at the UN Office on Drugs and Crime, Antonio Maria Costa, said that he saw evidence indicating that organized crime profits were "the only liquid investment capital" going into a number of banks which nearly collapsed during the 2008 financial crisis. Consequently, most of the $352 billion of drug trafficking profits were absorbed into the economic system.[21] Said Costa, "Inter-bank loans were funded by money that originated from the drugs trade and other illegal activities. . . . There were signs that some banks were rescued that way."[22] *The Guardian* surmises that Costa's statements, "will raise questions about crime's influence on the economic system at times of crisis."[23] Such anecdotes indicate that the flow of drug money into the banking system is a systemic feature of the global economy—one that is most noticeable when "normal" financial activity stops or is curtailed drastically. To the extent that such is the case, it suggests that the underworld often functions as a subsidiary of the overworld.

The underworld and the security state also have a history of collaborating to organize political assassinations. In 1955, the CIA's drug-trafficking KMT allies attempted to assassinate Zhou Enlai who was on his way to Sukarno's Bandung Conference. A saboteur put a bomb on the *Kashmir Princess* airliner. Zhou was tipped off and switched planes, but eleven passengers died when the bomb exploded. Although journalist Steve Tsang concluded that the CIA was not directly implicated,[24] other evidence points to possible US involvement, including the escape of the saboteur on a plane owned by the CIA/KMT proprietary airline Civil Air Transport (later renamed Air America).[25]

Perhaps the most infamous examples of intelligence-underworld collaboration were the Castro assassination plots in which the CIA enlisted Cuban exiles and top US organized crime figures to assassinate Fidel Castro. Castro survived the plots, but much evidence indicates that elements of the operations were incorporated into the assassination of President Kennedy. Robert Kennedy himself came to believe that such was the case.[26] Senator Kennedy had planned to reinvestigate his brother's assassination once he attained the presidency but before that could happen, he himself was assassinated.[27]

In 1976, former Chilean ambassador Orlando Letelier and journalist Ronnie Moffitt were killed by a car bomb on a Washington DC street. Letelier's murder had been ordered by DINA, Chile's CIA-created intelligence unit. The plot was executed by DINA members and Cuban exiles in conjunction with assets from Operation Condor, the CIA's outsourced supranational assassination apparatus. All of the parties involved were also engaged in drug trafficking.[28] Most history books in the US blame the assassination on Chile's Pinochet and Manuel Contreras, the DINA director. Contreras was eventually sentenced to seven years by a Chilean court for the murder. However, the CIA had been working with DINA since 1974. Contreras himself had been recruited as a CIA agent and met with CIA Deputy Director Vernon Walters on two occasions in Washington. During his trial, Contreras testified that Walters had declared Letelier a threat to the US. Further, Contreras testified that DINA assassin Michael Townley received CIA support for the car bombing operation that killed Letelier and Moffitt. To the present day, the CIA describes Townley as a

DINA agent while Latin American sources describe him as a CIA agent.[29] But a number of American authors like Peter Kornbluh have documented Washington's awareness of and responsibility for Operation Condor.[30] The strange personage of Michael Townley serves as a case study in the obscurantism of America's supranational deep state. In recent years, pop culture homage has been obliquely paid to the man: Michael Townley is the name of a video game protagonist—an underworld figure turned government informant in Rockstar's endlessly ported, *Grand Theft Auto 5*.

By now, the reader should not be surprised to learn that oil-rich Venezuela has been the target of similar deep state intrigues. In 1990, a CIA anti-drug unit was exposed as having shipped into the US a ton of cocaine, product which was eventually sold on the street. The head of the unit was General Ramon Guillen Davila.[31] DEA officials stated that the general confessed to establishing and profiting from the operation. Said one agent, "He cried, collapsed, admitted everything he had done . . . [Guillen] was trying to do exactly what Noriega did—no worse, no better."[32] The enterprise may have smuggled as much as 22 tons of cocaine into the US.[33] In 2007, the retired General Guillen was arrested, along with his son, for conspiring to assassinate President Hugo Chavez.[34] Guillen was able in 2007 to conspire to kill Chavez because he hadn't been indicted for his drug smuggling. The US had determined that Venezuelan relations were too important to risk in the 1990s—a time when the country was fighting against a rebellion being led by the same Hugo Chavez who Guillen would later plot to assassinate.[35] Though no authors raise this possibility, the circumstances around Guillen's drug smuggling operation and his oblique statements to the effect that he "was trying to do exactly what Noriega did," raise another possibility. Was the CIA attempting to establish a self-financing anti-Chavista force in Venezuela in the apparently likely event that the Chavez rebellion became a protracted conflict? The CIA subversion of DEA efforts at the time would seem to belie the explanation that this was purely a misguided but sincere interdiction operation gone wrong. In Latin America, Operation Condor and the Contras were both financed in similar ways for similar ends. Perhaps declassification or further research could establish whether there is more evidence to support this hypothesis.

Deep State Banking and Finance

Intertwined with the nexus of intelligence and organized crime are various types of clandestine financial infrastructure. Collectively, they represent another key component of the deep state. Former OSS officer, lawyer, and CIA officer Paul Helliwell was a key figure in the early establishment of the subterranean legal and financial institutions that would fund various covert operations around the world. After World War II, Helliwell facilitated the creation of the two legal entities which revived the East Asian opium connection. The first was Civilian Air Transport (CAT), an outfit which was built out of General Claire Chennault's World War II Flying Tigers unit. It was Helliwell who arranged for CAT to be made into a CIA propriety.[36] The second was Sea Supply Inc., a corporation set up to move arms to the KMT's opium traffickers in Burma and Thailand.[37] Helliwell was counsel to Meyer Lansky's Miami National Bank when KMT monies from the Burmese-Thai operation were coming in via Hong Kong and laundered through Lansky-connected property firms. Helliwell later established Castle Bank in the Bahamas, a company that laundered money on behalf of the CIA and organized crime.[38] When the Justice Department was pursuing Castle Bank for tax evasion, the investigation was eventually quashed, ending what may have been the largest tax evasion case in history. According to Jim Drinkhall in the *Washington Post*, the CIA successfully argued,

> [T]hat pursuit of the Castle Bank would endanger "national security." This was involved because that bank, besides its possible use as a haven for tax evaders, was the conduit for millions of dollars earmarked by the CIA for the funding of clandestine operations against Cuba and for other covert intelligence operations directed at countries in Latin America and the Far East. A major tax evasion investigation of the bank probably would have endangered these CIA operations.[39]

An official involved in the investigation claimed that Castle Bank was one of the channels used to finance anti-Cuban operations. Helliwell was reportedly one of the men in charge of financing the Bay of Pigs fiasco.[40]

In addition to the Lansky-connected Miami National Bank represented by Paul Helliwell, Miami was the location of another notorious conduit for illicit monies, the World Finance Corporation. This institution was established in 1970 by Bay of Pigs veteran Guillermo Hernandez-Cartaya.[41] Twelve or more employees of World Finance had intelligence connections, including Walter Sterling Surrey, one of the founding directors. Surrey was an OSS officer described by one journalist as "a charter member of the old boy network of US intelligence."[42] World Finance funded CORU, a Cuban exile terrorist outfit.[43] CORU's most notorious crime was its 1976 mid-flight bombing of a Cuban passenger plane which killed all 73 people aboard.[44] The two Cubans in the squad that assassinated Orlando Letelier were provided by CORU and the organization had also carried out the earliest planning for the assassination.[45] In the late 1970s, World Finance came under federal investigation for drug trafficking, money laundering, arms trafficking, political corruption and links to terrorism. As with Castle Bank, it appears that the CIA was able to derail the World Finance investigation. With national security as the justification, US Attorney R. Jerome Sanford was denied access to the FBI's CIA files pertaining to World Finance. The failed investigation so frustrated Sanford that he resigned.[46]

In 1973, Frank Nugan and Michael Hand—along with four Air America officials—established the Australian merchant bank, Nugan Hand.[47] In the Sydney bank's early days, Michael Hand told some younger colleagues that "it was his ambition that Nugan Hand become banker for the CIA."[48] In a short time, the bank expanded its capitalization of $1 million to $1 billion and opened offices in twenty-two countries.[49] One branch was in Chiang Mai, Thailand near the borders of Laos and Burma. On Australian television, the director of Nugan Hand's Chiang Mai branch said that the bank served as a "laundry" for the CIA-allied, Laotian Hmong as well as other opium traders.[50] The same director stated that Nugan Hand transferred various sums of $50 to 60 million for the CIA and that the bank was also involved in arms sales to the Third World.[51] Australian investigators found that Nugan Hand had financed major drug deals and laundered drug money.[52] The bank financed the first large-scale drug shipments into Australia. This occurred just as Nixon's

"War on Drugs" began effecting heroin traffic to the US.[53] With the previous Watergate discussion in mind, it would be interesting to know if this
redirection of the drug traffic was sanctioned by the Nixon administration
or if it was an independent deep state maneuver designed to maintain
lucrative drug-running operations in the face of Washington's decision to
finally combat the drug-trafficking of the CIA's allies.

A pivotal moment for Nugan Hand came in June of 1976 when the
bank was awarded a charter in the Cayman Islands. Eventually the Sydney
police and journalist Jonathan Kwitny of the *Wall Street Journal* came to
believe that there was a connection between the rise of Nugan Hand and
the collapse of Castle Bank.[54] Nugan Hand began its Caribbean operations at the same time as Castle was closing down. With its Caribbean
location and its hiring of "retired" CIA officers, Nugan Hand had a corporate structure strikingly similar to Castle. Kevin Mulcahy, a CIA agent
who testified in the Edwin Wilson case, informed the *National Times of
Sydney* "about the Agency's use of Nugan Hand for shifting money for
various covert operations around the globe."[55]

Nugan Hand also played a role in the CIA-backed 1975 overthrow
of Australia's Labor government. Pertaining to a moment earlier in the
crisis, a CIA contract employee told a newspaper that Michael Hand
paid him to forge cables that were politically damaging to Labor officials. The cables, he said, were forged at the instruction of CIA officer
Edwin Wilson.[56] A debate in the Australian parliament was scheduled
for November 11, 1975, during which the body was to discuss CIA
funding of Australian labor unions through Nugan Hand. The debate
never took place. That morning, the Governor General—a largely symbolic official—dismissed the Labor prime minister using legally dubious
powers never before asserted in the history of the Commonwealth.[57]
The Governor General had deep ties to US intelligence, dating back
to the OSS and later to CIA fronts including the Asia Foundation
and the Congress for Cultural Freedom.[58] When asked in 1981 about
Nugan Hand's collapse, CIA deputy director Bobby Inman stated that
he was worried that any deeper investigation of the bank would expose
various "dirty tricks" that had been played against Australia's Labor
government.[59]

The Nugan Hand bank collapsed following the death of Frank Nugan in 1980. Nugan was found dead in his late model Mercedes Benz on a remote, unpaved road ninety miles north of his $1 million Sydney home.[60] The business card of William Colby was found in the deceased Nugan's pocket. Colby had been employed as an advisor to Nugan Hand Limited on legal, political, and tax matters.[61] He was also a former director of the CIA and the man who had run the agency's notorious Phoenix Program during the Vietnam War.[62] With Nugan dead under highly suspicious circumstances, the bank's cofounder Michael Hand was in a precarious position. Hand—assisted by an ex-CIA officer—obtained a fake passport, put on a fake beard and mustache and then flew to Canada via Fiji before disappearing. An Australian intelligence document stated that Hand was working in Central America with the Contras in 1982.[63] This is logical given that in the 1980s a Senate Foreign Relations Committee investigation into Iran-Contra found that many of the men under investigation were subjects in a 1983 Australian report on Nugan Hand by the Commonwealth-New South Wales Joint Task Force on Drug Trafficking. Among the men involved with both Iran-Contra and Nugan Hand were Richard Secord, Theodore G. Shackley, Thomas G. Clines and Rafael Quintero. Hand, Shackley, Clines, and Secord were all involved in the heroin-riddled CIA operations in Laos in the late 1960s.[64]

In a strange postscript to the Nugan Hand story, Michael Hand was found alive and well in 2015 living in a small town in Idaho under name Michael Fuller. He had been earning a good living by selling tactical weapons to militaries around the world. Thus, one of the most wanted fugitives in Australian history was able to safely relocate to the United States and earn a decent living as a modest part of the military industrial complex. Australian author Peter Butt tracked Hand down, stating that "[T]he FBI could have dealt with Michael Hand long ago. A simple background check reveals Fuller's social security number is identical to the one allocated to Michael Hand in New York in 1960." Butt added, "The fact that Hand has been allowed to live the free life in the United States suggests that he belongs to a protected species, most likely of the intelligence kind."[65] Though Michael Hand was one of Australia's most wanted fugitives for over thirty years, there is no indication that he will be facing extradition.

After the collapse of Nugan Hand, the most notable deep state banking enterprise to emerge in the following era was the Bank of Credit and
Commerce International (BCCI). Though founded around the same time
as Nugan Hand, BCCI would outlast the Australian bank and play a prominent role in Iran-Contra intrigues. Discussed previously in chapter four,
BCCI was at the center of a supranational parapolitical meta-conspiracy
involving the 1980 "October Countersurprise," the illegal sale of arms to
Iran, the diversion of those funds to illegally arm the Contras, the facilita-
tion (or at least toleration) of cocaine trafficking to finance the Contras, and
the support of the heroin-financed Mujahedeen in Afghanistan. The upshot
of these all these banking enterprises—Castle Bank, Nugan Hand, BCCI—
is that they do not fit conceptually within a state/non-state binary. Nor
can they be thought of as simply components of what Glennon terms the
Trumanite network or what would otherwise be called the national security
state. The CIA routinely establishes proprietary firms. There is no reason that
the agency could not establish a bank with international branches to move
funds in and out of this or that country to fund this or that operation. If
these were fully state-sanctioned operations, it would seem that there would
be no reason why these enterprises should run afoul of authorities, but that
happened in all three cases. On many occasions, the public state eventually
detected criminal activity and then attempted to investigate under the auspices of state authority. Yet time and again, a full legal reckoning was eluded.

Today, it may be the case that these enterprises have become passé
given the de facto state of exception in which banks operate in the era
of "too big to fail." Two recent examples illustrate this point. Between
2004 and 2007, Wachovia was found to have failed to apply the legally
required anti-laundering strictures to $378.4 billion transferred into dol-
lar denominated accounts from Mexican currency exchange outlets. No
Wachovia official was prosecuted. The bank was forced to forfeit $110
million in funds proven to be connected to drug trafficking and to pay a
$50 million fine for not monitoring funds used to transport twenty-two
tons of cocaine. The total fine paid by Wachovia was less than 2 percent of
its $12.3 billion profit in 2009.[66]

In 2012, a similarly ineffectual fine was levelled against HSBC after
officials discovered that the bank had been providing financial services to

drug dealers, al Qaeda, and Russian organized crime.[67] Mexican HSBC branches transferred $7 billion to accounts in New York in 2007 and 2008. ICE found that in those years, HSBC moved $881 million of drug money into US accounts on behalf of a Columbian cartel and the Sinaloa Cartel. For its crimes, the Justice Department forced HSBC to pay $1.9 billion in fines and forfeitures. This is probably less money than HSBC made from the transactions as evidenced by an internal email in which an executive lamented the loss of $2.6 billion in revenue from the accounts they were forced to close.[68] The Hong Kong and Shanghai Banking Corporation (HSBC) has a uniquely drug-centric history. It was founded in 1865 after the second Opium War. The peace treaty forced China to legalize the opium trade whereupon HSBC became the biggest commercial bank in quasi-colonial Qing China.[69]

Netherworlds of Dark Money

In addition to all of these banks, there are other financial conduits of the deep state. Following World War II, a number of significant channels were established. The Marshall Plan had a secret codicil that provided funds for covert operations to be carried out by the CIA's Office of Policy Coordination (OPC). These monies were often channeled through foundations like Ford and Rockefeller with OPC personnel moving between intelligence and foundation positions.[70] Five percent of Marshall Plan funds (around $685 million) was diverted to fund these operations which included the creation of false front organizations, propaganda campaigns, the creation of unlawful underground organizations, and the infiltration of civil society—especially labor unions.[71] Part of these funds went to support Nightingale, a Nazi-created guerilla army in Ukraine which during the war had carried out thousands of murders in pursuit of its ultranationalist goals.[72] In addition, the US used $10 million of recovered Axis funds in the CIA's first covert operation, the successful campaign to determine the outcome of Italy's 1948 election.[73]

Japan's postwar political system was even more dramatically dominated through financing by deep political forces. During the second Sino-Japanese War, yakuza figure and ultra-rightist Yoshio Kodama was made a commissioned officer—eventually a rear admiral in the Japanese navy.

During the war, he amassed a fortune by selling the gold, diamonds, and platinum that he had procured in China through the traffic of opium and liquor as well as through outright looting. He transferred vast quantities of stolen diamonds and platinum to an associate before going to prison at the end of the war as a Class A war criminal. Kodama was released in 1948—reportedly following an intervention by the CIA. Kodama went on to become the CIA's top asset in Japan. Funds from the sale of the aforementioned materiel (around $175 million) were used to establish and fund Japan's Liberal Democratic Party (LDP). The right-wing LDP dominated Japanese politics for decades, making Japan into a de facto one-party state, firmly pro-US and anti-neutrality.[74] In postwar Japan, Kodama also used Yakuza gangs to crack down on labor unions and left-wing groups that opposed the US-Japan Security Pact.[75]

Kodama has links to other deep state financial conduits. He was a part of Golden Lily, an operation administered by Emperor Hirohito's brother Price Chichibu. Operation Golden Lily was the systematic looting of Japan's overseas empire in Asia. A vast, not precisely known portion of this wealth was recovered by OSS officer Edward Lansdale in the Philippines in the years after the war. It had been buried in hidden vaults by Japanese General Yamashita after the US had cut off the shipping lanes to Japan. Rather than reveal the existence of this vast amount of gold and other valuables, the US made a decision to obscure its existence and instead assert that Japan was financially wiped out after the war and thus unable to pay any reparations to members of victim nations. Uncompensated victims would even include Bataan Death March veterans and their families. Subsequently, the proceeds from the discoveries were stored in bank accounts all over the world to be used to fund various covert operations.[76] The full story of Golden Lily—sometimes called *Yamashita's gold*—has never been told. The most extensive account comes from the book *Gold Warriors* by Sterling and Peggy Seagrave.[77] While the Seagraves are not trained academic historians, they compensated for this by including with their book three CD-ROMs containing the source material on which their narrative is based. This supporting material, combined with the experiences of former US Deputy Attorney Norbert Schlei were enough to convince renowned Japan scholar Chalmers Johnson of the veracity of the Seagraves' central claims.[78]

Yoshio Kodama was also a key figure in another of the deep state's financial institutions—the Lockheed system of payoffs to key political figures. Rather than having its agents handing off suitcases full of cash, "the CIA used trusted American businessmen as go-betweens to deliver money to benefit its allies. Among these were executives from Lockheed, the company then building the U-2."[79] Five months prior to the 1965 overthrow of Indonesian President Sukarno, Lockheed reallocated a stream of funds from a Sukarno backer to a Suharto supporter. These political payoffs were laundered as commissions from arms sales. Lockheed records offer no explanation for the change which incidentally put the company at risk of being sued for violating the terms of a contract. However, a memo that surfaced later from the Jakarta office of the Economic Counselor of the US Embassy spoke of the Lockheed switch: "[There were] some political considerations behind it."[80] Kodama and Sasakawa Ryoichi were also instrumental in the overthrow of Sukarno and both were recipients of— and conduits for—Lockheed payments.[81] Eventually, the Lockheed payoff system would become a major scandal in Japan, leading to the 1983 criminal conviction of former prime minister Kakuei Tanaka for taking $4.5 million in bribes from the network.[82] The scandal also brought an end to Kodama's reign as the preeminent deep state fixer in Japan. Until the scandal broke in 1976, Kodama was unknown to the Japanese public. As for the $7 million in Lockheed bribes, the court's verdict was suspended owing to Kodama's poor health. He died in 1984.[83] It is worth noting that the Lockheed role in both Indonesia and Japan was only exposed through the Church Committee investigation.[84] This is another example of how the brief period following Watergate represented the most significant pushback from the public state against the national security state and deep state forces.

Lockheed is not the only private corporation to be involved in these sorts of intrigues involving arms sales and covert operations. In 1981, the US sold Boeing AWACS to Saudi Arabia for $8.5 billion. Reagan had to twist arms in the Senate to get the deal approved. Numerous sources reported that Reagan pushed the deal in exchange for a Saudi promise to fund the administration's covert operations and thereby avoid congressional oversight. This was not a direct kickback as with the Lockheed deals. Rather, the money went to other operations such as the funding of the Reagan's two infamous drug-trafficking terrorist proxy forces—the Contras and the Mujahedeen.[85]

More recently, the Saudis were also involved in another significant arms deal scandal. In 2004, Britain's Serious Fraud Office began an investigation into revelations that Saudi royals were receiving enormous secret payments from Britain's largest arms maker, BAE. The payments were essentially bribes to facilitate much larger arms sales to the kingdom. In 2006, British prime minister Tony Blair prevailed upon the Attorney General to end the investigation. It later emerged that Blair had intervened in response to threats from Prince Bandar—the chief of the Saudi National Security Council and the son of the kingdom's crown prince. Bandar was accused of receiving over $1 billion from BAE. Previously secret files revealed how Bandar had flown to London in 2006 to deliver threats to the effect that further investigation could cause "another 7/7" and would cost "British lives on British streets."[86] The least sinister way to interpret this would be as a threat to withhold from Britain the Saudi intelligence on terror networks that the kingdom so diligently and earnestly compiles. However, given Bandar's status as an éminence grise of the deep state, his threats lend themselves to darker interpretations. After all, it was Bandar who secured the AWACS deal and subsequently contributed over $30 million to fund the Contras.[87] It was Bandar who organized the USA-KSA plan to arm the Afghan Mujahedeen.[88] Bandar was also linked to 9/11 in different ways. Two unpublished phone numbers connected to Bandar were found in the phonebook of al Qaeda operative Abu Zubaydah. More troubling is the finding that in the years around 9/11, Prince Bandar and his wife gave tens of thousands of dollars to two Saudi families who lived on the same apartment block as two of the 9/11 hijackers. One of the men of these families, Omar al-Bayoumi, was suspected of being a covert Saudi agent. Al-Bayoumi greeted the hijackers upon their US arrival. He helped them get an apartment, helped them acquire social security cards, and helped them enroll in flight schools. The Basnans—the other of the two hijacker-friendly families—had once held a party for "blind sheik" Omar Abdel-Rahman, the Muslim cleric convicted for his role in the 1993 WTC bombing.[89] The "blind sheik" had previously helped the US by providing jihadi fighters for wars in Afghanistan and Bosnia.[90] And while under extremely tight surveillance in a US prison,[91] Abdel-Rahman ordered the drafting of a letter that would eventually lead to the September 9, 2001 assassination of Northern Alliance chief Ahmad Massoud. This cleared the way for the previously planned US invasion of Afghanistan which Massoud had categorically opposed. And of course, the pretext for America's Afghanistan War came two days later with the September 11 terror spectacle.[92]

As for Bandar, while none of the above proves that he was wittingly funding 9/11 hijackers, it does highlight, in several respects, how deep state actors are able to fund and carry out operations. These covert and illegal activities are rarely investigated or adjudicated even when substantial evidence surfaces. A rule of thumb for criminal investigations is that they should "follow the money." With apparently a different philosophy in mind, *The 9/11 Commission Report* stated, "To date, the U.S. government has not been able to determine the origin of the money used for the 9/11 attacks. Ultimately the question is of little practical significance."[93] At any rate, Bandar and KSA never became fully estranged from al Qaeda and associated groups. In 2007, Seymour Hersh wrote that Bandar was leading the Saudi side of a change in US policy that would utilize Salafi militants to attack US/Saudi adversaries in the Middle East. According to a US government consultant, "[Bandar's and the Saudis'] message to us was 'We've created this movement, and we can control it.' It's not that we don't want the Salafis to throw bombs; it's who they throw them at—Hezbollah, Moqtada al-Sadr, Iran, and at the Syrians, if they continue to work with Hezbollah and Iran."[94] This account could be dismissed as hearsay were it not for the fact that in subsequent years, US policy unfolded in just the way Bandar described, as al Qaeda and other Salafist types were unleashed in Libya and Syria with enormous support from the US and its allies, including Saudi Arabia.

The clandestine financial networks described here are obscure, widespread, and connected to various criminogenic operations involving a multinational cadre within and outside of the government. These channels often serve to fund nominally non-state organizations. Historically, top-down, deep political power has been brought to bear by diverse non-state entities. In previous eras of US history, this was accomplished through outfits like the Pinkerton National Detective Agency—a private firm that, beginning in the mid-nineteenth century, famously provided clients with a variety of services including strike-breaking, infiltration, intelligence gathering, and counterintelligence. The Pinkertons often worked with the wealthy overworld of its day, in addition to receiving government contracts. Since World War II, numerous types of organizations have been created to carry out legitimate and illegitimate activities on behalf of the state and/or overworld actors. Some of these are descendants, so to speak, of the Pinkertons—i.e., private intelligence or even paramilitary firms. These have included Wackenhut, Booz Allen, SAIC, Stratfor, and Blackwater. Officials in these companies may retain and utilize high-level security clearances. Other entities have been created by intelligence services but can eventually act with considerable autonomy. These include the various Anti-Communist Leagues established early in the Cold War.

In Europe, NATO's Operation Gladio created "stay behind" armies initially intended to resist Soviet occupation. When the Soviet invasion never came, Gladio assets were used to carry out false flag terror as part of a "strategy of tension" designed to move countries politically to the right.[95] In Italy, Gladio was connected to an even more obscure and infamous organization, the *Propaganda Due* (P2) Masonic Lodge. According to Swiss historian Daniele Ganser, "P2 was literally a state within the state and operated beyond any democratic controls."[96] The P2 lodge was comprised of powerful figures in Italian society, including many drawn from the legislative, executive, and judicial branches of the government. Its membership also included media figures, wealthy industrialists, military officials, and officers of the Carabinieri paramilitary police.[97] According to a German journalist, the ex-OSS officer and high-ranking Freemason Frank Gigliotti recruited and financed the leader who established the P2 lodge as an anti-Communist network.[98] It was apparently under the Nixon administration that US support for P2 most dramatically increased. Former CIA agent Richard Brennecke claimed that the US was financing P2 with as much as $10 million per month. He also stated, "We have used the P2 to create tensions which led to the explosion of terrorism in Italy and other countries during the 1970s."[99] This would be a reference to the

P2's relationship to Gladio. In the 1990s, an Italian parliament investigation concluded that Gladio members had conspired with ultra-rightists to engage in covert operations including terrorist attacks that were then blamed on communists to damage them in elections.[100] In 2001, Italy's former chief of counterintelligence, General Gianadelio Maletti, testified that after the Piazza Fontana bombing, Italian intelligence agents planted bomb components in the home of a leftist editor to blame him and the Italian left for the bombing.[101] While there have been a number of spectacular disclosures involving institutions like Gladio and P2, information about these entities remains sparse overall. In addition to the false flag terror of Italy's *strategy of tension*, there is reason to speculate whether these networks could have been involved in various other assassinations of European political figures such as Aldo Moro, Olaf Palme, and Alfred Herrhausen.

Every Day is Doomsday! COG and the Deep State

Situated more firmly within the government—but with links to the private sector—the "Doomsday Project" is another important and obscure component of the deep state. Also known as "Continuity of Government" (COG), the Doomsday Project began in the early days of the Cold War. Its initial purpose was to allow for the state's continued existence following a nuclear war. The Pentagon began implementing Doomsday plans shortly thereafter, notably with the construction of the huge underground complexes at Raven Rock and Mount Weather.[102]

COG planning under Eisenhower began to generate a series of Presidential Emergency Action Documents (PEADs) which could be issued by a president following the declaration of a national emergency.[103] It was under Eisenhower that Doomsday planning became even more secretive and absolutist. An FBI memo from 1958 revealed that one of the PEADs allowed the government to apprehend and detain "those dangerous alien enemies presently included in our security index."[104] Furthermore, in 1958 and 1959, President Eisenhower drafted and sent letters to ten Americans—mostly private citizens—bestowing on each of them the authority to exercise emergency executive powers in the wake of a catastrophic event (read: nuclear war). One of the ten authorized emergency dictators resigned. Of the nine that were left, two were presidential cabinet secretaries and one was the Chairman of the Board of Governors of the Federal Reserve. The other six were drawn from the pinnacle of the corporate rich, another striking confirmation of C. Wright Mills's *Power Elite* thesis. One of the letters remains classified but is known to have been sent to Theodore F. Koop, the man designated to be the "Administrator of the Emergency Censorship Agency."[105]

Kennedy inherited Eisenhower's Doomsday plans. A few months into JFK's presidency, his Special Assistant, Frederick G. Dutton, sent a letter to National Security Advisor McGeorge Bundy which spoke of the Doomsday plans. In August, after apparently receiving no response from Bundy, Dutton sent another memo.

> You may recall that in late May, I wrote advising of the existence of classified letters from President Eisenhower to ten private citizens throughout the country giving them authority over various parts of the economy and total society in the event of a declaration of a national emergency. The President subsequently asked that letters from him to the individuals involved terminating their contingent authority be held up until reorganization of [Doomsday plans]. I would appreciate notification by you as to whether that outstanding authority should be terminated, as I recommend; continued under new letters of instruction from the President; or what course you may desire to have taken.[106]

Bundy did respond to the second memo, sending a terse reply which stated that the Emergency Administrators' "outstanding authority" should be terminated. The Kennedy libraries have mail receipts suggesting that letters were sent to six of the men terminating their authority. But it is not known if the remaining three retained their emergency powers. On October 26, Kennedy's Director of Emergency Planning, Frank B. Ellis, told NBC that the president had authorized a number of men to take on administrative duties "in such areas as transportation, the mobilization of necessary foods, the re-establishment of communications and all of the other very critical aspects that are necessary to place into working order following an emergency" in the event of a nuclear attack or other disaster that could kill top US officials. Ellis did not identify these would-be emergency dictators, instead stating obliquely, "They are known."[107]

Preparations for Doomsday contingencies continued and accelerated during the tumultuous 1960s. These plans eventually evolved into Operation Garden Plot, issued shortly after the riots which followed the MLK assassination. Garden Plot allowed for two brigades to be kept at ready to quell unrest. The operation was discontinued after student protesters were shot at Kent State and Jackson State.[108] However, the plans were resurrected during the Carter administration by "Coordinator of Security" Samuel Huntington, a scholarly advocate of top-down (or "dark") power. In 1978, Huntington and Zbigniew Brzezinski redesigned the COG system, most notably by creating the Federal Emergency Management System (FEMA) to provide the infrastructure needed for a government takeover in the event of a crisis.[109]

Under the Reagan administration, COG planning was further ramped up as the "Doomsday Project."[110] Oliver North was working on these operations which included provisions to surveil political dissidents and detain undocumented aliens in the event of an emergency. This plan was given the codename Rex 84 and it entailed exceptionalist measures (i.e., suspension of the Constitution) under a number of pretexts, a US invasion of Nicaragua among them. In addition to spying on political opponents of Reagan's Central American policies, the plan called for the surveillance of environmentalists, anti-nuke activists, and refugee advocates. Some of the highest-level planning of this era was carried out by a parallel extra-governmental group. Echoing those Eisenhower provisions for a dictatorial committee-in-waiting, Reagan's privatization of the most sweeping security provisions serves to demonstrate the deep state essence of the Doomsday Project. Operating outside of regular government channels, this group included the CEO of G. D. Searle & Co., Donald Rumsfeld. It also included Dick Cheney, serving as a Wyoming congressman at the time. Official responsibility for the program resided with Vice President George H. W. Bush under an entity with an anodyne title: the National Program Office. Lieutenant Colonel Oliver North served as the National Security Council action officer.[111]

The most sweeping suspension of the constitution was to be asserted in the event of a nuclear war. However, in 1988, Reagan's Executive Order 12656 amended this to allow for constitutional suspension following "any occurrence, including natural disaster, military attack, technological emergency, or other emergency, that seriously degrades or seriously threatens the national security of the United States."[112] In 1994, it was reported in the *New York Times* that the Doomsday Project was a relic of the Cold War and thus was to be closed that year.[113] In reality, only the nuclear aspect of COG planning had ended. During the Clinton administration, planning continued with a $200 million annual budget. Soviet nukes were replaced by terrorists. Additionally, the specialists of the "shadow government" in waiting were no longer a bipartisan group, but instead were mostly Republican hawks including Cheney and Rumsfeld. In May of 2001, the Rumsfeld-Cheney COG planning team was essentially reunited in George W. Bush's administration as a terrorism task force. In this capacity, they presumably did a lot of planning (about which almost nothing is known) before a major terrorist attack resulted in the implementation of COG.[114] Since the September 11, 2001 terror spectacle, COG provisions have been implemented and renewed without transparency or debate. At present, it is impossible to know the extent to which secret decrees have overridden the US Constitution.[115]

Peter Dale Scott sees COG as a crucial component of the deep state—one with considerable impact on the course of postwar American history. Specifically, Scott asserts that COG has been an operational factor in four *structural deep events*, historical events that "are large enough to affect the whole fabric of society, with consequences that enlarge covert government, and are subsequently covered up by systematic falsifications in media and internal government records."[116] Scott's four structural deep events are: the Kennedy assassination, Watergate, Iran-Contra, and 9/11.[117] These events have served to facilitate key historical developments that have weakened and threatened democracy in the US. One of these negative developments is the transformation of the American economy into a plutonomy, an increasingly dizzying hierarchy of haves and have-nots. Another development is the drastic rise of secretive, top-down, state power in the US. A third is the rise of

American militarism and the tendency to launch wars in remote parts of the globe.[118]

In assessing all this, Peter Dale Scott views COG as an element of the deep state which has played a significant historical role in allowing deep political forces to eclipse the public state. Notably, there are provocative personnel overlaps between COG and structural deep events. These include figures like Jack Crichton—an army intelligence officer and the chief of intelligence for Dallas Civil Defense—who was in the president's Dallas motorcade on November 22, 1963. James McCord of the CIA was involved in high level COG planning. McCord figured in aspects of the Kennedy assassination and later more infamously in Watergate. John Dean of Watergate fame had been a participant in COG activities as associate deputy attorney general. Oliver North was deeply involved in some of the most sensitive aspects of the Doomsday Project. He was also a key Iran-Contra figure, during which he carried out illegal operations using Flashboard, the top-secret communications network of the Doomsday Project.[119] As mentioned above, Donald Rumsfeld and Dick Cheney were key COG figures during the 1980s and 1990s. They also played and obscure but important role in the post-Watergate "Halloween Massacre" of 1975. As detailed in a previous chapter, the Halloween Massacre can be viewed as the denouement of Watergate, marking as it did a decisive US political shift to the right under President Ford—a shift that is typically unrecognized today or is mistakenly attributed chiefly to Reagan's election to the presidency. Additionally, and more famously, Rumsfeld and Cheney were key 9/11 figures. Of this, Scott writes:

> [Cheney's and Rumsfeld's] behavior on 9/11 revives the question arising from their White House activity in the semiconspiratorial 1975 Halloween Massacre [. . .]. The question in both events is whether Cheney and Rumsfeld could have contrived such a major change on their own within the White House, or whether they were acting in concert with other aspects of the deep state. That is a key question for 9/11 [. . .] made even more urgent by [their] activities with respect to COG.[120]

On the surface, these appear to be alarmist statements, pregnant with grim implications. However, a close reading of Scott's work convincingly demonstrates that crucial information about 9/11 has been covered up. Given the extraordinary levels of government secrecy involved, it is impossible to say what exactly is being covered up, but subsequent to Scott's 2007 book on 9/11, high officials began to speak of various cover-ups related to the subject. For example, Senator Bob Graham stated in 2015, "One thing that irritates me is that the F.B.I. has gone beyond just covering up, trying to avoid disclosure, into what I call aggressive deception."[121] Graham had previously co-chaired the Joint Inquiry into Intelligence Community Activities before and after the Terrorist Attacks of September 11, 2001. John Farmer, the senior counsel of the 9/11 Commission, wrote, "At some level of the government, at some point in time [. . .] there was a decision not to tell the truth about what happened."[122]

While none of these critical insiders have placed a strong emphasis on COG operations and 9/11, the Doomsday angle remains part of the obscured story of 9/11. This and its relevance to prior cataclysmic events in recent US political history should be further scrutinized. As an institution in a supposedly democratic state, the Doomsday Project has remained mostly opaque. This opacity has persisted, even as the passage of time has seemingly nullified the arguments that might be made for keeping COG and related communications secret. For example, historically relevant communications over secure networks were withheld from the Warren Commission, the House Select Committee on Assassinations, the Assassination Records Review Board, and the 9/11 Commission regarding the Kennedy assassination and 9/11 respectively.[123] The Doomsday Project has had significant links to the private sector and has operated largely in the absence of meaningful congressional or other public state oversight. For these and other reasons, the Doomsday Project is a key constituent component of the American deep state.

Deep Sovereignty in the Imperium

Getting lost in the minutiae of these various political intrigues, one can miss the hegemonic forest for the conspiratorial trees. That is to say that the shocking details and mysteries pertaining to this or that episode can distract one from the ends toward which they are aimed. Drawing from Halford Mackinder, historian Alfred McCoy points out that US postwar geopolitical primacy rested upon control of both axial ends of the *world island*—the Eurasian landmass.[124] By controlling Western Europe (especially Germany) and East Asia (especially Japan), Americans created an international capitalist system over which the US reigned hegemonic. Trade and capital have flowed across two oceans with the US as the center of gravity, providing the global reserve currency and an historically unrivaled network of military bases concentrated in and around key strategic locations. While commonly understood as the postwar triumph of liberal democracy in the "free world," the preponderance of covert operations points to a much grimmer reality. In Europe and Japan, untold sums were spent to covertly manipulate political life. Japan was a de facto one-party state with war criminals serving as CIA-backed power brokers and fixers. Similarly, wartime fascists and Nazis were spared from legal reckoning in order to wield tremendous power in Italy and Germany, specifically in the personage of the fascist head of *P2*, Licio Gelli and the West German intelligence chief, Reinhard Gehlen. The establishment and operation of clandestine organizations and networks further confounds historiography and political sense-making in our time. However, the record is clear enough to establish that deep political forces have played a significant historical role. On balance, their activities have consistently served to undermine democracy and the rule of law while bolstering the deep state's drive for hegemony on its terms.

By now, it should be clear that mainstream journalists, social scientists, and historians cannot grapple with the dark realities of our historical epoch. Media outlets are either owned by massive corporate conglomerates or they depend on the corporate world for advertising. "Alternative" media is often dependent on the largesse of foundations whose wealth comes from the same capitalist system policed by the lawless deep state. Given these conditions, it should not be surprising that journalists cannot easily earn a living by exposing the illegitimacy of the regime that rules us. Without going too deeply into the realities of the modern corporate neoliberal university or, say, the role of capitalist foundations in academia, suffice it to say that academy is a pillar of the Establishment. The empire is not forced to deal with many true dissidents in academia. But the pretenses of academic freedom and the vestiges of the tenure system do allow for intellectual independence. Happily, there is a small number of scholars who overcome the stultifying processes of socialization. These free persons defy the odds by escaping the obscurantist, myopic orthodoxies of liberalism or postmodern "radicalism."

Oft cited throughout this book is my mentor, collaborator, and friend Peter Dale Scott. In 2006, Peter met the Norwegian scholar, Ola Tunander, at a conference in Melbourne, Australia. Tunander's work on the *deep state* informed Peter's thinking and the ideas presented in this book. In correspondence with Peter and me, Ola drafted a lengthy email full of important facts and incisive analysis. I find this material so fascinating that it warrants inclusion in this book.

When Tunander began looking into these areas in the 1990s, he noticed commonalities between the Turkish *deep state*,

[A]nd similar forces in Italy, Greece, and France—as well as in Sweden. What they all had in common were their close ties to corresponding forces in the US. In Italy, one had used the concept "*Stato parallelo*." In Sweden, there was no word for it. I saw a similarity between these forces and what Carl Schmitt called the "Sovereign," the one "who decides on the exception." As you know, this is the entity that decides on when to introduce a state of emergency or a military coup, as we experienced from Cold War Italy or Turkey or Greece. In other words, this is the entity that decides when the law should be applied or not. It was clear when these forces intervened with "coup attempts" in Italy in 1964, 1970, 1973 and 1974 that they acted in close collaboration with the Americans—primarily with the CIA but also with the DIA. Prince Junio Valerio Borghese's coup attempt in 1970, was preceded by the use of terrorist attacks (bombs exploding in public squares) that created a demand for order and for a strong leader. The "foreign minister" of the coup plotters, Adriano Monti, turned to CIA's man in Madrid Otto Skorzeny, who gave them green light for the coup (on the condition that Andreotti was given the top position). However, the coup plotters withdrew from the scene after Italian political leaders had accepted US demands. It is not clear who gave this order. A close collaborator to Borghese, Gaetano Lunetta, actually insisted that there had been a coup, and the political Italy had accepted a total subordination to the US. In this example, we find that the veto power of the security state acted outside or above the law to limit the range of the democratic state.

Tunander went on to state that powerful actors are able to "securitize" what had previously been in the domain of the public state by claiming that due to emergency circumstances, "no political alternatives exist—[i.e.,] democracy is no longer relevant, because there is no longer a political choice."

This complicates efforts to distinguish the concept of the *deep state* from that of the *security state*. In grappling with these ideas, Tunander turns to the example of Turkey:

> [T]he coup leader in Turkey in 1980, General Kenan Evren, also spoke about a "deep state" as something different from himself. The "deep state" appears here rather to have been a network of people linked to the Stay Behinds and directly to the Americans (i.e., to Gladio). It was an entity that already in late 1970s had started a terrorist campaign with bomb attacks to destabilize the country to make a military take-over "necessary." This is similar to what happened in Italy 10 years earlier.

At this point, Ola delves into some fascinating personal experiences with figures involved in these events.

> I once had a dinner with Ümit Halûk Bayülken in Turkey. He had been Evren's defense minister, and, according to Bayülken, Evren had called him late at night before the coup. Evren had said, "You have been a foreign minister and your father was a general, and I want you as defense minister tomorrow, or actually in a few hours." There had been too much bloodshed and violence and the military had to intervene, he argued. Mr. Bayülken's wife understood

that something was going on and tried to stop him, but Bayülken's father had been a general and so he felt he could not walk away from his responsibility. I also met Evren's foreign minister, who also was a civilian and a diplomat. General Evren certainly tried to give the coup a civilian legitimacy, but the brutal violence that had justified the coup was largely initiated by Abdullah Çatlı and his extreme rightwing Grey Wolves—utilized by Turkish Stay Behinds or Counter-Guerilla. They were linked to the Americans as well as to criminal activities like assassinations and drug trafficking, primarily heroin. As you know, Çatlı was later found dead in 1996 in the Susurluk incident, after the car crash in a Mercedes. He died with his girlfriend, the beauty queen Gonca Us. Also killed in the crash was the MP Sedat Bucak, a man with his own private army of supposedly 20,000 men. Also in the car was the Istanbul Chief of Police and former head of the Special Operations Department, Huseyin Kocadağ—as well as a number of sub machine guns, false passports, and identity cards. Çatlı was close to former Prime Minister and now Deputy Prime Minister Tansu Çiller. Çatlı's license to carry weapons was signed by former Minister of Interior Mehmet Ağar, who was forced to leave office because of this incident.

In this case, Tunander acknowledges that the evidence does support a tripartite conception of the state as the security state was subordinated to a higher power, or *deep state*. But he argues, for good reason, that the Turkish deep state was a US—or at least US intelligence—linked network that had penetrated the public state and the security state in Turkey. This leads to other fascinating subjects:

> The US-dominated *deep state* seems to enter the foreign state through very secret agreements, and in many cases by oral agreements, because these ties may be so secret that no formal agreement is possible. These secret agreements may be what actually constitutes the *deep state*. The deep state hierarchies are so secret that nothing about them can be regulated by legally binding agreements, making deep state activities necessarily extra-legal activities.

Former Chairman of Joint Chiefs of Staff General John Vessey told me at a dinner in Oslo that when it comes to US relations to Sweden, there was only one rule: "Nothing on paper." Several other high-ranking officers said the same, including former Chief of Naval Operations Admiral Elmo Zumwalt and Secretary of Defense Caspar Weinberger. The chairman of NATO's Military Committee, General Herman Fredrik Zeiner-Gundersen, said that this is a general rule: if something is written on paper, it is no longer secret. It could be leaked to a journalist, he said. According to this logic, "real secret information" or at least what is extremely secret (and also most important) exists only as oral information, but this means that a breach of discipline cannot be punished according to any law.

Obviously, this is not to say that such breaches will go unpunished. Violations of the secret agreements—including violations of the "code of silence"—will certainly not be tolerated by the sovereign power.

This brings to mind the example of criminal syndicates. Readers with good memories or those with social science backgrounds may recall that the modern capitalist state grew out of roving bands of protection racketeers.[125] This realm of state criminalization is essentially where Tunander proceeds to take his analysis.

There is no law that regulates this activity. All these functions have to be conducted as extra-legal activities: as mafia-like operations or deep state operations that are above the law. Anything that is above the formal hierarchy of secrecy is also above the law. This seems to situate these phenomena into a realm of "criminality." People that do not adhere to a secret oral agreement have to be punished by the use of extra-legal force; they may be assassinated or just threatened. To finance this activity you may have to use secret accounts hidden from the regular budget. You may use criminal activity like drug trafficking that cannot be tracked by any other state authority. Peter quoted a former DEA Investigator saying: "[I]n my 30-year history in the Drug Enforcement Administration and related agencies,

the major targets of my investigations almost invariably turned out
to be working for the CIA."[126] Of course, covert action could be
financed also through other kinds of criminal activities or sometimes by secret accounts hidden in the budget, but it is striking
that only security services or intelligence services are able to decide
who can cross national borders with large amounts of drugs without
being caught by law enforcement.

Parapolitical finance has already been discussed in this chapter. Another
relevant angle to ponder in passing is one that is maddening to consider
for people who are not on the political hard right. For every glaring US
social problem, any proposed solution is met with cries of "How are you
going to pay for that?" Meanwhile the US can run endless, massive military deficits thanks to dollar hegemony. Additionally, other types of murderous statecraft can be funded through criminal operations like drug
trafficking when said operations are simply too sinister to be funded in a
transparent way.

All this raises questions about how these enterprises can be managed
given the astounding levels of state secrecy. How can anyone steer the *ship
of state* (read: of *deep state*) if its operations are ultra-secretive or not even
formally documented?

When I was a civilian expert in the Swedish 2001 Submarine
Inquiry located at the Swedish Defense Ministry, we found that
there was an archive for documents above the formal levels of
secrecy. Formally speaking, these documents did not exist. They
had no legal existence. They existed in a realm between that of a
top-secret document and that of even more secret oral information. According to the responsible officer, some of these documents
were burnt after reading. Later, I found that other documents were
removed from the top-secret intelligence archives—probably into
"private archives" of one or another high-ranking officer. They no
longer existed in a legal sense. The security state and its hierarchy of
secrecy tends to develop very secret "need to know"-levels above the
formalized levels of secrecy.

Such activities would seem to place crucial knowledge about the state in a realm that is detached or just barely tethered to the authoritarian security state and far removed from democratic oversight. Thus does this sort of secrecy contribute to the problem of irresponsible top-down rule.

> These echelons of extreme secrecy in the security state tend to develop into a "deep state," and it seems to me that these echelons tend to be hijacked by foreign services like the Americans and perhaps also the British and the Israelis. If one looks at the Swedish experience, the informal, oral and very secret ties to the US (and to the British) were handled largely by officers loyal to the US and the UK. The Italian experience seems to have been very much the same. These networks of officers on the Swedish or Italian side, on all levels, were considered to be the relevant actors when the CIA or the Pentagon wanted to have something done in these very countries—whether they wanted to prepare for regime change or just manipulate the policies of these states according to the dictates of the US or, more specifically, the CIA.

So for Tunander, the access and control over state secrets, up to and including whether they shall even remain documented at all, helps to give rise to an overriding form of sovereignty that complicates liberal conceptions of democracy.

However, since Tunander sees the US as a plausibly deniable imperialist power vis-à-vis countries like Sweden, he does not fully embrace the idea of a tripartite state.

> This seems to indicate that the logic of the security and the logic of the *security state* bring us into the *deep state*. And while the *public state* may be infiltrated by the *deep state* (as in Turkey in the 1990s), the logic of this *public state* is relative openness—opposite to the logic of the *security state*'s secrecy, which accordingly, in the final analysis, acts as an opening for the *deep state*. To me, this means that I am at present hesitant to use the concept of the *tripartite state*. If one, as I did above, thinks in terms of classifications, one can divide

the state into three entities, but if one thinks about the essence or inner logic of these entities, I still believe that it is fruitful to use the concept of *dual state*.

Here, Tunander is getting into the heart of the matter from the perspective of social science theory. He returns to a very interesting conversation that bears on these matters.

Earlier, I referred to a lunch I had with former CIA Director and US Secretary of Defense James Schlesinger. I asked him about what his views on Sweden during the years he worked in the Nixon Administration. His answer was short and concise: "Which Sweden? the Political Sweden or the Military Sweden? The Military was planning for us to come as soon as possible." He obviously was not speaking about all Swedish political actors or all Swedish military officers. Rather, he was referring to a fundamental divide between a few very relevant political leaders who wanted to maintain Swedish neutrality and some military leaders that were directly linked up to the US agencies and identified themselves with the US and with US military force (and were planning for the US to come as soon as possible). These latter officers were not at the very top of the security state but they were able to run their own policy and to deceive the "Political Sweden," because of their very secret ties to US and British agencies. The logic of the public state (or the democratic state, which is never perfectly democratic) is rather the opposite to the secrecy logic of the security state, which provides and opening for the deep state as a criminal entity above the security state. I am not sure if this makes sense, but it is at least an attempt to approach this field of study. Of course, I have to think about it, and perhaps you also have some comments on this.

Indeed, I do have some commentary to provide. It is a very friendly critic who disagrees with your critical theory, while also acknowledging its strengths and providing examples that buttress it on the whole. I share his ambivalence, but obviously I come down on the side of a tripartite conception of the state. I do not wish to presume how Ola would respond to this, but I surmise that when speaking of the *dual state* vs. the *tripartite state*, one does not need to accept it as an either/or proposition. The deep state can and does exert its power over the public state and the security state. These dynamics do give rise to a dualistic state. i.e., a state that ostensibly operates along democratic, disguising the fact that true sovereignty in the Schmittian sense, is exercised by secretive, lawless institutions that can function in a covert, dictatorial fashion when the need arises. Tunander is correct to point out that outside of the US, the deep state presents as an American presence, overriding other countries' public and security states. But such does not explain what the American *deep state* is to America.

The case of James Schlesinger himself is instructive in this regard. Recall that he was appointed CIA chief by Nixon, in part because he thought Helms and the CIA were not helping him or were damaging him with the Watergate scandal. As DCI Schlesinger tried to compile all the dirt on the CIA that he could to assist his boss, the president. They were not very successful in terms of compiling the most damning CIA secrets. Here we see how the public state, personified by the president, could not take control of the regime even by asserting the presidency's direct control of the security state. Another part of the state proved more powerful than an elected president and the acting head of the intelligence apparatus. *Deep state* is the term I apply to those forces, the Trumpian stigma of the term notwithstanding.

I hope the reader finds theses exchanges worthwhile. For me, it has been very heartening to collaborate and work with scholars in these areas, people like Ola Tunander, Peter Dale Scott, and Lance deHaven-Smith. Opportunities for the free exchange of ideas are invaluable, especially at a time when disinformation and obfuscation prevail in politics, the media, in academia. These preceding passages are an attempt to share some of that with a readership.

An Unconstitutional Constitution

The material in this chapter is an attempt to offer glimpses into a dark quadrant connecting the overworld of private wealth, US intelligence agencies, the intelligence agencies of client states, organized crime, financial institutions, large corporations, private intelligence outfits, and secretive organizations designed for the clandestine manipulation of political life. In the US, covert operations are given official sanction by the National Security Council. To my knowledge, the NSC has never approved off-the-books financing of covert operations through, say, the trafficking of narcotics. Yet there have been numerous instances where CIA-allied entities took advantage of funding through various drug connections. In Southeast Asia, this was institutionalized, occurring over decades with the knowledge of multiple officials. And yet, no serious accounting ever took place, even when the reformist "Watergate Congress" was conducting investigations into the activities of US intelligence agencies.

An alternative explanation is that the CIA has been operating as an independent entity—a "rogue elephant" as Senator Frank Church described it. This is an explanation not too different from Glennon's *Trumanite network* construct that draws from the organizational politics model. That kind of framework posits a hermetically sealed network in which, say, the CIA and the Pentagon represent individual nodes. Nominal non-state entities like organized crime syndicates, private intelligence firms, and networks of overworld rich are, crucially, outside the scope of such a theory. Additionally, and as was shown in an earlier chapter, when the US Congress in the pivotal 1970s acted to curtail the excesses of the intelligence community excesses, various actors associated with the deep state simply found ways to carry on by working through new or extant organizations like the Safari Club, the Pinay Circle, or the World Anti-Communist League. These facts need to be confronted if the regime is to be understood and ultimately reformed or supplanted.

CHAPTER 12

LET US BRING LIGHT TO THE DARK SIDE

The Utility of *Tripartite State* Theory

This book grew out of a doctoral dissertation in the field of political science. Given the obscurantism of US political science, perhaps it would be better to describe this as an attempt at *parapolitical science*. That is to say that it is an attempt at sense-making—through the use of social science theory and empirical evidence—under conditions in which important political and historical events are intentionally obscured by powerful actors. Political science, and especially the subdiscipline of comparative politics, seeks to offer explanations and generalizations that apply to different political entities, typically nation-states. This presupposes that such units are of a type—an assumption that may be more or less realistic, depending on the character of the nation-states in question. The postwar US is a very unique case because of its role as systemic hegemon. More than other developed nations, its trajectory has been determined by domestic political forces that were not forced into subordination vis-à-vis other great powers. Instead, it is the political life of other nations which has been determined by each nation's relationship with the US hegemon. These other states may be America's allies, clients, rivals, or enemies.

Nevertheless, aspects of the tripartite state theory contained herein can be more or less applicable to other nation-states. Left out of the Glennon's examination of British "double-government" is the vague but real British notion of "the Establishment," the entrenched ruling class whose power does not stem from formal or transparent authority. Though its existence is widely acknowledged, its power and workings nevertheless represent deep political power. Most notable is the fact that many postwar US elites were Anglophiles who greatly admired the British empire. The structure and techniques of US intelligence services are most clearly descended from the British secret services. Like the British, the US became an economic world power through protectionist and mercantilist policies until the country had the economic strength to pursue and demand "free trade." If British elites have tried to argue that their empire was acquired absent-mindedly, the US takes this a step further by denying empire outright. Just as the sun never set on the British empire, the sun never sets on the US empire of bases—whether or not this is discussed in mainstream discourse.

In Turkey, the *deep state* came to be widely perceived by the public and the political class. This is why the country's political system served as the origin of the term itself. While in postwar Turkey there have been various elected governments and a formal security hierarchy, the Turkish deep state has repeatedly intervened to assert its sovereignty. A case mentioned earlier by Ola Tunander serves as a key example. Following years of terrorist attacks and assassinations, Turkish General Kenan Evren led a coup which installed him as President in 1980. Much of the violence preceding the coup was carried out by the Grey Wolves, a paramilitary terror organization. The Grey Wolves were intertwined with Turkey's Counter-Guerrilla, an element of the Turkish state that had engaged in domestic terrorism including a 1977 sniper assault on peaceful demonstrators that killed thirty-eight and injured hundreds more.[1] Counter-Guerrilla was the Turkish branch of Gladio, the NATO and CIA operation that established secret armies—ostensibly to resist a Soviet invasion but repurposed as parapolitical state actors. The significance of the US-Grey Wolves linkage is that they demonstrate how the postwar Turkish deep state was largely a US deep state franchise of sorts.

Postwar Italy also has structures quite compatible with tripartite state theory. Nominally a democracy, Italy has been subjected to infamous episodes of parapolitical violence. The original CIA covert operation was the massive campaign to subvert the Italian elections of 1948. Most significant were Italy's "Years of Lead" in which the security services and deep political elements deployed the "strategy of tension," utilizing false flag terror to discredit the Left and thereby manipulate Italian politics. Discussed in the previous chapter, the era's most notorious entity of the Italian deep state was the *P2* Masonic lodge, an organization which united ultra-rightists, business elites, security state officials, Gladio forces, and organized crime figures. This era of parapolitical violence reached an apex with the assassination of Prime Minister Aldo Moro who was kidnapped on the very day that he was to broker an historic compromise in the Italian parliament that would have allowed a power sharing compromise with the left. Though Moro was allegedly murdered by the "Red Brigade," his wife later revealed that a top US official had threatened to use "groups on the fringes" to kill the prime minister if he persisted with his compromise plan.[2] In a Rome court proceeding, Eleonora Moro testified, "[My husband] said that Kissinger had warned him heavily: either you stop courting the communists or you will pay dearly for it."[3] These and other episodes point to the heavy US presence in Italian politics, collectively suggesting that the country's deep state is subordinated to the imperatives of the imperial hegemonic American deep state.

The Japanese state likewise shares similarities with the US tripartite state. The US-written constitution had features which established a public state along with progressive programs such as land reform. However, the US also created institutions that allowed for minority rule to a considerable extent. Rural areas were weighted disproportionately in elections, empowering conservative political forces. Most notably, the ruling center-right Liberal Democratic Party was a US deep state project from the outset. As detailed in the last chapter, antidemocratic political forces survived the war and the US occupation. Most notable was the preservation of the Japanese overworld-underworld relationship as represented in the personage of Yoshio Kodama—the former Yakuza, ex-Imperial Admiral, CIA asset, and Lockheed bagman who founded the LDP and provided it with a deep war chest from vast amounts of Japan's wartime plunder. Post-World War II, the Japanese deep state was ultimately rehabilitated into a satellite of the US deep state.

Latin American cases provide useful confirmation of tripartite state theory. Bolivia had strengthened its democratic state during the presidency of Evo Morales. Just days before the 2019 elections, the *Washington Post* reported, "[I]t's indisputable that Bolivians are healthier, wealthier, better educated, living longer and more equal than at any time in this South American nation's history."[4] When Evo Morales won the election as polls had predicted, the US-dominated Organization of American States issued a press release alleging election fraud.[5] Shortly thereafter, Bolivian security officials essentially forced Morales to resign, effecting a coup of sorts. The key coup-plotting military officials had been trained by the US at Ft. Benning, Georgia—the infamous School of the Americas.[6] Two researchers from MIT's Election Data and Science Lab eventually conducted a study of the Bolivian election. They concluded, "There is not any statistical evidence of fraud that we can find," adding that, "the trends in the preliminary count, the lack of any big jump in support for Morales after the halt, and the size of Morales's margin all appear legitimate."[7] Clearly the Bolivian public state was not sovereign. The country's security state was subservient to deep political forces backed by the US. The putschists' extraconstitutional actions were aided and abetted by other deep state-dominated entities, most notably the Organization of American States. By contrast, the Venezuelan democratic state has been targeted for regime change since the George W. Bush administration. The difference between Venezuela and Bolivia is that up to this point, the Venezuelan security state has defended the public state. Despite various crises brought on by US hybrid warfare and other economic problems, the various coup attempts to date have failed. The Bolivian and Venezuelan cases offer more support to the notion that the security state is often the pivotal and decisive institution when it comes to whether democratic or deep political forces prevail in a country.

In more authoritarian US client states, the tripartite state construct may be less applicable. Saudi Arabia obviously has no democratic state. The complete absence of democratic oversight, the oil reserves to dominate global markets, and the kingdom's vast sums of petrodollars have made it an ideal vehicle for US deep statecraft. Thusly, the kingdom and its security services are by and large pillars of the American deep state. Within Saudi Arabia, elite theory is still applicable as various power struggles have played out between the royal family, foreign influences, and other prominent Saudis such as the assassinated Jamal Khashoggi—himself the nephew of the infamous deep state operator Adnan Khashoggi.

Russia, on the other hand, is a more complicated case. Following the disastrous Yeltsin presidency, the country was famously encumbered with a class of organized crime-linked oligarchs who constituted something of a *deep state* relative to Russia's anemic public state. When Putin came to power, he and the oligarchs famously made a deal that the oligarchs' holdings would not be nationalized if they stayed out of politics. Given Putin's approval ratings and Russia's greatly improved social and economic indicators since he came to power, it could be argued that he represents something of a public statesman in terms of mitigating the exploitative dominance of the Yeltsin-era oligarchs. Alternatively, the ersatz "common sense" that prevails in the West is that Putin may as well be a Russian Louis XIV, proclaiming "I am the deep state!" He is variously described as the richest man in Russia (if not the world), a despot guilty of every manner of criminal malfeasance, and/or a megalomaniac bent on world domination. Whatever the case, Russia has tripartite state elements and, as elsewhere, any strengthening of democratic forces would likely require the help of security state authority to reign in deep political institutions and personages.

While China lacks a democratic state, it is still a complex and historically crucial polity. The Chinese Communist Party (CCP) has functioned democratically in some respects. Namely, the CCP has pursued policies that have benefitted the majority of the population in ways that theoretically mirror what would be predicted in a democracy. Meanwhile, the opposite has often occurred in supposedly democratic nation-states that have pursued neoliberalism. The Chinese security state defends the hegemony of the CCP. While China has famously pursued market reforms, the state still controls key industries like oil and banking. Deep political forces may be emerging in the form of a billionaire class in control of vast sums of private wealth. Can the CCP manage and constrain these forces, or will Chinese elites increasingly identify more with the transnational corporate class and less with Chinese nationalist or socialist aims? The CCP's reforms have been—relative to the Maoist era—arguably truer to Marxist thought which posits capitalist-driven industrialization as a precondition for socialism. Will China become more socialist over time? Does the Belt and Road Initiative represent the foundation of a Chinese drive for imperial hegemony or is country truly pursuing "win-win" diplomacy of the internationalist variety favored by US statesmen like Franklin Roosevelt, Henry Wallace, or John Kennedy? Recently, the CCP has taken serious measures to raise living standards by cracking down of profiteering in the housing, health care, and education sectors. It speaks volumes that such moves are a non-starter in the "democratic" US. While China may never develop electoral democracy and a public state in the Western sense, the deep politics approach could still provide important insights into China's politics and historical development.

Surveying Our Situation

At the original time of this writing, October of 2019, human civilization was beset by crises to which its institutions were not responding. Subsequently, things have gotten worse. Since World War II, the US-led capitalist world order has presided over many technological and scientific advances. Tragically, the hegemonic American state has all too often been the decisive actor in managing the march of human civilization. US elites have run the world in such a way as to preclude the application of Enlightenment principles toward human progress. America's self-celebrated liberal institutions have failed the US and the rest of humanity. Humanity has had to exist in a world order most decisively shaped and dominated by the US. In part, this book has sought to address the deficiencies of liberal social science in explaining and understanding such problems. Of particular concern is the *high crime blindness* of social science. As Ola Tunander points out, "Liberal political science has been turned into an ideology of the [deep state], because undisputable evidence for [its existence] is brushed away as pure fantasy or *conspiracy.*"[8] In other words, the modern social scientist has made manifest the *The Zhuangzi's* astute Daoist pronouncement: "The sage is the sharpest tool of empire; he is not a means of bringing light to the empire."[9]

This criticism applies to America's chief sense-making institutions in general—academia and the media. It is exemplified in the way that that the term "conspiracy theory" has been weaponized as per CIA recommendations going back to the agency's efforts to control public discourse around the JFK assassination.[10] At present, the "conspiracy theory" epithet has achieved new levels of absurdity. One recent essay by a philosophy professor attempts to define conspiracy theories by asserting that "*conspiracy theories* [are explanations that] subvert received opinion and are based on the idea that things aren't as they seem."[11] Though muddled and vague in its argumentation, this seems to suggest that (A) "received opinion" should not be subverted, and (B) things must generally be as they seem to be. There is no guidance as to how an observer might grapple with the well-documented existence of clandestine activity, specifically those "plausibly deniable" operations where responsibility is deliberately obscured. The poverty of scholarly conspiraphobia is well-captured in the following statement: "The official account of 9/11 and the theory that the attacks were planned by the Bush administration are both theories about conspiracies but only the latter is a conspiracy theory."[12] Obviously both theories are "theories about a conspiracy," and thus both are "conspiracy theories." It is alarming enough that nonsensical idiocy like this could be written by a professor of philosophy. That it would then be published in a "progressive" media outlet should be shocking. But again—to cite *The Zhuangzi*—the philosophy professor "is not a means of bringing light to the empire."

With the so-called "Russiagate" conspiracy theory having fizzled out, the role of the "conspiracy theory" meme has been further clarified. As journalist Katie Halper observed while in conversation with a Russiagate critic, "[Y]ou guys are actually doing all the research and you guys are dismissed as conspiracy theorists, which is really ironic because you guys are skeptical of the conspiracy theory."[13] To summarize the Russiagate hoax: neoliberal Democrats and the corporate media expended much energy promoting an unsubstantiated conspiracy theory about Russia installing its "asset" Donald Trump as US President. While irresponsibly promoting this dangerous conspiracy theory about a nuclear-armed rival, the "Russiagate" proponents derisively dismissed the critics of their conspiracy theory as "conspiracy theorists." This has been frustrating to observers who believe or hope that reasoned public debate can illuminate social reality and thereby help solve human problems. At the very least, the Russiagate hoax demonstrates that the weaponization of the term "conspiracy theory" has become further detached from its literal meaning. The governing media has enlisted the term to serve as blunt propaganda instrument with which to bludgeon critics of official narratives. What is obvious, but rarely stated, is that any theory—conspiratorial or otherwise—should be evaluated in a disinterested fashion on the basis of its supporting evidence and logic.

The tripartite theory of the state and the concept of *exceptionism* have been developed herein to offer a means of understanding and explaining important historical and political realities. These matters include unadjudicated elite criminality, the ceaseless US pursuit of global dominance, and the prevailing regime's inability to address major crises—namely: economic inequality, ecological destruction, and the threat of nuclear omnicide. Empire, America's pursuit of global dominance, is at the root of these problems. Through its defaults, liberal political science has in effect been shaped into "an ideology of the deep state." In general, prevailing political science methodologies evince a worship of statistical data. They also carry an unstated assumption of pluralism. In other words, US political scientists implicitly presuppose the rule of law, transparency, and a Weberian state that holds a monopoly on legitimate violence. Given current political and historical realities, these methods are insufficient. They do not allow scholars to illuminate political orders characterized by elite criminality, widespread secrecy, and a cloaked illiberal state. As stated in the first chapter, the philosophy applied in this book is that the problem should define the methodology, not vice versa.

Institutionalized lawlessness, *exceptionism*, was established early on in the Cold War. In 1948, "plausibly deniable" CIA covert operations were authorized by NSC 10/2. In 1950, NSC-68 asserted: "The integrity of our system will not be jeopardized by any measures, covert or overt, violent or non-violent, which serve the purposes of frustrating the Kremlin design, nor does the necessity for conducting ourselves so as to affirm our values in actions as well as words forbid such measures."[14] These documents authorized and justified the establishment of a *state of exception*—in that they advocating and/or authorizing the state to covertly violate the law. The supremacy clause of the US Constitution establishes that ratified treaties are "the supreme law in the land." The US ratified the UN Charter which outlaws aggression or even the threat of aggression between states. Therefore, CIA covert operations are illegal; they are carried out in a state of exception. Given that the authority for these operations has never been suspended and the operations have been a significant structural component of the US-led world order, the term *exceptionism* was coined to describe the historical fact of institutionalized state criminality.

The US, like any civilization, has always had its observable, formal political institutions as well as its *deep* or unacknowledged political institutions. US democracy was always bourgeois. The overworld of private wealth always had outsized political power regardless of constitutional norms like equality under the law and such. Likewise, various underworld institutions have always been accommodated by elements of the US social structure—notably by the overworld and the state. The overworld, the underworld, and the state interacted and influenced each other in innumerable ways. Going back to the days of smuggling, the slave trade, "banana wars," and opium traffic—transnational capital has always been a key arena where the blurriness of sovereignty and the weakness of legal authority allowed deep political institutions to arise and thrive. When World War II broke out, the Anglophile Wall Street overworld—most notably represented by the Council on Foreign Relations—assessed the situation and chose to steer the US toward establishing a new capitalist world order over which it would reign hegemonic. The security state that emerged in World War II was never fully decommissioned before being reconstituted as the Cold War national security state. In particular, the Wall Street overworld was decisive in not only creating the CIA, but also in cryptically—one could say "covertly"—authorizing covert operations by way of an oblique reference to "other duties" in the National Security Act of 1947.

Animated by deep political forces, the open, democratic constitutional republic or *public state* accommodated the new, secretive, top-down security state. This gave rise to a *dual state* with the authoritarian security state heavily influenced by the overworld-driven pursuit of hegemony. That is to say that the dual state existed in tandem with America's deep political system—the emerging deep state. After a number of traumatic events like the JFK assassination, the Vietnam War, the 1968 MLK and RFK assassinations, and Watergate, the public state sought to investigate and reform the security state. These efforts came to naught for a number of reasons. They were not able to reveal any of the state's most explosive crimes. Perhaps most importantly, without a coherent critique of the deep political forces that animated the national security state, its critics were unable to illuminate the source of the problem. Namely, the problem was overworld dominance over (A) the national security state, (B) electoral politics, and (C) the media. The corporate rich overpowered American democracy. Reflexive anticommunism precluded the formation of a democratic consensus that could have allowed the public to successfully assert its constitutionally mandated sovereignty.

Recognizing in some sense that deep political forces were destroying his presidency, Nixon battled the CIA. He fired Richard Helms and had his new DCI attempt to dig up as much dirt as possible to bring the CIA to heel. He ultimately failed, but as a consequence, deep political actors created new institutions to pursue overworld objectives—all in such a way as to be unaccountable even to the US government. This led to the creation of a more organized, supranational deep state dominated by the American overworld but financed in part by unaccountable entities. Key among them were oil-rich US client states in the Middle East like Saudi Arabia—or Iran, where Richard Helms was stationed. This oil-financed supranational deep state included the Safari Club, BCCI, intelligence services of US client states, networks of erstwhile spooks like Ted Shackley, and arms dealers like Adnan Khashoggi. These institutions arose specifically to circumvent the will of US elected officials and their appointed security state officials.

Deep political forces also politically damaged President Carter. Specifically, big oil and the Federal Reserve exploded oil prices and interest rates, respectively. Overwhelming evidence indicates that anti-Carter elements successfully conspired to prevent the president from successfully negotiating the release of the Iranian hostages, contributing to Carter's defeat and Reagan's victory. Under Reagan, the deep state elements were brought back in from the cold, so to speak. The Fed's interest rates exploded Third World debt. When interest rates and gas prices were lowered dramatically, the US dominated the global economy anew. The economic turnaround was owed in no small part to the post–Bretton Woods *Dollar-Wall Street regime* and the military Keynesian spending bonanza it enabled. At this point, the tripartite state had been consolidated into a new regime. Previously, the US had been a liberal democratic political system coexisting with a deep political system. The pursuit of global dominance and the *exceptionism* of the security state eventually gave rise to a deep state system. Deep political institutions have systematically crushed progressive politics, dominating the public state and the security state. Therefore, deep political forces also dominated the domestic and international political economy. The Weberian model of the state is not operant in this case. The public state has no monopoly of the use of violence, but this is not because the US is a "failed state" in the conventional sense. The issue is not a "failed state," but America's hypertrophied deep state.

While these problems are considerable, they are not essentially novel or unique to the American experience. From the beginning, human civilization has been characterized by acute contradictions. All human advancements derive from the original sins of civilization, namely expropriation and exploitation. Without an exploited people toiling on expropriated land, there is no surplus to allow for material, intellectual, and technological progress. Thus far, civilization has proceeded on the basis of numerous social hierarchies legitimated by various myths. These legitimating myths facilitate denial of various forms of expropriation and exploitation. In America, these have included "whiteness" vis-à-vis Indians and black slaves, manifest destiny, scientific racism, social Darwinism, anti-Communism, counter-terrorism, American exceptionalism, and "humanitarian" interventionism.

Its famous hypocrisy notwithstanding, America was exceptional at its founding in terms of the Enlightenment principles embodied in the Declaration of Independence and the Bill of Rights. Indeed, democracy may offer hope if humanity could somehow establish systems of

governance that allow for the privileging of human needs over the interests of a tiny politico-economic elite of power. Unfortunately, the deep
state system has turned the politician into something like a modern analog of the priest-king. Rather than controlling and managing institutions
in the public interest, our contemporary priest-kings must scramble to
appease inscrutable forces that may as well be supernatural. These governing forces include the corporate media, the petroleum industry, high
finance, the national security bureaucracies, as well as various other foreign and domestic lobbies.

The power of America's deep political institutions provides the best
explanation for many of the failed presidencies that followed Kennedy's
assassination. President Kennedy served less than one term. Because JFK
was independent and adept enough to actually threaten America's deep
political system on multiple fronts, the deep state exercised its veto power
in Dallas. Johnson sought to accommodate deep political forces by waging the Vietnam War and unleashing the CIA in places where Kennedy
had restrained the agency. While Richard Nixon was undoubtedly criminal, liberals were joined by the establishment press, various bureaucrats,
powerful militarists, and commercial elites to bring about the president's
demise. For Carter, stagflation and the *October Counter-surprise* were
insurmountable. Reagan's scandals were more egregious than any previous president's, yet he completed two terms and is still celebrated across
what passes for a political spectrum in the US. This can be observed in the
form of President Obama's praise for Reagan.[15] By the time Bill Clinton
took office, the systems had been well established. When President-elect
Clinton was given the talk about the economic birds and the bees, he
dejectedly muttered, "You mean to tell me that the success of the economic program and my re-election hinges on the Federal Reserve and a
bunch of fucking bond traders?" As with Obama and Biden, very modest
New Deal–style reforms under Clinton were a non-starter.

The brazen Bush era violations of the Constitution were given a pass
owing to his administration's governance of, by, and for the deep state.
Only in 2007 when neoconservative forces were threatening an invasion
of Iran did an Establishment rift emerge, perhaps best encapsulated by
realist/neoliberal Zbigniew Brzezinski's warning to Congress. In testimony

before the body, Brzezinski described a "plausible scenario for a military collision with Iran" that could involve

> Iraqi failure to meet the benchmarks, followed by accusations of Iranian responsibility for the failure, *then by some provocation in Iraq or a terrorist act in the US blamed on Iran, culminating in a 'defensive' US military action against Iran* that plunges a lonely America into a spreading and deepening quagmire eventually ranging across Iraq, Iran, Afghanistan and Pakistan (emphasis added).[16]

Subsequently, the neoconservative pipe dream for a Bush administration-led war with Iran came to naught.

Bush's successor, Barack Obama, accommodated the deep state by consolidating the Bush-era security state expansion, by launching regime change operations in Libya and Syria, and by not prosecuting the criminals behind the financial crisis or the torture program. When asked by some progressive donors why he had failed to deliver the promised "change," Obama reportedly replied, "Don't you remember what happened to Dr. King?"[17]

The problem afflicting all elected officials, but presidents most acutely, is that the deep political system demands accommodations from leaders. These accommodations typically entail subverting the public good to the benefit of various rent-seeking overworld interests. The organized money people then channel a portion of their wealth into various enterprises that allow them to go on dominating the US political economy and American society. This is now so easily confirmed that two mainstream American political scientists recently published a major study finding that "economic elites and organized groups representing business interests have substantial independent impacts on U.S. government policy, while average citizens and mass-based interest groups have little or no independent influence.[18] *Structural deep events* or *SCADs* are the key unacknowledged driver of America's political decline. Historian James DiEugenio points out, "[S]omething did go wrong in 1963. [. . .] [I]n 1964, the year the Warren Report was issued, the percentage of people who said they trusted Washington to do the right thing most of the time was almost 80 percent.

But in that year, a toboggan slide began which resulted in the dwindling of that figure to below 20 percent by 1993."[19] As of 2019, according to the Pew Research Center, "Only 17 percent of Americans today say they can trust the government in Washington to do what is right 'just about always' (3 percent) or 'most of the time' (14 percent)."[20]

As Wolin argued, what has been established is *inverted totalitarianism*—created by demobilizing, rather than mobilizing, the great bulk of society. Wolin used the term *managed democracy* to describe the American political system.[21] This analysis is compatible with the arguments presented here, even if Wolin does not address endemic state criminality or the likelihood that the state has applied its clandestine arts to American democracy. In the Cold War, it became expedient to use the term *totalitarian* to describe regimes that allegedly had so much power that no element of society could pose any challenge to the state's hegemony. This allowed US sense-making institutions to name and describe an aberrant, illegitimate form of government. The same defining pathology of the Nazi state was attributed to Communism and socialism. Since the Soviet Union collapsed relatively peacefully, it turned out that the country was not *totalitarian* after all, according to the tautological Cold War definition.

In fact, it is the American tripartite state that has taken on more totalitarian characteristics. Any class of politico-economic elites will seek to identify and subvert potential threats to the prevailing order. Following the democratic upsurge of the 1960s, the empire *struck back*, so to speak. The Powell Memorandum is something of inverted totalitarian manifesto. Powell identifies all the problem areas facing the corporate rich: "the college campus, the pulpit, the media, the intellectual and literary journals, the arts and sciences, and from politicians." He bemoans the "bewildering paradox" that is the "extent to which the enterprise system tolerates, if not participates in, its own destruction." He points out that universities are funded by "tax funds generated largely from American business" as well as contributions from corporate America's capital funds. Additionally, most media outlets "are owned and theoretically controlled by corporations which depend upon profits, and the enterprise system to survive."[22] Powell called for the corporate rich to devote money toward neutering civil society such that corporate hegemony could not be threatened by critics with the temerity to criticize the "free enterprise system" that affords them their material wherewithal. To put it in blunt Marxist terms, it is as though Powell was scolding the base for being insufficiently attentive to curating the superstructure.

Likewise, the Trilateral Commission's *Crisis of Democracy* bemoaned the paradox that postwar material security may have afforded citizens the wherewithal to agitate for progressive, democratic reforms. By pointing out how prosperity was weakening "governability," Samuel Huntington and company were advocating—a la Sheldon Wolin—for a more studiously *managed* democracy.[23] The point here is not that either Powell or Huntington was an omnipotent, technocratic Svengali. Rather, these men simply produced the most straightforward and candid expressions of the emerging overworld consensus that American liberalism had outlived its usefulness and needed to go. By 1981, these forces had prevailed. The "Reagan Revolution," is more aptly termed the *Reagan Counterrevolution* for its consolidation of the American deep state system.

As a result of the catastrophic success of the deep state counterattack, the *higher immorality* identified by C. Wright Mills has become so entrenched that the political system cannot respond to the three crises facing Americans and the world: massive inequality, climate change, and the threat of nuclear omnicide. The extreme polarization of wealth has occurred in large part because of numerous deep state victories. After World War II, Anticommunism served as a pretext to police the Third World and overtly or covertly destroy progressive movements that sought to deviate from neocolonialism. The continuity of these policies—or even their intensification—following the collapse of the Soviet Union belies claims that such policies were reasoned responses to the "global communist conspiracy." Largely as a result of US-imposed systemic economic polarization, 25,000 people die of starvation and malnutrition per day.[24] As sociologist Peter Phillips points out, a 25 percent tax on the wealth of billionaires, "if efficiently distributed, would likely eliminate hunger in the world permanently."[25] Meanwhile, the major problem for the corporate rich is that they have accumulated so much wealth that it is difficult for them to find sufficient opportunities for investment. This leads capital to seek returns in financial speculation, military/war spending, and privatization of the public domain.[26] All three of these predatory, rent-seeking avenues of moneymaking entail accompanying efforts to dominate politics and society to facilitate these types of economic activities. On the whole, the corporate media tends to abet or run interference for this system of top-down domination. In 2019, the *Washington Post* provided a darkly humorous example of this with an Orwellian "fact-check." Bernie Sanders stated that "Three people in this country own more wealth than the bottom half of America." The newspaper dismissed Sanders' claim as "comparing apples to oranges" and "not especially meaningful" because "people in the bottom half have essentially no wealth," as if that impacts the literal veracity of the statement or mitigates the implicit critique.[27]

One remarkable aspect of US poverty and inequality stems from the structural fact of the *petrodollar/US Treasury Bill standard*. Momentarily forgetting the right-wing austerity cover story, Dick Cheney famously said, "Deficits don't matter." This is known to be the case by the small number of people who understand the dollar's position in the global economy. It begs the questioning of why such serious, solvable social problems persist in the US. For example, why does the US not have the world's best physical and social infrastructure to provide material security for all its citizens? Why has the US not lavishly funded its public education system to allow everyone to contribute to the disinterested pursuit of human knowledge and to the solving of humanity's problems? As stated above, the structural imposition of extreme economic inequality is not simply due to greed and zero-sum economic calculations by the corporate rich. Rather, widespread economic security endangers the "security" of the corporate rich because—as with any ruling elite—security for this class is defined as hegemony over society. If this analysis is correct, the end of US unipolarity may bring unprecedented social turmoil to the country. Without the exorbitant privilege of the dollar-Wall Street regime, the US may find itself unable to function politically or to adequately meet the material needs of the citizenry.

Climate change is an accelerating slow-motion crisis to which no rational policy response is forthcoming. The culpability of the oil companies is well known, but the deep state system collectively bears the greatest responsibility. Cleaner, publicly owned, localized energy solutions are called for. Such efforts would likely need to be financed by some combination of carbon taxes, wealth taxes, and/or credit creation. Unfortunately, all these rather obvious responses are anathema to US and global elites. The current system of dirty energy delivered over privately owned infrastructure has not only been an enormous source of rent-extraction for the corporate rich. Rather, the control of the global petroleum trade has also been a pillar of US dominance over the global capitalist system. In 2018, ex-president Obama told an audience at Rice University's Baker Institute that "suddenly America's like the biggest oil producer and the biggest gas [producer;] that was me, people."[28] Joseph Nye points out that the fracking boom has given the US a geopolitical boost, in part by giving the US leverage over non-compliant oil producing countries like Russia, Iran, and Venezuela.[29] As Philip K. Verleger points out, the fracking boom was a consequence of Federal Reserve quantitative easing (QE) policies, i.e., massive credit creation. Verleger argues that the Fed failed to predict that QE would lead to a fracking boom that would cause a price collapse.[30] The fracking boom's impact on oil prices was amplified by Saudi overproduction, alleged in the press to have been a Saudi strategy to undermine US energy producers by rendering new ventures unprofitable in a cheap oil market.[31] Alternatively, the historical record discussed in this book suggests that the QE-fueled fracking boom *and* KSA overproduction were collectively part of a deep state effort to collapse oil prices to the detriment of oil-producing US adversaries—namely Russia, Venezuela, and Iran. Either way, the effect was to further boost oil consumption and produce less market incentives for the desperately needed transition to green energy. Any efforts to address climate change must acknowledge the deep political forces that collectively oppose reform.

The threat of nuclear omnicide is not new, but it presently is a problem that warrants increased attention for a number of reasons. Specifically, recent US moves have been alarming. As filmmaker Oliver Stone and historian Peter Kuznick wrote in *The Nation*, there should have been more attention paid to President Trump's statements to the effect that he did not understand why the US had nuclear weapons if it couldn't use them. The 2018 Nuclear Posture Review actually expanded the role of nuclear weapons in the military posture of the United States, allowing nukes to be used in response to ill-defined "extreme circumstances" like cyberattacks or attacks on American or allied nations' infrastructure. This is especially troubling given that the 2018 National Defense Strategy deemed China and Russia to be the top security threats facing the US. This reorientation is happening after two decades of NATO expansion, obviously deemed threatening to nuclear-armed Russia. In the twenty-first century, the US has withdrawn from the Anti-Ballistic Missile treaty and the Intermediate Range Nuclear Forces Treaty. Stone and Kuznick point to other alarming nuclear items in the media. For example, a 2006 article in the Council on Foreign Relations' official magazine argued that the US could launch a successful nuclear first strike against Russia or China. The *Washington Post* reported that this "sent heads spinning [in Moscow] with visions of Dr. Strangelove."[32]

The US has a history of using nuclear bombs. This goes beyond Hiroshima and Nagasaki. As Daniel Ellsberg documents, the US has repeatedly threatened nations with nuclear destruction, using nuclear weapons in the same way that a robber uses a gun.[33] These and other sorts of imperial gambits may soon be unavailing for the hegemon. The end of US unipolarity seems to be inexorably nearing. No empire has gracefully retreated from its hegemony. The British may have eventually bowed to reality by giving up the British Empire, but the British ruling class preserved the great bulk of its interests under the postwar US-led world order. It appears that the US has not prepared for a post-hegemonic era, and this makes the nuclear issue all the more pressing.

How Might the Truth Help Revive Hopes for a Better World?

From a social science perspective, the historically informed conception of an exceptionist tripartite state offers useful predictions and analysis of future and recent events. The scholarship herein suggests that we have been living through the incremental imposition of a new kind of fascism or authoritarianism. The American deep state was greatly empowered by the 2001 terror attacks and subsequent "global war on terror" (GWOT). To an unknown extent, COG measures have superseded the constitution and amplified exceptionism. As with the Cold War, the GWOT allows the US the ability to define itself by its antithesis. Such was predicted with eerie prescience in 1988 by the Italian philosopher Guy Debord, who wrote:

> Such a perfect democracy constructs its own inconceivable foe, terrorism. Its wish is to be judged by its enemies rather than by its results. The story of terrorism is written by the state and it is therefore highly instructive. The spectators must certainly never know everything about terrorism, but they must always know enough to convince them that, compared to terrorism, everything else must be acceptable, or in any case more rational and democratic.[34]

It is unsettling to know that Debord wrote *Comments* after living through Italy's "Years of Lead," a period in which deep state actors engaged in the "fine-tuning of democracy" through the use of false flag terror that marginalized the political left and strengthened the security state.

The bugbear of the GWOT, Osama bin Laden, reportedly sought to weaken US hegemony but in the process somehow committed strategic blunders. By so viciously attacking the two most visible symbols of the US Empire—the World Trade Center and the Pentagon—bin Laden legitimized each of the sites' core deep state constituencies: neoliberalism and neoconservatism, respectively. Furthermore, the presumably fortuitous selection of the September 11 date meant that psychologically the attacks would come to be associated with 911, America's emergency phone number. Symbolically, this further allowed for the attacks to rationalize the subsequent "state of emergency" which necessitated reinforcing and strengthening *exceptionism*. Consequently, the state sought to achieve several exceptionist goals. These include the security state's Quixotic quest for "total information awareness," an aim to be achieved in part through massive data collection and warrantless surveillance. Torture and "extraordinary rendition" programs were created and utilized. Two long, legally dubious wars were launched. In sum, counterterrorism strengthened the already hypertrophied security state and thus, the American deep state.

If fascism is indeed capitalism in crisis, there's plenty of cause for concern if one accepts that fascism is not desirable. In that context, the collapse of US hegemony is cause for alarm. In 1997, Brzezinski asserted that "keep[ing] the barbarians from coming together" was a "grand imperative of imperial geostrategy."[35] The term "barbarians" refers to Russia and China, two countries that have indeed grown much closer in response to their grievances with the US-led world order. The election of Donald Trump has been an ominous development. Not only does Trump exhibit troubling, if clownish, fascistic tendencies, he has also elicited bellicose responses from the dominant, corporate wing of the Democratic Party which increasingly responds to critics on both the left and Trumpian right by employing neo-McCarthyist rhetoric.

The US is launching an unprecedented assault of press freedom with its persecution of Wikileaks publisher Julian Assange. Among other sins, Wikileaks published DNC emails revealing DNC corruption in the ill-fated 2016 primaries. The revelations led to the resignation of the DNC chair. Assange has stated categorically that the emails were provided by a DNC insider. On the basis of redacted reports received from an anti-Russian cybersecurity firm, a handpicked group of US intelligence officials assessed that the emails were acquired by a Russian hacker.[36] While Assange and Wikileaks have to date never published anything requiring a retraction, US intelligence agencies have often engaged in deceptive and/or criminal behavior. If Assange is telling the truth, Russiagate is essentially a hoax—a deep event of sorts.

The decline of US hegemony occurring in the cyberage raises the specter of new techno-authoritarianism. Silicon Valley monopolies like Google, Facebook, and Twitter operate on the basis of opaque and constantly revised algorithms that can determine what kind of content users are exposed to, what content they can effectively share, and who they share it with. Troublesome persons can be banned with no recourse under prevailing interpretations of free speech rights. The cyberage and/or the decline of US hegemony may also portend that future *state crimes against democracy* could be in the offing. Potential scenarios include election fraud by way of unauditable, paperless, electronic voting systems manufactured by politically connected corporate outfits. Deep political forces gave Italy its "Years of Lead" through the means of false-flag terror attacks. The American deep state may respond similarly in the US if circumstances deem it expedient. As Brzezinski alluded to in 2007 regarding

Iran, the state may manipulate intelligence and events to provide pretexts for foreign wars. Both Libya and Syria were presented as democratic protest movements necessitating "humanitarian" intervention. In both cases, reports about key episodes were incorrect and likely fabricated. In Libya, the US regime change campaign was justified by the false depiction of Ghaddafi as a criminal dictator who was planning to carry out a massacre of civilians, and who gave his soldiers Viagra so that they might do more raping of the populace.[37]

In Syria, the US and its allies have been similarly deceptive and lawless. Jeffrey Sachs summarizes, "While the Syrian War is often described as a civil war, it was in a fact a war of regime change led by the U.S. and Saudi Arabia under a U.S. presidential directive called Timber Sycamore." This US-orchestrated operation has killed around 500,000 people and displaced more than 10,000,000 Syrians.[38] One particularly cynical and oddly postmodern innovation of the Syrian War is the role played by the US and UK funded so-called "White Helmets." While the US and its allies have spent billions on the campaign to overthrow the Syrian government, the White Helmets have received millions of dollars, ostensibly to save Syrian lives. Founded by ex-British military officer and mercenary John Le Mesurier, the White Helmets are invariably lauded by the Western corporate media. A documentary on the group received an Oscar for Best Documentary Short. Critics like Max Blumenthal point to problems with the media narratives around the group, including the White Helmet's strange working relationship with al Qaeda-affiliated anti-government belligerents in Syria.[39] Besides the hagiographic Oscar-winning documentary, other efforts to have been taken to amplify the propaganda value of the White Helmets. These include an October 2016 effort by a PR company to enlist the support of Pink Floyd front man Roger Waters by inviting him to an elaborate dinner party hosted by a Saudi-born billionaire named Hani Farsi.[40] Given the evidence accumulated by the critics of the White Helmets and the corporate media's refusal to acknowledge the Western authorship of the Syrian War, it is reasonable to conclude that the White Helmets represent a devious deep state propaganda operation to legitimate the illegal overthrow of the Syrian government by al Qaeda-dominated proxy forces or through direct military intervention. Even for an experienced scholar of Western imperialism, this particular tactic is noteworthy. To state the obvious: It is an egregious violation of Enlightenment ideals to mobilize a field unit for the production of "humanitarian" flavored propaganda to justify unambiguously criminal aggression against another country. In the current political climate, to make public statements to this effect is to invite accusations that one is a Russian asset or a purveyor of "Russian talking points."[41]

While all these various spectacles have unfolded in the twenty-first century, the world has experienced a gigantic upward transfer of wealth that has been facilitated in no small part by deep political chicanery. Writing about this recently, I observed,

> The opacity of the higher circles means that we are never likely to know the extent to which the subprime crisis, subsequent bailouts, and failure to prosecute the fraudsters collectively represent something of a rolling deep state coup by a financial Power Elite. Suffice it to say that we should all be so lucky as to spectacularly "fail" in such a way as to effect an historically monumental transfer of wealth to ourselves. [To understand] big money's takeover of politics and society, [one must learn] about Blackstone, or more importantly, the "Big Three" capital firms—BlackRock, Vanguard, and State Street.[42]

Canadian journalist Paul Jay reported,

> Financialization of the economy produced two shadow banks that tower over the rest of the corporate world. Blackrock and Vanguard with other smaller money management firms, control 90 percent of the S&P 500 public companies, including fossil fuel companies, arms manufacturers and major U.S. media outlets that own 'mainstream' news. The top three financial services firms manage 15 trillion dollars of assets. That's more than China's 2019 GDP. Blackrock is the largest with 7.4 trillion, followed by Vanguard at 5.3 trillion and State Street Global Advisors at 2.5 trillion.[43]

As I argued in 2021, "The hegemony of organized money over society did not arise by accident. It involved a series of *coups d'etat profonde*, or strokes of the deep state."[44] Many of these events are documented in this book. They have contributed to the rise of the deep state system and they are continuing to concentrate more and more wealth and power in the deep state.

It is becoming so dire that even some former US high officials are sounding like scholars of deep politics these days. Retired Army Colonel and former Chief of Staff to Secretary of State Colin Powell recently said in an interview,

> [W]hat is really haunting us [is a] distribution of wealth, unprecedented in our history. But it really won't change much because . . . the deep state's in charge and the deep state ain't Donald Trump and it ain't Joe Biden. [. . .] The deep state is point zero zero one percent of the United States of America that owns the wealth equivalent to the GDP of Brazil. And they aren't going to let anything change that's against their purposes and their purposes are evolving and they scare me, they scare me to death because their purposes are looking more and more like IA and robotics, will eliminate what capitalism, predatory capitalism, in particular, has always wanted to eliminate—its most precisely component, labor, get rid of it. What does that mean? Well, it probably means a period of slavery. I mean, abject slavery for the average worker replaced by a period of we don't need you anymore, so let's conjure up a coronavirus or something, to get rid of you and let's replace you with technology. This is scary, but I really think that is part of what's happening right now. That's the new dimension of the 21st century that truly disturbs me, along with nuclear weapons and climate change.[45]

While it is difficult to know what to make of this, it is increasingly clear that these dynamics can only lead to a more totalizing form of despotism if they are not reversed.

In the face of these grim historical trends, what are the prospects for making the necessary changes? In conversation with Lance deHaven-Smith, he offered a novel suggestion: Use the state to uphold the law and prosecute the perpetrators of state crimes against democracy. Were it feasible, such would be quite an agreeable solution. Unfortunately, exceptionism and the weakness of the public state likely precludes such a course. Peter Dale Scott has advocated "visionary realism" or "realistic utopianism"—an effort built upon first strengthening civil society. As examples, he cites the Polish Solidarity movement and the US civil rights movement.[46] On the policy level, he proposes organizing to address income inequality, reform the US electoral process, reform drug laws, and end the doctrine of preemptive war. These are all urgently needed reforms, but his examples illustrate the magnitude of the problems faced by would be reformers. Polish Solidarity was given decisive support from the CIA.[47] The US civil rights movement was backed by the top of the US establishment, including decidedly non-woke figures like John Foster Dulles.[48] In essence, Jim Crow was a detriment to the neocolonial US agenda in the Third World and so the key political actors and national media allied with various politicians and social movement leaders to end segregation. A somewhat disheartening but apt explanation would be that the US ended the gratuitously cruel and economically backward Jim Crow system in order to have a better image in the more economically and geopolitically significant decolonizing world.

Peter Phillips and Ralph Nader offer a solution in the so-crazy-it-just-might-work mold; they make an appeal to the humanity and enlightened self-interest of politico-economic elites.[49] It is true that no one really benefits if human civilization is destroyed or forced to endure unprecedented calamity. The press and other potentially reformist liberal institutions are so impoverished that it is difficult to imagine the impact they might have if they were allowed to operate without first and foremost having to please the corporate rich. To visualize the potential for truly independent media, imagine media outlets like *The Intercept* if *The Intercept* were not controlled by a deep state-connected tech oligarch.[50]

Perhaps a more likely hopeful scenario would involve other nations escaping the orbit of US imperialism and achieving material prosperity as a result. Russia is saddled with its own rentier oligarchy. A large part of this reality stems from the US-rigged reelection of Boris Yeltsin as well as

US-imposed shock therapy. At any rate, Russia alone is not likely to lead a transition to a multipolar world governed by international law. China, on the other hand, appears to be the real rival to the US. The Chinese have experienced massive economic growth within the US-dominated global capitalist system. One key to Chinese success has been the country's refusal to follow the demonstrably disastrous dictates of neoliberalism. In China, the state controls the commanding heights of the economy. In the US—and wherever the US holds sway—it is the other way around. Recently, the Chinese leadership has taken steps to raise living standards by cracking down on profiteering in the education, health care, and housing sectors. In America, these sectors extract vast sums of wealth from those Americans who choose to get an education, see a doctor, or not be homeless. But unlike China, these parasitic rentier interests in America enjoy a divine right of racketeering. China, we are told, is "authoritarian." Having "democracy" apparently means that the vast majority of the population must submit to being exploited by a tiny, privileged elite. But perhaps China is becoming that which the US has tried so hard to pre-empt or crush anywhere and everywhere: a good economic example that could provide a model and a lifeline for other long-suffering peoples in the Global South.

As for the Americans, perhaps a way forward could involve some kind of revelation that would expose the scope of the totalizing subversion of US democracy by deep political forces. The political assassinations of the 1960s have that potential. This explains why they are still obscured through ongoing disinformation operations even more than fifty years after the fact.[51] Perhaps a whistleblower or a coalition of high-level officials could collaborate to orchestrate just such a revelation or series of revelations. Another possibility would involve using the electoral system to affect some sort of novel form of *democratic state capture*. Imagine if democratic forces were to seize control of the government and use its authority to assert and apply the rule of law throughout the various organs of the state—even going so far as to force *exceptionist* deep state persons and entities to operate transparently and lawfully!

As a corollary, state secrecy must be radically reformed. Overriding access to state secrets should be vested in elected officials and divested from deep state apparatchiks. Few things are as emblematic of our Kafkaesque system as the fact that two presidents—Nixon and Clinton—tried unsuccessfully to pry JFK assassination secrets out of the CIA. Overriding secrecy and *the exception* must be divested from opaque and unaccountable entities. In the meantime, all of the tripartite state's efforts to further centralize surveillance, economic power, and social control should be resisted. The tripartite state is not humanity's protector. In 1973, CIA-psychological operatives in Chile scrawled graffiti on the sides of buildings that read "*Jakarta se acerca*"—"Jakarta is coming." This was a reference to the massive CIA orchestrated 1965 bloodletting in Indonesia which overthrew Sukarno and made the country safe for US corporations like Freeport Sulphur. The American and Indonesian governments have never acknowledged the truth of those events. But we must confront these sorts of dark truths if we are to move forward as a civilization. To paraphrase Peter Dale Scott, we must *Come to Jakarta*.[52]

To that end, the role of the intellectual in these times is to rekindle the Enlightenment and thereby illuminate the political dark age wrought by the exceptionist tripartite state. Given the magnitude of our present crises, some kind of Truth and Reconciliation process is desperately needed, perhaps with broad amnesty in exchange for full disclosure. Without fundamental redirection, the US is driving Western civilization toward a very grim future. In sum, deep state dominance has derailed the hopes articulated by Lord Acton that "all information is within reach, and every problem [. . .] capable of solution."[53] American society must supplant the higher immorality which currently prevails. The master task of the twenty-first century scholar is to reacquaint power and wisdom.

GLOSSARY

deep events: mysterious events that involve violence and/or lawbreaking, are embedded in extant covert activities, serve to enlarge state secrecy, and are subsequently obscured systematically by the state and the media.[1]

deep political system: a system in which governance entails habitual resort to "decision-making and enforcement procedures outside as well as inside those publicly sanctioned by law and society," i.e., a system of governance that includes "collusive secrecy and law-breaking."[2]

deep politics: "all those political practices and arrangements, deliberate or not, which are usually repressed rather than acknowledged."[3]

deep state: misappropriated in the Trump era, the term herein refers to the various institutions that collectively exercise undemocratic power over state and society. Pluralistic to varying degrees, the deep state is an outgrowth of the overworld of private wealth. It includes most notably the institutions that advance overworld interests through the nexuses connecting the overworld, the underworld, and the national security organizations that mediate between them. In 2015, I described the deep state as follows:

An obscured, dominant, supra-national source of antidemocratic power. It is debatable whether this phenomenon has arisen due to (a) unique historical circumstances, (b) innate dynamics of capitalism, or (c) unresolved contradictions within human civilization.

The Weberian state's monopoly on violence does not stay confined to the democratic state or even the formal security state. There is sufficient empirical evidence to suggest that the U.S.-led world order has entailed systemic violence which has undermined democratic sovereignty.[4]

To these interventions, I would add relevant and valid variations:
deep state (organizational): supranational or supragovernmental structural components of the deep state system, e.g., the Adnan Khashoggi-centered "off-the-books" intelligence entities (most notably the Safari Club) which Peter Dale Scott (2015) described as:

> A supranational deep state, whose organic links to the CIA may have helped consolidate it. . . . [D]ecisions taken at this level . . . were in no way guided by the political determinations of those elected to power in Washington [and were instead] expressly created to overcome restraints established by political decisions in Washington.[5]

The "Doomsday Project" or Continuity of Government provisions are hypothesized here and in the work of Peter Dale Scott[6] as representing a supragovernmental deep state component whose opacity and overriding authority may have been utilized in key deep events such as the JFK assassination, Watergate, Iran-Contra, and 9/11.
deep state (systemic): a system of governance in which deep state predominance has been institutionalized via the co-optation or subversion of state, civil society, and liberal institutions. In this broadest sense, elements of organized religion, the educational system, the corporate media (and much of the "independent" media) can be considered part of the deep state. This is largely congruous with the age-old concept of "the Establishment."
dual state: derived from Carl Schmitt (1985), the theory that alongside the democratic (or public) state, there exists a security state that is able to exercise supralegal prerogative powers in any instance it deems to be a "state of emergency."[7]

public state: the visible and formally organized institutions that comprise our elected federal, state, and local governments as well as the civil service bureaucracies associated with them.

security state: those institutions in charge of maintaining "security" domestically and internationally—e.g. the Pentagon, the Central Intelligence Agency, and the Federal Bureau of Investigation.

state crimes against democracy (SCADs): "concerted actions or inactions by government insiders intended to manipulate democratic processes and undermine popular sovereignty."[8]

parapolitics: "a system or practice of politics in which accountability is consciously diminished."[9]

exceptionism: "the institutionalization of the interminable state of exception" and "of securitized supra-sovereignty or Lockean 'prerogative' although not to a fixed or determinate source."[10]

overworld: the upper strata of politically active wealth, comprised of the richest persons and their representatives[11] —i.e., an amalgamation of C. Wright Mills's concepts of the *corporate rich* and the *power elite*.[12]

tripartite state: a system of governance in which the state has come to be comprised of the *democratic/public state*, the *security state*, and the *deep state*.[13]

underworld: organized crime entities; in a deep political system of governance, relevant state institutions and overworld interests interact with elements of the underworld through various modes of discursive accommodation.[14]

ENDNOTES

FOREWORD

1. Good, "Deep Fake Politics: Getting Adam Curtis Out of Your Head."

CHAPTER 1

1. C. Wright Mills, *The Power Elite* (New York, NY: Oxford University Press, 1956).
2. Sheldon Wolin, *Democracy Incorporated: Managed Democracy and the Specter of Inverted Totalitarianism* (Princeton, NJ: Princeton University Press, 2008).
3. Juan J. Linz and Alfred Stepan, *Problems of Democratic Transition and Consolidation: Southern Europe, South America, and Post-Communist Europe* (Baltimore, MD: Johns Hopkins University Press, 1996).
4. Robert A. Dahl and Charles E. Lindblom, *Politics, Economics and Welfare* (New York, NY: Harper and Brothers, 1953).
5. Mills, *The Power Elite*.
6. Harold D . Lasswell, "The Garrison State," *The American Journal of Sociology* 46, no. 4 (1941): 455–68.
7. Lance deHaven-Smith, ed., *The Battle for Florida: An Annotated Compendium of Materials from the 2000 Presidential Election* (Gainesville, FL: University Press of Florida, 2005).
8. Mark Crispin Miller, *Fooled Again: How the Right Stole the 2004 Election & Why They'll Steal the Next One Too (Unless We Stop Them)* (New York, NY: Basic Books, 2005).
9. Mills, *The Power Elite*.
10. Martin Gilens and Benjamin I. Page, "Testing Theories of American Politics: Elites, Interest Groups, and Average Citizens," *Perspectives on Politics* 12, no. 3 (2014): 564–81.

11. Michael Hudson, "The Road to Debt Deflation, Debt Peonage, and Neofeudalism," 2012, http://www.levyinstitute.org/pubs/wp_708.pdf.

12. See: Chalmers Johnson, *Blowback: The Costs and Consequences of American Empire* (New York, NY: Metropolitan Books, 2000); Chalmers Johnson, *The Sorrows of Empire: Militarism, Secrecy, and the End of the Republic* (New York, NY: Metropolitan Books, 2004); Chalmers Johnson, *Nemesis: The Last Days of the American Republic* (New York, NY: Metropolitan Books, 2006).

13. Aaron Good, "American Exception: Hegemony and the Dissimulation of the State," *Administration & Society* 50, no. 1 (January 17, 2018): 4–29, https://doi.org/10.1177/0095399715581042.

14. Good, "American Exception: Hegemony and the Dissimulation of the State." I use the term *supra-national* to indicate that the *deep state* exercises power above national boundaries. This applies not only to the nations targeted by US aggression, but also to US administrations in which the deep state intervened in opposition to a US President—the nominal head of the US state. As chronicled in Chapter 4, the Kennedy, Nixon, and Carter administrations were most decisively impacted by deep state operations.

15. Grant Barrett, "A Wordnado of Words in 2013," *New York Times*, December 21, 2013, https://www.nytimes.com/2013/12/22/opinion/sunday/a-word nado-of-words-in-2013.html.

16. Peter Dale Scott, *The American Deep State: Wall Street, Big Oil, and the Attack on U.S. Democracy* (New York, NY: Rowman & Littlefield, 2015), 3; Peter Dale Scott, *The Road to 9/11: Wealth, Empire, and the Future of America* (Berkeley, CA: University of California Press, 2007), 267.

17. Good, "American Exception: Hegemony and the Dissimulation of the State," 16.

18. Oliver Stone and Peter Kuznick, *The Untold History of the United States*, 2nd ed. (New York, NY: Gallery Books, 2019), 37.

19. Good, "American Exception: Hegemony and the Dissimulation of the State," 15.

20. John Kelly, "Crimes and Silence: The CIA's Criminal Acts and the Media's Silence," in *Into the Buzzsaw: Leading Journalists Expose the Myth of a Free Press*, ed. Kristina Borjesson (Amherst, NY: Prometheus Books, 2002), 311.

21. "'We Lied, Cheated and Stole': Pompeo Comes Clean About CIA," *Telesur*, April 24, 2019, accessed July 1, 2019, https://www.telesureng-lish.net/news/We-Lied-Cheated-and-Stole-Pompeo-Comes-Clean-About -CIA-20190424-0033.html

22. Gary Kamiya, "When the CIA ran a LSD sex-house in San Francisco," *San Francisco Chronicle*, April 1, 2016, accessed July 1, 2019, https://www .sfchronicle.com/bayarea/article/When-the-CIA-ran-a-LSD-sex-house-in -San-Francisco-7223346.php

23. Lance deHaven-Smith, "When Political Crimes Are Inside Jobs: Detecting State Crimes against Democracy," *Administrative Theory & Praxis* 28, no. 3 (2006): 330–55, https://www.jstor.org/stable/25610803.

24. deHaven-Smith, "When Political Crimes Are Inside Jobs: Detecting State Crimes against Democracy," 338.

25. Francis A. Boyle, *Biowarfare and Terrorism* (Atlanta, GA: Clarity Press, Inc., 2005).

26. deHaven-Smith, *The Battle for Florida: An Annotated Compendium of Materials from the 2000 Presidential Election.*

27. Miller, *Fooled Again: How the Right Stole the 2004 Election & Why They'll Steal the Next One Too (Unless We Stop Them).*

28. Lance deHaven-Smith, *Conspiracy Theory in America* (Austin, TX: University of Texas Press, 2013), 20.

29. Scott, *The American Deep State: Wall Street, Big Oil, and the Attack on U.S. Democracy*, 117.

30. Scott, *The American Deep State: Wall Street, Big Oil, and the Attack on U.S. Democracy*, 121.

31. Peter Dale Scott, *Deep Politics and the Death of JFK* (Berkeley, CA: University of California Press, 1993).

32. Peter Phillips, *Giants: The Global Power Elite* (New York, NY: Seven Stories Press, 2018), 31.

33. Good, "American Exception: Hegemony and the Dissimulation of the State."

34. John Mearsheimer, *The Tragedy of Great Power Politics* (New York, NY: W. W. Norton, 2001).

35. Michael Sullivan, *American Adventurism Abroad: Invasions, Interventions, and Regime Changes Since World War II*, Rev. ed (Malden, MA, 2008).

36. Charles Kindleberger, *The World in Depression, 1929–1939* (Berkeley, CA: University of California Press, 1973).

37. Susan Strange, *States and Markets*, 2nd ed. (New York, NY: Continuum, 1994).

38. Strange, *States and Markets.*

39. Robert W. Cox, "Social Forces, States and World Orders: Beyond International Relations Theory," *Millennium: Journal of International Studies* 10, no. 2 (June 23, 1981): 126–55, https://doi.org/10.1177/0305829881 0100020501.

40. Giovanni Arrighi and Beverly Silver, *Chaos and Governance in the Modern World System* (Minneapolis: University of Minnesota Press, 1999).

41. Matthew Connelly, "The New Imperialists," in *Lessons of Empire: Imperial Histories and American Power*, ed. Craig Calhoun, Frederick Cooper, and Kevin W. Moore (New York, NY: The New Press, 2006), 19–33.

42. Charles S. Maier, *Among Empires: American Ascendancy and Its Predecessors* (Cambridge, MA: Harvard University Press, 2006), 62–64.

43. Michael Doyle, *Empires* (Ithaca, New York: Cornell University Press, 1986), 30.

44. Doyle, *Empires*, 12.

45. G. John Ikenberry, *Liberal Leviathan: The Origins, Crisis and Transformation of the American World Order* (Princeton, NJ: Princeton University Press, 2011), 66–68.

46. Ikenberry, *Liberal Leviathan: The Origins, Crisis and Transformation of the American World Order*, 71–72.

47. Ikenberry, *Liberal Leviathan: The Origins, Crisis and Transformation of the American World Order*, 225.

48. John A. Hobson, *Imperialism: A Study* (New York, NY: James Pott & Company, 1902).

49. Vladimir Ilyich Lenin, *Imperialism: The Highest Stage of Capitalism*, 1917.

50. Joseph A. Schumpeter, *Imperialism and Social Classes*, trans. Heinz Norden (New York, NY: Augustus M. Kelley, 1951).

51. Andre Gunder Frank, "The Development of Underdevelopment," *Monthly Review* 18, no. 4 (September 2, 1966): 17–31, https://doi.org/10.14452/MR-018-04-1966-08_3.

52. Walt Whitman Rostow, *The Stages of Economic Growth: A Non-Communist Manifesto* (Cambridge, England: Cambridge University Press, 1960)

53. Michael Parenti, *Against Empire* (San Francisco, CA: City Lights Books, 1995), 1.

54. Michael Hardt and Antonio Negri, *Empire* (Cambridge, MA: Harvard University Press, 2000).

55. Borrowing from Peter Dale Scott, I use this term to describe those typically leftist writers who see the structural forces of capitalism to be so powerful and decisive that they reflexively dismiss any discussion of individual elites or of elite schisms. For hyperstructuralists, governance is essentially all structure, no agency.

56. Jennifer Pitts, "Political Theory of Empire and Imperialism," *Annual Review of Political Science* 13, no. 1 (May 2010): 211–35, https://doi.org/10.1146/annurev.polisci.051508.214538.

57. David Harvey, *The New Imperialism* (New York, NY: Oxford University Press, 2003), 26.

58. David Harvey, *The New Imperialism* (New York, NY: Oxford University Press, 2003), 26.

59. For numerous examples, see: William Blum, *Killing Hope: U.S. Military and C.I.A. Interventions Since World War II*, 2nd ed. (Monroe, ME: Common Courage Press, 2004); Stephen Kinzer, *Overthrow: America's Century of Regime Change from Hawaii to Iraq* (New York, NY: Times Books, 2006);

Sullivan, *American Adventurism Abroad: Invasions, Interventions, and Regime Changes Since World War II.*

60. Good, "American Exception: Hegemony and the Dissimulation of the State."

61. Ole R. Holsti, "Theories of International Relations," in *Explaining the History of American Foreign Relations*, ed. Michael J. Hogan and Thomas G. Patterson, Second (New York, NY: Cambridge University Press, 2004).

62. Holsti, "Theories of International Relations."

63. Hans Morgenthau, *Politics among Nations*, 4th ed. (New York, NY: Knopf, 1970).

64. Kenneth Waltz, *Theory of International Politics* (New York, NY: McGraw-Hill, 1979).

65. Mearsheimer, *The Tragedy of Great Power Politics.*

66. Holsti, "Theories of International Relations," 62.

67. Stephen D. Krasner, "State Power and the Structure of International Trade," *World Politics* 28, no. 3 (April 18, 1976): 317–47, https://doi.org/10.2307/2009974.

68. Kindleberger, *The World in Depression, 1929–1939.*

69. E.g., Robert O. Keohane and Joseph S. Nye, *Power and Interdependence: World Politics in Transition* (Boston, MA: Little, Brown & Co., 1977).

70. Charles Glasser, "The G-20 Is Discussing the 'International Liberal Order.' That's a Bad Place to Start a Debate," *Washington Post*, June 28, 2019, https://www.washingtonpost.com/politics/2019/06/28/g-is-discussing-international-liberal-order-thats-bad-place-start-debate/.

71. Andre Gunder Frank, *Capitalism and Underdevelopment in Latin America* (New York, NY: Monthly Review Press, 1967).

72. Immanuel Wallerstein, *The Modern World-System I: Capitalist Agriculture and the Origins of the European World Economy in the Sixteenth Century* (Berkeley, CA: University of California Press, 2011).

73. See, e.g.: Edward N. Muller, "Dependent Economic Development, Aid Dependence on the United States, and Democratic Breakdown in the Third World," *International Studies Quarterly* 29, no. 4 (December 1985): 445, https://doi.org/10.2307/2600381; Peter M. Sanchez, "Bringing the International Back in: US Hegemonic Maintenance and Latin America's Democratic Breakdown in the 1960s and 1970s," *International Politics* 40, no. 2 (2003): 223–47, https://doi.org/10.1057/palgrave.ip.8800015.

74. Christina Lin, "White Helmets: Instrument for Regime Change in Syria?" *Asia Times*, October 24, 2016, https://www.asiatimes.com/2016/10/opinion/white-helmets-instrument-regime-change-syria/.

75. Holsti, "Theories of International Relations," 88.

76. Holsti, "Theories of International Relations," 82.

77. Olmsted, *Challenging the Secret Government: The Post-Watergate Investigations of the CIA and FBI*, 99.

CHAPTER 2

1. Michael J. Hogan and Thomas G. Paterson, "Introduction," in *Explaining the History of American Foreign Relations*, ed. Michael J. Hogan and Thomas G. Paterson (New York, NY: Cambridge University Press, 2004),.

2. Samuel Flagg Bemis, *A Diplomatic History Of The United States* (New York, NY: Henry Holt and Company, 1936).

3. Dexter Perkins, *The Monroe Doctrine 1826–1867* (Baltimore, MD: Johns Hopkins University Press, 1933).

4. Hogan and Paterson, "Introduction," 1.

5. For example: Charles A. Beard and Mary R. Beard, *America in Midpassage*, vol. 1 (New York, NY: Macmillan Company, 1939).

6. Hogan and Paterson, "Introduction," 2.

7. George Kennan, *American Diplomacy* (Chicago, IL: University of Chicago Press, 1951).

8. Morgenthau, *Politics among Nations*.

9. Hogan and Paterson, "Introduction," 2–3.

10. William Appleman Williams, *The Tragedy of American Diplomacy* (Cleveland, OH: World Publishing Company, 1959).

11. Hogan and Paterson, "Introduction," 4–5.

12. John Lewis Gaddis, "The Emerging Post-Revisionist Synthesis on the Origins of the Cold War," *Diplomatic History* 7, no. 3 (1983): 171–190.

13. Hogan and Paterson, "Introduction," 5.

14. Hogan and Paterson, "Introduction," 5.

15. Cited from: Lloyd C. Gardner et al., "Responses to John Lewis Gaddis, 'The Emerging Post-Revisionist Synthesis on the Origins of the Cold War,'" *Diplomatic History* 7, no. 3 (1983): 198, https://doi.org/10.1111/j.1467–7709.1983.tb00390.x.

16. Melvyn P. Leffler, *A Preponderance of Power: National Security, the Truman Administration, and the Cold War* (Stanford, CA: Stanford University Press, 1992).

17. Melvyn P. Leffler, "National Security," in *Explaining the History of American Foreign Relations*, ed. Michael J. Hogan and Thomas G. Paterson (New York, NY: Cambridge University Press, 2004), 124.

18. Bruce Cumings, "'Revising Postrevisionism,' or, The Poverty of Theory in Diplomatic History," *Diplomatic History* 17, no. 4 (October 1993): 562, https://doi.org/10.1111/j.1467–7709.1993.tb00599.x.

19. Aaron Good, Ben Howard, and Peter Dale Scott, "How the U.S. Used Radical Islam and 9/11 to Advance Imperialism and Override the Constitution," CovertAction Magazine, The Twenty Year Shadow of 9/11, September 11, 2021, https://covertactionmagazine.com/2021/09/11/the-twenty-year-shadow-of-9-11-u-s-complicity-in-the-terror-spectacle-and-the-urgent-need-to-end-it/.

20. Mills, *The Power Elite*.

21. Robert Buzzanco, "What Happened to the New Left? Toward a Radical Reading of American Foreign Relations," *Diplomatic History* 23, no. 4 (1999): 576, https://www.jstor.org/stable/24913642.

22. Buzzanco, "What Happened to the New Left? Toward a Radical Reading of American Foreign Relations," 577.

23. Michael J. Hogan and Thomas G. Paterson, eds., *Explaining the History of American Foreign Relations* (New York, NY: Cambridge University Press, 2004).

24. Charles A. Beard, *Contemporary American History* (New York, NY: Macmillan Company, 1914), 55–59.

25. Charles A. Beard, *President Roosevelt and the Coming of the War, 1941* (New Haven, CT: Yale University Press, 1948).

26. Cumings, "'Revising Postrevisionism,' or, The Poverty of Theory in Diplomatic History," 544–545.

27. Kai Bird, *The Chairman: John J. McCloy & The Making of the American Establishment* (New York, NY: Simon & Schuster, 1992), 387–388.

28. Peter Dale Scott, *The Road to 9/11: Wealth, Empire, and the Future of America* (Berkeley, CA: University of California Press, 2007), 32.

29. Jim Hougan, *Spooks: The Haunting of America : The Private Use of Secret Agents* (New York, NY: William Morrow and Co., 1978), 435–436.

30. Cumings, "'Revising Postrevisionism,' or, The Poverty of Theory in Diplomatic History," 564.

31. Cumings, "'Revising Postrevisionism,' or, The Poverty of Theory in Diplomatic History," 565.

32. Lloyd C. Gardner, *Arcitects of Illusion: Men and Ideas in American Foreign Policy, 1941–1949* (Chicago, IL: Quadrangle Books, 1970), 301.

33. Gardner et al., "Responses to John Lewis Gaddis, 'The Emerging Post-Revisionist Synthesis on the Origins of the Cold War,'" 198.

34. Buzzanco, "What Happened to the New Left? Toward a Radical Reading of American Foreign Relations," 581.

35. Michael T. Klare, "The Traders Versus the Prussians," *Seven Days*, 1977, 32–33.

36. Scott, *The Road to 9/11: Wealth, Empire, and the Future of America*.

37. See, for example: Scott, *The Road to 9/11: Wealth, Empire, and the Future of America*.

38. Wolin, *Democracy Incorporated: Managed Democracy and the Specter of Inverted Totalitarianism*.

39. John Glaser, "The Amnesia of the U.S. Foreign Policy Establishment," *The New Republic*, March 15, 2019, https://newrepublic.com/article/153323/amnesia-us-foreign-policy-establishment.

40. Howard Friel and Richard Falk, *The Record of the Paper: How the "New York Times" Misreports US Foreign Policy* (New York, NY: Verso, 2004), 16.

41. "The Senate Select Committee to Study Governmental Operations with Respect to Intelligence Activities," vol. II (Washington D.C., April 26, 1976), 10–13, https://www.intelligence.senate.gov/sites/default/files/94755_II.pdf.

42. "The Senate Select Committee to Study Governmental Operations with Respect to Intelligence Activities," vol. II (Washington D.C., April 26, 1976), 14, https://www.intelligence.senate.gov/sites/default/files/94755_II.pdf.

43. Jessica Schulberg, "The U.S. Is Still Violating the Anti-Torture Treaty It Signed 20 Years Ago," *The New Republic*, October 21, 2014, https://newrepublic.com/article/119928/us-violates-un-convention-against-torture-signed-20-years-ago.

44. Bruce Ackerman, "Trump's War Against Iran Is an Impeachable Offense," *The American Prospect*, January 6, 2020, https://prospect.org/impeachment/trump-war-against-iran-impeachable-offense/.

45. Mills, *The Power Elite*.

46. See: Ernst Fraenkel, *The Dual State: A Contribution to the Study of Dictatorship* (New York, NY: Oxford University Press, 1941); Hans Morgenthau, "A State of Insecurity," *The New Republic* 132, no. 16 (1955): 8–14; Ola Tunander, "Democratic State vs. Deep State: Approaching the Dual State of the West," in *Government of the Shadows: Parapolitics and Criminal Sovereignty*, ed. Eric Wilson (New York, NY: Pluto Press, 2009), 56–722; Scott, *The Road to 9/11: Wealth, Empire, and the Future of America*; Michael J. Glennon, *National Security and Double Government* (New York, NY: Oxford University Press, 2015).

47. deHaven-Smith, "When Political Crimes Are Inside Jobs: Detecting State Crimes against Democracy."

48. Mills, *The Power Elite*; G. William Domhoff, *Who Rules America?* (Englewood Cliffs, NJ: Prentice-Hall, 1967); Phillips, *Giants: The Global Power Elite*.

49. Franz Neumann, *Behemoth: The Structure and Practice of National Socialism, 1933–1944* (New York, NY: Oxford University Press, 1944). Of the book, C. Wright Mills wrote that "if you read his book thoroughly, you see the harsh outlines of possible futures close around you. With leftwing thought confused and split and dribbling trivialities, he locates the enemy with a 500 watt glare. And Nazi is only one of his names." See C. Wright Mills, "The Nazi Behemoth Dissected," *Partisan Review* 9, no. 5 (1942): 437, http://archives.bu.edu/collections/partisan-review/search/detail?id=283940.

50. Mills, *The Power Elite*, 361.

51. David Wise and Thomas B. Ross, *The Invisible Government* (New York, NY: Random House, 1964).

52. G. William Domhoff, "There Are No Conspiracies," Who Rules America?, March 2005, https://whorulesamerica.ucsc.edu/theory/conspiracy.html.

53. Carl Schmitt, *Political Theology*, trans. George Schwab (Chicago, IL: University of Chicago Press, 1985).

54. Glennon, *National Security and Double Government.*

55. "NSC 68: United States Objectives and Programs for National Security" (Washington D.C., April 14, 1950), https://www.mtholyoke.edu/acad /intrel/nsc-68/nsc68-1.htm.

56. Mills, *The Power Elite*, 356.

57. Scott, *Deep Politics and the Death of JFK*, 7.

58. Scott, *Deep Politics and the Death of JFK*, xi-xii.

59. Laurence H. Shoup and William Minter, *Imperial Brain Trust: The Council on Foreign Relations and United States Foreign Policy* (Lincoln, NE: Authors Choice Press, 2004).

60. C. Wright Mills, *The Politics of Truth: Selected Writings of C. Wright Mills*, ed. John H. Summers (New York, NY: Oxford University Press, 2008), 142–143.

61. Scott, *The Road to 9/11: Wealth, Empire, and the Future of America*, 267.

62. Ian S. Lustick, "History, Historiography, and Political Science: Multiple Historical Records and the Problem of Selection Bias," American Political Science Review 90, no. 03 (September 1, 1996): 605–18, https://doi.org /10.2307/2082612.

63. Peter Dale Scott, *The War Conspiracy* (New York, NY: Bobbs Merrill, 1972), 171.

64. David N. Gibbs, "Researching Parapolitics: Replication, Qualitative Research and Social Science Methodology," in *The Dual State: Parapolitics, Carl Schmitt and the National Security Complex* (Surrey, England: Ashgate Publishing Limited, 2012), 103.

65. Gibbs, "Researching Parapolitics: Replication, Qualitative Research and Social Science Methodology," 114.

66. Gibbs, "Researching Parapolitics: Replication, Qualitative Research and Social Science Methodology," 114.

67. Gary King, "Replication, Replication," *PS: Political Science and Politics* 28, no. 3 (September 1995): 444, https://doi.org/10.2307/420301; Gary King, Robert Keohane, and Sidney Verba, *Designing Social Inquiry: Scientific Inference in Qualitative Research* (Princeton, NJ: Princeton University Press, 1994).

68. Gibbs, "Researching Parapolitics: Replication, Qualitative Research and Social Science Methodology," 102.

69. Gibbs, "Researching Parapolitics: Replication, Qualitative Research and Social Science Methodology," 115.

70. Herbert A. Simon, "Rational Choice and the Structure of the Environment.," *Psychological Review* 63, no. 2 (1956): 129–38, https://doi.org/10.1037 /h0042769. *Satisficing* is a social science term in the rational choice litera-ture which describes how people often devote minimal energy to making decisions based on imperfect information. They *satisfice.* My mentor and

friend Lance deHaven-Smith was once amused listening to me complain about political science graduate work. Laughing, he asked, "Oh God, did you learn about *satisficing*?"

CHAPTER 3

1. Carl Schmitt, *Political Theology*, trans. George Schwab (Chicago, IL: University of Chicago Press, 1985), 5.
2. Schmitt, *Political Theology*, 5.
3. Fraenkel, *The Dual State: A Contribution to the Study of Dictatorship*.
4. Hans Morgenthau, "A State of Insecurity," *The New Republic* 132, no. 16 (1955), 12.
5. Tunander, "Democratic State vs. Deep State: Approaching the Dual State of the West."
6. Glennon, *National Security and Double Government*.
7. Walter Bagehot, *The English Constitution* (Ithaca, New York: Cornell University Press, 1966); Glennon, *National Security and Double Government*, 5.
8. Glennon, *National Security and Double Government*, 5.
9. Glennon, *National Security and Double Government*, 6.
10. Glennon, *National Security and Double Government*, 6.
11. Glennon, *National Security and Double Government*, 6–7.
12. Glennon, *National Security and Double Government*, 7.
13. Glennon, *National Security and Double Government*, 7.
14. Glennon, *National Security and Double Government*, 7–8.
15. Glennon, *National Security and Double Government*, 8.
16. Glennon, *National Security and Double Government*, 11.
17. Glennon, *National Security and Double Government*, 12.
18. Glennon, *National Security and Double Government*, 12–13.
19. Glennon, *National Security and Double Government*, 13.
20. Glennon, *National Security and Double Government*, 14.
21. Glennon, *National Security and Double Government*, 14–15.
22. Glennon, *National Security and Double Government*, 15.
23. Daniel Ellsberg, *The Doomsday Machine: Confessions of a Nuclear War Planner* (New York, NY: Bloomsbury, 2017), 90.
24. Ellsberg, *The Doomsday Machine: Confessions of a Nuclear War Planner*, 92.
25. Ellsberg, *The Doomsday Machine: Confessions of a Nuclear War Planner*, 94.
26. Ellsberg, *The Doomsday Machine: Confessions of a Nuclear War Planner*, 128.
27. Ellsberg, *The Doomsday Machine: Confessions of a Nuclear War Planner*.
28. Dana Priest and William M. Arkin, *Top Secret America: The Rise of the New American Security State* (New York, NY: Little, Brown, 2011).
29. Priest and Arkin, *Top Secret America: The Rise of the New American Security State*; Glennon, *National Security and Double Government*, 16.
30. Glennon, *National Security and Double Government*, 16.

31. Glennon, *National Security and Double Government*, 17.
32. Glennon, *National Security and Double Government*, 17–18.
33. Glennon, *National Security and Double Government*, 18; C. Wright Mills, *The Power Elite* (New York, NY: Oxford University Press, 1956), 222.
34. Glennon, *National Security and Double Government*, 19.
35. Glennon, *National Security and Double Government*, 19.
36. Glennon, *National Security and Double Government*, 21.
37. Glennon, *National Security and Double Government*, 21.
38. Glennon, *National Security and Double Government*, 22.
39. Glennon, *National Security and Double Government*, 22.
40. Glennon, *National Security and Double Government*, 23.
41. Glennon, *National Security and Double Government*, 147.
42. Glennon, *National Security and Double Government*, 23.
43. Glennon, *National Security and Double Government*, 24.
44. Glennon, *National Security and Double Government*, 24; C. Wright Mills, *The Power Elite* (New York, NY: Oxford University Press, 1956), 190.
45. Glennon, *National Security and Double Government*, 24.
46. Glennon, *National Security and Double Government*, 25.
47. Glennon, *National Security and Double Government*, 26–27.
48. Glennon, *National Security and Double Government*, 28.
49. Glennon, *National Security and Double Government*, 28.
50. Glennon, *National Security and Double Government*, 29–30.
51. Glennon, *National Security and Double Government*, 30.
52. Glennon, *National Security and Double Government*, 30–31.
53. Glennon, *National Security and Double Government*, 32.
54. Glennon, *National Security and Double Government*, 32–34.
55. Glennon, *National Security and Double Government*, 36.
56. Glennon, *National Security and Double Government*, 37.
57. Glennon, *National Security and Double Government*, 39.
58. Glennon, *National Security and Double Government*, 39.
59. Glennon, *National Security and Double Government*, 40.
60. Glennon, *National Security and Double Government*, 40.
61. Glennon, *National Security and Double Government*, 41.
62. Glennon, *National Security and Double Government*, 41.
63. Glennon, *National Security and Double Government*, 42.
64. Glennon, *National Security and Double Government*, 42.
65. Glennon, *National Security and Double Government*, 42.
66. Glennon, *National Security and Double Government*, 43.
67. Glennon, *National Security and Double Government*, 44.
68. Glennon, *National Security and Double Government*, 46.
69. Glennon, *National Security and Double Government*, 47.
70. Glennon, *National Security and Double Government*, 47.

71. Glennon, *National Security and Double Government*, 47–48.
72. Glennon, *National Security and Double Government*, 48.
73. Glennon, *National Security and Double Government*, 49.
74. Glennon, *National Security and Double Government*, 50.
75. Glennon, *National Security and Double Government*, 51.
76. Glennon, *National Security and Double Government*, 51.
77. Glennon, *National Security and Double Government*, 52, 173.
78. Glennon, *National Security and Double Government*, 48.
79. Glennon, *National Security and Double Government*, 52.
80. Glennon, *National Security and Double Government*, 52–53.
81. Glennon, *National Security and Double Government*, 53, 176.
82. Glennon, *National Security and Double Government*, 54.
83. Glennon, *National Security and Double Government*, 54.
84. Glennon, *National Security and Double Government*, 55.
85. Glennon, *National Security and Double Government*, 56; Amy Zegart and Julie Quinn, "Congressional Intelligence Oversight: The Electoral Disconnection," *Intelligence and National Security* 25, no. 6 (December 16, 2010): 744–66, https://doi.org/10.1080/02684527.2010.537871.
86. Glennon, *National Security and Double Government*, 57.
87. Arthur M. Schlesinger, *The Imperial Presidency* (Boston, MA: Houghton Mifflin, 1973); Chalmers Johnson, *Nemesis: The Last Days of the American Republic* (New York, NY: Metropolitan Books, 2006), 14–18.
88. Glennon, *National Security and Double Government*, 58.
89. Glennon, *National Security and Double Government*, 58–59.
90. Glennon, *National Security and Double Government*, 59.
91. Joan Mellen, *A Farewell to Justice: Jim Garrison, JFK's Assassination, and the Case That Should Have Changed History*, 2nd ed. (New York, NY: Skyhorse Publishing, 2013), 162.
92. Schlesinger, *The Imperial Presidency*.
93. Glennon, *National Security and Double Government*, 59.
94. Glennon, *National Security and Double Government*, 59.
95. Glennon, *National Security and Double Government*, 60.
96. Glennon, *National Security and Double Government*, 61–62. Additionally, Robert Gates was Bush's DCI during the congressional October Surprise investigation. As such, he could stymie inquiries from that position if Lee Hamilton et al requested information about Gates' or Bush's or Donald Gregg's activities in the Fall of 1980. Also, Gates was made Casey's Chief of Staff in 1981. Casey was another central October Surprise character and Reagan's campaign manager. See: Robert Parry, "Second Thoughts on October Surprise," *Consortium News*, June 8, 2013, https://consortiumnews.com/2013/06/08/second-thoughts-on-october-surprise/.
97. Glennon, *National Security and Double Government*, 64.

98. Glennon, *National Security and Double Government*, 64.
99. Glennon, *National Security and Double Government*, 68.
100. Glennon, *National Security and Double Government*, 69.
101. Glennon, *National Security and Double Government*, 70.
102. Glennon, *National Security and Double Government*, 71.
103. Glennon, *National Security and Double Government*, 71–72.
104. Glennon, *National Security and Double Government*, 74.
105. Glennon, *National Security and Double Government*, 74; Graham Allison and Philip Zelikow, *Essence of Decision: Explaining the Cuban Missile Crisis*, 2nd ed. (New York, NY: Longman, 1999), 19–20.
106. Allison and Zelikow, *Essence of Decision: Explaining the Cuban Missile Crisis*, 36.
107. Allison and Zelikow, *Essence of Decision: Explaining the Cuban Missile Crisis*, 27–28; Morgenthau, *Politics among Nations*.
108. Allison and Zelikow, *Essence of Decision: Explaining the Cuban Missile Crisis*, 30.
109. Allison and Zelikow, *Essence of Decision: Explaining the Cuban Missile Crisis*, 31. Waltz, *Theory of International Politics*.
110. Allison and Zelikow, *Essence of Decision: Explaining the Cuban Missile Crisis*, 33.
111. Robert O. Keohane, *After Hegemony: Cooperation and Discord in the World Political Economy* (Princeton, NJ: Princeton University Press, 1984); Allison and Zelikow, *Essence of Decision: Explaining the Cuban Missile Crisis*, 34–35.
112. Glennon, *National Security and Double Government*, 75.
113. Glennon, *National Security and Double Government*, 76.
114. Glennon, *National Security and Double Government*, 77.
115. Glennon, *National Security and Double Government*, 78.
116. Glennon, *National Security and Double Government*, 80.
117. Allison and Zelikow, *Essence of Decision: Explaining the Cuban Missile Crisis*, 255.
118. Glennon, *National Security and Double Government*, 80.
119. Glennon, *National Security and Double Government*, 81.
120. Glennon, *National Security and Double Government*, 81.
121. Allison and Zelikow, *Essence of Decision: Explaining the Cuban Missile Crisis*, 143.
122. Glennon, *National Security and Double Government*, 81.
123. Glennon, *National Security and Double Government*, 81–82.
124. Glennon, *National Security and Double Government*, 82–83.
125. Glennon, *National Security and Double Government*, 83–84.
126. Glennon, *National Security and Double Government*, 84.
127. Glennon, *National Security and Double Government*, 84–85.
128. Glennon, *National Security and Double Government*, 85.

129. Glennon, *National Security and Double Government*, 85.

130. Glennon, *National Security and Double Government*, 86.

131. Glennon, *National Security and Double Government*, 86–87.

132. Glennon, *National Security and Double Government*, 87.

133. Glennon, *National Security and Double Government*, 87–88.

134. G. William Domhoff, "C. Wright Mills, Power Structure Research, and the Failures of Mainstream Political Science," *New Political Science* 29, no. 1 (March 9, 2007): 97–114, https://doi.org/10.1080/07393140601170867.

135. Valeri M. Hudson and Benjamin S. Day, *Foreign Policy Analysis: Classic and Contemporary Theory*, 3rd ed. (New York, NY: Rowman & Littlefield, 2020) 35.

136. See: Gerald Horne, *The Counter-Revolution of 1776* (New York, NY: New York University Press, 2014).

137. James Huang, "Real Reason for Syria War Plans, from Gen. Wesley Clark," Who. What. Why., August 31, 2013, https://whowhatwhy.org/2013/08/31/classic-why-real-reason-for-syria-war-plans-from-gen-wesley-clark/.

138. Alan J. Kuperman, "A Model Humanitarian Intervention? Reassessing NATO's Libya Campaign," *International Security* 38, no. 1 (July 2013): 105–36, https://doi.org/10.1162/ISEC_a_00126.

139. Oliver Stone and Peter Kuznick, *The Untold History of the United States*, 2nd ed. (New York, NY: Gallery Books, 2019), 648–649.

140. David Brennan, "Trump Says U.S. Troops Stayed In Syria 'Because I Kept the Oil,'" *Newsweek*, January 15, 2020, https://www.newsweek.com/donald-trump-us-troops-syria-oil-bashar-al-assad-kurds-wisconsin-rally-1482250.

141. Michael Parenti, *Contrary Notions: The Michael Parenti Reader* (San Francisco, CA: City Lights Books, 2007), 309–310.

142. Mills, *The Power Elite*, 343.

143. Samuel P. Huntington, "The Clash of Civilizations?," *Foreign Affairs* 72, no. 3 (1993): 22, https://doi.org/10.2307/20045621.

144. Robert Dreyfuss, *Devil's Game: How the United States Helped Unleash Fundamentalist Islam* (New York, NY: Henry Holt and Company, 2005), 51.

145. This formulation rests upon the debatable assessment that Israel functions as an element of US hegemony under which Britain is a junior partner.

146. Peter Dale Scott and Aaron Good, "Was the Now-Forgotten Murder of One Man on September 9, 2001 a Crucial Pre-Condition for 9/11?" CovertAction Magazine, December 9, 2020, https://covertactionmagazine.com/2020/12/09/was-the-now-forgotten-murder-of-one-man-on-september-9-2001-a-crucial-pre-condition-for-9-11/.

147. Zbigniew Brzezinski, *The Grand Chessboard: American Primacy and Its Geostrategic Imperatives* (New York, NY: Basic Books, 1997).

148. C. Wright Mills, *The Politics of Truth: Selected Writings of C. Wright Mills*, ed. John H. Summers (New York, NY: Oxford University Press, 2008), 204.

149. Mills, *The Politics of Truth: Selected Writings of C. Wright Mills*, 205.

150. Mills, *The Politics of Truth: Selected Writings of C. Wright Mills*, 206.
151. Inderjeet Parmar, *Foundations of the American Century* (New York Chichester, West Sussex: Columbia University Press, 2012), 261, https://doi .org/10.7312/parm14628.
152. Frances Stonor Saunders, *The Cultural Cold War: The CIA and the World of Arts and Letters* (New York, NY: The New Press, 2000).
153. Hudson and Day, *Foreign Policy Analysis: Classic and Contemporary Theory*, 167.
154. Mills, *The Politics of Truth: Selected Writings of C. Wright Mills*, 2.

CHAPTER 4

1.   Mills, *The Power Elite*.
2.   Mills, *The Power Elite*, 22, 24.
3.   Mills, *The Power Elite*, 5.
4.   Mills, *The Power Elite*, 5.
5.   Mills, *The Power Elite*, 7.
6.   Mills, *The Power Elite*, 10.
7.   Mills, *The Power Elite*, 18.
8.   Mills, *The Power Elite*, 19.
9.   Mills, *The Power Elite*, 19.
10. Mills, *The Power Elite*, 19–20.
11. Mills, *The Power Elite*, 21.
12. Mills, *The Power Elite*, 27.
13. Mills, *The Power Elite*, 27.
14. Mills, *The Power Elite*, 27.
15. Mills, *The Power Elite*, 269.
16. Mills, *The Power Elite*, 269–270.
17. Mills, *The Power Elite*, 270.
18. Mills, *The Power Elite*, 271.
19. Mills, *The Power Elite*, 271–272.
20. Mills, *The Power Elite*, 272–273.
21. Mills, *The Power Elite*, 273.
22. Mills, *The Power Elite*, 273–274.
23. Mills, *The Power Elite*, 274–275.
24. Mills, *The Power Elite*, 274–275.
25. Mills, *The Power Elite*, 275.
26. Mills, *The Power Elite*, 275–276.
27. Mills, *The Power Elite*, 276.
28. Mills, *The Power Elite*, 277.
29. Mills, *The Power Elite*, 324.
30. Mills, *The Power Elite*, 268.
31. Mills, *The Power Elite*, 283.

32. Mills, *The Power Elite*, 408; James Stewart Martin, *All Honorable Men: The Story of the Men on Both Sides of the Atlantic Who Successfully Thwarted Plans to Dismantle the Nazi Cartel System*, ed. Mark Crispin Miller, vol. 21, Forbidden Bookshelf (New York, NY: Open Road Media, 2016).

33. Tom Bower, *The Paperclip Conspiracy: The Hunt for the Nazi Scientists* (Boston, MA: Little, Brown & Co., 1987).

34. Christopher Simpson, *Blowback: America's Recruitment of Nazis and Its Destructive Impact on Our Domestic and Foreign Policy*, ed. Mark Crispin Miller, vol. 4, Forbidden Bookshelf (New York, NY: Open Road Media, 2014).

35. David Talbot, *The Devil's Chessboard: Allen Dulles, the CIA, and the Rise of America's Secret Government* (New York, NY: Harper Collins, 2015).

36. Bird, *The Chairman: John J. McCloy & The Making of the American Establishment*.

37. Mills, *The Power Elite*, 311.
38. Mills, *The Power Elite*, 313.
39. Mills, *The Power Elite*, 314.
40. Mills, *The Power Elite*, 315.
41. Mills, *The Power Elite*, 317.
42. Mills, *The Power Elite*, 315.
43. Mills, *The Power Elite*, 317–318.
44. Mills, *The Power Elite*, 318.
45. Mills, *The Power Elite*, 319.
46. Mills, *The Power Elite*, 319–320.
47. Mills, *The Power Elite*, 326.
48. Mills, *The Power Elite*, 329.
49. Mills, *The Power Elite*, 331.
50. Mills, *The Power Elite*, 332.
51. Mills, *The Power Elite*, 333.
52. Mills, *The Power Elite*, 336–337.
53. Mills, *The Power Elite*, 338.
54. Mills, *The Power Elite*, 342.
55. Mills, *The Power Elite*, 345.
56. Mills, *The Power Elite*, 343.
57. Mills, *The Power Elite*, 345.
58. Mills, *The Power Elite*, 346.
59. Mills, *The Power Elite*, 347.
60. Mills, *The Power Elite*, 348.
61. Mills, *The Power Elite*, 349.
62. Mills, *The Power Elite*, 350.
63. Mills, *The Power Elite*, 351.
64. Mills, *The Power Elite*, 351.

65. Mills, *The Power Elite*, 293.

66. Mills, *The Power Elite*, 294.

67. Mills, *The Power Elite*, 294.

68. Mills, *The Power Elite*, 356.

69. Mills, *The Power Elite*, 328.

70. Ellsberg, *The Doomsday Machine: Confessions of a Nuclear War Planner*.

71. Mills, *The Power Elite*, 356.

72. C. Wright Mills, *The Causes of World War Three* (London, England: Secker & Warburg, 1959), 89–90.

73. Mills, *The Causes of World War Three*, 90.

74. E.g., Priest and Arkin, *Top Secret America: The Rise of the New American Security State*.

75. Lasswell, "The Garrison State."

76. Lasswell, "The Garrison State," 462.

77. Lasswell, "The Garrison State," 455.

78. Mills, *The Power Elite*, 27.

79. Mills, *The Power Elite*, 343.

80. Mills, *The Power Elite*, 356.

81. Matthew T. Witt and Lance deHaven-Smith, "Conjuring the Holographic State," *Administration & Society* 40, no. 6 (October 29, 2008): 547–85, https://doi.org/10.1177/0095399708321682.

82. Shoup and Minter, *Imperial Brain Trust: The Council on Foreign Relations and United States Foreign Policy*.

83. Mills, *The Power Elite*, 293.

84. Robert A. Dahl, *Who Governs?: Democracy and Power in an American City* (New Haven, CT: Yale University Press, 1961).

85. Charles E. Lindblom, *Politics and Markets: The World's Political Economic Systems* (New York, NY: Basic Books, 1977).

86. Jurgen Habermas, *Legitimation Crisis*, trans. Thomas McCarthy (Boston, MA: Beacon Press, 1973).

87. Lance deHaven-Smith, "From a Fabric of Suspicion: The U.S. Constitution and Other Founding Dilemmas," in *State Crimes Against Democracy: Political Forensics in Public Affairs*, ed. Alexander Kouzmin, Matthew T. Witt, and Andrew Kakabadse (New York, NY: Palgrave Macmillan, 2013).

88. Guido Giacomo Preparata, *The Ideology of Tyranny: The Use of Neo-Gnostic Myth in American Politics* (New York, NY: Palgrave Macmillan, 2011); deHaven-Smith, "From a Fabric of Suspicion: The U.S. Constitution and Other Founding Dilemmas."

89. Michel Foucault, "Governmentality," in *Power*, ed. James D. Faubion, trans. Robert Hurley, vol. 3, *The Essential Works of Foucault, 1954–1984* (New York, NY: The New Press, 2001), 201–22.

90. deHaven-Smith, "From a Fabric of Suspicion: The U.S. Constitution and Other Founding Dilemmas"; Michel Foucault, *The Order of Things: An Archaeology of the Human Sciences* (London, England: Tavistock, 1970).

91. Jane Mayer, *The Dark Side: The Inside Story of How The War on Terror Turned into a War on American Ideals* (New York, NY: Anchor Books, 2009); deHaven-Smith, "From a Fabric of Suspicion: The U.S. Constitution and Other Founding Dilemmas."

92. John D. Marks, *The Search for the Manchurian Candidate: The CIA and Mind Control*, ed. W. W. Norton (New York, NY, 1979); deHaven-Smith, "From a Fabric of Suspicion: The U.S. Constitution and Other Founding Dilemmas."

93. Mills, *The Power Elite.*

94. For a critique of Chomsky views, see: Michael Parenti, *Dirty Truths: Reflections on Politics, Media, Ideology, Conspiracy, Ethnic Life and Class Power* (San Francisco, CA: City Lights Books, 1996), 188.

95. Michael Parenti, *Dirty Truths: Reflections on Politics, Media, Ideology, Conspiracy, Ethnic Life and Class Power* (San Francisco, CA: City Lights Books, 1996) 174–175.

96. Mills, *The Power Elite*, 361.

CHAPTER 5

1. Good, "American Exception: Hegemony and the Dissimulation of the State."

2. Peter Dale Scott, *The Road to 9/11: Wealth, Empire, and the Future of America* (Berkeley, CA: University of California Press, 2007), 267.

3. Scott, *The Road to 9/11: Wealth, Empire, and the Future of America*, 267.

4. Gareth Jenkins, "Susurluk and the Legacy of Turkey's Dirty War," *Terrorism Monitor* 6, no. 9 (2008), https://jamestown.org/program/susurluk-and-the-legacy-of-turkeys-dirty-war/.

5. Barrett, "A Wordnado of Words in 2013."

6. Mike Lofgren, "Anatomy of the Deep State," *Bill Moyers*, February 21, 2014, https://billmoyers.com/2014/02/21/anatomy-of-the-deep-state/.

7. Mike Lofgren, *The Deep State* (New York, NY: Viking, 2016), 5.

8. Lofgren, *The Deep State*, 5.

9. Lofgren, *The Deep State*, 49–50.

10. Peter Dale Scott, *American War Machine: Deep Politics, the CIA Global Drug Connection, and the Road to Afghanistan* (New York, NY: Rowman & Littlefield, 2010), 30.

11. Peter Dale Scott, *The War Conspiracy* (New York, NY: Bobbs Merrill, 1972), 171.

12. Peter Dale Scott, *Deep Politics and the Death of JFK* (Berkeley, CA: University of California Press, 1993), 7.

13. Scott, *American War Machine: Deep Politics, the CIA Global Drug Connection, and the Road to Afghanistan*, 8.

14. Scott, *The Road to 9/11: Wealth, Empire, and the Future of America*, xvi.

15. Lofgren, "Anatomy of the Deep State."

16. Lofgren, "Anatomy of the Deep State."

17. Scott, *American War Machine: Deep Politics, the CIA Global Drug Connection, and the Road to Afghanistan*, 14.

18. Scott, *American War Machine: Deep Politics, the CIA Global Drug Connection, and the Road to Afghanistan*, 13.

19. Scott, *Deep Politics and the Death of JFK*, xi-xii.

20. Scott, *American War Machine: Deep Politics, the CIA Global Drug Connection, and the Road to Afghanistan*, 14.

21. Peter Dale Scott, *The American Deep State: Wall Street, Big Oil, and the Attack on U.S. Democracy* (New York, NY: Rowman & Littlefield, 2015), 145.

22. Scott, *The American Deep State: Wall Street, Big Oil, and the Attack on U.S. Democracy*, 30.

23. Scott, *The American Deep State: Wall Street, Big Oil, and the Attack on U.S. Democracy*, 199–200: n. 63.

24. Good, "American Exception: Hegemony and the Dissimulation of the State," 20.

25. Good, "American Exception: Hegemony and the Dissimulation of the State."

26. Hannah Arendt, *Between Past and Future: Eight Exercises in Political Thought* (New York, NY: Penguin Books, 1993); Scott, *The American Deep State: Wall Street, Big Oil, and the Attack on U.S. Democracy*, 3.

27. Arendt, *Between Past and Future: Eight Exercises in Political Thought*, 93.

28. Karl R. Popper, *The Open Society and Its Enemies*, 5th ed. (Princeton, NJ: Princeton University Press, 2013).

29. Scott, *The American Deep State: Wall Street, Big Oil, and the Attack on U.S. Democracy*, 3.

30. Samuel P. Huntington, *American Politics: The Promise of Disharmony* (Cambridge, MA: Belknap Press, 1981), 75; Scott, *The American Deep State: Wall Street, Big Oil, and the Attack on U.S. Democracy*, 3.

31. Scott, *The American Deep State: Wall Street, Big Oil, and the Attack on U.S. Democracy*, 3.

32. Glenn R. Morrow, *Plato's Cretan City: A Historical Interpretation of the "Laws"* (Princeton, NJ: Princeton University Press, 1993).

33. Ernest Barker, *Greek Political Theory: Plato and His Predecessors*, 4th ed. (London, England: Methuen & Co., 1951), 349.

34. George Klosko, "The Nocturnal Council in Plato's Laws," *Political Studies* 36, no. 1 (March 24, 1988): 76, https://doi.org/10.1111/j.1467–9248.1988.tb00217.x.

35. Matt Peppe, "Hillary Clinton, the Council on Foreign Relations and the Establishment," *Counterpunch*, February 24, 2016, https://www.counterpunch.org/2016/02/24/hillary-clinton-the-council-on-foreign-relations-and-the-establishment/.

36. Barker, *Greek Political Theory: Plato and His Predecessors*, 349.

37. See: Scott, *The Road to 9/11: Wealth, Empire, and the Future of America*; Scott, *The American Deep State: Wall Street, Big Oil, and the Attack on U.S. Democracy.*

38. Harry S. Truman, "Limit CIA Role To Intelligence," *The Washington Post*, December 22, 1963, https://archive.org/stream/LimitCIARoleToIntelligenceByHarrySTruman/Limit CIA Role To Intelligence by Harry S Truman_djvu.txt.

39. Lance deHaven-Smith, "From a Fabric of Suspicion: The U.S. Constitution and Other Founding Dilemmas," in *State Crimes Against Democracy: Political Forensics in Public Affairs*, ed. Alexander Kouzmin, Matthew T. Witt, and Andrew Kakabadse (New York, NY: Palgrave Macmillan, 2013), 48.

40. deHaven-Smith, "From a Fabric of Suspicion: The U.S. Constitution and Other Founding Dilemmas," 48–49.

41. Lofgren, *The Deep State*, 36.

42. David Usborne, "WMD Just a Convenient Excuse for War, Admits Wolfowitz," *The Independent*, May 30, 2003, https://www.independent.co.uk/news/world/middle-east/wmd-just-a-convenient-excuse-for-war-admits-wolfowitz-106754.html.

43. Leo Strauss, *Natural Right and History*, paperback (Chicago, IL: University of Chicago Press, 1965), 106.

44. Richard N. Haass (@RichardHaass), "International order for 4 centuries . . ." Twitter, July 14, 2018, https://twitter.com/RichardHaass/status/1018245342989516805.

45. Caitlyn Johnstone, "Ex-CIA Director Thinks US Hypocrisy About Election Meddling Is Hilarious," Caitlyn Johnstone, February 17, 2018, https://caityjohnstone.medium.com/ex-cia-director-thinks-us-hypocrisy-about-election-meddling-is-hilarious-3262692029fe.

46. Jurgen Habermas, *Legitimation Crisis*, trans. Thomas McCarthy (Boston, MA: Beacon Press, 1973); DeHaven-Smith, "From a Fabric of Suspicion: The U.S. Constitution and Other Founding Dilemmas," 58.

47. deHaven-Smith, "From a Fabric of Suspicion: The U.S. Constitution and Other Founding Dilemmas," 58.

48. Zbigniew Brzezinski, "The Global Political Awakening," *New York Times*, 2008, https://www.nytimes.com/2008/12/16/opinion/16iht-YEbrzezinski.1.18730411.html.

49. deHaven-Smith, "From a Fabric of Suspicion: The U.S. Constitution and Other Founding Dilemmas," 48.

50. deHaven-Smith, "From a Fabric of Suspicion: The U.S. Constitution and Other Founding Dilemmas," 48–49.

51. deHaven-Smith, "From a Fabric of Suspicion: The U.S. Constitution and Other Founding Dilemmas," 59.

52. Good, "American Exception: Hegemony and the Dissimulation of the State."

53. Charles Tilly, "War Making and State Making as Organized Crime," in *Bringing the State Back In*, ed. Peter B. Evans, Dietrich Rueschemeyer, and Theda Skocpol (Cambridge: Cambridge University Press, 1985), 169–91, https://doi.org/10.1017/CBO9780511628283.008.

54. Charles Tilly, "Reflections on the History of European State Making," in *The Formation of National States in Western Europe*, ed. Charles Tilly (Princeton, NJ: Princeton University Press, 1975), 42.

55. Good, "American Exception: Hegemony and the Dissimulation of the State," 3.

56. Good, "American Exception: Hegemony and the Dissimulation of the State," 3.

57. John Locke, *The Second Treatise of Government and A Letter Concerning Toleration*, ed. Tom Crawford (Mineola, NY: Dover Publications, 2002), 74.

58. Mark Neocleous, "Security, Liberty and the Myth of Balance: Towards a Critique of Security Politics," *Contemporary Political Theory* 6, no. 2 (May 7, 2007), 135, https://doi.org/10.1057/palgrave.cpt.9300301.

59. Neocleous, "Security, Liberty and the Myth of Balance: Towards a Critique of Security Politics," 137.

60. Locke, *The Second Treatise of Government and A Letter Concerning Toleration*, 77.

61. Locke, *The Second Treatise of Government and A Letter Concerning Toleration*, 77.

62. Locke, *The Second Treatise of Government and A Letter Concerning Toleration*, 77.

63. Neocleous, "Security, Liberty and the Myth of Balance: Towards a Critique of Security Politics," 139–140.

64. Carl Schmitt, *Political Theology*, trans. George Schwab (Chicago, IL: University of Chicago Press, 1985), 5.

65. Schmitt, *Political Theology*, 6.

66. Schmitt, *Political Theology*, 6.

67. Schmitt, *Political Theology*, 7.

68. Schmitt, *Political Theology*, 13.

69. Schmitt, *Political Theology*, 14.

70. Lasswell, "The Garrison State"; Scott, *The Road to 9/11: Wealth, Empire, and the Future of America*; Wolin, *Democracy Incorporated: Managed Democracy and the Specter of Inverted Totalitarianism*.

71. Hans Morgenthau, "A State of Insecurity," *The New Republic* 132, no. 16 (1955), 12.
72. Hans Morgenthau, "A State of Insecurity," *The New Republic* 132, no. 16 (1955), 12.
73. Tunander, "Democratic State vs. Deep State: Approaching the Dual State of the West."
74. Tunander, "Democratic State vs. Deep State: Approaching the Dual State of the West," 57.
75. Scott, *The War Conspiracy*, 171.
76. Tunander, "Democratic State vs. Deep State: Approaching the Dual State of the West," 68.
77. Tunander, "Democratic State vs. Deep State: Approaching the Dual State of the West," 68.
78. Good, "American Exception: Hegemony and the Dissimulation of the State," 6; Tunander, "Democratic State vs. Deep State: Approaching the Dual State of the West."
79. Tilly, "Reflections on the History of European State Making"; Tilly, "War Making and State Making as Organized Crime."

CHAPTER 6

1. Shoup and Minter, *Imperial Brain Trust: The Council on Foreign Relations and United States Foreign Policy*.
2. Henry Luce, "The American Century," *Life*, February 17, 1941, https://books.google.com/books?id=I0kEAAAAMBAJ&printsec=frontcover#v=onepage&q&f=false.
3. Mike Lofgren, *The Deep State* (New York, NY: Viking, 2016), 49.
4. Alfred W. McCoy, *The Politics of Heroin: CIA Complicity in the Global Drug Trade*, Rev. ed. (Chicago, IL: Lawrence Hill Books, 1991); Scott, *American War Machine: Deep Politics, the CIA Global Drug Connection, and the Road to Afghanistan*.
5. Scott, *American War Machine: Deep Politics, the CIA Global Drug Connection, and the Road to Afghanistan*, 55.
6. Curt Cardwell, *NSC 68 and the Political Economy of the Cold War* (New York, NY: Cambridge University Press, 2011).
7. Shoup and Minter, *Imperial Brain Trust: The Council on Foreign Relations and United States Foreign Policy*, 173.
8. Shoup and Minter, *Imperial Brain Trust: The Council on Foreign Relations and United States Foreign Policy*, 173–174.
9. Jerry W. Sanders, *Peddlars of Crisis: The Committee on the Present Danger and the Politics of Containment* (Cambridge, MA: South End Press, 1983), 37.
10. Cardwell, *NSC 68 and the Political Economy of the Cold War*, 24.
11. Sanders, *Peddlars of Crisis: The Committee on the Present Danger and the Politics of Containment*, 37–38.

12. Sanders, *Peddlars of Crisis: The Committee on the Present Danger and the Politics of Containment*, 38; "NSC 68: United States Objectives and Programs for National Security" (Washington D.C., April 14, 1950), https://www.mtholyoke.edu/acad/intrel/nsc-68/nsc68-1.htm.

13. Frank Kofsky, *Harry S. Truman and the War Scare of 1948: A Successful Campaign to Deceive the Nation* (New York, NY: St. Martin's Press, 1995).

14. Kofsky, *Harry S. Truman and the War Scare of 1948: A Successful Campaign to Deceive the Nation*, 13–14.

15. Kofsky, *Harry S. Truman and the War Scare of 1948: A Successful Campaign to Deceive the Nation*, 15.

16. Kofsky, *Harry S. Truman and the War Scare of 1948: A Successful Campaign to Deceive the Nation*, 15.

17. Kofsky, *Harry S. Truman and the War Scare of 1948: A Successful Campaign to Deceive the Nation*, 40–41.

18. Kofsky, *Harry S. Truman and the War Scare of 1948: A Successful Campaign to Deceive the Nation*, 41.

19. Kofsky, *Harry S. Truman and the War Scare of 1948: A Successful Campaign to Deceive the Nation*, 42.

20. Kofsky, *Harry S. Truman and the War Scare of 1948: A Successful Campaign to Deceive the Nation*, 43–45.

21. Kofsky, *Harry S. Truman and the War Scare of 1948: A Successful Campaign to Deceive the Nation*, 8.

22. Cumings, "'Revising Postrevisionism,' or, The Poverty of Theory in Diplomatic History."

23. George Kennan, *At Century's Ending: Reflections, 1982–1995* (New York, NY: Norton, 1996), 118; James W. Carden, Marshall Auerback, and Patrick Lawrence, "'The Russia Question,'" Consortium News, May 12, 2021, https://consortiumnews.com/2021/05/12/the-russia-question/.

24. George Orwell, *1984* (New York, NY: Plume/Harcourt Brace, 1984), 193.

25. Michael Hudson, *J Is for Junk Economics: A Guide to Reality in an Age of Deception* (Glashütte, Germany: ISLET-Verlag, 2017), 85.

26. Hudson, *J Is for Junk Economics: A Guide to Reality in an Age of Deception*, 105.

27. Orwell, *1984*, 194.

28. Orwell, *1984*, 195.

29. Orwell, *1984*, 195–196.

30. George Carlin, "Jamming in New York," *HBO* (US, 1992), https://scrapsfromtheloft.com/comedy/george-carlin-jamming-new-york-1992-full-transcript/.

31. Orwell, *1984*, 196–197.

32. Sanders, *Peddlars of Crisis: The Committee on the Present Danger and the Politics of Containment*, 13.

33. Truman, "Limit CIA Role To Intelligence."

34. Douglas Frantz and David McKean, *Friends in High Places: The Rise and Fall of Clark Clifford* (New York, NY: Little, Brown & Co., 1995), 67–68.

35. Scott, *The American Deep State: Wall Street, Big Oil, and the Attack on U.S. Democracy*, 18.

36. Scott, *The American Deep State: Wall Street, Big Oil, and the Attack on U.S. Democracy*, 19.

37. Stephen Kinzer, *All the Shah's Men: An American Coup and the Roots of Middle East Terror* (Hoboken, NJ: John Wiley & Sons, 2003).

38. Scott, *The American Deep State: Wall Street, Big Oil, and the Attack on U.S. Democracy*, 19.

39. Scott, *The American Deep State: Wall Street, Big Oil, and the Attack on U.S. Democracy*, 19.

40. E.g., Samuel P. Huntington, *Political Order in Changing Societies* (New Haven, CT: Yale University Press, 1968).

41. James Risen, "SECRETS OF HISTORY: The C.I.A. in Iran -- A Special Report.; How a Plot Convulsed Iran in '53 (and in '79)," *New York Times*, April 16, 2000, https://www.nytimes.com/2000/04/16/world/secrets-history-cia-iran-special-report-plot-convulsed-iran-53-79.html.

42. Scott, *The American Deep State: Wall Street, Big Oil, and the Attack on U.S. Democracy*, 20.

43. Peter Dale Scott, "The Dulles Brothers, Harry Dexter White, Alger Hiss, and the Fate of the Private Pre-War International Banking System," *The Asia-Pacific Journal: Japan Focus* 12, no. 16 (April 20, 2014), https://apjjf.org/2014/12/16/Peter-Dale-Scott/4109/article.html.

44. Stephen Kinzer, *The Brothers: John Foster Dulles, Allen Dulles, and Their Secret World War* (New York, NY: Times Books, 2013), 164.

45. Mills, *The Power Elite*.

46. Gerard Colby, *Thy Will Be Done: The Conquest of the Amazon: Nelson Rockefeller and Evangelism in the Age of Oil* (New York, NY: Harper Collins, 1995), 343.

47. Stephen R. Weissman, "What Really Happened in Congo," *Foreign Affairs* 93, no. 4 (2014): 14–24.

48. Richard D. Mahoney, *JFK: Ordeal in Africa* (New York, NY: Oxford University Press, 1983).

49. Colby, *Thy Will Be Done: The Conquest of the Amazon: Nelson Rockefeller and Evangelism in the Age of Oil*, 343.

50. Scott, *The Road to 9/11: Wealth, Empire, and the Future of America*, 13.

51. Daniel Schorr, "In Havana, Old Foes Come Together for a Bay of Pigs Reunion," *Christian Science Monitor*, March 30, 2001, http://www.csmonitor.com/2001/0330/p11s1.html.

52. Truman, "Limit CIA Role To Intelligence."

53. David Talbot, *Brothers: The Untold History of the Kennedy Years* (New York, NY: Free Press, 2007), 51; Robert F. (Jr.) Kennedy, "John F. Kennedy's Vision

of Peace," *Rolling Stone*, November 20, 2013, https://www.rollingstone. com/politics/politics-news/john-f-kennedys-vision-of-peace-109020/.

54. John M. Newman, *JFK and Vietnam: Deception, Intrigue, and the Struggle for Power* (New York, NY: Warner Books, 1992).

55. John F. Kennedy, "Commencement Address at American University," *John F. Kennedy Presidential Library and Museum* (Washington D.C., June 10, 1963), https://www.jfklibrary.org/archives/other-resources /john-f-kennedy-speeches/american-university-19630610.

56. Oliver Stone and Peter Kuznick, *The Untold History of the United States*, 1st ed. (New York, NY: Gallery, 2012), 326.

57. James DiEugenio, "How Max Holland Duped the Daily Beast," Kennedys and King, June 23, 2017, https://kennedysandking.com /john-f-kennedy-articles/how-max-holland-duped-the-daily-beast.

58. M.D. Gary Aguilar et al., "A Joint Statement on the Kennedy, King, and Malcolm X Assassinations and Ongoing Cover-Ups," The Truth and Reconciliation Committee, 2019, https://www.americantruthnow.org/sign -the-petition.

59. Lance deHaven-Smith, "Beyond Conspiracy Theory: Patterns of High Crime in American Government," *American Behavioral Scientist* 53, no. 6 (February 16, 2010), 796, https://doi.org/10.1177/0002764209353274.

60. Peter Dale Scott, *The American Deep State: Wall Street, Big Oil, and the Attack on U.S. Democracy* (New York, NY: Rowman & Littlefield, 2015), 110.

61. Peter Dale Scott, *Deep Politics and the Death of JFK* (Berkeley, CA: University of California Press, 1993), 220; Thurston Clarke, "'It Will Not Be Lyndon': Why JFK Wanted to Drop LBJ for Reelection," Daily Beast, November 18, 2013, https://www.thedailybeast.com/ it-will-not-be-lyndon-why-jfk-wanted-to-drop-lbj-for-reelection?ref=scroll.

62. James K. Galbraith, "Exit Strategy," *Boston Review*, 2003, https://bostonre-view.net/archives/BR28.5/galbraith.html.

63. Stone and Kuznick, *The Untold History of the United States*, 344.

64. Hugh Wilford, *The Mighty Wurlitzer: How the CIA Played America* (Cambridge, MA: Harvard University Press, 2008), 246.

65. Aleksandr Fursenko and Timothy Naftali, *"One Hell of a Gamble": Khrushchev, Castro, and Kennedy, 1958–1964* (New York, NY: W.W. Norton & Company, 1997), 344–345.

66. Talbot, *Brothers: The Untold History of the Kennedy Years*.

67. Tom Jackman, "CIA May Have Used Contractor Who Inspired 'Mission: Impossible' to Kill RFK, New Book Alleges," *Washington Post*, February 9, 2019, https://www.washingtonpost.com/history/2019/02/09/cia-may

-have-used-contractor-who-inspired-mission-impossible-kill-rfk-new
-book-alleges/.

CHAPTER 7

1. Lewis H. Lapham, "Tentacles of Rage: The Republican Propaganda Mill, a Brief History," *Harper's Magazine*, September 2004, https://harpers.org/archive/2004/09/tentacles-of-rage/.
2. Robert Buzzanco, "What Happened to the New Left? Toward a Radical Reading of American Foreign Relations," *Diplomatic History* 23, no. 4 (1999), 593–595, https://www.jstor.org/stable/24913642.
3. Peter Dale Scott, *The Road to 9/11: Wealth, Empire, and the Future of America* (Berkeley, CA: University of California Press, 2007), 31.
4. John A. Farrell, "Nixon's Vietnam Treachery," *New York Times*, December 31, 2016, https://www.nytimes.com/2016/12/31/opinion/sunday/nixons-vietnam-treachery.html%0D.
5. Scott, *The Road to 9/11: Wealth, Empire, and the Future of America*, 31.
6. Klare, "The Traders Versus the Prussians."
7. Scott, *The Road to 9/11: Wealth, Empire, and the Future of America*, 31.
8. Jim Hougan, "Strange Bedfellows," Counterpunch, June 8, 2005, https://www.counterpunch.org/2005/06/08/strange-bedfellows/.
9. Lewis F. Powell, "Powell Memorandum: Attack On American Free Enterprise System," Washington & Lee University School of Law Scholarly Commons, August 23, 1971, https://scholarlycommons.law.wlu.edu/powellmemo/1/.
10. Buzzanco, "What Happened to the New Left? Toward a Radical Reading of American Foreign Relations," 595.
11. Michel Crozier, Samuel P. Huntington, and Joji Watanuki, *The Crisis of Democracy: Report on the Governability of Democracies to the Trilateral Commission* (New York, NY: New York University Press, 1975), 113.
12. Crozier, Huntington, and Watanuki, *The Crisis of Democracy: Report on the Governability of Democracies to the Trilateral Commission*, 114.
13. Lance deHaven-Smith, "When Political Crimes Are Inside Jobs: Detecting State Crimes against Democracy," *Administrative Theory & Praxis* 28, no. 3 (2006), 337, https://www.jstor.org/stable/25610803.
14. "Steel: The Ides of April," *Fortune*, May 1962, https://ratical.org/ratville/JFK/Unspeakable/IdesOfApril.html#s3; Donald Gibson, *Battling Wall Street: The Kennedy Presidency* (New York, NY: Sheridan Square Press, 1994) 15–16.
15. Gibson, *Battling Wall Street: The Kennedy Presidency*, 75.
16. David Talbot, *The Devil's Chessboard: Allen Dulles, the CIA, and the Rise of America's Secret Government* (New York, NY: Harper Collins, 2015), 467–468.
17. Talbot, *The Devil's Chessboard: Allen Dulles, the CIA, and the Rise of America's Secret Government*, 476.

18. Ken Hughes, "Richard Nixon: Domestic Affairs," Miller Center at UVA, 2019, https://millercenter.org/president/nixon/domestic-affairs.
19. Talbot, *The Devil's Chessboard: Allen Dulles, the CIA, and the Rise of America's Secret Government*, 145–146.
20. Gibson, *Battling Wall Street: The Kennedy Presidency*, 71–72.
21. Mohammad Homayounvash, *Iran and the Nuclear Question: History and Evolutionary Trajectory* (New York, NY: Routledge, 2017), 59.
22. Peter Dale Scott, "The Vietnam War and the CIA-Financial Establishment," in *Remaking Asia: Essays on the American Use of Power*, ed. Mark Selden (Pantheon Books, 1971) 118.
23. Scott, "The Vietnam War and the CIA-Financial Establishment," 119.
24. Scott, "The Vietnam War and the CIA-Financial Establishment," 119.
25. Richard Parker, "Galbraith and Vietnam," *The Nation*, February 24, 2005, https://www.thenation.com/article/archive/galbraith-and-vietnam/.
26. Scott, "The Vietnam War and the CIA-Financial Establishment," 131.
27. Scott, "The Vietnam War and the CIA-Financial Establishment," 130–131.
28. Scott, "The Vietnam War and the CIA-Financial Establishment," 131–133.
29. Scott, "The Vietnam War and the CIA-Financial Establishment," 133.
30. Michael Hudson, *Super Imperialism: The Origin and Fundamentals of US Dominance* (Sterling, VA: Pluto Press, 2003), 203, 305–307.
31. Yanis Varoufakis, *The Global Minotaur: America, Europe and the Future of the Global Economy*, 2nd ed. (London, England: Zed Books, 2015) 94.
32. Leonard Jay Santow, *Do They Walk on Water?: Federal Reserve Chairmen and the Fed* (Westport, CT: Praeger, 2009), 95.
33. Varoufakis, *The Global Minotaur: America, Europe and the Future of the Global Economy*, 94.
34. Kevin Hebner, "The Dollar Is Our Currency, but It's Your Problem," *IPE*, October 2007, https://www.ipe.com/the-dollar-is-our-currency-but-its-your-problem/25599.fullarticle.
35. Michael Hudson, *Killing the Host: How Financial Parasites and Debt Bondage Destroy the Global Economy* (Petrolia, CA: Counterpunch Books, 2015), vi.
36. Hudson, *Killing the Host: How Financial Parasites and Debt Bondage Destroy the Global Economy*, iii-iv.
37. Hudson, *Killing the Host: How Financial Parasites and Debt Bondage Destroy the Global Economy*, iv.
38. Hudson, *Killing the Host: How Financial Parasites and Debt Bondage Destroy the Global Economy*, iv-v.
39. Michael Hudson, "The New Road to Serfdom: An Illustrated Guide to the Coming Real Estate Collapse," *Harper's Magazine*, May 2006.
40. See, for example: Hudson, *J Is for Junk Economics: A Guide to Reality in an Age of Deception*.
41. Peter Gowan, *The Global Gamble: Washington's Faustian Bid for World Dominance* (London, England: Verso, 1999), 18.

42. Gowan, *The Global Gamble: Washington's Faustian Bid for World Dominance*, 20.

43. Gowan, *The Global Gamble: Washington's Faustian Bid for World Dominance*, 21.

44. The Observer, "Saudi Dove in the Oil Slick," *The Guardian*, January 13, 2001, https://www.theguardian.com/business/2001/jan/14/globalrecession.oilandpetrol.

45. "Saltsjoebaden Conference," May 1973, 27–28, https://info.publicintelligence.net/bilderberg/BilderbergConferenceReport1973.pdf.

46. "Saltsjoebaden Conference," 31.

47. Gowan, *The Global Gamble: Washington's Faustian Bid for World Dominance*, 21.

48. Gowan, *The Global Gamble: Washington's Faustian Bid for World Dominance*, 21–22.

49. Gowan, *The Global Gamble: Washington's Faustian Bid for World Dominance*, 23.

50. David E. Spiro, *The Hidden Hand of American Hegemony: Petrodollar Recycling and International Markets* (Ithaca, New York: Cornell University Press, 1999), 107.

51. Spiro, *The Hidden Hand of American Hegemony: Petrodollar Recycling and International Markets*, 124.

52. Yanis Varoufakls, *The Global Minotaur; America, Europe and the Future of the Global Economy*, 2nd ed. (London, England: Zed Books, 2015), 97–90.

53. Gowan, *The Global Gamble: Washington's Faustian Bid for World Dominance*, 23–24.

54. Aaron Good, "American Exception: Hegemony and the Dissimulation of the State," *Administration & Society* 50, no. 1 (January 17, 2018): 9, https://doi.org/10.1177/0095399715581042.

55. Gowan, *The Global Gamble: Washington's Faustian Bid for World Dominance*, 25.

56. Gowan, *The Global Gamble: Washington's Faustian Bid for World Dominance*, 26.

57. Gowan, *The Global Gamble: Washington's Faustian Bid for World Dominance*, 26, 29–30.

58. "The CIA's Family Jewels," The National Security Archive, June 26, 2007, https://nsarchive2.gwu.edu/NSAEBB/NSAEBB222/.

59. Seymour M. Hersh, "Huge C.I.A. Operation Reported in U.S. Against Antiwar Forces, Other Dissidents in Nixon Years," *New York Times*, December 22, 1974, https://www.nytimes.com/1974/12/22/archives/huge-cia-operation-reported-in-u-s-against-antiwar-forces-other.html.

60. Emma Best, "Amid Scandal, Former CIA Director Admitted That You Can Never Really Know What the CIA's Up To," Muckrock, August 26, 2017, https://www.muckrock.com/news/archives/2017/apr/26/cia-layers/.

61. Kathryn Olmsted, *Challenging the Secret Government: The Post-Watergate Investigations of the CIA and FBI* (Chapel Hill, NC: University of North Carolina Press, 1996), 49–50.

62. Olmsted, *Challenging the Secret Government: The Post-Watergate Investigations of the CIA and FBI*, 59.

63. Olmsted, *Challenging the Secret Government: The Post-Watergate Investigations of the CIA and FBI*, 66.

64. John Prados and Arturo Jimenez-Bacardi, "The Rockefeller Commission, the White House and CIA Assassination Plots," National Security Archive, February 29, 2016, https://nsarchive.gwu.edu/briefing-book/intelligence /2016-02-29/gerald-ford-white-house-altered-rockefeller-commission-report.

65. "C. D. Jackson Dies; Time, Inc., Official; Adviser to Eisenhower Had Been Publisher of Fortune," *New York Times*, September 20, 1964, https: //www.nytimes.com/1964/09/20/archives/c-d-jackson-dies-time-inc-offi-cial-adviser-to-eisenhower-had-been.html.

66. Carl Bernstein, "The CIA and the Media," *Rolling Stone*, October 20, 1977, http://www.carlbernstein.com/magazine_cia_and_media.php.

67. Jefferson Morley, "When Was the Zapruder Film First Shown to the American People?," JFK Facts, July 3, 2017, https://jfkfacts.org/when -was-the-zapruder-film-first-shown-to-the-american-people/.

68. "The Senate Select Committee to Study Governmental Operations with Respect to Intelligence Activities," vol. 5, 1976, 6–7, https://history-matters .com/archive/church/reports/book5/html/ChurchVol5_0001a.htm.

69. John Prados and Arturo Jimenez-Bacardi, "White House Efforts to Blunt 1975 Church Committee Investigation into CIA Abuses Foreshadowed Executive-Congressional Battles after 9/11," National Security Archive, July 20, 2015, https://nsarchive2.gwu.edu/NSAEBB/NSAEBB522-Church-Committee-Faced-White-House-Attempts-to-Curb-CIA-Probe/.

70. Olmsted, *Challenging the Secret Government: The Post-Watergate Investigations of the CIA and FBI*, 109.

71. Nicholas M. Horrock, "Colby Describes C.I.A. Poison Work," *New York Times*, September 17, 1975, https://www.nytimes.com/1975/09/17/archives /colby-describes-cia-poison-work-he-tells-senate-panel-of-secret.html.

72. James L. Otis, *Secrets of the CIA* (Turner Original Productions, 1998), https://youtu.be/rOfeq0HhaxE.

73. Olmsted, *Challenging the Secret Government: The Post-Watergate Investigations of the CIA and FBI*, 107.

74. John Prados and Arturo Jimenez-Bacardi, "The CIA's Constitutional Crisis: The Pike Committee's Challenge to Intelligence Business as Usual," National Security Archive, June 2, 2017, https://nsarchive.gwu.edu/briefing-book /intelligence/2017-06-02/white-house-cia-pike-committee-1975.

75. Lisa Pease, "When the CIA's Empire Struck Back," Consortium News, February 6, 2014, https://consortiumnews.com/2014/02/06/when-the-cias -empire-struck-back/?print=pdf.

76. Olmsted, *Challenging the Secret Government: The Post-Watergate Investigations of the CIA and FBI*, 139.

77. "Mr. Pike Goes Too Far," *Washington Post*, November 19, 1975, http://jfk .hood.edu/Collection/Weisberg Subject Index Files/P Disk/Pike Committee 10–75 to 03–76/Item 095.pdf.

78. John M. Crewdson, "Church Doubts Plot Links to Presidents," *New York Times*, July 19, 1975, https://www.nytimes.com/1975/07/19/archives /church-doubts-plot-links-to-presidents-church-doubtful-on-links-to.html.

79. Olmsted, *Challenging the Secret Government: The Post-Watergate Investigations of the CIA and FBI*, 142.

80. Olmsted, *Challenging the Secret Government: The Post-Watergate Investigations of the CIA and FBI*, 143.

CHAPTER 8

1. Paul Bleau, "Oswald's Intelligence Connections: How Richard Schweiker Clashes with Fake History," Kennedys and King, July 29, 2017, https: //kennedysandking.com/john-f-kennedy-articles/oswald-s-intelligence-connections-how-richard-schweiker-clashes-with-fake-history.

2. Gaeton Fonzi, *The Last Investigation* (New York, NY: Thunder's Mouth Press, 1993), 31–32.

3. Bleau, "Oswald's Intelligence Connections: How Richard Schweiker Clashes with Fake History."

4. Olmsted, *Challenging the Secret Government: The Post-Watergate Investigations of the CIA and FBI*, 99.

5. Fonzi, *The Last Investigation*, 5.

6. Jefferson Morley, "Suspicious JFK Deaths: CIA Colleague Suspected Bill Harvey in Mobster Murder," JFK Facts, May 11, 2013, https://jfkfacts. org/suspicious-jfk-deaths-cia-colleague-suspected-bill-harvey-in-mobster-murder/.

7. Talbot, *Brothers: The Untold History of the Kennedy Years*, 274–276.

8. Fonzi, *The Last Investigation*, 375.

9. Jeff Woodburn, "Examining NH's Own JFK Assassination Mystery," nhmagazine.com, November 16, 2017, https://www.nhmagazine.com /examining-nhs-own-jfk-assassination-mystery/.

10. Fonzi, *The Last Investigation*, 189–192.

11. James DiEugenio, *Destiny Betrayed: JFK, Cuba, and the Garrison Case*, 2nd ed. (New York, NY: Skyhorse Publishing, 2012), 152; Fonzi, *The Last Investigation* 50–51.

12. DiEugenio, *Destiny Betrayed: JFK, Cuba, and the Garrison Case*, 153.

13. "George de Mohrenschildt: Staff Report of the Select Committee on Assassinations U.S. House of Representatives," March 1979, 70, http: //www.aarclibrary.org/publib/jfk/hsca/reportvols/vol12/pdf/HSCA _Vol12_deMohren.pdf.

14. Fonzi, *The Last Investigation*, 176–177.

15. Fonzi, *The Last Investigation*, 179.

16. Fonzi, *The Last Investigation*, 194, 432.

17. Robert Sam Anson, "The Insider Interview: Richard Sprague," *New Times*, May 13, 1977, http://jfk.hood.edu/Collection/Weisberg Subject Index Files/K Disk/Kershaw Jack/Item 09.pdf.

18. Fonzi, *The Last Investigation*, 196–197.

19. Fonzi, *The Last Investigation*, 197–198.

20. Joan Mellen, *A Farewell to Justice: Jim Garrison, JFK's Assassination, and the Case That Should Have Changed History*, 2nd ed. (New York, NY: Skyhorse Publishing, 2013), 345.

21. "Final Report of the House Select Committee on Assassinations" (Washington D.C., January 2, 1979), https://history-matters.com/archive /contents/hsca/contents_hsca_report.htm.

22. G. Robert Blakey and Richard Billings, *The Plot to Kill the President: Organized Crime Assassinated JFK - The Definitive Story* (New York, NY: Times Books, 1981).

23. Michael Parenti, *Dirty Truths: Reflections on Politics, Media, Ideology, Conspiracy, Ethnic Life and Class Power* (San Francisco, CA: City Lights Books, 1996), 159.

24. Gary Aguilar et al., "A Joint Statement on the Kennedy, King, and Malcolm X Assassinations and Ongoing Cover-Ups."

25. Scott Shane, "C.I.A. Is Still Cagey About Oswald Mystery," *New York Times*, October 16, 2009, https://www.nytimes.com/2009/10/17/us/17inquire .html?hp&_r=0.

26. Laurence H. Shoup, "Jimmy Carter and the Trilateralists: Presidential Roots," in *Trilateralism: The Trilateral Commission and Elite Planning for World Management* (Boston, MA: South End Press, 1980), 201.

27. Shoup, "Jimmy Carter and the Trilateralists: Presidential Roots," 203.

28. Crozier, Huntington, and Watanuki, *The Crisis of Democracy: Report on the Governability of Democracies to the Trilateral Commission*, 96; Shoup, "Jimmy Carter and the Trilateralists: Presidential Roots," 203.

29. Shoup, "Jimmy Carter and the Trilateralists: Presidential Roots," 206–207.

30. "#1: Jimmy Carter and the Trilateral Commission," Project Censored, July 8, 2015, https://www.projectcensored.org/1-jimmy-carter-and-the-trilat- eral-commission/; Noam Chomsky, *Radical Priorities*, ed. Carlos-Peregrine Otero, 3rd ed. (Oakland, CA: AK Press, 2003) 136–137.

31. Christopher Lydon, "Jimmy Carter Revealed: Rockefeller Republican," *The Atlantic*, July 1977, https://www.theatlantic.com/magazine/archive /1977/07/jimmy-carter-revealed-rockefeller-republican/404908/.

32. Lydon, "Jimmy Carter Revealed: Rockefeller Republican."

33. Timothy A. Canova, "The Transformation of U.S. Banking and Finance: From Regulated Competition to Free-Market Receivership," *Brooklyn Law Review* 60, no. 4 (1995), 1309, https://poseidon01

.ssrn.com/delivery.php?ID=39108408712408401507
61081051190761190410270200350830290740640290021121220
93004001101106062010057062109039088004014011110608705
60370480100771150930821170640900190910850600960041
34. 20119068001001082110025124006000871.
35. Michael Sherman, "A Short History of Financial Deregulation in the United States," July 2009, 1, http://cepr.net/documents/publications/dereg-timeline-2009-07.pdf.
36. Varoufakis, *The Global Minotaur: America, Europe and the Future of the Global Economy*, 99.
37. George C. Wilson, "Carter Is Converted To a Big Spender On Defense Projects," *Washington Post*, January 29, 1980, https://www.washingtonpost.com/archive/politics/1980/01/29/carter-is-converted-to-a-big-spender-on-defense-projects/6a04fed3-ca48-433e-a972-cca13bdf83a0/.
38. Robert M. Gates, *From the Shadows: The Ultimate Insider's Story of Five Presidents and How They Won the Cold War* (New York, NY: Simon & Schuster, 1996), 143–149.
39. Jeffrey St. Clair and Alexander Cockburn, "How Jimmy Carter and I Started the Mujahideen," Counterpunch, January 15, 1998, https://www.counterpunch.org/1998/01/15/how-jimmy-carter-and-i-started-the-mujahideen/.
40. Scott, *The Road to 9/11: Wealth, Empire, and the Future of America*, 90.
41. Kai Bird, *The Chairman: John J. McCloy & The Making of the American Establishment* (New York, NY: Simon & Schuster, 1992), 644–645.
42. Bird, *The Chairman: John J. McCloy & The Making of the American Establishment*, 648.
43. Bird, *The Chairman: John J. McCloy & The Making of the American Establishment*, 652.
44. Scott, *The Road to 9/11: Wealth, Empire, and the Future of America*, 90.
45. Scott, *The Road to 9/11: Wealth, Empire, and the Future of America*, 91.
46. David D. Kirkpatrick, "How a Chase Bank Chairman Helped the Deposed Shah of Iran Enter the U.S.," *New York Times*, December 29, 2019, https://www.nytimes.com/2019/12/29/world/middleeast/shah-iran-chase-papers.html.
47. Kirkpatrick, "How a Chase Bank Chairman Helped the Deposed Shah of Iran Enter the U.S."
48. Robert Parry, "Clouds Over George Bush," Consortium News, December 29, 1998, https://www.consortiumnews.com/1990s/c122898a.html.
49. Joseph J. Trento, *Prelude to Terror: The Rogue CIA and the Legacy of America's Private Intelligence Network* (New York, NY: Carroll & Graf Publishers, 2005), 314.
50. Scott, *The American Deep State: Wall Street, Big Oil, and the Attack on U.S. Democracy*, 26.

51. Trento, *Prelude to Terror: The Rogue CIA and the Legacy of America's Private Intelligence Network*, 101.

52. Trento, *Prelude to Terror: The Rogue CIA and the Legacy of America's Private Intelligence Network*, 61.

53. Trento, *Prelude to Terror: The Rogue CIA and the Legacy of America's Private Intelligence Network*, 194.

54. Scott, *The American Deep State: Wall Street, Big Oil, and the Attack on U.S. Democracy*, 27; Kevin Phillips, "The Barreling Bushes," *L.A. Times*, January 11, 2004, https://www.latimes.com/archives/la-xpm-2004-jan-11-op-phillips11-story.html.

55. Trento, *Prelude to Terror: The Rogue CIA and the Legacy of America's Private Intelligence Network*, 113–117.

56. Peter Carlson, "International Man of Mystery: The Ex-CIA Agent And Current Convict Has Many Stories To Tell. Some May Even Be True.," *Washington Post*, June 22, 2004, http://www.washingtonpost.com/wp-dyn/articles/A59212-2004Jun21_5.html.

57. Robert Parry, "Jimmy Carter's October Surprise Doubts," Consortium News, May 12, 2011, https://consortiumnews.com/2011/05/12/jimmy-carters-october-surprise-doubts/.

58. Robert Parry, *Trick or Treason: The October Surprise Mystery* (New York, NY: Sheridan Square Press, 1993); Scott, *The American Deep State: Wall Street, Big Oil, and the Attack on U.S. Democracy*, 27–28.

59. Scott, *The Road to 9/11: Wealth, Empire, and the Future of America*, 99.

60. Gary Sick, *October Surprise: America's Hostages in Iran and the Election of Ronald Reagan* (New York, NY: Times Books, 1991).

61. Barbara Honegger, *October Surprise* (New York, NY: Tudor Communications Trade, 1989).

62. Alexandre de Marenches and David A. Andelman, *The Fourth World War: Diplomacy and Espionage in the Age of Terrorism* (New York, NY: William Morrow and Co., 1992).

63. Scott, *The Road to 9/11: Wealth, Empire, and the Future of America*, 106.

64. Abolhassan Bani-Sadr, "'Argo' Helps Iran's Dictatorship, Harms Democracy," *Christian Science Monitor*, March 5, 2013, https://www.csmonitor.com/Commentary/Global-Viewpoint/2013/0305/Argo-helps-Iran-s-dictatorship-harms-democracy.

65. Nicholas Schou, "The 'October Surprise' Was Real, Legendary Spymaster Hints in Final Interview," *Newsweek*, April 24, 2016, https://www.newsweek.com/duane-dewey-clarridge-october-surprise-spies-cia-451611.

66. Ari Ben-Menashe, *Profits of War Inside the Secret U.S.-Israeli Arms Network* (Sheridan Square Press, 1992).

67. Robert Parry, "A CIA Hand in an American 'Coup'?" Consortium News, August 26, 2013, https://consortiumnews.com/2013/08/26/a-cia-hand-in-an-american-coup/.

68. For a compendium of much of Parry's work on the subject see: Robert Parry, "October Surprise Series," Consortium News, 2016, https://consortiumnews .com/the-new-october-surprise-series/.

69. Scott, *The American Deep State: Wall Street, Big Oil, and the Attack on U.S. Democracy*, 28–29.

70. Robert Sherrill, *The Oil Follies of 1970–1980: How the Petroleum Industry Stole the Show (and Much More Besides)* (Garden City, NY: Anchor Press /Doubleday, 1983) 435–437; Scott, *The American Deep State: Wall Street, Big Oil, and the Attack on U.S. Democracy*, 28.

71. Scott, *The Road to 9/11: Wealth, Empire, and the Future of America*, 90.

72. Jimmy Carter, "Crisis of Confidence," July 15, 1979, https://www.pbs.org /wgbh/americanexperience/features/carter-crisis/.

73. Newman, *JFK and Vietnam: Deception, Intrigue, and the Struggle for Power*; James K. Galbraith, "Exit Strategy."

74. James K. Galbraith, "JFK Had Ordered Full Withdrawal from Vietnam: Solid Evidence," WhoWhatWhy, September 26, 2017, https://whowhatwhy.org/politics/government-integrity/jfk-ordered-full -withdrawal-vietnam-solid-evidence/.

75. Noam Chomsky, "Vain Hopes, False Dreams," *Z Magazine*, September 1992, https://chomsky.info/199209__/; Noam Chomsky and James K. Galbraith, "Letters from Chomsky and Galbraith on JFK and Vietnam," *Boston Review*, December 1, 2003, https://bostonreview.net/world/chom-sky-galbraith-letters-vietnam-jfk-kennedy; Robert S McNamara and Brian VanDeMark, *In Retrospect: The Tragedy and Lesson of Vietnam* (New York, NY: Times Books, 1996).

76. Andrew Gavin Marshall, "Controlling the Global Economy: Bilderberg, the Trilateral Commission and the Federal Reserve," Global Research, Global Power and Global Government: Part 3, August 3, 2009, https: //www.globalresearch.ca/controlling-the-global-economy-bilderberg-the-trilateral-commission-and-the-federal-reserve/14614; Joseph B. Treaster, *Paul Volcker: The Making of a Financial Legend* (Hoboken, NJ: John Wiley & Sons, 2004), 57–60.

CHAPTER 9

1. Hougan, "Strange Bedfellows."

2. Joan Hoff, "The Nixon Story You Never Heard," Counterpunch, January 7, 2001, https://www.counterpunch.org/2001/01/07/the-nixon-story-you-never -heard/.

3. Len Colodny, "Woodwardgate: Still Protecting the Right Wing," Counterpunch, November 29, 2005, https://www.counterpunch.org/2005/11/29/woodwardgate -still-protecting-the-right-wing/.

4. Hougan, "Strange Bedfellows."

5. Hougan, "Strange Bedfellows."

6. Shane O'Sullivan, *Dirty Tricks: Nixon, Watergate, and the CIA* (New York, NY: Hot Books, 2018), 108–110.
7. Daniel Ellsberg, Peter Dale Scott, and Aaron Good, "Empire, the Deep State, and the Doomsday Machine," in *Media Freedom Summit 2.0: Critical Media Literacy for Social Justice* (San Francisco, CA: Project Censored, 2018).
8. Jim Hougan, *Secret Agenda: Watergate, Deep Throat, and the CIA* (New York, NY: Random House, 1984).
9. Peter Dale Scott, *The Road to 9/11: Wealth, Empire, and the Future of America* (Berkeley, CA: University of California Press, 2007), 47.
10. Hougan, *Secret Agenda: Watergate, Deep Throat, and the CIA*, 18.
11. Carl Oglesby, *The Yankee and Cowboy War: Conspiracies from Dallas to Watergate and Beyond* (New York, NY: Berkley Medallion Books, 1976), 293–294.
12. Hougan, *Secret Agenda: Watergate, Deep Throat, and the CIA*, 16.
13. See: Scott, *The Road to 9/11: Wealth, Empire, and the Future of America*; Scott, *The American Deep State: Wall Street, Big Oil, and the Attack on U.S. Democracy*.
14. Hougan, *Secret Agenda: Watergate, Deep Throat, and the CIA*, 16.
15. Russ Baker, *Family of Secrets: The Bush Dynasty, the Powerful Forces That Put It in the White House, and What Their Influence Means for America* (New York, NY: Bloomsbury Press, 2009), 199.
16. John Newman, *Oswald and the CIA* (New York, NY: Skyhorse Publishing, 2008), 95.
17. Hougan, *Secret Agenda: Watergate, Deep Throat, and the CIA*, 58.
18. Hougan, *Secret Agenda: Watergate, Deep Throat, and the CIA*, 213.
19. Hougan, *Secret Agenda: Watergate, Deep Throat, and the CIA*, 24.
20. Hougan, *Secret Agenda: Watergate, Deep Throat, and the CIA*, 22–23.
21. Scott, *The American Deep State: Wall Street, Big Oil, and the Attack on U.S. Democracy*, 118.
22. Kathryn Olmsted, *Challenging the Secret Government: The Post-Watergate Investigations of the CIA and FBI* (Chapel Hill, NC: University of North Carolina Press, 1996), 77–78.
23. H.R. Haldeman and Joseph DiMona, *The Ends of Power* (New York, NY: Times Books, 1978), 109.
24. Hougan, *Secret Agenda: Watergate, Deep Throat, and the CIA*, 59; Haldeman and DiMona, *The Ends of Power*, 204–205.
25. Oliver Stone and Peter Kuznick, *The Untold History of the United States*, 1st ed. (New York, NY: Gallery, 2012), 390.
26. Baker, *Family of Secrets: The Bush Dynasty, the Powerful Forces That Put It in the White House, and What Their Influence Means for America*, 181.

27. Jefferson Morley, "Nixon Asked CIA About the 'Who Shot John Angle,'" JFK Facts, 2014, https://jfkfacts.org/nixon-asked-cia-about-the-who-shot-john-angle/.

28. Morley, "Nixon Asked CIA About the 'Who Shot John Angle.'"

29. Morley, "Nixon Asked CIA About the 'Who Shot John Angle.'"

30. Scott, "The Vietnam War and the CIA-Financial Establishment."

31. Garrick Alder, "How the Washington Post Missed the Biggest Watergate Story of All," Consortium News, February 20, 2018, https://consortiumnews.com/2018/02/20/how-the-washington-post-missed-the-biggest-watergate-story-of-all/.

32. Robert Parry, "The October Surprise Mysteries," Consortium News, October 22, 2012, https://consortiumnews.com/2012/10/22/the-october-surprise-mysteries/.

33. Richard Nixon and H.R. Haldeman, "The Smoking Gun Tape," Watergate.info, June 23, 1972, https://watergate.info/1972/06/23/the-smoking-gun-tape.html.

34. Haldeman and DiMona, *The Ends of Power*, 37–38.

35. Haldeman and DiMona, *The Ends of Power*, 39.

36. Peter Dale Scott, "From Dallas to Watergate: The Longest Cover-Up," *Ramparts*, December 1973, 12.

37. Michael Carlson, "James McCord Obituary," *The Guardian*, April 28, 2019, https://www.theguardian.com/us-news/2019/apr/28/james-mccord-obituary.y

38. O'Sullivan, *Dirty Tricks: Nixon, Watergate, and the CIA*, 405.

39. Hougan, *Secret Agenda: Watergate, Deep Throat, and the CIA*, 303–304.

40. UPI, "Watergater Blames CIA," *San Francisco Chronicle*, May 5, 1977, http://jfk.hood.edu/Collection/White Materials/Security-CIA/CIA 1779.pdf.

41. Peter Dale Scott, "From Dallas to Watergate: The Longest Cover-Up," *Ramparts*, December 1973, 13.

42. Peter Dale Scott, "From Dallas to Watergate: The Longest Cover-Up," *Ramparts*, December 1973, 13, 15.

43. John Newman, "Oswald, the CIA, and Mexico City," *Frontline*, November 20, 2003, https://www.pbs.org/wgbh/frontline/article/oswald-the-cia-and-mexico-city/#return27.

44. O'Sullivan, *Dirty Tricks: Nixon, Watergate, and the CIA*, 270.

45. O'Sullivan, *Dirty Tricks: Nixon, Watergate, and the CIA*, 272.

46. O'Sullivan, *Dirty Tricks: Nixon, Watergate, and the CIA*, 202.

47. Hougan, *Secret Agenda: Watergate, Deep Throat, and the CIA*, 22.

48. O'Sullivan, *Dirty Tricks: Nixon, Watergate, and the CIA*, 241.

49. O'Sullivan, *Dirty Tricks: Nixon, Watergate, and the CIA*, 307.

50. Ray Locker, *Nixon's Gamble: How a President's Own Secret Government Destroyed His Administration* (Guilford, Connecticut: Lyons Press, 2016), 179.

51. Locker, *Nixon's Gamble: How a President's Own Secret Government Destroyed His Administration*, 188–189.

52. "The CIA's Family Jewels."

53. Christopher Moran, "Nixon's Axe Man: CIA Director James R. Schlesinger," *Journal of American Studies* 53, no. 1 (February 9, 2019): 95–121, https://doi.org/10.1017/S002187581700086X.

54. Hougan, "Strange Bedfellows."

55. Bernstein, "The CIA and the Media."

56. Bernstein, "The CIA and the Media."

57. Bernstein, "The CIA and the Media."

58. "Ray Cline's Efforts with Certain of the Press to Improve Public Confidence in Agency," September 17, 1965, https://www.cia.gov/library/readingroom/docs/CIA-RDP80B01676R001700030003-0.pdf.

59. See: Olmsted, *Challenging the Secret Government: The Post-Watergate Investigations of the CIA and FBI*.

60. Robert Parry, "How the Washington Press Turned Bad," Consortium News, October 28, 2014, https://consortiumnews.com/2014/10/28/how-the-washington-press-turned-bad/.

61. Brian Covert, "Played by the Mighty Wurlitzer: The Press, the CIA, and the Subversion of Truth," in *Censored 2017*, ed. Mickey Huff and Andy Lee Roth (New York, NY: Seven Stories Press, 2016), 277.

62. Hugh Wilford, *The Mighty Wurlitzer: How the CIA Played America* (Cambridge, MA: Harvard University Press, 2008), 226.

63. Normon Soloman, "Snow Job: The Establishment's Papers Do Damage Control for the CIA," FAIR, January 1, 1997, https://fair.org/extra/snow-job/.

64. Robert Parry, "The CIA/MSM Contra-Cocaine Cover-Up," Consortium News, September 26, 2014, https://consortiumnews.com/2014/09/26/the-ciamsm-contra-cocaine-cover-up/.

65. Frank Konkel, "The Details About the CIA's Deal With Amazon," *The Atlantic*, July 17, 2014, https://www.theatlantic.com/technology/archive/2014/07/the-details-about-the-cias-deal-with-amazon/374632/.

66. Jeff Frieden, "Economics and Politics in the 1970s," in *Trilateralism: The Trilateral Commission and Elite Planning for World Management*, ed. Holly Sklar (Boston, MA: South End Press, 1980), 66.

67. Frieden, "Economics and Politics in the 1970s," 68–69.

68. Frieden, "Economics and Politics in the 1970s," 69.

69. Cardwell, *NSC 68 and the Political Economy of the Cold War*; William Borden, *The Pacific Alliance: United States Foreign Economic Policy and Japanese Trade Recovery, 1947–1955* (Madison, Wisconsin: University of Wisconsin Press, 1984).

70. O'Sullivan, *Dirty Tricks: Nixon, Watergate, and the CIA*, 392–393.

71. Hougan, *Secret Agenda: Watergate, Deep Throat, and the CIA*.

72. Len Colodny and Robert Gettlin, *Silent Coup: The Removal of a President* (New York, NY: St. Martin's Press, 1991).

73. Jim Hougan, *Spooks: The Haunting of America : The Private Use of Secret Agents* (New York, NY: William Morrow and Co., 1978), 261.

74. O'Sullivan, *Dirty Tricks: Nixon, Watergate, and the CIA*, 405–406.

75. Hougan, *Secret Agenda: Watergate, Deep Throat, and the CIA*, 112.

76. Peter Dale Scott, *Deep Politics and the Death of JFK* (Berkeley, CA: University of California Press, 1993), 236.

77. Hougan, *Secret Agenda: Watergate, Deep Throat, and the CIA*, 118.

78. Scott, *Deep Politics and the Death of JFK*, 240.

79. Phil Willon and Michael Fechter, "Watergate: The Untold Story," *Tampa Tribune*, January 19, 1997.

80. O'Sullivan, *Dirty Tricks: Nixon, Watergate, and the CIA*, 179.

81. Scott, *Deep Politics and the Death of JFK*, 240.

82. O'Sullivan, *Dirty Tricks: Nixon, Watergate, and the CIA*, 180.

83. O'Sullivan, *Dirty Tricks: Nixon, Watergate, and the CIA*, 378.

84. O'Sullivan, *Dirty Tricks: Nixon, Watergate, and the CIA*, 378.

85. O'Sullivan, *Dirty Tricks: Nixon, Watergate, and the CIA*, 379.

86. O'Sullivan, *Dirty Tricks: Nixon, Watergate, and the CIA*, 378.

87. Scott, *Deep Politics and the Death of JFK*, 239.

88. Hougan, *Secret Agenda: Watergate, Deep Throat, and the CIA*, 173.

89. Hougan, *Secret Agenda: Watergate, Deep Throat, and the CIA*, 174.

90. O'Sullivan, *Dirty Tricks: Nixon, Watergate, and the CIA*, 373.

91. Colodny and Gettlin, *Silent Coup: The Removal of a President;* Jim Hougan, "Hougan, Liddy, the Post and Watergate," Investigative Notes, June 22, 2011, http://jimhougan.com/wordpress/?p=11.

92. O'Sullivan, *Dirty Tricks: Nixon, Watergate, and the CIA*, 376.

93. O'Sullivan, *Dirty Tricks: Nixon, Watergate, and the CIA*, 377.

94. Hougan, *Secret Agenda: Watergate, Deep Throat, and the CIA*, 306.

95. Hougan, *Secret Agenda: Watergate, Deep Throat, and the CIA*, 307.

96. Hougan, *Secret Agenda: Watergate, Deep Throat, and the CIA*, 307.

97. Hougan, *Secret Agenda: Watergate, Deep Throat, and the CIA*, 310.

98. Hougan, *Secret Agenda: Watergate, Deep Throat, and the CIA*, 310–312.

99. Hougan, *Secret Agenda: Watergate, Deep Throat, and the CIA*, 312–313.

100. Ray Locker, *Haig's Coup: How Richard Nixon's Closest Aide Forced Him from Office.* (Lincoln, NE: University of Nebraska Press, 2019), http://www.jstor.org/stable/j.ctvd58ttx.

101. Ray Locker, "Haig's Coup: How Gen. Alexander Haig Aided a Military 'Spy Ring' and Covered It Up to Save Himself," *Garrison: The Journal of History and Deep Politics* 1, no. 2 (2019): 58–68.

CHAPTER 10

1. Peter Dale Scott and Aaron Good, *A History of the Deep State: From the Hiss Case to 9/11*, 2019, 50.
2. Tim Weiner, *Legacy of Ashes: The History of the CIA* (New York, NY: Anchor Books, 2008), 371.
3. Haldeman and DiMona, *The Ends of Power*; Hougan, *Secret Agenda: Watergate, Deep Throat, and the CIA*; Scott and Good, *A History of the Deep State: From the Hiss Case to 9/11*, 50.
4. Scott and Good, *A History of the Deep State: From the Hiss Case to 9/11*, 50.
5. Carl Bernstein and Bob Woodward, "Special Report: Watergate - the Untold Story," *The Independent*, June 13, 2012, https://www.independent.co.uk /news/world/americas/special-report-watergate-the-untold-story-7844900. html.
6. Alfred W. McCoy, *The Politics of Heroin: CIA Complicity in the Global Drug Trade*, 2nd Rev. e (Chicago, IL: Lawrence Hill Books, 2003), 19.
7. Scott and Good, *A History of the Deep State: From the Hiss Case to 9/11*, 67.
8. McCoy, *The Politics of Heroin: CIA Complicity in the Global Drug Trade*, 283–285.
9. Peter Dale Scott, *American War Machine: Deep Politics, the CIA Global Drug Connection, and the Road to Afghanistan* (New York, NY: Rowman & Littlefield, 2010), 52.
10. Scott and Good, *A History of the Deep State: From the Hiss Case to 9/11*, 67.
11. McCoy, *The Politics of Heroin: CIA Complicity in the Global Drug Trade*, 288.
12. Scott and Good, *A History of the Deep State: From the Hiss Case to 9/11*, 68.
13. Alfred W. McCoy and Cathleen B. Read, *The Politics of Heroin in Southeast Asia* (New York, NY: Harper and Row, 1972).
14. McCoy, *The Politics of Heroin: CIA Complicity in the Global Drug Trade*, xix.
15. Douglas Valentine, *The Strength of the Pack: The Personalities, Politics and Espionage Intrigues That Shaped the DEA* (Walterville, OR: Trine Day, 2009), 125.
16. Peter Dale Scott, "Drugs, Anti-Communism and Extra-Legal Repression in Mexico," in *Government of the Shadows: Parapolitics and Criminal Sovereignty*, ed. Eric Wilson (New York, NY: Pluto Press, 2009), 179–181.
17. Scott and Good, *A History of the Deep State: From the Hiss Case to 9/11*, 69.
18. Scott and Good, *A History of the Deep State: From the Hiss Case to 9/11*, 73; Renata Adler, "Searching for the Real Nixon Scandal," *Atlantic Monthly*, December 1976, https://archive.org/stream/nsia-WatergateFile/nsia-Water-gateFile/Watergate File 037_djvu.txt.
19. Scott and Good, *A History of the Deep State: From the Hiss Case to 9/11*, 52.
20. Scott and Good, *A History of the Deep State: From the Hiss Case to 9/11*, 73; Alan A. Block, *Masters of Paradise* (New Brunswick, NJ: Transaction Publishers, 1991), 227.

21. Scott and Good, *A History of the Deep State: From the Hiss Case to 9/11*, 73.
22. Scott and Good, *A History of the Deep State: From the Hiss Case to 9/11*, 52; Fred Emery, *Watergate: The Corruption of American Politics and the Fall of Richard Nixon* (New York, NY: Times Books, 1994), 111–112, 148, 162, 188.
23. Scott and Good, *A History of the Deep State: From the Hiss Case to 9/11*, 55–56; J. Anthony Lukas, *Nightmare: The Underside of the Nixon Years* (New York, NY: Viking Press, 1976), 190, 229.
24. Scott and Good, *A History of the Deep State: From the Hiss Case to 9/11*, 56.
25. Scott and Good, *A History of the Deep State: From the Hiss Case to 9/11*, 56–57.
26. Scott and Good, *A History of the Deep State: From the Hiss Case to 9/11*, 57–59.
27. Douglas Valentine, "CIA and the Drug Business," Consortium News, September 10, 2015, https://consortiumnews.com/2015/09/10/cia-and-the-drug-business/.
28. George Volsky, "Cuban Exiles Recall Domestic Spying and Picketing for C.I.A.," *New York Times*, January 4, 1975, https://www.nytimes.com/1975/01/04/archives/cuban-exiles-recall-domestic-spying-and-picketing-for-cia.html.
29. Scott and Good, *A History of the Deep State: From the Hiss Case to 9/11*, 69–70.
30. Lamar Waldron, *Watergate: The Hidden History: Nixon, the Mafia, and the CIA* (Berkeley, CA: Counterpoint, 2012), 293–295.
31. Richard Nixon, *The Memoirs of Richard Nixon* (New York, NY: Grosset & Dunlap, 1978), 643–644.
32. Peter Dale Scott, "From Dallas to Watergate: The Longest Cover-Up," *Ramparts*, December 1973, 12.
33. Hougan, *Secret Agenda: Watergate, Deep Throat, and the CIA*, 120.
34. Michael Hedges and Jerry Sepe, "Power Broker Served Drugs, Sex at Parties Bugged for Blackmail," *The Washington Times*, June 30, 1989, http://www.futile.work/uploads/1/5/0/1/15012114/power-broker-served-drugs.pdf.
35. Hedges and Sepe, "Power Broker Served Drugs, Sex at Parties Bugged for Blackmail."
36. Whitney Webb, "Government by Blackmail: Jeffrey Epstein, Trump's Mentor and the Dark Secrets of the Reagan Era," Mint Press News, June 25, 2019, https://www.mintpressnews.com/blackmail-jeffrey-epstein-trump-mentor-reagan-era/260760/.
37. Vicky Ward, "Jeffrey Epstein's Sick Story Played Out for Years in Plain Sight," Daily Beast, July 9, 2019, https://www.thedailybeast.com/jeffrey-epsteins-sick-story-played-out-for-years-in-plain-sight.
38. Nixon and Haldeman, "The Smoking Gun Tape."

39. Stephen Kinzer, "From Mind Control to Murder? How a Deadly Fall Revealed the CIA's Darkest Secrets," *The Guardian*, September 6, 2019, https://www.theguardian.com/us-news/2019/sep/06/from-mind-control-to-murder-how-a-deadly-fall-revealed-the-cias-darkest-secrets.

40. Tamsin Shaw, "The Bitter Secret of 'Wormwood,'" *The New York Review of Books*, January 18, 2018, https://www.nybooks.com/daily/2018/01/18/the-bitter-secret-of-wormwood/.

41. John M. Crewdson, "Hunt Says CIA Had Assassin Unit," *New York Times*, December 26, 1975, https://www.nytimes.com/1975/12/26/archives/hunt-says-cia-had-assassin-unit-watergate-figure-tells-of-small.html.

42. Newman, *Oswald and the CIA*, 96.

43. Newman, *Oswald and the CIA*, 289.

44. Hougan, *Secret Agenda: Watergate, Deep Throat, and the CIA*, 16.

45. Hougan, *Secret Agenda: Watergate, Deep Throat, and the CIA*, 307; Carl Bernstein and Bob Woodward, *All the President's Men* (New York, NY: Simon & Schuster, 1974), 317, 348–349.

CHAPTER 11

1. Michel Crozier, Samuel P. Huntington, and Joji Watanuki, *The Crisis of Democracy: Report on the Governability of Democracies to the Trilateral Commission* (New York, NY: New York University Press, 1975), 162.

2. Jon Schwarz, "A New Biography Traces the Pathology of Allen Dulles and His Appalling Cabal," *The Intercept*, 2015, https://theintercept.com/2015/11/02/the-deepest-state-the-safari-club-allen-dulles-and-the-devils-chessboard/.

3. Peter Gribbin, "Brazil and CIA," *CounterSpy* 3, no. 4 (1979): 20.

4. Tanya Harmer, *Allende's Chile and the Inter-American Cold War* (Chapel Hill, NC: University of North Carolina Press, 2011), 17–18, 184–186.

5. Douglas Valentine, *The Strength of the Wolf: The Secret History of America's War on Drugs* (New York, NY: Verso, 2004), 40.

6. Peter Dale Scott, *American War Machine: Deep Politics, the CIA Global Drug Connection, and the Road to Afghanistan* (New York, NY: Rowman & Littlefield, 2010), 68–70.

7. Scott, *American War Machine: Deep Politics, the CIA Global Drug Connection, and the Road to Afghanistan*, 27.

8. Scott, *American War Machine: Deep Politics, the CIA Global Drug Connection, and the Road to Afghanistan*, 70–71.

9. Scott, *American War Machine: Deep Politics, the CIA Global Drug Connection, and the Road to Afghanistan*, 77.

10. McCoy and Read, *The Politics of Heroin in Southeast Asia*; McCoy, *The Politics of Heroin: CIA Complicity in the Global Drug Trade*, 1991; McCoy, *The Politics of Heroin: CIA Complicity in the Global Drug Trade*, 2003.

11. Gary Webb, *Dark Alliance: The CIA, the Contras, and the Crack Cocaine Explosion* (New York, NY: Seven Stories Press, 1998).

12. McCoy, *The Politics of Heroin: CIA Complicity in the Global Drug Trade*, 2003, 475.

13. Nafeez Mosaddeq Ahmed, "Our Terrorists," New Internationalist, October 1, 2009, https://newint.org/features/2009/10/01/blowback-extended-version.

14. Howard Witt, "Oil Firms Find New Wild West, In Azerbaijan," *Chicago Tribune*, June 21, 1992, http://articles.chicagotribune.com/1992-06-21/business/9202250031_1_western-oil-companies-azeri-oil-oil-bureaucracy.

15. Ahmed, "Our Terrorists."

16. Peter Dale Scott, *Drugs, Oil, and War: The United States in Afghanistan, Colombia, and Indochina* (New York, NY: Rowman & Littlefield, 2003), 164.

17. Ahmed, "Our Terrorists."

18. Peter Dale Scott, *The Road to 9/11: Wealth, Empire, and the Future of America* (Berkeley, CA: University of California Press, 2007), 163.

19. Richard V. Secord and Charles J. Wurts, *Honored and Betrayed: Irangate, Covert Affairs, and the Secret War in Laos* (New York, NY: John Wiley & Sons, 1992).

20. Lawrence Walsh, "Final Report of the Independent Counsel for Iran/Contra Matters," vol. 1 (Washington D.C., August 4, 1993), https://fas.org/irp/offdocs/walsh/chap_09.htm.

21. Rajeev Syal, "Drug Money Saved Banks in Global Crisis, Claims UN Advisor," *The Guardian*, December 12, 2009, https://www.theguardian.com/global/2009/dec/13/drug-money-banks-saved-un-cfief-claims.

22. Syal, "Drug Money Saved Banks in Global Crisis, Claims UN Advisor."

23. Syal, "Drug Money Saved Banks in Global Crisis, Claims UN Advisor."

24. Steve Tsang, "Target Zhou Enlai: The "Kashmir Princess' Incident of 1955," *The China Quarterly* 139 (September 12, 1994): 766–82, https://doi.org/10.1017/S0305741000043150.

25. Wendell L. Minnick, "Target: Zhou Enlai - Was America's CIA Working with Taiwan Agents to Kill Chinese Premier?" *Far Eastern Economic Review*, July 13, 1995, reprinted at: http://www.namebase.net:82/ppost07.html.

26. David Talbot, *Brothers: The Untold History of the Kennedy Years* (New York, NY: Free Press, 2007); Robert F. (Jr.) Kennedy, *American Values: Lessons I Learned from My Family* (New York, NY: Harper Collins, 2018), 267–268.

27. Talbot, *Brothers: The Untold History of the Kennedy Years*.

28. Scott, *American War Machine: Deep Politics, the CIA Global Drug Connection, and the Road to Afghanistan*, 5.

29. Scott, *American War Machine: Deep Politics, the CIA Global Drug Connection, and the Road to Afghanistan*, 36–37.

30. Scott, *American War Machine: Deep Politics, the CIA Global Drug Connection, and the Road to Afghanistan*, 37; Peter Kornbluh, *The Pinochet File: A Declassified Dossier on Atrocity and Accountability* (New York, NY: New Press, 2003).

31. Tim Weiner, "Anti-Drug Unit of C.I.A. Sent Ton of Cocaine to U.S. in 1990," *New York Times*, November 20, 1993, https://www.nytimes .com/1993/11/20/world/anti-drug-unit-of-cia-sent-ton-of-cocaine-to-us -in-1990.html.

32. Howard G. Chua-Eoan and Elaine Shannon, "Confidence Games: How Venezuelan Traffickers Allegedly Colluded with the CIA to Smuggle Coke into the U.S.," *Time*, November 29, 1993.

33. Jose de Cordoba, "Former CIA Ally Faces Drug Charge: Ex-Venezuelan General Said to Smuggle Cocaine With Agency's Approval," *Wall Street Journal*, November 22, 1996.

34. Chris Carlson, "Is The CIA Trying to Kill Venezuela's Hugo Chávez?," Venezuelanalysis.com, April 19, 2007, https://venezuelanalysis.com/ analysis/2345.

35. Douglas Valentine, *The Strength of the Pack: The Personalities, Politics and Espionage Intrigues That Shaped the DEA* (Walterville, OR: Trine Day, 2009), 400.

36. Scott, *Drugs, Oil, and War: The United States in Afghanistan, Colombia, and Indochina*, 7.

37. McCoy, *The Politics of Heroin: CIA Complicity in the Global Drug Trade*, 2003, 168.

38. Scott, *Drugs, Oil, and War: The United States in Afghanistan, Colombia, and Indochina,* 61.

39. Jim Drinkhall, "CIA Helped Quash Major, Star-Studded Tax Evasion Case," *Washington Post*, April 24, 1980, https://www.washingtonpost.com/archive /politics/1980/04/24/cia-helped-quash-major-star-studded-tax-evasion -case/a55ddf06-2a3f-4e04-a687-a3dd87c32b82/?noredirect=on&utm _term=.b8b12b265c67.

40. Drinkhall, "CIA Helped Quash Major."

41. Pete Brewton, *The Mafia, CIA and George Bush* (New York, NY: S.P.I. Books, 1992), 181.

42. Brewton, *The Mafia, CIA and George Bush*, 182.

43. Scott, *American War Machine: Deep Politics, the CIA Global Drug Connection, and the Road to Afghanistan*, 37.

44. Peter Dale Scott and Jonathan Marshall, *Cocaine Politics: Drugs, Armies, and the CIA in Central America*, Updated ed (Berkeley, CA: University of California Press, 1998), 31.

45. Scott, *American War Machine: Deep Politics, the CIA Global Drug Connection, and the Road to Afghanistan*, 37.

46. Brewton, *The Mafia, CIA and George Bush,* 181–182.

47. James A. Nathan, "Dateline Australia: America's Foreign Watergate?" *Foreign Policy*, no. 49 (1982): 168, https://doi.org/10.2307/1148494, 182.

48. McCoy, *The Politics of Heroin: CIA Complicity in the Global Drug Trade*, 1991, 465–466.

49. Nathan, "Dateline Australia: America's Foreign Watergate?", 182.
50. Nathan, "Dateline Australia: America's Foreign Watergate?", 182.
51. Scott, *American War Machine: Deep Politics, the CIA Global Drug Connection, and the Road to Afghanistan*, 167.
52. Scott, *American War Machine: Deep Politics, the CIA Global Drug Connection, and the Road to Afghanistan*, 166.
53. Scott, *Drugs, Oil, and War: The United States in Afghanistan, Colombia, and Indochina*, 40–41.
54. McCoy, *The Politics of Heroin: CIA Complicity in the Global Drug Trade*, 1991, 469.
55. McCoy, *The Politics of Heroin: CIA Complicity in the Global Drug Trade*, 1991, 470.
56. Nathan, "Dateline Australia: America's Foreign Watergate?", 177.
57. Michael Sullivan, *American Adventurism Abroad: Invasions, Interventions, and Regime Changes Since World War II*, Rev. ed (Malden, MA, 2008), 148–149.
58. Nathan, "Dateline Australia: America's Foreign Watergate?", 176.
59. Nathan, "Dateline Australia: America's Foreign Watergate?", 177.
60. Nathan, "Dateline Australia: America's Foreign Watergate?", 170; McCoy, *The Politics of Heroin: CIA Complicity in the Global Drug Trade*, 1991, 461.
61. Nathan, "Dateline Australia: America's Foreign Watergate?", 170.
62. Douglas Valentine, *The Phoenix Program* (New York, NY: William Morrow and Co., 1990).
63. ProPublica, "Decades After Disappearing From Australia, a CIA-Linked Fugitive Is Found in Idaho," ProPublica, November 10, 2015, https://www.propublica.org/article/after-disappearing-from-australia-a-cia-linked-fugitive-found-in-idaho.
64. Keith Schneider, "North's Aides Linked to Australia Study," *New York Times*, August 9, 1987, https://www.nytimes.com/1987/03/08/world/north-s-aides-linked-to-australia-study.html.
65. Damien Murphy, "Nugan Hand Bank Mystery: Michael Hand Found Living in the United States," *The Sydney Morning Herald*, November 9, 2015, https://www.smh.com.au/business/banking-and-finance/nugan-hand-bank-mystery-michael-hand-found-living-in-the-united-states-20151108-gkthas.html.
66. Ed Vulliamy, "How a Big US Bank Laundered Billions from Mexico's Murderous Drug Gangs," *The Guardian*, April 2, 2011, https://www.theguardian.com/world/2011/apr/03/us-bank-mexico-drug-gangs.
67. Matt Taibbi, "Gangster Bankers: Too Big to Jail," *Rolling Stone*, February 14, 2013, https://www.rollingstone.com/politics/politics-news/gangster-bankers-too-big-to-jail-102004/.
68. John Burnett, "Awash In Cash, Drug Cartels Rely On Big Banks To Launder Profits," NPR: All Things Considered, March 20, 2014,

https://www.npr.org/sections/parallels/2014/03/20/291934724 /awash-in-cash-drug-cartels-rely-on-big-banks-to-launder-profits.

69. Taibbi, "Gangster Bankers: Too Big to Jail."

70. Sallie Pisani, *The CIA and the Marshall Plan* (Lawrence, KS: University Press of Kansas, 1991).

71. Tim Weiner, *Legacy of Ashes: The History of the CIA* (New York, NY: Anchor Books, 2008), 32–3, 40.

72. Oliver Stone and Peter Kuznick, *The Untold History of the United States*, 1st ed. (New York, NY: Gallery, 2012), 214.

73. Peter Dale Scott, *The American Deep State: Wall Street, Big Oil, and the Attack on U.S. Democracy* (New York, NY: Rowman & Littlefield, 2015), 15.

74. Chalmers Johnson, Norbert A. Schlei, and Michael Schaller, "The CIA and Japanese Politics," *Asian Perspective* 24, no. 4 (2000): 79–103, http://www.jstor.org/stable/42705308; Chalmers Johnson, "The Looting of Asia," *London Review of Books* 25, no. 22 (2003): 3–6, https://www.lrb.co.uk/v25/n22/chalmers-johnson/the-looting-of-asia.

75. Terry McCarthy, "Japan's Political Thugs Exposed," *The Independent*, September 26, 1992, https://www.independent.co.uk/news/world/japans-political-thugs-exposed-1553629.html; Johnson, Schlei, and Schaller, "The CIA and Japanese Politics," 87.

76. Johnson, "The Looting of Asia"; Sterling Seagrave and Peggy Seagrave, *Gold Warriors: America's Secret Recovery of Yamashita's Gold* (New York, NY: Verso, 2003).

77. Seagrave and Seagrave, *Gold Warriors: America's Secret Recovery of Yamashita's Gold*.

78. Johnson, "The Looting of Asia"; see also: Johnson, Schlei, and Schaller, "The CIA and Japanese Politics."

79. Weiner, *Legacy of Ashes: The History of the CIA*, 137.

80. Peter Dale Scott, "The United States and the Overthrow of Sukarno, 1965–1967," *Pacific Affairs* 58, no. 2 (1985): 239–64, https://doi.org/10.2307/2758262, 255–256.

81. Scott, *American War Machine: Deep Politics, the CIA Global Drug Connection, and the Road to Afghanistan*, 170.

82. James Sterngold, "Kakuei Tanaka, 75, Ex-Premier and Political Force in Japan, Dies," *New York Times*, December 17, 1993, https://www.nytimes.com/1993/12/17/obituaries/kakuei-tanaka-75-ex-premier-and-political-force-in-japan-dies.html.

83. Wolfgang Saxon, "Yoshio Kodama: Was Rightist," *New York Times*, January 18, 1984, https://www.nytimes.com/1984/01/18/obituaries/yoshio-kodama-was-rightist.html.

84. David Leigh and Rob Evans, "The Lockheed Scandal," *The Guardian*, The BAE Files, June 8, 2007, https://www.theguardian.com/world/2007/jun/08/bae35.

85. Jonathan Marshall, "Saudi Arabia and the Reagan Doctrine," *Middle East Report*, no. 155 (November 1988): 12–17, https://doi.org/10.2307/3012078.

86. David Leigh and Rob Evans, "BAE: Secret Papers Reveal Threats from Saudi Prince," *The Guardian*, The BAE Files, February 15, 2008, https://www.theguardian.com/world/2008/feb/15/bae.armstrade.

87. "Prince Bandar Bin Sultan: Larger-than-Life Diplomacy," *The Economist*, November 6, 2008, https://www.economist.com/books-and-arts/2008/11/06/larger-than-life-diplomacy.

88. David Plotz, "Saudi Ambassador Prince Bandar," Slate, October 24, 2001, http://www.slate.com/articles/news_and_politics/assessment/2001/10/saudi_ambassador_prince_bandar.html.

89. Scott, *The American Deep State: Wall Street, Big Oil, and the Attack on U.S. Democracy*, 75.

90. Scott and Good, "Was the Now-Forgotten Murder of One Man on September 9, 2001 a Crucial Pre-Condition for 9/11?"

91. Aaron Good et al., "The 9/9/2001 Massoud Assassination," *CovertAction Bulletin* (CovertAction Magazine, November 25, 2021), https://www.patreon.com/posts/episode-2-9-9-59070932.

92. Scott and Good, "Was the Now-Forgotten Murder of One Man on September 9, 2001 a Crucial Pre-Condition for 9/11?"

93. Thomas H. Kean and Lee H. Hamilton, "The 9/11 Commission Report" (Washington D.C., 2004), https://www.9-11commission.gov/report/911Report.pdf.

94. Seymour M. Hersh, "The Redirection: Is the Administration's New Policy Benefitting Our Enemies in the War on Terrorism?," *The New Yorker*, March 5, 2007, https://www.newyorker.com/magazine/2007/03/05/the-redirection.

95. Daniele Ganser, *NATO's Secret Armies: Operation GLADIO and Terrorism in Western Europe* (New York, NY: Frank Cass, 2005).

96. Daniele Ganser, "Beyond Democratic Checks and Balances: The 'Propaganda Due' Masonic Lodge and the CIA in Italy's First Republic," in *Government of the Shadows: Parapolitics and Criminal Sovereignty*, ed. Eric Wilson (New York, NY: Pluto Press, 2009), 256–75, 257.

97. Ganser, "Beyond Democratic Checks and Balances: The 'Propaganda Due' Masonic Lodge and the CIA in Italy's First Republic," 260–261.

98. Ganser, "Beyond Democratic Checks and Balances: The 'Propaganda Due' Masonic Lodge and the CIA in Italy's First Republic," 266.

99. Ganser, "Beyond Democratic Checks and Balances: The 'Propaganda Due' Masonic Lodge and the CIA in Italy's First Republic," 265.

100. Ganser, "Beyond Democratic Checks and Balances: The 'Propaganda Due' Masonic Lodge and the CIA in Italy's First Republic," 269.

101. Ganser, "Beyond Democratic Checks and Balances: The 'Propaganda Due' Masonic Lodge and the CIA in Italy's First Republic," 270.

102. Tim Weiner, "Pentagon Book For Doomsday Is to Be Closed," *New York Times*, April 18, 1994, https://www.nytimes.com/1994/04/18/us/penta-gon-book-for-doomsday-is-to-be-closed.html.

103. Scott, *The American Deep State: Wall Street, Big Oil, and the Attack on U.S. Democracy*, 147.

104. Scott, *The American Deep State: Wall Street, Big Oil, and the Attack on U.S. Democracy*, 148.

105. "The Eisenhower Ten," CONELRAD, Atomic Secrets, n.d., http://conel-rad.com/atomicsecrets/secrets.php?secrets=05.

106. Frederick G. Dutton, "Memorandum for Honorable McGeorge Bundy," *The White House* (Washington D.C., August 19, 1961), http://conelrad.com/atomicsecrets/secrets.php?secrets=e17.

107. "The Eisenhower Ten."

108. Scott, *The American Deep State: Wall Street, Big Oil, and the Attack on U.S. Democracy*, 148–149.

109. Scott, *The American Deep State: Wall Street, Big Oil, and the Attack on U.S. Democracy*, 149.

110. Weiner, "Pentagon Book For Doomsday Is to Be Closed."

111. Scott, *The Road to 9/11: Wealth, Empire, and the Future of America*, 183–184.

112. Scott, *The Road to 9/11: Wealth, Empire, and the Future of America*, 186.

113. Weiner, "Pentagon Book For Doomsday Is to Be Closed."

114. Scott, *The Road to 9/11: Wealth, Empire, and the Future of America*, 186.

115. Scott, *The Road to 9/11: Wealth, Empire, and the Future of America*, 40–41.

116. Scott, *The American Deep State: Wall Street, Big Oil, and the Attack on U.S. Democracy*, 117, 121.

117. Scott, *The American Deep State: Wall Street, Big Oil, and the Attack on U.S. Democracy*, 109.

118. Scott, *The American Deep State: Wall Street, Big Oil, and the Attack on U.S. Democracy*, 109–110.

119. Scott, *The American Deep State: Wall Street, Big Oil, and the Attack on U.S. Democracy*, 117–118.

120. Scott, *The Road to 9/11: Wealth, Empire, and the Future of America*, 235.

121. Carl Hulse, "Florida Ex-Senator Pursues Claims of Saudi Ties to Sept. 11 Attacks," *New York Times*, April 13, 2015, https://www.nytimes.com/2015/04/14/world/middleeast/florida-ex-senator-pursues-claims-of-saudi-ties-to-sept-11-attacks.html.

122. James Ridgeway, "The 9/11 Questions That Remain," *Mother Jones*, September 11, 2009, https://www.motherjones.com/politics/2009/09/911-questions-remain/.

123. Scott, *The American Deep State: Wall Street, Big Oil, and the Attack on U.S. Democracy*, 119.

124. Alfred W. McCoy, *In the Shadows of the American Century: The Rise and Decline of US Global Power* (Chicago, IL: Haymarket Books, 2017).

125. Tilly, "War Making and State Making as Organized Crime."

126. Scott, *American War Machine: Deep Politics, the CIA Global Drug Connection, and the Road to Afghanistan*, 121.

CHAPTER 12

1. Ganser, *NATO's Secret Armies: Operation GLADIO and Terrorism in Western Europe*, 236.

2. Ola Tunander, "Democratic State vs. Deep State: Approaching the Dual State of the West," in *Government of the Shadows: Parapolitics and Criminal Sovereignty*, ed. Eric Wilson (New York, NY: Pluto Press, 2009), 56–722, 58.

3. "Eleonora Moro," *The Telegraph*, July 2010.

4. Anthony Faiola, "Socialism Doesn't Work? An Emerging Middle Class of Bolivians Would Beg to Differ.," *Washington Post*, October 2019.

5. Joe Emersberger, "WaPo Prints Study That Found Paper Backed an Undemocratic Bolivia Coup," FAIR, March 2020.

6. Jeb Sprague, "Top Bolivian Coup Plotters Trained by US Military's School of the Americas, Served as Attachés in FBI Police Programs," The Grayzone, November 2019.

7. John Curiel and Jack R. Williams, "Bolivia Dismissed Its October Elections as Fraudulent. Our Research Found No Reason to Suspect Fraud.," *Washington Post*, February 2020.

8. Tunander, "Democratic State vs. Deep State: Approaching the Dual State of the West," 68.

9. A.C. Graham, *Chuang-Tzu: The Inner Chapters* (Indianapolis, IN: Hackett Publishing Company, 2001), 208.

10. deHaven-Smith, *Conspiracy Theory in America*.

11. Quassim Cassam, "Why Conspiracy Theories Are Deeply Dangerous," *New Statesman*, October 7, 2019, https://www.newstatesman.com/world /north-america/2019/10/why-conspiracy-theories-are-deeply-dangerous.

12. Cassam, "Why Conspiracy Theories Are Deeply Dangerous."

13. Katie Halper, "Trump Couldn't Have Asked for a Bigger Gift Than Russiagate," Truthdig, March 29, 2019, https://www.truthdig.com/articles /matt-taibbi-and-aaron-mate-on-how-russiagate-helped-trump/.

14. "NSC 68: United States Objectives and Programs for National Security."

15. See for example: Michael Duffy and Michael Scherer, "The Role Model: What Obama Sees in Reagan," *Time*, January 27, 2011, http://content .time.com/time/magazine/article/0,9171,2044712,00.html.

16. Barry Grey, "A Political Bombshell from Zbigniew Brzezinski," World Socialist Web Site, February 2, 2007, https://www.wsws.org/en/articles /2007/02/brze-f02.html.

17. Ray McGovern, "Doubting Obama's Resolve to Do Right," Consortium News, May 28, 2013, https://consortiumnews.com/2013/05/28/doubting -obamas-resolve-to-do-right/.

18. Gilens and Page, "Testing Theories of American Politics: Elites, Interest Groups, and Average Citizens."

19. James DiEugenio, *Destiny Betrayed: JFK, Cuba, and the Garrison Case*, 2nd ed. (New York, NY: Skyhorse Publishing, 2012), 396.

20. "Public Trust in Government: 1958–2019," Pew Research Center, April 11, 2019, https://www.people-press.org/2019/04/11/public-trust-in-government-1958-2019/.

21. Wolin, *Democracy Incorporated: Managed Democracy and the Specter of Inverted Totalitarianism.*

22. Powell, "Powell Memorandum: Attack On American Free Enterprise System."

23. Much of Wolin's (2008) analysis of *managed democracy* and *inverted totalitarianism* is in accordance with this dissertation. To summarize, he describes US democracy as being managed by corporate power in anti-democratic fashion such that it has created a new form of totalitarianism. It is described as *inverted* because it neutralizes all countervailing political forces by demobilizing and depoliticizing the public rather than by actively mobilizing them as the famous totalitarian systems of the 20th century did. The most obvious differences between this work and Wolin's is the emphasis here on the *exceptionist deep state*. By contrast, Wolin (2008) does not explore or elaborate on state criminality, even though his critical interrogation of the Hobbesian *sovereign* would not have precluded delving into such matters (74–75).

24. Peter Phillips, *Giants: The Global Power Elite* (New York, NY: Seven Stories Press, 2018), 31.

25. Phillips, *Giants: The Global Power Elite*, 32.

26. William I. Robinson, *Global Capitalism and the Crisis of Humanity* (New York, NY: Cambridge University Press, 2014); Phillips, *Giants: The Global Power Elite*, 29.

27. Glenn Kessler et al., "Fact-Checking the First Democratic Debate (Night 2)," *Washington Post*, June 28, 2019, https://www.washingtonpost.com/politics/2019/06/28/fact-checking-first-democratic-debate-night/?noredirect=on&utm_term=.a6b9f811636c.

28. Valerie Richardson, "Obama Takes Credit for U.S. Oil-and-Gas Boom: 'That Was Me, People,'" AP News, November 28, 2018, https://www.apnews.com/5dfbc1aa17701ae219239caad0bfefb2.

29. Joseph S. Nye, "Shale Gas Is America's Geopolitical Trump Card," *Wall Street Journal*, June 8, 2014, https://www.wsj.com/articles/joseph-nye-shale-gas-is-americas-geopolitical-trump-card-1402266357.

30. Philip K. Verleger, "QE and Oil Prices," *The International Economy*, 2015, http://www.international-economy.com/TIE_Sp15_Verleger.pdf.

31. Chico Harlan, "How Plunging Oil Prices Have Created a Volatile New Force in the Global Economy," *The Guardian*, July 21, 2015,

https://www.theguardian.com/business/2015/jul/21/falling-oil-prices
-fracking-us-iran-saudi-arabia-opec.

32. Oliver Stone and Peter Kuznick, "2 Minutes and Counting," *The Nation*, April 3, 2019, https://www.thenation.com/article/untold-history -of-the-united-states-rerelease/.

33. Ellsberg, *The Doomsday Machine: Confessions of a Nuclear War Planner*.

34. Guy Debord, *Comments on the Society of the Spectacle*, trans. Malcolm Imrie (London, England: Verso, 1988), 24.

35. Zbigniew Brzezinski, *The Grand Chessboard: American Primacy and Its Geostrategic Imperatives* (New York, NY: Basic Books, 1997), 40.

36. Ray McGovern, "FBI Never Saw CrowdStrike Unredacted or Final Report on Alleged Russian Hacking Because None Was Produced," Consortium News, June 17, 2019, https://consortiumnews.com/2019/06/17/fbi-never- saw-crowdstrike-unredacted-or-final-report-on-alleged-russian-hacking -because-none-was-produced/.

37. Maximillian Forte, "The Top Ten Myths in the War Against Libya," Counterpunch, August 31, 2011, https://www.counterpunch.org/2011/08 /31/the-top-ten-myths-in-the-war-against-libya/.

38. Jeffrey D. Sachs, "America's Economic Blockades and International Law," Worth, June 28, 2019, https://www.worth.com/americas-economic -blockades-and-international-law/.

39. Max Blumenthal, "How the White Helmets Became International Heroes While Pushing U.S. Military Intervention and Regime Change in Syria," AlterNet, October 2, 2016, https://www.alternet.org/2016/10/how-white -helmets-became-international-heroes-while-pushing-us-military/.

40. Max Blumenthal, "Exclusive Emails Show How the White Helmets Tried to Recruit Roger Waters with Saudi Money," The Grayzone, April 19, 2018, https://thegrayzone.com/2018/04/19/exclusive-emails-show-how-the -white-helmets-tried-to-recruit-roger-waters-with-saudi-money/.

41. See for example: Susan Glasser, "Https://Twitter.Com/Sbg1/Status/1184 277045972537344?Lang=en," Twitter, October 15, 2019, https://twitter .com/sbg1/status/1184277045972537344?lang=en.

42. Aaron Good, "Deep Fake Politics: Getting Adam Curtis Out of Your Head," Kennedys and King, April 6, 2021, https://kennedysandking.com/reviews /deep-fake-politics-getting-adam-curtis-out-of-your-head.

43. Paul Jay, "Three Investment Banks Contrl More Wealth Than GDP of China—and Threaten Our Existence," theAnalysis.news, January 22, 2020, https://theanalysis.news/commentary/the-lords-of-finance-own-the -media-arms-and-big-oil-and-threaten-our-existence-paul-jay-theanalysis/.

44. Good, "Deep Fake Politics: Getting Adam Curtis Out of Your Head."

45. Lawrence Wilkerson and Paul Jay, "Did Trump Walk Into a Trap?— Wilkerson and Jay," theAnalysis.news, January 8, 2021, https://theanalysis. news/did-trump-walk-into-a-trap-wilkerson-and-jay/.

46. Scott, *The Road to 9/11: Wealth, Empire, and the Future of America*, 256–257.

47. Seth G. Jones, *A Covert Action Reagan, the CIA, and the Cold War Struggle in Poland* (New York, NY: W.W. Norton & Company, 2018).

48. Mary L. Dudziak, *Cold War Civil Rights* (Princeton, NJ: Princeton University Press, 2000).

49. Phillips, *Giants: The Global Power Elite*; Ralph Nader, *Only the Super-Rich Can Save Us!* (New York, NY: Seven Stories Press, 2009).

50. Alexander Rubinstein and Max Blumenthal, "Pierre Omidyar's Funding of Pro-Regime-Change Networks and Partnerships with CIA Cutouts," Mint Press News, February 20, 2019, https://www.mintpressnews.com/pierre-omidyar-funding-of-pro-regime-change-networks-and-partnerships-with-cia-cutouts/255337/.

51. See for example: Philip Shenon and Larry J. Sabato, "How the CIA Came to Doubt the Official Story of JFK's Murder," Politico, August 3, 2017, https://www.politico.com/magazine/story/2017/08/03/jfk-assassination-lone-gunman-cia-new-files-215449.

52. Peter Dale Scott, *Coming to Jakarta: A Poem About Terror* (New York, NY: New Directions Books, 1989).

53. Scott, *The Road to 9/11: Wealth, Empire, and the Future of America*, 17.

GLOSSARY

1. Scott, *The American Deep State: Wall Street, Big Oil, and the Attack on U.S. Democracy*, 1.

2. Scott, *Deep Politics and the Death of JFK*, xi-xii.

3. Scott, *Deep Politics and the Death of JFK*, 7.

4. Good, "American Exception: Hegemony and the Dissimulation of the State," 19–20.

5. Scott, *The American Deep State: Wall Street, Big Oil, and the Attack on U.S. Democracy*, 30.

6. E.g., Scott, *The Road to 9/11: Wealth, Empire, and the Future of America*.

7. Schmitt, *Political Theology*; Tunander, "Democratic State vs. Deep State: Approaching the Dual State of the West," 56.

8. deHaven-Smith, "Beyond Conspiracy Theory: Patterns of High Crime in American Government,"methodological, and practical implications of research on state crimes against democracy (SCADs 796.

9. Scott, *The War Conspiracy*, 171.

10. Good, "American Exception: Hegemony and the Dissimulation of the State," 16.

11. Scott, *The Road to 9/11: Wealth, Empire, and the Future of America*, 268.

12. Mills, *The Power Elite*.

13. Good, "American Exception: Hegemony and the Dissimulation of the State."

14. See: Scott, *Deep Politics and the Death of JFK*.

INDEX